Randall Thomas Davidson

The Lambeth Conferences of 1867, 1878, and 1888 :

With the Official Reports and Resolutions, Together with the Sermons Preached at

the Conferences

Randall Thomas Davidson

The Lambeth Conferences of 1867, 1878, and 1888 :
With the Official Reports and Resolutions, Together with the Sermons Preached at the Conferences

ISBN/EAN: 9783337084349

Printed in Europe, USA, Canada, Australia, Japan

Cover: Foto ©Lupo / pixelio.de

More available books at **www.hansebooks.com**

The Lambeth Conferences.

The Lambeth Conferences

OF

1867, 1878, *and* 1888.

With the Official Reports and Resolutions, together with the Sermons preached at the Conferences.

EDITED BY

RANDALL T. DAVIDSON,

DEAN OF WINDSOR.

LONDON:
SOCIETY FOR PROMOTING CHRISTIAN KNOWLEDGE,
NORTHUMBERLAND AVENUE, CHARING CROSS, W.C.;
43, QUEEN VICTORIA STREET, E.C.
BRIGHTON: 135, NORTH STREET.

NEW YORK: E. & J. B. YOUNG & Co.
1889.

WYMAN AND SONS, PRINTERS,
GREAT QUEEN STREET, LINCOLN'S-INN FIELDS,
LONDON, W.C.

CONTENTS.

PART I.

NARRATIVE.

	Page
CHAP. I.—The First Conference, 1867	9
CHAP. II.—The Second Conference, 1878	20
CHAP. III.—The Third Conference, 1888.	34

PART II.

DOCUMENTS, REPORTS, AND RESOLUTIONS, ILLUSTRATING THE HISTORY OF THE CONFERENCES.

	Page
I.—Letters from the Canadian Bishops: Reply of the Archbishop of Canterbury	51
II.—Action taken by the Convocation of Canterbury	55
III.—Official "Programme of Arrangements" issued by the Archbishop of Canterbury for the Conference of 1867	56
IV.—Sermon by the Bishop of Illinois, Sept. 24, 1867	61
V.—Archbishop Longley's Opening Address, Sept. 24, 1867	77
VI.—Amended Programme adopted during the Sessions	83
VII.—Formal "Address to the Faithful" from the Bishops attending the Conference of 1867	88
VIII.—Latin and Greek Versions of the Address	92

	Page
IX.—Resolutions formally passed by the Conference of 1867	97
X.—Correspondence with Dean Stanley about the use of Westminster Abbey, 1867	101
XI.—Sermon by the Bishop of Montreal, Sept. 28, 1867	106
XII.—Reports of the Committees appointed by the Conference of 1867	110
(A) Synodical System	110
(B) Voluntary Spiritual Tribunals	117
(C) Courts of Metropolitans	122
(D) Election of Bishops	124
(E) Declaration of submission to Synods ...	126
(F) Provincial Subordination	128
(G) Missionary Bishoprics	130
(H) Condition of the Church in Natal ...	133
(J) Letters Dimissory	136
XIII.—Resolutions of the Conference adopted at the Adjourned Session, Dec. 10, 1867	136
XIV.—Addresses from the Canadian and West Indian Houses of Bishops, 1872 and 1873	139
XV.—Correspondence between the Bishops of the Protestant Episcopal Church in the United States and the Archbishop of Canterbury, 1874 and 1875	141
XVI.—Memorandum of the Canadian House of Bishops, 1874	148
XVII.—Action of the Convocations of Canterbury and York with reference to the proposed Second Conference	149
XVIII.—Circular Letter of Inquiry addressed by the Archbishop of Canterbury to all the Anglican Bishops, March 28, 1876	151

Contents.

		Page
XIX.—Letter of Invitation to the Conference of 1878, dated July 10, 1877	...	153
XX.—Sermon by the Archbishop of York, on July 2, 1878	...	154
XXI.—Official "Letter" of the Bishops attending the Conference of 1878, including the Reports	...	163
(1) Best mode of maintaining union	...	164
(2) Voluntary Boards of Arbitration	...	171
(3) Missionary Bishops and Missionaries	...	174
(4) Anglican Chaplains on the Continent	...	179
(5) Answers to questions submitted during the Conference	...	180
XXII.—Latin and Greek Versions of the Letter	...	191
XXIII.—Official List of the Bishops present at the Conference of 1878	...	204
XXIV.—Order of precedence observed at the Conference of 1878	...	206
XXV.—Sermon by the Bishop of Pennsylvania, July 27, 1878	...	208
XXVI.—Prayer issued for use before and during the Conference	...	222
XXVII.—Papers issued to the Bishops in connection with the Conference of 1888	...	223
XXVIII.—Sermon by the Archbishop of Canterbury, on July, 2, 1888	...	228
XXIX.—Sermon by the Bishop of Minnesota, on July, 3, 1888	...	241
XXX.—Address to the Queen, July 27, 1888, and Her Majesty's Reply	...	252

	Page
XXXI.—Official List of the Bishops present at the Conference of 1888 ...	256
XXXII.—Official List of the Bishops present at the Conference, arranged according to Provinces	260
XXXIII.—Encyclical Letter from the Assembled Bishops, issued July 27, 1888...	264
XXXIV.—Resolutions formally adopted by the Conference of 1888 ...	277
XXXV.—Reports of Committees :—	
(1) Intemperance ...	285
(2) Purity ...	292
(3) Divorce ...	296
(4) Polygamy ...	298
(5) Observance of Sunday ...	301
(6) Socialism ...	303
(7) Care of Emigrants ...	311
(8) Mutual Relations of Dioceses and Branches of the Anglican Communion...	321
(9) Home Reunion ...	331
(10) Scandinavian Church, Old Catholics, &c....	339
(11) Eastern Churches ...	347
(12) Authoritative Standards of Doctrine and Worship ...	352
XXXVI.—Statement in regard to Ordinations performed by Dr. Cummins, &c. ...	359
XXXVII.—Sermon by the Archbishop of York, July 28, 1888 ...	364
XXXVIII.—Latin and Greek Versions of the Encyclical Letter and Resolutions of 1888 ...	376

NARRATIVE.

CHAPTER I.

THE FIRST CONFERENCE. 1867.

PERHAPS it is not too much to say that a decennial Conference of the bishops of the Anglican Communion, under the presidency of the Archbishop of Canterbury, has now become a recognised part of the organisation of our Church, and the general attention which has been directed to the third of these Conferences seems to afford a suitable opportunity for recalling the history and doings of the earlier gatherings of 1867 and 1878.

The first official step in connexion with the assembling of such a Conference was taken, not in England, but in Canada. The notion had, indeed, been "in the air" for many years,[1] both in England and abroad, and the final impulse which brought about a Conference was eminently significant of the changed conditions of the Church.

It arose, strange to say, from the interest awakened in North America by the Church affairs of South Africa.

At the Provincial Synod of the Canadian Church, held on September 20, 1865, it was unanimously agreed, upon the motion of the Bishop of Ontario, to urge upon the Archbishop of Canterbury and the Convocation of his Province that means should be adopted "by which the members of our Anglican

---

[1] A reference to some of the earlier suggestions on the subject will be found in the *Guardian* of June 19, 1878, p. 857.

Communion in all quarters of the world should have a share in the deliberations for her welfare, and be permitted to have a representation in one General Council of her members gathered from every land."[1]

To a more personal appeal which accompanied this address, Archbishop Longley replied in guarded terms. "The meeting of such a Synod," he said, "is not by any means foreign to my own feelings .... I cannot, however, take any step in so grave a matter without consulting my episcopal brethren in both branches of the united Church of England and Ireland, as well as those in the different colonies and dependencies of the British Empire."

In May, 1866, the Convocation of Canterbury appointed a committee to "consider and report upon" the Canadian address, and the whole subject was fully debated in Convocation in the following spring. Obvious difficulties and dangers were suggested, but in the end the Lower House conveyed to the Archbishop of Canterbury "a respectful expression of an earnest desire that he would be pleased to issue an invitation to all the bishops in communion with the Church of England, to assemble at such time and place, and accompanied by such persons as may be deemed fit, for the purpose of Christian sympathy and mutual counsel on matters affecting the welfare of the Church at home and abroad."[2]

In the Upper House, Archbishop Longley took the utmost pains to "diminish the doubts and difficulties" of some of his brethren. "It should be distinctly understood," he said, "that at this meeting no declaration of faith shall be made, and no decision come to which shall affect generally the interests of

---

[1] For the full text of the address and reply, see Part II., No. I., p. 51, and Chronicle of Convocation of Canterbury, May 2, 1866, p. 286 ; Feb. 12, 1867, p. 696.

[2] Chronicle of Convocation, Feb. 14, 1867, p. 793.

the Church, but that we shall meet together for brotherly counsel and encouragement . . . . I should refuse to convene any assembly which pretended to enact any canons, or affected to make any decisions binding on the Church . . . . I feel I undertake a great responsibility in assenting to this request, and certainly if I saw anything approaching to what [is apprehended] as likely to result from it, I should not be disposed to sanction it, but I can assure [my brethren] that I should enter on this meeting in the full confidence that nothing would pass but that which tended to brotherly love and union, and would bind the Colonial Church, which is certainly in a most unsatisfactory state, more closely to the Mother Church."[1]

A week later the Archbishop issued the following invitation to all the bishops of the Anglican Communion, then 144 in number :—

"LAMBETH PALACE, *Feb.* 22, 1867.

RIGHT REV. AND DEAR BROTHER,—

"I request your presence at a meeting of the bishops in visible communion with the United Church of England and Ireland, purposed (God willing) to be holden at Lambeth, under my presidency, on the 24th of September next and the three following days

"The circumstances under which I have resolved to issue the present invitation are these :—The Metropolitan and Bishops of Canada, last year, addressed to the two Houses of the Convocation of Canterbury the expression of their desire that I should be moved to invite the bishops of our Indian and Colonial Episcopate to meet myself and the Home bishops for brotherly communion and conference.

"The consequence of that appeal has been that

---

[1] Chronicle of Convocation, Feb. 15, 1867, p. 807.

both Houses of the Convocation of my province have addressed to me their dutiful request that I would invite the attendance, not only of our Home and Colonial bishops, but of all who are avowedly in communion with our Church. The same request was unanimously preferred to me at a numerous gathering of English, Irish, and Colonial archbishops and bishops recently assembled at Lambeth; at which,—I rejoice to record it,—we had the counsel and concurrence of an eminent bishop of the Church in the United States of America,—the Bishop of Illinois.

"Moved by these requests, and by the expressed concurrence therein of other members both of the Home and Colonial episcopate, who could not be present at our meeting, I have now resolved,—not, I humbly trust, without the guidance of God the Holy Ghost,—to grant this grave request, and call together the meeting thus earnestly desired. I greatly hope that you may be able to attend it, and to aid us with your presence and brotherly counsel thereat.

"I propose that, at our assembling, we should first solemnly seek the blessing of Almighty God on our gathering, by uniting together in the highest act of the Church's worship. After this, brotherly consultations will follow. In these we may consider together many practical questions, the settlement of which would tend to the advancement of the kingdom of our Lord and Master Jesus Christ, and to the maintenance of greater union in our missionary work, and to increased intercommunion among ourselves.

"Such a meeting would not be competent to make declarations or lay down definitions on points of doctrine. But united worship and common counsels would greatly tend to maintain practically the unity of the faith; whilst they would bind us in straiter bonds of peace and brotherly charity.

"I shall gladly receive from you a list of any subjects you may wish to suggest to me for consideration and discussion. Should you be unable to attend, and desire to commission any brother bishop to speak for you, I shall welcome him as your representative in our united deliberations.

"But I must once more express my earnest hope that, on this solemn occasion, I may have the great advantage of your personal presence.

"And now I commend this proposed meeting to your fervent prayers; and, humbly beseeching the blessing of Almighty God on yourself and your diocese, I subscribe myself,

"Your faithful brother in the Lord,
"C. T. CANTUAR."

The invitation was accepted by seventy-six bishops, and as soon as those who came from the Colonies and the United States began to arrive in England, a series of preliminary meetings was held to discuss and arrange the details of a Conference for which no precedent existed to serve as a guide. The strong divergence of opinion upon the legal aspect of Bishop Colenso's deposition and excommunication, and the fact that the Bishop of Capetown had come to England on purpose to secure, if possible, the synodical sanction of the Conference to the course he had himself adopted, made the agenda-paper a matter of no small difficulty, if it was to be kept within the limits laid down by the Archbishop of Canterbury in the Convocation speech which has been quoted above. Not a few of the English bishops felt so sure of the increased confusion such a Conference must cause in an already tangled web that they declined to attend its deliberations. Among these were the Archbishop of York and the Bishops of Durham, Carlisle, Ripon, Peterborough, and Manchester. Others, including Bishop Thirlwall, of St. David's, postponed their acceptance until the official agenda-paper or programme should be published,[1] a fact to which they afterwards called attention when the programme had unexpectedly been changed.

The Conference met on Tuesday, September 24,

---

[1] For its full text, see Part II., No. III., p. 56.

the opening service being preceded by a Celebration of Holy Communion in Lambeth Palace Chapel, with a sermon from Bishop Whitehouse, of Illinois.[1] The meetings of the Conference were held in the upstairs dining-hall, or "guard-room," of Lambeth Palace, not (as was the case in 1878) in the great library. On the Archbishop of Canterbury's right sat the Archbishop of Armagh, the Bishop of London, the Presiding Bishop of the American Church, the Primus of the Scottish Episcopal Church, the Bishop of Calcutta, and the Bishop of Sydney. On the left were the Archbishop of Dublin, and the Bishops of Montreal, New Zealand, and Capetown. The other bishops sat in front. The Bishop of Gloucester and Bristol acted as episcopal secretary to the meeting throughout its deliberations.

In his opening address,[2] Archbishop Longley again defined, with some care, the position of the Conference. "It has never been contemplated," he said, "that we should assume the functions of a general synod of all the churches in full communion with the Church of England, and take upon ourselves to enact canons that should be binding upon those here represented. We merely propose to discuss matters of practical interest, and pronounce what we deem expedient in resolutions which may serve as safe guides to future action. Thus it will be seen that our first essay is rather tentative and experimental, in a matter in which we have no distinct precedent to direct us."

Special importance attached to the discussions of the first day, when, in the form of a preamble to the subsequent resolutions, the standpoint taken by the Anglican Church was in general terms described. All the leading bishops took part in the debate, and its outcome will be best seen by placing the paragraph, as it was first drafted, side by side with the form which was finally agreed upon.

---

[1] See Part II., No. IV., p. 61. [2] See Part II., No. V., p. 77.

As originally drafted.

"We, Bishops of Christ's Holy Catholic Church, professing the faith of the primitive and undivided Church, as based on Scripture, defined by the first four General Councils,[1] and reaffirmed by the Fathers of the English Reformation, now assembled by the good providence of God at the Archiepiscopal Palace of Lambeth, under the presidency of the Primate of all England, desire, first, to give hearty thanks to Almighty God for having thus brought us together for common counsels and united worship; secondly, we desire to express the deep sorrow with which we view the divided condition of the flock of Christ throughout the world; and, lastly, we do here solemnly declare our belief that the best hope of future reunion will be found in drawing each of us for ourselves closer to our common Lord, in giving ourselves to much prayer and intercession, in the cultivation of a spirit of charity, and in seeking to diffuse through every part of the Christian community that desire and resolution to return to the faith and discipline of the undivided Church which was the principle of the English Reformation."

---

[1] *See* 1 Eliz. c. i. xxxvi.

As ultimately carried.

"We, Bishops of Christ's Holy Catholic Church, in visible Communion with the United Church of England and Ireland, professing the faith delivered to us in Holy Scripture, maintained by the primitive Church and by the Fathers of the English Reformation, now assembled by the good providence of God, at the Archiepiscopal Palace of Lambeth, under the presidency of the Primate of all England, desire, first, to give hearty thanks to Almighty God for having thus brought us together for common counsels and united worship; secondly, we desire to express the deep sorrow with which we view the divided condition of the flock of Christ throughout the world, ardently longing for the fulfilment of the prayer of our Lord: 'That all may be one, as Thou, Father, art in me, and I in Thee, that they also may be one in us, that the world may believe that Thou has sent me'; and, lastly, we do here solemnly record our conviction that unity will be most effectually promoted, by maintaining the faith in its purity and integrity, as taught in the Holy Scriptures, held by the primitive Church, summed up in the Creeds, and affirmed by the undisputed General Councils, and by drawing each of us closer to our common Lord, by giving ourselves to much prayer and intercession, by the cultivation of a spirit of charity, and a love of the Lord's appearing."

On the second day—Wednesday, September 25—the president consented, notwithstanding the strenuous protest of several bishops, to a complete change of programme, in accordance with the wish of the Bishop of Capetown and others,[1] and the discussions were thus diverted into an unexpected channel. A long day was occupied in discussing the due gradation of synodal authority, diocesan, provincial, and perhaps patriarchal, within the Anglican Communion. After the failure of successive attempts to obtain the formal sanction of the Conference to the definite schemes proposed, it was found necessary to fall back upon a perfectly general resolution proposed by Bishop Selwyn, of New Zealand, in the following terms :—" That, in the opinion of this Conference, unity of faith and discipline will be best maintained among the several branches of the Anglican Communion by due and canonical subordination of the synods of the several branches to the higher authority of a synod or synods above them."

This was carried *nem. con.*, and a committee was appointed to consider the whole subject.

On the following day (Thursday, Sept. 26), the "burning question" of Bishop Colenso's position was the subject of prolonged debate. The Archbishop of Canterbury had declined to allow any distinct resolution of condemnation to be put to the Conference, and he ruled out of order a motion to that effect which was proposed by the Presiding Bishop of the American Church. After several hours discussion, it was resolved, by 49 votes to 10, " that, in the judgment of the bishops here assembled, the whole Anglican Communion is deeply injured by the present condition of the Church in Natal ; and that a committee be now appointed at this general meeting to report on the best mode by which the

---

[1] See Part II., No. VI., p. 83.

Church may be delivered from the continuance of this scandal, and the truth maintained. That such report be forwarded to his Grace the Lord Archbishop of Canterbury with the request that his Grace will be pleased to transmit the same to all the bishops of the Anglican Communion, and to ask for their judgment thereon."

The next matter dealt with was the possible constitution of what was described as a Spiritual Court of Appeal; and on this subject it was found necessary, after long debate, to await the report of a committee before any formal recommendation could be made. Such a committee was accordingly appointed "to consider the constitution of a voluntary spiritual tribunal, to which questions of doctrine may be carried by appeal from the tribunals for the exercise of discipline in each Province of the Colonial Church."

It had, upon the previous day, been informally decided that a short "Encyclical" Letter or Address should be drafted by a Committee[1] for the signature of the Bishops attending the Conference. This Address was adopted by the whole body before the adjournment on Thursday evening, and was formally signed at the morning session on the following day.[2] It was suggested in the Conference that it should be publicly read by the Archbishop from the altar of Lambeth Parish Church; but this course was not adopted. After other resolutions[3] had been carried with respect to the due notification of the establishment of new dioceses, the provision of Letters Commendatory, and the proper measure of publicity to

---

[1] The Committee consisted of the Archbishop of Canterbury and the Bishops of London, Winchester, Oxford, North Carolina, Grahamstown, Ohio, Ely, St. Andrews, Cape Town, Moray and Ross, and New Zealand.

[2] The complete document, as signed, is given below. Part II., No. VII., p. 88.

[3] See Part II., No. IX., p. 98.

be given to the proceedings of the Conference, a second and unexpected debate arose upon the position of Bishop Colenso, and a resolution was carried expressing the acquiescence of the Conference in certain advice given by the Convocation of Canterbury a year before, respecting the steps to be taken " if it be decided that a New Bishop should be consecrated " for the Diocese of Natal.

After the *Gloria in Excelsis* had been sung by the assembled Bishops, the Primate dismissed the Conference with the Benediction, on the understanding that those members of it who could remain in England should reassemble in December to receive the Reports of the various Committees.

On the following day, Saturday, September 28, thirty-four Bishops attended a closing service in Lambeth Parish Church, when the Holy Communion was celebrated by the Archbishop, and a sermon was preached by Bishop Fulford, of Montreal. It had originally been proposed that this service should be held in Westminster Abbey; but Dean Stanley, in a correspondence published at the time,[1] gave his reasons for objecting to the use of the Abbey in the manner proposed, and the Conference fell back on Lambeth Church as an alternative.

The several Committees were in frequent session during the next two months under the direction of Bishop Selwyn, of New Zealand;[2] Bishop Fulford, of Montreal; and Bishop Cotterill, of Grahamstown, the last-named of whom had undertaken the onerous work of " Secretary of Committees " to the Conference.

On December 10 a further session of the Conference, or such members of it as had remained in

---

[1] See Part II., No. X., p. 101.
[2] Bishop Selwyn had been nominated in November, 1867, to the See of Lichfield; but he was not enthroned till January 9, 1868.

England, was held at Lambeth Palace, when eight Reports were presented.[1] With reference to the first seven of these, a resolution was in each case formally passed: "That this adjourned meeting of the Conference receives the Report (No. —) of the Committee now presented, and directs the publication thereof, commending it to the careful consideration of the Bishops of the Anglican Communion, as containing the result of the deliberations of that Committee; and returns the members of the same its thanks for the care with which they have considered the various important questions referred to them."

Upon the presentation of Report No. VIII., which referred to Bishop Colenso's deposition, it was resolved "that the Report be received and printed; that the thanks of this meeting be given to the Committee for their labours, and that his Grace be requested to communicate the Report to the Council of the Colonial Bishoprics Fund."

The further resolutions, which will be found in full elsewhere,[2] were for the most part of a formal character. It was, indeed, impossible, considering the small number of Bishops who were able to attend, that any important motions should at this stage be brought before them. The session lasted for a few hours only, and it became evident that in any future Conference some different arrangement must be adopted. Reiterated thanks were expressed to the Bishops of Gloucester and Grahamstown, the Episcopal Secretaries; and to Mr. Philip Wright and Mr. Isambard Brunel, who had acted as their lay assistants and advisers. The Conference had been attended, in all, by seventy-six Bishops out of one hundred and forty-four who had received invitations. Of these seventy-six, eighteen were English Bishops,

---

[1] See Part II., No. XII., p. 110.
[2] See Part II., No. XIII., p. 136.

five were Irish, and six were Scotch. The Colonial Church sent twenty-four, including five Metropolitans. The United States sent nineteen. At no one session of the Conference were all the Bishops present, but the Encyclical Address received the signatures of all, and the President was subsequently authorised to affix the names of several others who had been reluctantly prevented from attending.[1]

CHAPTER II.

THE SECOND CONFERENCE. 1878.

THE circumstances in which the first Conference had been held were exceptionally difficult, and some of the interests at stake were of so keen and even personal a sort that the Bishops found it hard to give undistracted attention to the wider questions of policy and practice which had been included in Archbishop Longley's programme. The allotted time also had been far too short for dealing adequately with such subjects. Eight Committees had indeed reported; but their Reports, as has been seen, were presented to less than a score of Bishops at one brief session on a single day. Due discussion of them was thus impossible, and Bishop Selwyn, who had been foremost perhaps among the promoters

---

[1] See Part II., No. XIII., p. 138.

of the gathering, could only suggest the postponement to a future Conference of any debate upon these weighty documents.[1]

The inquiry soon became common, Will there be a second Conference, and if so, when? Once again, as in 1865, it was the Canadian Church which took the first official step. In December, 1872, the Bishops of the Ecclesiastical Province of Canada made formal appeal to the Convocation of Canterbury to join with them in a request to Archbishop Tait, who had in 1869 succeeded to the Primacy, that he would summon as soon as possible a second meeting of the Conference.[2]

Taking this Canadian letter as his text, Bishop Selwyn, in a memorable speech in Convocation, endorsed and expanded the appeal. He had visited America in 1871. He was to pay a second and more formal visit in 1874, and his experience in every part of the world led him to long for such confederation and unity of action as could, he believed, be best secured by a second Conference, or, as he called it, "A General Council of the Bishops of the Anglican Communion, to carry on the work begun by the Lambeth Conference of 1867."[3]

The matter was, by common consent, adjourned for a time; and in the following year (1874) Bishop Kerfoot, of Pittsburgh, as representing the American Church, was in constant communication upon the subject with Archbishop Tait, whom he visited at Addington, and to whom he was authorised to write officially from America.[4] The Bishop of Lichfield's formal attendance in that year at the meetings, first

---

[1] See *e.g.*, Chronicle of Convocation, Feb. 13, 1873, p. 172.
[2] See Part II., No. XIV., p. 139.
[3] See Chronicle of Convocation, Feb. 13, 1873, pp. 168–174.
[4] See Part II., No. XV., p. 141, and "Life of Bishop Kerfoot," vol. ii., pp. 581–587.

of the Provincial Synod of Canada and then of the General Convention in New York,[1] brought the question again into prominence, and it had now become practically certain that a second Conference would be held in 1877 or 1878 if the necessary conditions could be agreed upon.

Some of these conditions were suggested by the Canadian House of Bishops;[2] others were laid down by the Archbishop himself in an important Convocation speech, and in his written reply to a formal request signed by no less than 42 Bishops of the American Church.[3] Speaking in Convocation on April 16, 1875, he said:—

"No one can doubt that very great good has arisen from the friendly intercourse which took place during the last Lambeth Conference. At the same time, it must be remembered that it is a serious matter to gather the Bishops together from all parts of the globe, unless there is some distinct object for their so gathering. I therefore am disposed, by the advice of my brethren, to request that our brethren at home, and also those at a distance, will state to me as explicitly as possible what the subjects are that it is desirable to discuss at such meeting. They are of a somewhat limited character. There is no intention whatever on the part of anybody to gather together the Bishops of the Anglican Church for the sake of defining any matter of doctrine. Our doctrines are contained in our formularies, and our formularies are interpreted by the proper judicial authorities, and there is no intention whatever at any such gathering that questions of doctrine should be submitted for interpretation in any future Lambeth Conference any more than they were at the previous Lambeth Conference. My predecessor had a very

---

[1] See "Life of Bishop Selwyn," vol. ii., pp. 319-324.
[2] See Part II., No. XVI., p. 148.
[3] See Part II., No. XV., p. 144.

difficult task in defining the exact duty of the Bishops who came together on the former occasion, and with great firmness, and at the same time with that remarkable courtesy and kindliness for which he was so eminent, he steered the somewhat difficult course which was before him, and it was distinctly settled that matters of that kind were not to be entered upon. Well, then, with regard to discipline, of course our discipline is exercised by ourselves and by the constituted Courts of the Church at home, and the discipline of the various Colonial and more independent Churches is exercised by these Churches according to fixed rules which have been established by themselves, and we have no intention whatever of interfering with these matters of discipline. We are, therefore, perhaps naturally, anxious to know tolerably distinctly the subjects which any would wish to bring before us. . . . . Friendly intercourse must, of course, be of great value. But it is possible that Bishops at a very great distance—such as the Bishop of Athabasca, who, I believe, can scarcely reach his diocese under a year—might perhaps, under a misapprehension, think it was necessarily their duty to come to such a Conference unless it was distinctly stated what was to be done. . . . . I cannot doubt that there are many points respecting the connection between the Mother Church and the Colonial Churches on which a friendly Conference would be very valuable indeed. . . . . With regard to our brethren in America, no such difficulties exist: what we enjoyed so much during the late Conference was the friendly intercourse and exchange of sentiment between us and them. We have no desire to interfere with their affairs, and I am sure they have no desire to interfere with ours. As far as they are concerned, I think it would be a work of love in which we should be engaged—the extension of Christ's kingdom—and that we may be able by friendly intercourse to strengthen each other's hands

But I think it important that there should be no misunderstanding, and none of that difficulty which, I am bound to say, did exist at the last Lambeth Conference as to what subjects might and what subjects might not be introduced ; that we should know what it is that our brethren wish to bring before us, and what we wish to bring before them, before they give themselves the trouble of coming from the ends of the earth, happy as the results of such a meeting are, under God's Providence, likely to be." [1]

Fortified by the concurrence of the Northern Convocation,[2] which had held aloof in 1867, the Archbishop of Canterbury issued a formal letter on March 28th, 1876, to all the Bishops of the Anglican Communion, intimating his readiness to hold a Conference in 1878, " if it shall seem expedient, after the opinions of all our brethren have been ascertained," and inviting an expression of opinion.[3] These letters to the Bishops throughout the world were not, as heretofore, sent direct from Lambeth ; but were forwarded to the various Metropolitans and presiding Bishops, with a request that they would transmit them officially to the Bishops entitled to receive them in each branch or Province of the Church—a rule which has since been followed in all similar circulars of an official kind.

Before the close of the year about ninety letters of reply were received by the Archbishop, from all parts of the world, showing, as had been anticipated, an overwhelming preponderance of opinion in favour of a second Conference, provided a longer period of session could be arranged for than "the four short days" of 1867.

---

[1] See Chronicle of Convocation, April 16, 1875, pp. 132–134.

[2] For the formal resolution passed in the Convocation of York on Feb. 26, 1875, see Part II., No. XVII., p. 150.

[3] See Part II., No. XVIII., p. 151.

Most of the Bishops also suggested subjects for discussion, and on these the Archbishop took counsel with an Episcopal Committee, and especially with Bishop Selwyn. After the fullest deliberation, the following definite invitation was issued :—

LAMBETH PALACE,
July 10, 1877.

RIGHT REVEREND AND DEAR BROTHER,

It is proposed to hold a Conference of Bishops of the Anglican Communion, at this place, beginning on Tuesday, the second day of July, eighteen hundred and seventy-eight.

The Conference, it is proposed, shall extend over four weeks; the first week, of Four Sessions, to be devoted to discussions, in Conference, of the subjects submitted for deliberation; the second and third weeks to the consideration of these subjects in Committees; and the fourth week to final discussions in Conference, and to the close of the meeting.

The subjects selected for discussion are the following :—

1. The best mode of maintaining Union among the various churches of the Anglican Communion.
2. Voluntary Boards of Arbitration for Churches to which such an arrangement may be applicable.
3. The relations to each other of Missionary Bishops and of Missionaries, in various branches of the Anglican Communion acting in the same country.
4. The position of Anglican Chaplains and Chaplaincies on the Continent of Europe and elsewhere.
5. Modern forms of infidelity, and the best means of dealing with them.
6. The condition, progress, and needs of the various Churches of the Anglican Communion.

I shall feel greatly obliged if, at your early convenience, you will inform me whether we may have the pleasure of expecting your presence at the Conference.

I am,
Right Reverend and dear Brother,
Yours faithfully in Christ,
A. C. CANTUAR.

It was evidently not without intention that the subjects selected for discussion, though grouped under such all-embracing headings, coincided in some parts so closely with the Resolutions of the Conference of 1867. The Reports presented in that year had never, as has been seen, received adequate discussion, nor had any one of them been "adopted" by the Conference. By a recurrence to these subjects a certain measure of continuity was secured, and a basis was laid for the practical deliberations of 1878. The plan adopted in 1867 of drafting and publishing beforehand the Resolutions which were to be moved, had not worked altogether well, and it was arranged that in 1878 the formal motion should in each case be for the appointment of a Committee which, after considering some branch of the selected subjects, should report to the Conference in its final week of session.

One hundred and eight Bishops accepted the Archbishop's invitation. Some of these, however, were at the last moment prevented from attending, and the actual number present at the Conference was exactly one hundred.[1]

On Saturday, June 29, St. Peter's Day, the proceedings of the Conference began with a gathering of Bishops at Canterbury, for what had been described as a "Service of Welcome" in the Cathedral.

Archbishop Tait, four weeks before, had lost his only son, who had recently returned from a visit to America, and the fear that the Archbishop would himself be unable to attend the Service, which would

---

[1] See Part II., No. XXIII., page 204.

thus be deprived of much of its interest and completeness, kept away many Bishops who had intended to be present. The Archbishop, however, went to Canterbury as arranged, and was met by thirty-six Bishops,[1] and an immense gathering of clergy.

A service was held in the morning in St. Augustine's Missionary College, with a sermon by Bishop Cleveland Coxe, of Western New York, and at the Special Evensong in the Cathedral at three o'clock, the Archbishop gave an official welcome to the assembled Bishops. The ancient marble throne, known as "St. Augustine's Chair," was moved from its ordinary position in the south transept, and placed in the centre of the altar steps. The Bishops were grouped on either side of it, and the Archbishop addressed them as follows:—

"My brothers, representatives of the Church throughout the world, engaged in spreading the Gospel of Jesus Christ wherever the sun shines, I esteem it a very high privilege to welcome you here to-day, to the cradle of Anglo-Saxon Christianity. . . I am addressing you from St. Augustine's chair. This thought carries us back to the time when that first missionary to our Anglo-Saxon forefathers, amid much discouragement, landed on these barbarous shores. More than twelve centuries and a-half have rolled on since then. The seed he sowed has borne an abundant harvest, and this great British nation, and our sister beyond the ocean, have cause to render thanks to God for the work begun by him here. And how full of encouragement to you is St. Augustine's work. What difficulties greater than those that confronted him can stand in your path? And you have blessings that he had not. You stand nearer the pure primitive Christianity of the Apostles. You have a motive power to touch the heart denied

---

[1] Nearly all of these came from abroad. Only three of the home Diocesans were present.

to him. . . . . The varied history of the Church has recorded many failures and many successes, and we learn from the past neither to be elated by the one nor discouraged by the other. The monuments which surround us speak of a chequered history. They tell of dark times and of great times. But they all testify to the superintending power of God, Who works all things according to the pleasure of His will, after His own plan for the building up of His one Kingdom in His own way. . . . . It is my privilege to welcome you to Christ Church, Canterbury. . . . . Gregory sent St. Augustine here that he might mark England with the name of Christ, "that Name which is above every name." God grant that that Name may be ever more and more acknowledged among us; that its glories may shine more and more brightly here, and in your distant dioceses, triumphing over all obstacles, and reconciling all petty divisions, uniting all hearts in the truth of our Lord and Saviour, Jesus Christ. My Brethren from across the Atlantic,—you especially from the great Republic,—to you a particular welcome is due from me. Partly for our Church's sake, partly for my sake, partly also for something you discerned in himself, you welcomed one very dear to me last autumn.[1] The bond that unites us is not the less sacred because so many hopes of earthly joy have withered and disappeared. God unite us all more closely in His own great Family. And now let us to prayer."

At eleven o'clock, on Tuesday, July 2, the Bishops met at Lambeth. They were marshalled in the Guard-room, where the actual Sessions of 1867 had been held, and passed thence in procession to the Chapel, the Bishops from the United States walking alongside of the English Diocesan Bishops as their

---

[1] The Archbishop's son, the Rev. Craufurd Tait, had been formally welcomed by the House of Bishops assembled at Boston on Oct. 5, 1877.

guests, all due precedence being given in the processional arrangements to the Metropolitans and presiding Bishops.[1] After the *Veni Creator* had been sung, the Holy Communion was celebrated by the Archbishop of Canterbury, assisted by the Bishops of London, Winchester, Salisbury, and Rochester, as officers of the Provincial College. With the exception of the Archbishop of Canterbury's Chaplains,[2] none but Bishops were present in the Chapel. The sermon was preached by the Archbishop of York, the text being Galatians ii. 11 : " But when Peter was come to Antioch, I withstood him to the face, because he was to be blamed."[3]

The Sessions of the Conference were held in the Great Library, not, as in 1867, in the Guard-room. The arrangement of hours and subjects was as follows :—

Tuesday, July 2.
- 11 a.m. Holy Communion and sermon in Lambeth Palace Chapel.
- 1.30 p.m. Archbishop's opening address.
- 2 p.m.—4.45 p.m. *Subject I.*— The best mode of maintaining union among the various Churches of the Anglican Communion.

Wednesday, July 3.
- 10.30 a.m. Litany in Chapel.
- 11 a.m. *Subject II.*—Voluntary Boards of Arbitration for Churches to which such an arrangement may be applicable.
- 1.30 p.m. *Subject III.*—The relation to each other of Missionary Bishops and of Missionaries in various Branches of the Anglican Communion, acting in the same country.

---

[1] See Part II., No. XXIV., p. 206.
[2] Archdeacon Fisher, Rev. F. G. Blomfield, Hon. and Rev. W. H. Fremantle, Rev. W. F. Erskine Knollys, Rev. Randall T. Davidson.
[3] See Part II., No. XX., p. 154.

Thursday, July 4.
- 10.30 a.m. Litany in Chapel.
- 11 a.m. *Subject IV.*—The position of Anglican Chaplains and Chaplaincies on the Continent of Europe and elsewhere.
- 1.30 p.m. *Subject V.*—Modern forms of Infidelity, and the best means of dealing with them.

Friday, July 5.
- 10.30 a.m. Litany in Chapel.
- 11 a.m. and 1.30 p.m. *Subject VI.*—The condition, progress, and needs of the various Churches of the Anglican Communion.

It was decided, almost unanimously, that the proceedings of the Conference should, as in 1867, be private. A shorthand report was made of all the speeches, and it was arranged that this should be preserved by the Archbishop along with the other manuscripts belonging to Lambeth Library, but should in no way be made public.[1]

The secretarial work of the Conference was again, as in 1867, under the charge of Bishops Ellicott and Cotterill,[2] assisted by Dr. Isambard Brunel, and, unofficially, by the Archbishop's resident Chaplain.[3] For the avoidance of discussions irrelevant to the programme it was arranged, with general consent, that if any memorials or petitions—and there were not a few—should be forwarded to the Conference, they should be placed, without further remark than a bare statement of their purport, in the hands of the

---

[1] A long account of the debates which had taken place in 1867 was unexpectedly published in the *Guardian* of June 19, 1878, under circumstances explained in a letter from the Rev. W. Benham to the Archbishop, which appeared in the *Guardian* of the following week, June 26, 1878, p. 900.

[2] Bishop of Grahamstown 1856–1871; Bishop of Edinburgh 1871–1886.

[3] The Rev. R. T. Davidson.

President, and that the memorialists should be informed that in no case could any answer be returned.

In the opening debates during the first week the formal motion was in each case for the appointment of a Committee to consider the particular subject under discussion, and to report to the Conference during the closing week of Session. On the final and very wide subject—(No. VI.)—" The condition, progress, and needs of the various Churches of the Anglican Communion," the order was varied by the appointment of an influential Committee presided over by the Archbishop of Canterbury, which sat *de die in diem* at Lambeth, "to receive questions submitted in writing by Bishops desiring the advice of the Conference on difficulties or problems they have met with in their several Dioceses."

The various Committees met at Lambeth, Fulham, Farnham, and elsewhere during the fortnight which intervened between the first and last groups of Sessions, and their Reports were, for the most part, ready when the Conference re-assembled in Lambeth Library on Monday, July 22nd. On subject No. V. alone—" Modern forms of Infidelity, and the best means of dealing with them,"—the Committee, as was natural, announced that they had not found it possible to prepare in the time allotted for their deliberations a detailed Report upon so vast a question. To judge, however, from the published opinions of the Bishops present at the Conference[1] the debates upon this subject were among the most useful of any that took place.

As the outcome of much discussion it was decided that the Reports, when adopted by the Conference, should be incorporated as a whole in a combined

---

[1] See, for example, "The Second Lambeth Conference: A Personal Narrative," by Bishop Stevens Perry, of Iowa, pp. 27, &c.

"Letter," and put forth to the world in the name of the hundred Bishops assembled. This course was rendered possible by the almost complete unanimity with which the five Reports in their ultimate shape received the imprimatur of the Conference. Bishop Wordsworth of Lincoln, who, as Archdeacon of Westminster, had in 1867 translated into Greek and Latin the Address then published[1] undertook in like manner to make translations of this document of 1878, condensing or omitting such portions of the Reports as would be inappropriate or uninteresting to those outside the Anglican Communion.[2]

The final paragraphs of the official letter, which will be found in its complete form elsewhere,[3] were as follows :—

"These are the Reports of the Conference, and the practical conclusions at which we have arrived. Some of these conclusions have reference to the special circumstances of different branches of the One Church of Christ, according to peculiarities of their various missionary work for the heathen, or their labours among their own people ; some embody principles which apply to all branches of the Church Universal. They are all limited in their scope to those subjects which have been distinctly brought before the assembled Bishops. We invite to them the attention of the various Synods and other governing powers in the several Churches, and of all the faithful in Christ Jesus throughout the world.

"We do not claim to be lords over God's heritage, but we commend the results of this our Conference to the reason and conscience of our brethren as enlightened by the Holy Spirit of God, praying that all throughout the world who call upon the Lord Jesus Christ may be of one mind, may be united in

---

[1] See Part II., No. VIII., p. 92.
[2] See Part II., No. XXII., p. 191.
[3] See Part II., No. XXI. p. 163.

one fellowship, may hold fast the Faith once delivered to the Saints, and worship their one Lord in the spirit of purity and love.

" Signed on behalf of the Conference,

" A. C. CANTUAR."

The Letter having been thus formally signed, the *Gloria in Excelsis* was sung by the assembled Bishops, the Benediction was pronounced, and the deliberations of the Conference were at an end.

On the following day (Saturday, July 27) a grand closing service was held in St. Paul's Cathedral. The Bishops who were able to be present—about eighty-five in number—received the Archbishop of Canterbury at the West door, and the hymn, " The Church's One Foundation," was sung as the long procession walked up the nave. The *Te Deum*[1] followed, and the Holy Communion was then celebrated by the Archbishop of Canterbury, who was assisted in the service and administration by the Bishops of London, Moray and Ross, Sydney, Montreal, Christ Church (New Zealand), Capetown, Rupertsland, and Delaware. The sermon was preached by Bishop Stevens, of Pennsylvania, from the text, " I, if I be lifted up from the earth, will draw all men unto Me " (St. John xii. 32).[2] The service over, the Bishops assembled in the apse of the Cathedral, when a few farewell words were spoken by the Archbishop. " I feel confident," he said, " that the effect of our gathering will be that the Church at home and abroad will be strengthened by the mutual counsel which we have taken together. May the blessing of Almighty God, the Father, the Son, and the Holy Ghost attend each one of us in our several spheres when we depart from this place. On behalf of the Bishops

---

[1] Stainer in E flat.
[2] See Part II., No. XXV., p. 208.

of England I offer to those of our brethren who have come hither from foreign lands our heartfelt thanks, and bid them, in the name of God, Farewell!"

So ended the second Lambeth Conference. It had been attended, as has been seen, by exactly one hundred Bishops. Thirty-five of these were English,[1] nine were Irish, seven were Scottish, thirty were Colonial and Missionary, and nineteen belonged to the Church of the United States.[2] The expenses of the Conference, so far as they did not devolve upon the Archbishop of Canterbury, were defrayed by the English Diocesan Bishops. A committee of laymen, under the guidance of Mr. J. G. Talbot, M.P., undertook to arrange for all possible hospitality to the American and Colonial Bishops. This organization, however, as well as the visits paid to the English Universities and Cathedral cities, lay altogether outside the official arrangements for the Conference.

CHAPTER III.

THE THIRD CONFERENCE, 1888.

IT was virtually settled at the Conference of 1878 that a third Conference should be held at Lambeth, ten years later, and the death of Archbishop Tait, on December 3, 1882, made no difference in these arrangements.

---

[1] Namely, two Archbishops, twenty-six English Diocesans, three Bishops Suffragan, and four ex-Colonial Bishops holding "Commissions" in England.

[2] For the numbers attending the Conference of 1867, see above, page 19.

Invitation to the Conference of 1888.

In July, 1886, Archbishop Benson issued the following formal letter, which was sent, as on previous occasions, through the various Metropolitans and Presiding Bishops, to all members of the Anglican Episcopate "exercising superintendence over Dioceses, or lawfully commissioned to exercise Episcopal functions therein":—

"RIGHT REVEREND AND DEAR BROTHER,

"There appears to be a general desire that a Conference of the Bishops of the Anglican Communion should again be held at Lambeth within the next few years.

"I have accordingly decided (following the precedents of 1867 and 1878) to issue next year an invitation to such a Conference, which would assemble, according to our present plan, in the summer of 1888.

"It will be of material assistance to myself and to those who are good enough to co-operate with me in making the necessary arrangements, if you can, at your early convenience, inform me whether it seems to you probable that you will be able to take part in our deliberations, and whether there are any subjects of general importance which appear to you specially appropriate for discussion in the Conference.

"I am in hopes that the suggestions which may reach me in answer to this circular letter will enable me to issue, next spring, the formal invitations to the Conference, together with an intimation as to the definite subjects which will, in the following year, come before us for discussion.

"I have made these preliminary arrangements in conjunction with the Archbishop of York and the English Bishops, and I am glad to be able to inform you that the Bishop of Gloucester and Bristol, whose efficient aid as hon. Episcopal Secretary both in 1867 and 1878 will be gratefully remembered, has again kindly consented to act in that capacity. We have associated with him as Hon. Assistant Secretary the Dean of Windsor, who, as resident chaplain to Archbishop Tait, was responsible for many of the arrangements of the Conference of 1878.

"It is not necessary that I should assure you of our earnest desire that you will unite with us in humble prayer to Almighty God that His guidance and blessing may be vouchsafed in rich measure, both to our ultimate deliberations and to the arrangements necessary to secure their efficiency.

"I remain,
"Your faithful Brother and Servant in Christ,
"EDW: CANTUAR:

In the twenty years that had elapsed since the first Conference, the number of Bishops entitled to receive an invitation had increased from 144 to 200, and nine more were added before the third Conference actually assembled. Most of the Bishops, in replying, suggested subjects for discussion, and these suggestions were examined with the utmost care by the Archbishop of Canterbury, and by other Bishops whose assistance he invited. The result of this examination was the following formal letter, sent through the Metropolitans as before :—

"LAMBETH PALACE,
"9th November, 1888.

"RIGHT REVEREND AND DEAR BROTHER,

"I am now able to send you definite information with regard to the Conference of Bishops of the Anglican Communion to be held at Lambeth, if God permit, in the summer of next year.

"In accordance with the precedent of 1878, it has been arranged that the Conference shall assemble on Tuesday, July 3rd, 1888. After four days' session there will be an adjournment, in order that the various Committees appointed by the Conference may have opportunity of deliberation. The Conference will re-assemble on Monday, July 23rd, or Tuesday, July 24th, and will conclude its session on Friday, July 27th.

"Information as to the Services to be held in connection with the Conference, and other particulars will be made public as the time draws near.

"I have received valuable suggestions from my Episcopal brethren in all parts of the world as to the subjects upon which it is thought desirable that we should deliberate.

"These suggestions have been carefully weighed by myself and by the Bishops who have been good enough to co-operate with me in making the preliminary arrangements, and the following are the subjects definitely selected for discussion :—

"I. The Church's practical work in relation to (A) Intemperance, (B) Purity, (C) Care of Emigrants, (D) Socialism.

"II. Definite Teaching of the Faith to various classes, and the means thereto.

"III. The Anglican Communion in relation to the Eastern Churches, to the Scandinavian and other Reformed Churches, to the Old Catholics, and others.

"IV. Polygamy of heathen converts. Divorce.

"V. Authoritative standards of Doctrine and Worship.

"VI. Mutual relations of Dioceses and Branches of the Anglican Communion.

"May I venture again to invite your earnest prayer that the Divine Head of the Church may be pleased to prosper with His blessing this our endeavour to promote His glory, and the advancement of His Kingdom upon earth.

"I remain,
"Your faithful Brother and Servant in Christ,
"EDW: CANTUAR:"

No less than 147 Bishops signified their intention of being present at the Conference. One of these died after accepting the invitation.[1] Three others were at the last moment prevented from leaving their Dioceses. On the other hand, two Bishops were consecrated [2] during the actual month of Conference, and the total number who took part in its deliberations was thus 145. This was proportionally a much larger attendance than at either of the previous Conferences. In 1867, 144 Bishops were invited, and 76 attended. In 1878, 173 were invited, and 100 attended. In 1888, 211 were invited, and 145 attended.

The official proceedings began, as in 1878, with a service held at Canterbury, on Saturday, June 30. After hospitable entertainment in St. Augustine's Missionary College, the Bishops assembled and robed in the Chapter-house, and walked in procession through the cloisters to the great west door of the Cathedral, where they were received by the Archbishop, and by the Cathedral Clergy. The Archbishop was attended by his Chaplains, but the arrangements as to space in the choir of the Cathedral did not admit of such attendance in the case of the other Bishops. As the long procession, including, besides the Bishops, the members of the Cathedral body, the City clergy, and the Mayor and Corporation of Canterbury, moved up the nave and choir, Psalm lxviii. was chanted, and the hymn "Onward, Christian Soldiers," sung. The Bishops, about a hundred in number, were ranged on either side upon the altar-steps, and the Archbishop took his place in St. Augustine's Chair, which had once again been placed for the purpose in the centre of the altar-steps. The *Te Deum* having been chanted, the Archbishop, seated in his chair, delivered the following address :—

---

[1] The Bishop of Fond du Lac, U.S.A.
[2] The Bishops of Bedford and Leicester.

"Brethren most dear, and to me most reverend, few privileges of my office can surpass that which, though unworthy, I exercise to-day. It is to bid you welcome in the name of the Lord. Happy should my soul be if it were given me to take in all that such welcome means. Welcome from all continents, and seas, and shores, where the English tongue is spoken. Welcome, bearers of the great commission to be His witnesses unto the end of the earth. Welcome, disciples of the great determination to 'refuse fables,' and seek the inspiration of the Church at the fountain-head of inspired reason. Welcome to the chair, which, when filled least worthily, most takes up its own parable, and speaks of unbroken lines of government and law and faith, and forgets not the yet earlier Christianity of the land whose own lines soon flowed into and blended with the Roman and the Gallic and the Saxon strains. Round this chair have clustered the glorious memorials you see through ages, none more dear than his who spoke from it last with a pathos and courage quite his own His simple words to you, our brethren of the great Republic, 'the particular welcome from himself,' which his great sorrow and your love privileged him to give you, still shed a tender human light upon the solemn matters we are to treat of, and the heavenly enterprises to which we and our successors are pledged. We know how dear to you is this sanctuary of our fathers and yours,—yes, of 'your Father and our Father.' And even because of the potency of its deep appeal to us to be holy in worship, pure in doctrine, strong in life—even for this appeal's sake we bid you here remember the pregnant words of Gregory to Augustine himself, 'Non pro locis res, sed pro bonis rebus loca amanda sunt.' Love not the things for the sake of the genius of the place, love the place for the good things wrought there. This he said in answer to Augustine's question—'The faith being one, are there different customs in different Churches?' The answer was worthy of him who has been called the greatest of the Popes, and called the first of the Methodists. He says, you remember, 'What thou hast found in any Church more pleasing to the Almighty God, that do thou solicitously choose out, and in the English Church, young in the faith, pour in with excellent instruction what thou gatherest from many Churches.' For the moment, while his Church was young, Augustine stood in a strange, unique position, commissioned to represent in one person the very Church itself which sent him, and bound to represent the future Church for which he was responsible. Were not the words prophetic and characteristic? The task assigned him has surely fulfilled itself in the manifoldness of his Church, the embracingness, the comprehensiveness, and the integrity of her spirit—the versatility with which she enters into the life of new nations, the readiness with which she receives them to herself, the simplicity of the unvarying rule of her faith, yet the steadfastness of the claim she makes for other Churches, as well as for herself, that they may have liberty in things doubtful or indifferent. We honour her when we say she has all the right which the most venerable Churches have to order her service of God, as they did, "according to the diversities of countries, times, and men's manners," so that nothing be ordained against God's word. We vindicate her dignity when we say the right is hers, not ours. It is for her to choose for us, and not we for ourselves; for her in her lasting power, not for us separately in our passing weakness. We honour her when we say that her right is the right of all Churches, and of no individuals. If this voice of Gregory to Augustine be worked into the fabric of our Church, it may well be the "sermon in stones" which we shall hear to-day as the last echoes of the service tremble along the arches, and seem to fancy's ear to quiver with anxiety to leave one true tone with us for comfort and for strength. It is this,—liberty for all the holy Churches of God, loyal allegiance of Churchmen each to his own.

Lastly, may He inspire and bless the work of all believers, be they Churchmen or no, who love the Lord Jesus Christ in sincerity and truth."

Evensong followed, the Anthem being Mendelssohn's "The Sorrows of Death," and the Hymn, "The Church's one Foundation." As the great procession moved outwards from the choir, the Archbishop pronounced the Benediction a second time over the multitude assembled in the nave.

A second great service was held in Westminster Abbey on Monday evening, July 2nd, when the Sermon was preached by the Archbishop of Canterbury, who took for his text Ephesians iv. 16, "All the body, fitly framed and knit together, through that which every joint supplieth."[1]

Nearly all the Bishops who had accepted the invitation to the Conference were present at this service, each attended by his Chaplain. They were marshalled in long procession at the west end of the nave, and during the service were seated in the choir and under the lantern, the general congregation occupying the transepts. The Archbishops and Metropolitans, with their Chaplains, had places assigned them in the sacrarium. The special Psalms and Lessons were: Psalms civ. cxlv. Isaiah xlix. 1-24. Acts ii. 1-22. Sterndale Bennett's Anthem, "God is a Spirit," and Bishop Cleveland Coxe's Hymn, "Saviour, sprinkle many Nations," had also been specially chosen for the occasion.

On the following morning, Tuesday, July 3rd, the Conference opened with a Celebration of Holy Communion in Lambeth Palace Chapel, the introductory sermon or address being delivered by Bishop

---

[1] See Part II., No. XXVIII., page 228.

Whipple, of Minnesota, who had been deputed to this office by the Presiding Bishop of America, at the request of the Archbishop of Canterbury. The closing sentences of the sermon [1] were as follows:—

"To none is this Council so dear as to those whose lives are spent in the darkness of heathenism, or who have gone out to new lands to lay foundation for the work of the Church of God. In loneliness, with deferred hopes, neglected by brethren, your only refuge to cry as a child to God, it is a joy for you to feel the beating of a brother's heart, and hear the music of a brother's voice, and kneel with brothers at the dear old trysting-place, the Table of our Lord. Let us consecrate all we have and are to Him; let us remember loved ones far away; let us gather the work we have so long garnered in our hearts and lay it at His feet. We shall not have met in vain if out of the love learned of Him we give each to other and to all fellow-labourers for Him a brother's love, a brother's sympathy, and a brother's prayers. I do not know how to clothe in words the thronging memories which cluster round us in this holy place, what searchings of heart, what cries to God, what communions with Christ, what consolations of the Holy Spirit, have been witnessed in this sacred place. I cannot call over the long roll of saints, confessors, and martyrs, whose 'names are written in the Lamb's Book of Life.' Two names will be remembered to-day by us all. One that gentle Archbishop Longley, who in the greatness of his love saw with a prophet's eye the mission of the Church, and planned these Conferences, that our hearts might beat as one in the battle of the last time. The other, the wisest of counsellors, and the most loving of brethren, the great-hearted Archbishop Tait, whose dying legacy to his brethren was 'love one another.' They

---

[1] See Part II., No. XXIX., page 241.

have finished their course and entered into rest. A little more work, a few more trials, and we, too, shall finish our course. We are not two companies: the militant and triumphant are one. We are the advance and rear of one host, travelling to the Canaan of God's rest. God grant that we, too, may so follow Christ that we may have an abundant entrance to His eternal kingdom."

The historic chapel was filled to overflowing by the Bishops in their robes, no one else being present, except the Chaplains of the Archbishop of Canterbury. He was himself the Celebrant, assisted by his Provincial Officers, the Bishops of London, Winchester, Rochester, Lincoln, and Salisbury.

The order of procession adopted at all these services was the same, and was simpler than that of the former Conferences. Due precedence was given to Archbishops, to Metropolitans and Presiding Bishops, and to the Bishops of London, Durham, and Winchester, all other Bishops without distinction being arranged according to date of consecration.[1]

The great Library had been prepared, as in 1878, for the sessions of the Conference, a low platform having on this occasion been specially erected, with places for the three Archbishops and the seven Metropolitans, in a semi-circle on either side of the President's chair.

The secretarial work was, for the third time, undertaken by the Bishop of Gloucester and Bristol,[2] who was assisted by the Dean of Windsor,[3] and the Archdeacon of Maidstone,[4] the last-named having been added as Assistant-Secretary a few weeks before the Conference, owing to the unexpected pressure of correspondence.

---

[1] See Part II., No. XXXI., page 256.
[2] The Right Rev. C. J. Ellicott, D.D.
[3] The Very Rev. Randall T. Davidson, M.A.
[4] The Ven. B. F. Smith, M.A.

A shorthand writer, as on the two previous occasions, made a verbatim report of all the discussions for preservation at Lambeth.

The proceedings during the first week of session followed exactly upon the lines laid down by Archbishop Tait in 1878. Certain speakers had been selected, specially qualified to open the several discussions, the motion being in each case for the appointment of a Committee to consider the particular subject, and to report to the Conference in its closing week of session. Twelve such Committees were appointed in all, some of the subjects being, by general consent, divided into two, or varied in form from the wording of the official agenda paper.[1]

A strong "Committee of Reference" was appointed in case any important questions, not covered by the programme, should be suggested, in the form of questions, for consideration and reply. But its work was light, and had reference mainly to the procedure of the Conference itself. In accordance with the unanimous recommendation of this Committee, it was decided that no attempt should be made to secure the "adoption" of the various Reports presented by the Committees, but that formal resolutions should in each case be moved by the several Chairmen.

The memorials and petitions which arrived each day were notified to the Conference by the President's direction, but it was made clear, as on former occasions, that no answer could in any case be returned.

The Committees met frequently during the fortnight which intervened between the two weeks of full session. Some of them were accommodated in the newly-opened "Church House," in Dean's Yard, which was thus put in its first days to one of the most important of the uses that its promoters had in view. Other Committees met at Lambeth, at

---

[1] See Part II., No. XXXV., page 285.

Farnham, at Ely, and at London House. When the Conference re-assembled on Monday, July 23rd, the Reports were all in print, and were circulated in time for the respective discussions.

The substitution of carefully-worded resolutions in place of motions for the actual "adoption" of the several Reports worked very successfully. It was agreed that when any of the minority desired it, the numbers voting for and against the adoption of any of the resolutions ultimately carried should be made public. But in the case of three only, out of the thirty-two resolutions of the Conference,[1] was such a request made. Resolutions or amendments lost on a division were not made public in any form. It was also decided that the Reports of the Committees, though not formally adopted, should, unless otherwise decided by vote of Conference, be printed and circulated with the official resolutions. The names of the members of Committee were to be printed on the Reports, which were all, however, to be prefaced by a note, for the protection of minorities, pointing out that the Reports had not in all cases been unanimously adopted by the Committees responsible for them.

The Archbishop of Canterbury was requested to draft, with such assistance as he might invite, an Encyclical Letter, embodying the results of the deliberations of the Conference in a form suited for general circulation. This was done, and on the last day of session, Friday, July 27th, the draft Encyclical Letter was considered, paragraph by paragraph, and, after certain alterations had been made, the Archbishop was requested, without one dissentient voice, to sign it on behalf of the Conference.[2] An Address to the Queen,[3] which had lain in the gallery

---

[1] Part II., No. XXXIV., page 277.
[2] Part II., No. XXXIII., page 264.
[3] Part II., No. XXX., page 252.

for signature during the sessions of the Conference was formally read by the Archbishop, and the Conference closed with the Doxology and Benediction.

A solemn valedictory and thanksgiving service was held next day in St. Paul's Cathedral. It was attended not only by the Bishops,[1] and their chaplains, but by the Lower Houses of Convocation both of Canterbury and York, by the House of Laymen of the Province of Canterbury, and by the legal and other officers of the Primate. All these walked in procession from the west door of the Cathedral to the choir. The service consisted of Holy Communion and Sermon, followed by a grand *Te Deum*.[2] The Celebrant was the Archbishop of Canterbury. The Bishop of Minnesota read the Epistle; the Bishop of London the Gospel. The Sermon was preached by the Archbishop of York, who took as his text Romans viii. 19, "The earnest expectation of the creature waiteth for the manifestation of the sons of God."[3]

An enormous congregation crowded the space under the dome, as well as the nave, transepts, and both aisles. The service lasted more than three hours. After the *Te Deum*, the long procession returned to the west door, and the third Lambeth Conference was at an end.

Of the 145 Bishops who took part in it, 46 belonged to England and Wales,[4] 11 to Ireland, 6 to Scotland, 29 to the United States of America, and 53 to Colonial and Missionary Dioceses throughout the world.

---

[1] About 130 Bishops were present.
[2] Gounod.
[3] Part II., No. XXXVII., page 364.
[4] Viz., 32 Diocesan Bishops, 8 Bishops Suffragan, and 6 ex-Colonial Bishops holding Commissions in England.

Warm thanks were tendered to all those on whom the business arrangements of the Conference had devolved ; and, not least, to the Committee of laymen who had again, as in 1878, under Mr. Talbot's guidance, made themselves responsible for the organisation of the hospitality offered to American and Colonial Bishops. Mr. Tallents acted as Hon. Secretary of this important Committee.

The Encyclical Letter and Reports were immediately published by the Society for Promoting Christian Knowledge, and obtained a wide and rapid circulation, more than 18,000 having been sold before the close of the year.

The Encyclical Letter and the Resolutions of the Conference were translated into Greek and Latin by Bishop Wordsworth of Salisbury, who thus carried on the work undertaken on the two previous occasions by his father, the Bishop of Lincoln. These versions are reproduced below.[1]

The foregoing narrative has dealt simply with the three Conferences in their bare official aspect. The indirect results which accrue from such gatherings are probably at least as great as those of an official kind. For an estimate of these indirect results, however, and for the impression made by the debates of the earlier Conferences upon those who attended them, the reader must turn to the accounts which have been published in ample number in the Biographies of Bishops on both sides of the Atlantic.[2]

The keen interest aroused on every side by the Conference of 1888 has given evidence enough, were

---

[1] See Part II., No. XXXVIII., page 376.

[2] *E.g.*, Lives of Bishops Sumner, Gray, Hopkins, Ewing Selwyn, Kerfoot, Wilberforce, Wordsworth, &c.

such required, that those who planned in faith and courage the first of these decennial gatherings were right in believing that a solid gain must follow, not to the Anglican Communion only, but to the Church of Christ throughout the world.

PART II.

Letters and Documents illustrating the History of the Lambeth Conferences.

No. I. (See page 10.)

Addresses from the Provincial Synod of the United Church of England and Ireland in Canada, assembled at Montreal in September, 1865; with the Reply of the Archbishop of Canterbury.

To the Most Reverend the Archbishop, the Right Reverend the Bishops, and the Reverend the Clergy of the Convocation of the Province of Canterbury.

We, the Bishops, Clergy, and Laity of the Canadian Branch of the United Church of England and Ireland, in Synod assembled, would approach your Venerable Body with the deepest sentiments of reverence and affection.

We are engaged, like yourselves, in endeavouring, in this distant dependency of the Crown, to uphold the truth of Religion, as our Common Church maintains it, and that Apostolic Order which is so essential a safeguard in the preservation and diffusion of the Catholic Faith. Recent declarations in high places in our Mother-land, in reference to the position of the Colonial Branches of the Mother Church, have created amongst us feelings of regret and apprehension, as tending to shake the conviction, always so dear to us, that we in the Colonies were, in all respects, one with the Church of our parent country.

No statute or decision, we beg solemnly to assure you, much as it may serve to weaken our outward connection with the Church of our fathers, can impair the integrity and vigour of those principles in doctrine and fellowship which constitute her inward life. We are one with her in the great Articles of Christian Belief, and one with her in that Episcopal Order which binds her members in unity throughout the world.

In desiring most earnestly to retain this connection, we believe that it would be most effectually preserved and perpetuated if means could be adopted by which the members of our Anglican Communion in all quarters of the world should have a share in the deliberations for her welfare, and be permitted to have a representation in one General Council of her members gathered from every land. Deeply affected by the threat of isolation which recent declarations in high places have indicated, we earnestly solicit this measure of relief, as maintaining that test of inward communion which is to us the most precious.

But while we look with hope to such concession, we readily affirm our belief that the manner and measure of the relief and encouragement we solicit will be left most wisely to the deliberate judgment of those ancient Convocations of the Church to whom, under God, the cause of true religion at home and abroad is so largely indebted.

Dated at the City of Montreal, in the Province of Canada, this twentieth day of September, in the year of our Lord one thousand eight hundred and sixty-five.

  F. MONTREAL, JAMES BEAVEN, D.D.,
   Metropolitan.   *Prolocutor.*

To His Grace Charles Thomas, Archbishop of Canterbury, D.D., Primate of all England, and Metropolitan.

May it please your Grace,—

We, the Bishops, Clergy, and Laity of the Province of Canada, in Triennial Synod assembled, desire to represent to your Grace, that in consequence of the recent decisions of the Judicial Committee of the Privy Council in the well-known case respecting the *Essays and Reviews*, and also in the case of the Bishop of Natal and the Bishop of Cape Town, the minds of many members of the Church have been unsettled or painfully alarmed; and that doctrines hitherto believed to be Scriptural, and undoubtedly held by the members of the Church of England and Ireland, have been adjudicated upon by the Privy Council in such a way as to lead thousands of our brethren to conclude that, according to this decision, it is quite compatible with membership in the Church of England to discredit the historical facts of Holy Scripture, and to disbelieve the eternity of future punishment; moreover, we would express to your Grace the intense alarm felt by many in Canada lest the tendency of the revival of the active powers of Convocation should leave us governed by canons different from those in force in England and Ireland and thus cause us to drift into the status of an independent branch of the Catholic Church—a result which we would at this time most solemnly deplore.

In order, therefore, to comfort the souls of the faithful, and reassure the minds of wavering members of the Church, and to obviate, as far as may be, the suspicion whereby so many are scandalised, that the Church is a creation of Parliament, we humbly entreat your Grace, since the assembling of a General Council of the whole Catholic Church is at present impracticable, to convene a National Synod of the Bishops of the Anglican Church at home and abroad, who, attended by one or more of their presbyters or laymen, learned in ecclesiastical law, as their advisers, may meet together, and, under the guidance of the Holy Ghost, take such counsel and adopt such measures as may be best fitted to provide for the present distress in such Synod, presided over by your Grace.

F. MONTREAL,   JAS. BEAVEN, D.D.,
Metropolitan, President.   *Prolocutor.*

Reply of the Archbishop.

To the Bishops, Clergy, and Laity of the Province of Canada, lately assembled in their Triennial Synod.

ADDINGTON PARK, *December*, 1865.

My Right Rev., Rev., dear Brethren,—

I have duly received the Address forwarded to me by your Metropolitan, from the late Triennial Provincial Synod of the Province of Canada, requesting me to convene a Synod of the Bishops of the Anglican Church, both at home and abroad, in order that they may meet together, and, under the guidance of the Holy Ghost, take such counsel, and adopt such measures, as may be best fitted to provide for the present distress.

I can well understand your surprise and alarm at the recent decisions of the Judicial Committee of the Privy Council in grave matters bearing upon the doctrine and discipline of our Church, and I can comprehend your anxiety, lest the recent revival of action in the two Provincial Convocations of Canterbury and York should lead to the disturbance of those relations, which have hitherto subsisted between the different branches of the Anglican Church.

The meeting of such a Synod as you propose is not by any means foreign to my own feelings, and I think it might tend to prevent those inconveniences, the possibility of which you anticipate. I cannot, however, take any step in so grave a matter without consulting my episcopal brethren in both branches of the United Church of England and Ireland, as well as those in the different colonies and dependencies of the British Empire.

I remain, your faithful and affectionate friend and brother in Christ,

C. T. CANTUAR,
Primate of All England.

No. II. (See page 10.)

Proceedings of the Convocation of Canterbury with respect to the Canadian Address of September, 1865.

On May 2, 1866, the Lower House unanimously resolved, " That his Grace the President be respectfully requested to direct the appointment of a Committee to consider and report upon the Address of the Canadian Branch of the United Church of England and Ireland, dated at Montreal, September 20, 1865."—(*Chronicle of Convocation*, May 2, 1866, *p.* 290.)

The President having granted this request, a Committee of fifteen members was appointed. The Committee presented its report on June 29, 1866, but the debate upon it was postponed until the following group of sessions.

On February 14, 1867, the Lower House, after a prolonged discussion, agreed by a majority of 29 to the following resolution :—

" That this House tenders its sincere thanks to the Committee on the Address of the Canadian Church, for the labour which they have bestowed on the subject, and for the Report which they have framed and presented to this House, and desires to convey to his Grace the Archbishop of Canterbury a respectful expression of an earnest desire that he would be pleased to issue an invitation to all the Bishops in communion with the Church of England to assemble at such time and place, and accompanied by such persons as may be deemed fit, for the purpose of Christian sympathy and mutual counsel on matters affecting the welfare of the Church at home and abroad ; and that this resolution be forwarded to the Upper House."

A debate upon the subject took place in the Upper House on the following day. No formal resolution was proposed, but the Archbishop announced his intention of acceding to the request which had been made.—(*Chronicle of Convocation, February* 14 and 15, 1867, *pp*. 767–793, 800–808.)

No. III.   (See page 13.)

Official Arrangements for the Conference of Bishops of the Anglican Communion, to be holden at Lambeth Palace, on September 24, 1867, *and following days.*

FIRST DAY.—Tuesday, September 24, at eleven o'clock, a.m. Prayers and Holy Communion. Sermon, by the Bishop of Illinois.

General Subject for the Day's Discussion,

INTERCOMMUNION BETWEEN THE CHURCHES OF THE ANGLICAN COMMUNION.

Opening Address of the President: specifying the general principles and rules of the Conference, and inviting any introductory remarks from Home Metropolitans and from distant Bishops.

General agreement as to the arrangement of the time and subjects.

Resolution :—

We, Bishops of Christ's Holy Catholic Church, professing the faith of the primitive and undivided Church, as based on Scripture, defined by the first four General Councils,[1] and reaffirmed by the Fathers of the English Reformation, now assembled by the good providence of God at the Archiepiscopal Palace of Lambeth, under the presidency of the Primate of all England, desire, First, to give hearty thanks to Almighty God for having thus brought us together for common counsels, and united worship; Secondly, we desire to express the deep sorrow with which we view the divided condition of the flock of Christ throughout the world ; and, Lastly, we do here solemnly declare our belief that the best hope of future reunion will be found in drawing each of us for ourselves closer to our common Lord, in giving ourselves to much prayer and intercession, in the cultivation of a spirit of charity, and in seeking to diffuse through every part of the Christian community that desire and resolution to return to the faith and discipline of the undivided Church which was the principle of the English Reformation.

Resolution :—

Notification of New Sees and Bishops.

That it appears to us expedient, for the purpose of maintaining brotherly intercommunion, that all cases of establishment of new Sees, and appointment of new Bishops, be notified to all Archbishops and Metropolitans of the Home and Colonial Church

---

[1] See 1 Eliz., c. i. xxxvi.

of England and Ireland, the Primus of the Protestant Episcopal Church in Scotland, and the Presiding Bishop of the Protestant Episcopal Church in the United States of America.

Resolution :—
Letters Commendatory.

That, having regard to the conditions under which intercommunion between Members of the Church passing from one distant Diocese to another may be duly maintained, we hereby deem it desirable—

(1) That forms of Letters Commendatory on behalf of clergymen visiting other Dioceses be drawn up and agreed upon, and that no strange clergyman should officiate in any Diocese without exhibiting such Commendatory Letters to the Bishop thereof;

(2) That a form of Letters Commendatory for such Laymen as may desire to avail themselves of them be in like manner prepared.

The Benediction.

SECOND DAY.—Wednesday, September 25.

General Subject for the Day's Discussion,

COLONIAL CHURCHES.

Resolution :—
Subordination to Metropolitans.

That it be a matter for the consideration of this Conference, and of the Bishops of the Colonial Church especially—

(1) Whether it be desirable that such Colonial and Missionary Dioceses as have not as yet been gathered into Provinces be formed into any Province; and

(2) Whether any, and if so what, steps should be taken.

Resolution :—

Discipline to be exercised by Metropolitans.

That, whereas schemes for conducting Ecclesiastical Affairs and for the exercising of Discipline have been embodied in the Letters Patent granted by the Crown to the Metropolitans of Canada, India, Australasia, New Zealand, and South Africa, it appears to us to be desirable that the aforesaid schemes so embodied in the Letters Patent be, for the present, and until the local authorities, spiritual and temporal, have otherwise provided, as much as possible adhered to; and that in all cases where the power of coercive jurisdiction is not conveyed by such Letters Patent it is desirable to provide by voluntary agreement for the enforcement of discipline, and that with a view to secure this end, all Bishops at their Consecration, and clergymen of those Dioceses at their ordination or institution to the cure of souls, should be required to pledge themselves to submit to the provisions of such schemes.

Resolution :—

Court of Metropolitans.

That in the case of any charges being preferred against a Suffragan Bishop of any Province, it appears to us desirable that the Metropolitan thereof should summon all the Bishops of his Province to sit with him for the hearing of the case, and that he should not proceed to the hearing of it without the aid and concurrence of all the Bishops of his Province that can be assembled.

The question of any charge being brought against a Metropolitan should also be considered.

Resolution :—

Question of Appeal.

That it be a matter for the consideration of this Conference whether, in cases where no Letters

Patent have been issued, any, and if any what, Appeal should lie from such Provincial Decisions.

Resolution :—

Conditions of Union.

That it be a matter for the consideration of this Conference, in reference to Colonial Churches not legally united to the United Churches of England and Ireland, what safeguards as to their continued soundness in Doctrine and Discipline be required by the Mother Church as the condition of the maintenance of full spiritual and ecclesiastical communion.

The Benediction.

THIRD DAY.—Thursday, September 26th.

General Subject for the Day's Discussion,

CO-OPERATION IN MISSIONARY ACTION.

Resolution :—

Notification of proposed Missionary Bishoprics.

That in case it should be proposed to found a Missionary Bishopric by any of the branches of the Church represented in this Conference, it seems to us desirable—

(1) That notification of such intention be sent to all Archbishops and Metropolitans of the Home and Colonial Church of England and Ireland, the Primus of the Protestant Episcopal Church in Scotland, and the Presiding Bishop of the Protestant Episcopal Church in the United States ; and

(2) That, so soon as any person is consecrated to such Bishopric, the announcement of such Consecration be made to the same parties.

Resolution :—

Subordination of Missionaries.

That, in the case of the establishment of any Missionary Bishopric, and consecration of a Bishop to the same, we deem it expedient that all Missionaries should place themselves under the general superintendence of such Missionary Bishop, subject always to their obedience to such written instructions as may be sent to them by those in authority at home.

Concluding resolution :—

That we desire to render our hearty thanks to Almighty God for the blessings vouchsafed to us in and by this Conference; and we desire to express our hope that this our Meeting may hereafter be followed by other Meetings to be conducted in the spirit of the same brotherly love.

The Closing Benediction.

No. IV.

Sermon of Bishop Whitehouse, of Illinois, preached in Lambeth Palace Chapel, on September 24, 1867.

"Who now rejoice in my sufferings for you, and fill up that which is behind of the afflictions of Christ in my flesh for his body's sake, which is the Church."—*Col.* i. 24.

There is something very startling at the first glance in the leading phraseology of this verse, and we challenge it with almost a suspicion that it cannot consist with the humility of the man who chides himself as " less than the least of all saints."

"Fill up" what is behind of the sufferings of Christ! "Fill up" the sufferings of the "Man of sorrows!" "Fill up" the pains of poverty, exposure, anxiety, betrayal, and agony which,—speaking in the light of this world,—scarce left a sunny spot in the life of Jesus! "Fill up" the sufferings of One who drank drop by drop the mysterious cup of the Divine wrath, while mind and body agonized in the terrible struggle! "Fill up" the precious sufferings which bought and healed a world!

This cannot be, and by every trait of the Apostle's character, as well as by the perfection and triumph of the Cross, we are warned off from any such construction. Yet the words stand written for our learning. There is a sense in which the spirit sealed them as eternal truth, and like the other parts of the same Testament they are living words for our hearts, consciences, and lives.

What Paul did, and realized in his experience, belongs, we may be assured, to the true spirit and compass of our profession. The affection which bound him thus to the Church and Christ must find a responsive place in our hearts, as successors in his calling of trust and sacrifice, which, though exercised in the midst of less "fiery trials" may still require us to be "armed with the same suffering mind." It at least may show, in the deep-toned and mystical relations it involves, what is the hereditary commission of the Elect, and the burden on their generations of discharging a long entail of "afflictions" for His body's sake, which is the Church.

I am placed to-day in one of the most trying, as well as the most honourable, positions of, my life. The delicate courtesy of His Grace of Canterbury transferred the trust of the opening sermon to the American Episcopate, and the friendship of our own Presiding Bishop devolved it on me, because to some extent I had been identified with this plan of demonstrative unity, and had been adopted into the earlier councils which determined and shaped it,—selected thus by a courtesy, which did not stop to weigh merit or estimate capacity, but regarded only the antecedent of a remoter accident and privilege.

I know, brothers beloved, that I am standing in the circle of my peers in the rank of ministration of Christ's Church, and that officially we are equal. But I cannot keep down the consciousness to how limited an extent that peerage applies to an equality of learning, manhood, grace, experience, and power in the "rhetoric of life," the lovely and profound graces of your "holy conversation." I cannot clear myself from an inward rebuke that I should be speaking as the father of Fathers, when I ought to sit in silence, learning as "a child." Each impulse has been checked, each thought has been crippled by the haunting majesty of this strange secluded assembly, and the vision of my own "presence" so weak among you.

But, while I have prayed and striven to "glory in my infirmities" that the power of Christ may rest upon me, I still cast myself upon a consciousness that you have all learned through a life's tears, no matter how gifted you are, an experience taught by all the huge discrepancy between the proud aggression of the "young Melancthon," daring for success, and the subdued Apostle with the care of all the Churches. What a sympathy we instinctively acquire with words which breath of pity for sinfulness, and help for labour, of a closer union with the unseen, of steps guided on a great appointed course, of fellowship in sufferings, begun in the holy flesh and holy soul of our own Lord, and of the spirit of Grace, which is continually teaching in discipline and soothing with comfort, offering us sweet thorns that may be woven into an angel's crown, and transmuting each sanctified care and struggle into a coronal, rayed with the glory of Christ.

Hence then may I preach as communing with my

own tried and feeble nature, to chasten and cheer it; believing that we are more nearly one on the "hidden man of the heart," then we may be divided on your eminence of scholarship or well-earned human dignity. I trust more to touch the finer association of your experience, than afford any instruction; but in our brotherhood with the great apostle, as "keepers of the flocks" we may meditatively appreciate his divine words, and sympathize with his invigorating experience.

Because Paul was made an apostle and minister, "the afflictions" follow of necessity; they are inherent of the office, as much as are the aggressive duties and systematic labours. The enduring them is fruit to the Church which is Christ's Body; and we cannot properly estimate a labour or affliction without regarding both as the ὑστερήματα which, like the "fragments" supernatural in the wilderness banquet of the five barley loaves and small fishes, are gathered up by apostolic hands, each in his own basket, until the whole be fulfilled in the completed elect. The apostle calls himself διάκονος, *of* the Church, and *for* the Church, but *where* that Church is ὀικονόμια θέου, a family to be administered, and a trust involved of stewardship and implication, which, even if unjustly handled, still involves relations of personal profit.

But the ὑστερήματα mentioned are not the "filling up" of παθήματα, the passion and sufferings, for the expiation of sin, of the Incarnate and Crucified, which none could fill up and none can have, except in the transferred experience of a crucified, buried, and risen soul. Neither are they "sufferings" which malice and violence even to martyrdom may wreak on the flesh, and hurl on the quivering nerves. But, they are θλίψεις, afflictions of the inner nature and the heart's consciousness, which are not to be met in the bravery of a stern endurance, which casts them off as a very little thing, in the anasthesia of the flesh from the inward hope of glory. They are "afflictions" which it were treachery not to feel, and loss not to cherish; where the inner man must be seared to the right spiritual sensibility, if it does not respond to them, not only in the pang of the sword, which goeth through the heart, but in a quickened heart to casket them in the tenderness, which saddens but elevates the whole nature.

Christ and His ministry constitute one mystical personality, and the identity runs through every relation—as He is, so are they in this world. The servant is not greater than his Lord, and separation even to cruelty and hate, may be a natural sequence, as we carry about in our body the mortification of Christ, that His life may be manifested in us. But far deeper is this, a community of liegemen and servants sharing loyally in the struggle and attainder of the Lord, for Christ says, I call you not servants but friends, for the servant knoweth not what his Lord doeth. It is the fellowship of the inner and spiritual; the co-operative in counsel and purpose, the ancestral of an ever-returning feast with hereditary dignity, and the noble responsibility of a heritage faithfully transmitted in integrity and honour. It is the consciousness inspiring every power, that while the leadership is resistless and the result triumph, each individual effort exerted, and specially every "affliction" garnered in the watchful breast in sympathy with the Head, is graciously allowed as contribution of individual partnership, accelerating the issue and filling up the measure of the hours of contest.

The sufferings of Christ are thus to be doubly taken —those which He sustained in His own body, where nothing remains to be fulfilled; the other to be suffered in His mystical Body to the end of the ages;—and so there remain many sufferings to be fulfilled. Of this the Church as the appointed agency, the ministry as the delegated headship, the members as the instruments of work, must, severally and incorporate, carry the burthen, as the Church represents Christ fulfilling, both in receptiveness and activity, the work which the Father gave Him to do. But the spirit in which the "afflictions" are borne and the work done, is rejoicing, the "joy in tribulation," the winnowing of the elect. Hence the filling up of what is behind of the afflictions of Christ in "my flesh" has the two-fold relation of sufferings of ours assumed by Christ, and afflictions of His bequeathed to us in the grace of reciprocal endurance.

The visible Church, "the body of Christ," instinct with life, guidance, and sympathy from its visible Head, is now witnessing in sackcloth. At every point in the million million pores of sensibility, and the deep capacity of a worn and anguished soul, the "body" is fulfilling through its organism, the heirloom of the suffering state imparted by Him,—who touched earth "to begin to do and to teach," who lived the "Man of sorrows," baptized His body into His own baptism of blood, and left that Body to work out, in its ages of discipline and mercy, the mission begun over the hills and valleys of Palestine.

The three years of the Lord's earthly manifestation were type and pattern of all to follow. Had that ministry continued for centuries; had those precious feet trodden worn and bleeding all earth's highways and acres; had that voice rung in its awful immensity from heaven to hell, or pleaded with sweet gentleness in the household ear, still would the mysterious history have been the same,—afflictions, rejection, crucifying afresh, and the few cross-bearers following with holy chaunt the same pathway, and gathering up the "fragments" of their Master's afflictions as a manna creation for earthly wants, support for duty, memorial of tenderness, and earnest of power, triumphant through weakness.

Such is and will be the position of the Church which is Christ's body in this world, which world in all its plans and policy, its heart and intellect, is opposed to Christ; such in some familiar or strange forms will be the experience of the visible headship of the undying Episcopate; such will be, in the experience of the believer's soul, the *stigmata* that testify his fellowship in suffering, and the pulsations of the infused current of the resurrection life.

The sufferings of the Redeemer, personal and propitiatory, terminated on the cross. Heaven and earth, time and eternity, took the indelible record, "*It is finished.*" But as He is one with the holy cause of His truth and Church, given back in the hour of universal dominion as Head over all things, to be the living Head of His living Body, the Church, the measure of suffering is *not* fulfilled, the lien of afflictions *not* discharged until the reproach, persecution, and distress of the militant Church, and the far sorer trials of her inner struggles have ended, and her honoured faithful are the crowned conquerors of the spotless church above. In the whole militant Church, distributed through its offices and membership, through its work and feeling; under the blow from without or the rending pang within; in the stern hour of fierceness, impotent to crush, or in the ceaseless burthen of infirmity and sins; in the common griefs, or the thorn betrayed only in the lone cry of a thrice pressed anguish; for you, for me, for Christ's ministers and Christ's "little ones" are the sufferings of Christ, one day to be "filled up," completed gloriously sealed.

St. Paul represents himself as affording his flesh, —in its old nature, spiritually crucified, and, in its power of labour and endurance, activity, and influence freely consecrated,—to press on this consummation, and hasten the coming hour of victory and peace. Paul shrank neither from a suffering Messiah nor a suffering Church, but, appreciating in both the highest attributes of excellence and honour, cast body and soul into the mould, to be used by Christ, as well as to be "formed after the image of Him who created him." He rejoiced in his calling, magnified his office, glorified his Saviour for His work and His love, discerned and cherished His mystical Body, vindicated his apostleship with the might of his intellect and the heroism of his gigantic mission, irradiated Judaism and subdued the heathen, preached far and wide the exhaustless Gospel, and then in hallowed egoism threw open his own breast, that with the blood of the sufferings—love warm and joy dyed,— he might still feed his precious nestlings and nourish children's children. "I now rejoice in my sufferings for you, and fill up that which is behind of the afflictions of Christ in my flesh for His body's sake, which is the Church."

And we, successors of his ministry and heirs of his faith, glorying in our calling and moaning apart, "Not worthy—not worthy to be called an apostle!" we, when century has heaped on century the wrecks of all human institutions, and buried them beneath the dying verdure of fresh spring-times, only to be crushed with more crumbling ruins, we who live when material progress scorns the past, when Mammon builds Babel towers; and science utters oracles from rocks and graves, to confuse the old faiths, and dishonour old trusts,—we stand in our unbroken line, witness by the same sacramental altars of eighteen centuries agone, confess in the same creeds, teach from the same inspired word, recognize the mystical spouse ever young and beautiful, and are folded to her breast as a dear and holy mother; we find perpetuated in Christ's visible body, each function of its living organism, each susceptibility of its complex being and individual experience, and encounter "the dangers and chances of the world" in the same conflict with the same suffering Church. As we catch this single gush of heart-revealing it is fresh for us as a living spring to thirsty lip. We drink it in, and then down among all our heart sickness and bewildered struggles, our wearying shame and spectral responsibility, where perhaps years have withered the flowers, and dried even perennial roots, *there* are we conscious of response to joy in sufferings.

We rejoice in sympathy, because for us also, this single verse is the experience of the believing soul, because it explains our place in this world, because it opens our sufficient consolation and because it defines our honourable trust.

How much of our understanding and enjoyment of Gospel righteousness depends on the proper view of our real oneness with Christ. When we know Him, not alone "after the flesh" as a being of singular and isolated excellence, of noble character, sweet benevolence and lofty power, as the great Teacher to a band of disciples, the bright example of purity and love, standing off from us to be studied, imitated, honoured, and adored—but, when we know Him in the spirit as united to us, our wisdom, our righteousness, our sanctification, our redemption, acting for us and acting in us, and our spiritual nature entering into the same condition as that of our great representative, as it is written "If any man be in Christ he is a new creature,"—then indeed, the travail and the victory of Christ are his. He is the son of God and heir of the kingdom; he has become the beloved child in whom the Father is well pleased. He has eternal life abiding in him; he has come unto Mount Sion and the new Jerusalem, and the brotherhood of the living dead; his enemies are overcome, and he is the conqueror of death and hell; his portion is to be where Christ is, and his progress, even now is "from glory to glory;" already he is exercising his priesthood and his kingship, he reigns with Christ.

It doth not indeed yet "appear" what we shall be. Much of this germing glory is and will be hidden. The new creatures carry to outward observation the soiled and beggar dress of the hedge and the wilderness. To man they look even as others who have no such hope, and even to themselves they seem only weak, unfaithful and chief of sinners. It doth not appear to us, but it does appear to the Father, the Lamb and the Spirit. They regard the true Christian as thus transformed into Christ's image, clothed with Christ's righteousness, united to Him in the reciprocal crucifixion and the new life of the resurrection, dead in Christ, in Him quickened, justified, and raised, the new and heavenly being called into life within; with a struggling but conquering holiness pressing him towards the mark for the prize of the high calling. In proportion as he sees and feels this precious mystical and spiritual union, will the believer learn to rejoice with "joy unspeakable and full of glory." It explains our place in the world in its perpetual separation and inevitable antagonism. Oh! awful vastness and penetrative subtilty of the world! We are not marshalled sharp and defiant as hostile armies, flaunting their standards, serried in rank and battle cry. But the world is all around us, the enveloping medium, and with elemental forces,—the world *around* the Church, the world *within* the Church, and the world in each heart of struggle and grace. But no matter where, no matter in what form; no matter how bold in cruelty, how seductive in blandishment, how tangled in interest, and blended in counsels, how co-operative in social advances, and mutually dependent in the instruments, still the enmity of the world is deep and permanent, according to that significant saying of the Saviour,—the world hated Me before it hated you. Hence our age and condition will be necessarily a period of multiplied and distributed "afflictions," minutely ramified and keenly penetrative, boundless in area as exhaustless in ingenuity. The Church is alive and the world is alive. Each grapples the other or permeates the other as the case may be, on contact at myriad points, with forces and influences, silent as the dew, and leaping as the cloud-flash; internal as the blood current and sensitive as the nerves; wise as the serpent and grand in intellect and research; tender as the dove and fascinating as household loves. This is our heritage for "afflictions," this is our treasure-house for rejoicing in sufferings.

The mummy may lie in the sarcophagus, and the sick cripple lie still on the couch, but the active, the vigorous, the busy want space and motion, conflict and antagonism. They will race hither and thither to be filled. This is our "hour" and in such an age "numbers numberless" will be the afflictions of Christ.

Not ours the time, when the light through the casement or the "song in the night" of solitary faith betrayed the watcher of the Church in the wilderness of heathenism or corruption; nor ours the fellowship in suffering, doing and bearing for the truth, as we would in the dungeon, at the stake, in the amphitheatre or in the disciplinary solitude of the cave on the mountain. Ours is the superb energy of revival, when the Church God inspired, challenges, wrestles, and works; when the Church claims her inheritance, and vows to retrieve it; when she moves aggressively as a recognised power, rallies her men, women and children for work through society, on the summits of refinement, in the places of learning, in the throng of cities down to their gloomiest dens, over the fields and hamlets, in mines and factories, following enterprise to the distant colony and reclaiming the waste; when she cheers with prayers the wayfarer of the cross into heathenism refined or brutal, and enlarges the heart so long exiled from the brotherhood of Christendom with plans and pleadings for restoring unity. This is an age of vigour, materialism, science, and breadth; this is an age of thrift, refinement, and liberty, which quickens the individual to intense development and drives the mass with impassioned tread;—can we wonder that we of the Anglican Communion have the yearnings, the griefs, the temptations, the betrayals, the false purposes and misguided minds, the inadequate resources, all the indescribable conflicts which darken our atmosphere? Can we deny how much we deserve the rebuke, ridicule, and correction of the sharp world around us? Can we hush our sobs when we know in our poor experience how Christ is wounded in the house of His friends? Can we cheer ourselves in selfish gladness, when there is so much to be done, so much to be endured, and the strife seems so unequal with our shepherd sling? No, brothers, no; we bless God in our heart of hearts that He has poured around light and heat, even if it does quicken spawn of evil, if it does shame us in its brightness, and make us faint in its glow; you wish no change in the strife that tends not to victory, no higher honour than to gather the fragments of the sufferings of Jesus, no more sufficient consolation than the pledge which covers all infirmities and reaches our heart sins. "My grace is sufficient for thee." This is for us "Our song in the night," the force of the day's work, a consciousness within not to be uttered;—"I *now* rejoice in my sufferings for you, and fill up that which is behind of the afflictions of Christ in my flesh for his body's sake which is the Church."

And these words open our sufficient consolation. As Downe quaintly says, "The joy of that text is germinal and ariseth out of the bosom and womb of the sorrow itself. It is not that I rejoice because I am afflicted; it is not because I shall sink in my calamity and be buried in that valley, but because my calamity raises me, and makes my valley a hill bringing me nearer to God." Even so! St. Paul said, "I now rejoice in my sufferings for you." Not that suffering ceased to be such, and physically his nerve did not quiver with pain or his heart sink in much weariness. The "perils often" were noted and felt. The "care of all the Churches" pressed sore on an aching brow, and the "thorn in the flesh" pierced with its hidden point the heart of hearts. Yet welcome all! The union with Christ in all these things changed them into seeds of light, earnests of peace, and the noble martyr-soul could glow and nerve itself with the honourable mission and anticipated victory.

Such is our earthly trial when sanctified, such our labour and discipline and afflictions as ministers of Christ. Received in faith, sustained in hope, handled with disciplinary and bracing power, they make us better and meet for rest. We are assured that our Saviour sees them, that we and ours are known and regarded, that succour and recompense are alike included, and so may we bear and do, "to fill up these afflictions of Christ in our flesh," for Christ's afflictions end in glory.

Thus is defined our honourable trust, and this union to Christ, the membership with His body, the Church, and our peculiar calling of apostleship culminate in our obligations to others. St. Paul's whole estimate of human nature was changed by these relations to the covenant salvation. Henceforth we hear him say, "I know no man after the flesh." Once he had loved or rejected qualities inherent in the individual, and, on principles of his own taste or wisdom, he had admired the properties most honourable and useful to society, and within the restricted sphere of national prejudice and association. But this was changed. All men and each individual were now estimated as they were related to Christ. In the good he saw the Saviour's righteousness and honour; in the ignorant and impenitent, he saw only that they were "afar off," and alienated from Christ by wicked works. The whole moral creation was to him not as written in the flesh but in the spirit. Hence the joy was *in* suffering, not in the midst of it. It was for others, not for himself. It was in his flesh, not in spirit and disposition, but actually endured in the flesh. It was not for his own salvation but for edifying the Church, and *that*

Christ's visible body. He might have escaped it, if he would have been satisfied to have had his faith, in this sense to himself, before God, but he could not; he read himself, "debtor to the Greek and barbarian, the bond and free," and, specially, his "kinsmen after the flesh," and through much tribulation he must press to fulfil it. Hence the diffusive love of the commissioned heart. All qualities are worthless, if debased by unrepented sin, all distinctions nothing, if they stand on the dead level of impenitence or unbelief. All sorrows are small in comparison with eternal danger, and the present degradation of "the wrath of God abiding." All relief is but superficial, which knows only the flesh, and weeps only from eyes which have been dimmed with no genuine tears of a faithful repentance. To know ourselves we must know Christ. To appreciate human nature in its realities for good and its fearful exposures to evil, we must enter into the same mind that was in Christ Jesus. To minister to what is useful, kind and loving, in our place of activity we must know men, not after the flesh, but in the worth and woe so awfully revealed and contrasted in the "sufferings of Christ." A living union to Him, to which we are invited, drawn and changed by a tenderness which passeth conception, is the fountain head of just relations to the world in its struggle and to our fellow-men in their claims. No one goes out over their length and breadth with such success and power, as the one who has attained experience of that happy, thrice happy state of soul, to love and forget himself in the Saviour, to live and act as Christ is, all and in all, and himself a member of the great body, through which the life is sent and perpetuated, by the ever-present Redeemer, in the oneness of work, suffering, and joy. And no bishop will grapple resolutely with a course of godly work, or adventure honestly in sacrifice of charity, or plead a heart message, or gently admonish in discipline, or even move on an earnest track of functional duty, without finding, in and under all, sufferings, which, rightly interpreted, are the "afflictions of Christ," and "implement" of the appointed measure of His suffering body.

In relations which I have thus so feebly sketched, does the apostolic brotherhood of to-day gather under the roof which, for six centuries, has been the abode in wealth and power of the highest ecclesiastical dignity; where the mitred brows have ached with burthens grave enough to find large place in history, and hearts have wrestled in grief and pang written only in the Book of God. We meet in the solemn chapel, whence from Boniface onwards the same old line has defiled to the other high places of the church; and from which have deployed over the broad Atlantic the four score who have verified in a new world the experience of the apostle, and the colonial band which is girdling the earth. Could the solemn possession of that Episcopate, from the place of the departed, utter their testimony, sure I am, it would be in accord with the Prisoner in Rome, and whenever work was true and spirit loyal, deep would answer to deep— "Filling up the afflictions of Christ"—"Rejoicing in sufferings."

And meet it was that the first appeal for a conclave of the likeminded Brotherhood should spring from a sense of anxiety, hazard, and bewildered responsibility. Canada asked in weakness—God answered in strength. From the undefined and scattered afflictions, He summoned the joy of a grand demonstrative Unity. He collected the ὑστερήματα, "fragments,"—so that the might and majesty of the supernatural creation might be disclosed, and the abundance be carried back on the homeward way for fresh hunger, and expanded multitudes. We have come from afar to this Conference in humility and weakness, bearing our personal and corporate griefs, and anxious to find in spiritual fellowship what by God's grace may inform and strengthen us. But we have also come to demonstrate for ever a fact, existent indeed, but one never before exhibited or made foederal in energy—the Co-operative Unity of the Anglican Communion.

And, if we are permitted to secure the effect of the first of these to the extent only, that, as we each have need, our inner nature may go home refreshed in holiness and peace, and our working power be increased in confidence and extent, by the larger observation and more assured fraternity;—and if we should fulfil the other to the issue, that in equal and loving reality we had sealed together the Holy Sacrament the visible unity of the Anglo-Catholic Church, then—however in our consciousness we might be disappointed of larger results, or the world might cry, "what meaneth this waste," or the Church might chide that we had not borne home more fruits for token,—still thoughtfully and in reverence, patiently waiting God's time for His uses, manifold of this energized and visible potency, might we magnify Him for His goodness, that had made us partakers in mission thus honoured and blest.

But whether such an assembly speak trumpet-tongued from the high atmosphere of foederated liberty, or in tones chastened and restricted by consciousness of personal and national prescription, there will be experience of sorrow, rebuke without and misgiving within. In whatever we may do or say, or withhold in humble fervency of love and zeal, with soul intent on the welfare and woe of Christ's Mystical Body, in recognized oneness with Him, in the "fear and trembling" of a rejoicing heart, must there be a mingling of suffering "the filling up of the afflictions of Christ." But "such grief is the mother of joy," and Bernard says, "as the cells of the honeycomb wall in the honey, and the shell preserveth the kernel, so that joy collected and multiplied by the grace of our Lord, is prepared and preserved for the joys of Paradise."

No. V. (See page 14.)

Opening Address delivered by the Archbishop of Canterbury in the first Session of the first Lambeth Conference, September 24, 1867.

My Most Reverend and Right Reverend Brethren,

In opening the proceedings of the first Conference that has ever taken place of the Bishops of the Reformed Church in visible communion with the United Church of England and Ireland, my prevailing feeling is one of profound gratitude to our Heavenly Father for having thus far prospered the efforts which have been made to promote this solemn assembling of ourselves together. Many have been the anxious thoughts and great the heart-searchings which have attended the preparations for this remarkable manifestation of life and energy in the several branches of our communion. Many also have been the prayers, and fervent, I trust, will continue to be the prayers, offered up by us, severally and collectively, that He will prosper our deliberations, to the advancement of His glory and the good of His Church. Having met together, as I truly believe we have done, in a spirit of love to Christ, and to all those who love Him, with an earnest desire to strengthen the bonds which unite the several branches of our Reformed Church, to encourage each other in our endeavours to maintain the faith once delivered to the saints, and to advance the kingdom of Christ upon earth, I will not doubt that a blessing from above will rest upon our labours, and that the guidance of the Holy Spirit, whose aid we have invoked, will direct, sanctify, and govern our counsels.

The origin of this Conference has already been stated in the circular of invitation which I addressed to you all. It was at the instance of the Metropolitan and the Bishops of the Church of Canada, supported by the unanimous request of a very large meeting of Archbishops and Bishops of the Home and Colonial Church—a request confirmed by addresses from both the Houses of Convocation of my Province of Canterbury—that I resolved upon convening it. Further encouragement to venture upon this unprecedented step was afforded when the petition from the Canadian Church was first discussed, a plain intimation being given by a distinguished member of the Protestant Episcopal Church in the United States of America, that it would be regarded as a very graceful act, and would be hailed with general satisfaction in that Church, if the invitation to the Conference were extended to our Episcopalian brethren in those States.

Fully conscious, however, of all the difficulties which must surround the attempt to organise and superintend an assembly of so novel a character, I might well have hesitated to incur so great a risk; but to have refused to yield to wishes thus fully and forcibly expressed, to have shrunk from undertaking the consequent responsibility, would have been unworthy of the position in which, by God's providence, I am placed. In faith and prayer has the task been undertaken, and I humbly trust it will please God to prosper our work to a successful conclusion. The result, indeed, has thus far more than justified the expectations raised. We rejoice to find that so many of our brethren from distant parts of the globe have been moved to respond to the call, and we welcome with feelings of cordial affection and genuine sympathy the presence of so large a proportion of the American Episcopate. From very many also, who, owing to various circumstances, have been prevented from joining us, I have received letters expressing the profound satisfaction and thankfulness with which they regard the opportunities afforded by this gathering for conferring together upon topics of mutual interest; for discussing the peculiar difficulties and perplexities in which our widely-scattered Colonial Churches are involved, and the evils to which they are exposed; for cementing yet more firmly the bonds of Christian communion between Churches acknowledging one Lord, one faith, one baptism—connected not only by the ties of kindred, but by common formularies; 'and for meeting, through their representatives, from the most distant regions of the earth, to offer up united prayers and praise to the Most High in the mother tongue common to us all, and to partake together of the Holy Communion of the Body and Blood of our Saviour Christ.

It has never been contemplated that we should assume the functions of a General Synod of all the Churches in full communion with the Church of England, and take upon ourselves to enact canons that should be binding upon those here represented. We merely propose to discuss matters of practical interest, and pronounce what we deem expedient in resolutions which may serve as safe guides to future action. Thus it will be seen that our first essay is rather tentative and experimental, in a matter in which we have no distinct precedent to direct us.

The subjects which will be brought under your consideration have already been laid before you in the Prospectus of Arrangements for our proceedings. They may be briefly comprised under the following heads :—(1) The best way of promoting the Reunion of Christendom. (2) The Notification of the Establishment of New Sees. (3) Letters commendatory from Clergymen and Laymen passing to distant Dioceses. (4) Subordination in our Colonial Church to Metropolitans. (5) Discipline to be exercised by Metropolitans. (6) Court of the Metropolitan. (7) Question of Appeal. (8) Conditions of Union with the Church at home. (9) Notification of proposed Missionary Bishoprics. (10) Subordination of Missionaries. In the selection of topics regard has been chiefly had to those which bear on practical difficulties seeming to require solution. It has been found impossible to meet all views, and embrace every recommendation that has been suggested. Some may be of opinion that subjects have been omitted which ought to have found a place in our deliberations; that we should have been assembled with the view of defining the limits of Theological Truth; but it has been deemed far better, on the first occasion of our meeting in such form, rather to do too little than attempt too much, and instead of dealing with propositions which can lead to no efficient result, to confine ourselves to matters admitting of a practical and beneficial solution.

The unexpected position in which our Colonial Churches have recently found themselves placed has naturally created a great feeling of uneasiness in the minds of many. I am fully persuaded that the idea of any essential separation from the Mother Church is universally repudiated by them; they all cling to her with the strongest filial affection, while they are bound to her Doctrines and Form of Worship by cogent motives of interest. At the same time I have good reason to believe that there are various shades of opinion as to the best modes in which the connection between the daughter Churches and their common mother can be maintained; and I trust that the interchange of thought between those who are chiefly interested in those important questions will lead to some profitable conclusions. I may also state my belief that legislation on the subject of the Colonial Churches has been postponed until the view taken by this Conference shall have been declared. These matters have been regarded under various aspects in the voluminous correspondence which I have had with many of my Colonial brethren; they will all, no doubt, be fully developed in the course of our discussion by those who represent these several opinions. I trust that, under a deep sense of the solemnity of the occasion on which we are assembled, our discussions will be characterised by mutual forbearance, if sentiments at variance with our own shall be advanced, so that by the comparison, rather than the conflict of opinions, we may be drawn nearer to each other in brotherly harmony and concord. With the arrangement that certain subjects shall, after a brief consideration, be referred to Committees, I believe that the various topics for consideration may be profitably discussed.

Doubtless there is much in these latter days, even as we have all been taught to expect, which is dark and dispiriting to the mind that has not been exercised to discern the meaning of such signs. The enemy is on every side, plying his insidious arts to sap the foundations of belief, to hinder the cause of God's Church, and prevent the Word of God from doing its work in the conversion of the soul of sinful man. No effort is spared to disparage the authority of those who witness for the truth and uphold the dogmatic teaching for which the Apostolic writings are at once the model and the warrant. Though it be not our purpose to enter upon theological discussion, yet our very presence here is a witness to our resolution to maintain the faith, which we hold in common as our priceless heritage, set forth in our Liturgy and other formularies; and this our united celebration of offices common to our respective Churches in each quarter of the globe, is a claim, in the face of the world, for the independence of separate Churches, as well as a protest against the assumption by any Bishop of the Church Catholic of dominion over his fellows in the Episcopate.

Not one of us, I am persuaded, can fail to respond to that earnest desire for unity which is expressed in the introduction to our resolutions. It is but the echo of the petition which the Saviour of the world offered in behalf of His Church when He prayed the Father that those who should believe in Him might all be one in the Father and the Son. And while we deplore the divided state of Christendom, and mourn over the obstacles which at present exist to our all being joined together in the unity of the Spirit and in the bond of peace, this very feeling should be our most powerful motive to urge our petitions at the Throne of Grace, that it may please God, in His own good time, to remove such hindrances as at present render that union impracticable.

And now may our Almighty Father shed abroad upon us the spirit of wisdom, peace, and love, and inspire us with such counsels as may most tend to edification; so that, being knit together more closely in the bonds of brotherly affection and Christian communion, and animated with a more fervent zeal for the Saviour's honour and the salvation of souls, we may do our endeavour to prepare His Church for the coming of Him whom we lovingly adore, and whose advent in power and glory we ardently look to and long for.

No. VI. (See page 16.)

Amended Programme adopted during the Sessions.

SECOND DAY.—Wednesday, September 25.

General Subject for the Day's Discussion,

COLONIAL CHURCHES.

Resolution I. :—

Alteration of Order.

That His Grace the President of this meeting be requested to allow the last Resolution headed "*Conditions of Union*," to be first taken into consideration.

Resolution II. :—

Conditions of Union.

(*a*) That in the opinion of this Conference, "Unity in the Faith," and fellowship in the one Body of Christ, will be best maintained among the several branches of the Anglican Communion in the manner already pointed out by the Convocation of the Province of Canterbury: viz., by the due and Canonical subordination of the Synods of the several Branches to the higher authority of the Synods above them, the Diocesan Synod being recognised as inferior to the Provincial Synod, and the Provincial Synod to some higher Synod or Synods of the Anglican Communion.

Appointment of Committee.

(*b*) That a Committee of   members (with power to add to their number, and to obtain the assistance of men learned in Ecclesiastical and Canon Law) be appointed to inquire into and report upon the whole subject; and that such report be forwarded to His Grace the Lord Archbishop of Canterbury, with a request that, if possible, it may be communicated to any adjourned meeting of this Conference.

Proposed Inquiry into Disunion in Natal.

(*c*) That in the judgment of the Bishops now assembled, the whole Anglican Communion is deeply injured by the present condition of the Church in Natal; and that a Committee be now appointed at this General Meeting to consider the whole case, and inquire into all the proceedings which have been taken therein; and to report on the best mode by which the Church may be delivered from the continuance of this scandal, and the true faith maintained. That such Report be forwarded to his Grace the Lord Archbishop of Canterbury, with a request that, if possible, it may be communicated to any adjourned meeting of the Conference; and

Further, that his Grace be requested to transmit the same to all the Bishops[1] of the Anglican Communion, and to ask for their judgment thereupon.

Resolution III.:—

Question of Appeal.

That in the opinion of this Conference, it is very desirable that there should be a Board of Reference,

---

[1] ? Convocations, Conventions, and Synods.

or a Spiritual Tribunal for final appeal and decision in all matters of Faith; including Representatives from all Branches of the Anglo-Catholic Church; and the Bishops here assembled earnestly recommend this most important matter to the deliberate consideration of the Convocations, Conventions, and Synods of the said Anglo-Catholic Church.

Or, if Resolution III. should not be carried, then—Question of Appeal.

III. That in order to the maintenance of the strictest union between the Mother-Church of England and her daughter Churches in the Colonies, it is desirable that in questions of doctrine there should be an appeal from the tribunals for the exercise of Discipline in each Province to a spiritual tribunal in England.

That such tribunal be presided over by the Primate of all England (for the time being), and be composed of Bishops only.

Appointment of Committee.

And—

That a Committee be appointed to consider the details of the Constitution of such tribunal, and that their Report be forwarded to His Grace the Lord Archbishop of Canterbury, with a request that, if possible, it may be communicated to any adjourned meeting of the Conference.

Circulation of Report.

And further, that his Grace be requested to transmit the same to the Convocations and Synods of all the Provinces of the United Church of England and Ireland, and to all Bishops (if any) of the said Church not included in any Ecclesiastical Province.

Election of Members of Tribunal.

That His Grace the Archbishop of Canterbury be requested to invite the several Provinces of the Church to elect Bishops for the said Tribunal.

Resolution IV. :—

This Meeting to be followed by other Meetings.

That, in order to give effect to the above Resolutions, it is desirable that a General Synod of the Bishops of the Anglican Communion, accompanied, if it be thought fit, by other representatives from each Diocese, should be assembled from time to time under the Presidency of the Primate of all England.

Resolution V. :—

Time of First Meeting, &c.

That His Grace the Lord Archbishop is hereby requested to summon the First Meeting of such Synod for the year 187 ; and that in the opinion of this Conference the Primate of all England should be authorised to summon any Special Synod within that time, should the needs of the Church seem to require it; or should his Grace be requested to do so by   or more Bishops.

Resolution VI. :—

Conditions of Union.

That, in order to the binding of the Churches of our Colonial Empire and the Missionary Churches beyond them in the closest union with the Mother-Church, it is necessary that they receive and maintain without alteration the standards of Faith and Doctrine, as they are in use in that Church. That nevertheless each

Province should have the right to make such adaptations and additions to the services of the Church as its peculiar circumstances may require.

Provided, That no change or addition be made inconsistent with the spirit and principles of the Book of Common Prayer, and that all such changes be liable to revision by any Synod of the Anglican Communion in which the said Province shall be represented.

Resolution VII.:—

Court of Metropolitans.

That in case of charges being brought against a Suffragan Bishop of any Province it appears to be desirable that the Metropolitan thereof should summon all the Bishops of his Province to sit with him for the hearing of the case, and that he should not proceed to the hearing of it without the aid of all the Bishops of the Province that can be assembled, who shall sit with him as judges.

That the question of any charge brought against a Metropolitan be referred to the Committee appointed by Resolution III.

Resolution VIII.:—

Scheme for conducting Election of Bishops, when not otherwise provided for.

That it is the opinion of this Conference that the election of a Bishop of any Colonial Diocese should be made by the Synod of the Diocese convened for that purpose, with liberty to delegate this power to others. But that no such election should be deemed canonically valid until it shall have been confirmed by the Bishops of the Province.

That the rules for the regulation of such elections be made by the Synods of the several Provinces.

Resolution IX. :—

Declaration of Submission to Regulations of Synods.

That all Bishops at their Consecration should be required to make a written Declaration of adhesion and submission to the regulations agreed upon by the General Synod of the Anglican Communion; and that a form of such Declaration be prepared by the Committee appointed by Resolution III.

No. VII. (See page 17.)

Formal "Address to the Faithful" from the Bishops attending the Conference of 1867.

To the Faithful in Christ Jesus, the Priests and Deacons, and the Lay Members of the Church of Christ in Communion with the Anglican Branch of the Church Catholic,—

We the undersigned Bishops, gathered under the good providence of God for prayer and conference at Lambeth, pray for you that ye may obtain grace, mercy, and peace from God our Father, and from the Lord Jesus Christ our Saviour.

We give thanks to God, brethren beloved, for the faith in our Lord Jesus Christ, and the love towards the saints, which hath abounded amongst you; and for the knowlege of Christ which through you hath been spread abroad amongst the most vigorous races of the earth; and with one mouth we make our supplications to God, even the Father, that by the power of the Holy Ghost He would strengthen us with His might, to amend amongst us the things which are amiss, to supply the things which are lacking, and to reach forth unto higher measures of love and zeal in worshipping Him, and in making known His name; and we pray that in His good time He would give back unto His whole Church the Blessed gift of Unity in Truth.

And now we exhort you in love that ye keep whole and undefiled the faith once delivered to the saints, as ye have received it of the Lord Jesus. We entreat you to watch and pray, and to strive heartily with us against the frauds and subtleties wherewith the faith hath been aforetime and is now assailed.

We beseech you to hold fast, as the sure word of God, all the canonical Scriptures of the Old and New Testament; and that by diligent study of these oracles of God, praying in the Holy Ghost, ye seek to know more of the Lord Jesus Christ our Saviour, very God and very Man, ever to be adored and worshipped, whom they reveal unto us, and of the will of God, which they declare.

Furthermore, we entreat you to guard yourselves and yours against the growing superstitions and additions with which in these latter days the truth of God hath been overlaid; as otherwise, so especially by the pretension to universal sovereignty over God's heritage asserted for the See of Rome, and by the practical exaltation of the Blessed Virgin Mary as mediator in the place of her Divine Son, and by the addressing of prayers to her as intercessor between God and man. Of such beware, we beseech you, knowing that the jealous God giveth not His honour to another.

Build yourselves up, therefore, beloved, in your most holy faith; grow in grace and in the knowledge and love of Jesus Christ our Lord. Show forth before all men by your faith, self-denial, purity, and godly conversation, as well as by your labours for the people amongst whom God hath so widely spread you, and by the setting forth of His Gospel to the unbelievers and the heathen, that ye are indeed the servants of Him who died for us to reconcile His Father to us, and to be a sacrifice for the sins of the whole world.

Brethren beloved, with one voice we warn you: the time is short; the Lord cometh; watch and be sober. Abide steadfast in the Communion of Saints, wherein God hath granted you a place. Seek in faith for oneness with Christ in the blessed Sacrament of His body and blood. Hold fast the Creeds and the pure worship and order, which of God's grace ye have inherited from the Primitive Church. Beware of causing divisions contrary to the doctrine ye have received. Pray and seek for unity amongst yourselves, and amongst all the faithful in Christ Jesus; and the good Lord make you perfect, and keep your bodies, souls, and spirits, until the coming of the Lord Jesus Christ.

(Signed)

C. T. Cantuar.
M. G. Armagh.
R. C. Dublin.
A. C. London.
C. R. Winton.
C. St. David's
J. Lichfield.
S. Oxon.
Thomas Vowler, St. Asaph.
A. Llandaff.
John Lincoln.
W. K. Sarum.
John T. Norwich.
J. C. Bangor.
H. Worcester.
Charles Wordsworth, D.C.L., Bishop of St. Andrew's, Dunkeld, and Dumblane.
Thos. G. Suther, Bishop of Aberdeen and Orkney.
William S. Wilson, Bishop of Glasgow and Galloway.
Thomas B. Morrell, Coadjutor Bishop of Edinburgh.
F. Montreal, Metropolitan of Canada.
G. A. New Zealand, Metropolitan of New Zealand.
R. Capetown, Metropolitan of South Africa.
Aubrey G. Jamaica.
T. Barbados.
J. Bombay.
H. Nova Scotia.
F. T. Labuan.
H. Grahamstown.
H. J. C. Christchurch.
Mathew Perth.
Benj. Huron.
W. W. Antigua.
E. H. Sierra Leone.
T. N. Honolulu.
J. T. Ontario.

"Address to the Faithful," 1867.

J. W. Quebec.
W. J. Gibraltar.
H. L. Dunedin.
Edward, Bishop Orange River Free State.
A. N. Niagara.
William George Tozer, Missionary Bishop.
James B. Kelly, Coadjutor of Newfoundland.
S. Angl. Hierosol.

John H. Hopkins, Presiding Bishop of Pr. Ep. Church, in the United States.
Chas. P. McIlvaine, Bishop of Ohio.
G. J. Gloucester and Bristol.
E. H. Ely.
William Chester.
T. L. Rochester.
Horace Sodor and Man.
Samuel Meath.
H. Kilmore.
Charles Limerick Ardfert and Aghadoe.

Robert Eden, D.D., Bishop of Moray, Ross, and Caithness, Primus.
Alexander Ewing, Bishop of Argyll and the Isles.
Manton Eastburn, Bishop of Massachusetts.
J. Payne, Bishop of Cape Palmas and parts adjacent.
H. J. Whitehouse, Bishop of Illinois.
Thomas Atkinson, Bishop of North Carolina.
Henry W. Lee, Bishop of Iowa.
Horatio Potter, Bishop of New York.
Thomas M. Clark, Bishop of Rhode Island.
Alexander Gregg, Bishop of Texas.
W. H. Odenheimer, Bishop of New Jersey.
G. T. Bedell, Assistant Bishop of Ohio.
Henry C. Lay, Missionary Bishop of Arkansas and the Indian Territory.
Jos. C. Talbot, Assistant Bishop of Indiana.
Richard H. Wilmer, Bishop of Alabama.
Charles Todd Quintard, Bishop of Tennessee.
John B. Kerfoot, Bishop of Pittsburgh.
J. P. B. Wilmer, Bishop of Louisiana.
C. M. Williams, Missionary Bishop to China.
J. Chapman, Bishop.
George Smith, late Bishop of Victoria (China).
David Anderson, late Bishop of Rupert's Land.
Edmund Hobhouse, Bishop of New Zealand.

No. VIII. (See page 32.)

LATIN AND GREEK VERSIONS OF THE ADDRESS.

Archdeacon Wordsworth, afterwards Bishop of Lincoln, translated the Episcopal Address into Latin and Greek, as follows:—

EPISTOLA ENCYCLICA.

EPISCOPORUM IN ANGLIA CONGREGATORUM DIEBUS XXIV.–XXVII. MENSIS SEPTEMBRIS, ANNO SALUTIS MDCCCLXVII.

Fidelibus in Christo Jesu, Presbyteris, Diaconis, et Laicis, cum Anglicanâ parte Ecclesiæ Catholicæ communicantibus, salutem in Domin

Nos, qui subscripsimus, Episcopi, benignâ Dei providentiâ communium orationum et consiliorum causâ unanimiter consociati, in Palatio Archiepiscopi Cantuariensis Lambethano, obsecrationes pro vobis facimus, ut gratiam, misericordiam et pacem consequamini a Deo Patre Nostro, et a Nostro Salvatore Domino Jesu Christo.

Gratias Deo agimus, fratres carissimi, propter fidem in Domino Jesu Christo, et in sanctos dilectionem, quæ abundavit in vobis; et propter Christi agnitionem, quæ per vos inter valentissimas orbis universi nationes dimanavit; et uno ore supplicationes offerimus Deo et Patri, ut potentia Spiritûs Sancti virtute Suâ nos confortet, ut, quæ sint apud nos depravata, emendare, et, quæ desint, supplere valeamus; et ut nosmet ipsos ad sublimiores dilectionis et zeli mensuras erigamus in Illo adorando, et in Nomine Ejus declarando; et enixè Eum apprecamur, ut, beneplacito Ipsius tempore, universæ Suæ Ecclesiæ beatum restituat donum Unitatis in Veritate.

Jam verò, fratres dilecti, vos in caritate cohortamur, ut fidem semel sanctis traditam integram atque illibatam conservetis, quemadmodum eam accepistis a Jesu Christo Domino Nostro. Obsecramus vos, vigilate, orate, et nobiscum toto corde certate contra fallacias atque argutias, quibus jampridem et in hoc ipso tempore fides impugnatur.

Obtestamur vos, constanter tenete, utpote firmum Dei Verbum, omnes Canonicas Scripturas Veteris et Novi Testamenti; et diligenti meditatione scrutantes hæc Dei Oracula, orantes in Spiritu Sancto, quæratis abundantiùs cognoscere Dominum Jesum Christum, Verum Deum et Verum Hominem, semper colendum atque adorandum, Quem nobis illa revelant, et Voluntatem Dei in eis patefactam.

Insuper vos obsecramus, vosmet ipsos et vestros custodite contra indies gliscentes superstitiones atque additamenta quibus in hisce novissimis temporibus Veritas Dei incrustatur; quùm in aliis, tùm præcipuè per universi principatûs affectationem dominantis in clero Dei, qui Romanæ sedi a nonnullis asseritur; et per exaltationem, re ipsâ manifestam, Beatæ Virginis Mariæ in locum Mediatoris, vice Filii ipsius Divini, et per orationes ei oblatas tanquam inter Deum et homines Interpellatoris munere fungenti. Cavete a talibus, vos obtestamur, probè scientes honorem Suum Ipsius non alii dare Deum zelotem.

Superædificamini, igitur, fratres carissimi, sanctissimæ fidei vestræ; crescite in gratiâ et in agnitione et dilectione Jesu Christi Domini Nostri. Manifestum facite omnibus, per fidem, abstinentiam, puritatem et sanctum conversationem, et per vestros labores pro populis inter quos Deus vos tam latè propagavit, et per Evangelii prædicationem incredulis atque ethnicis, vos reverâ esse servos Illius Qui mortuus est pro nobis ut Patrem nobis reconciliaret, et ut pro peccatis totius mundi sacrificium Semet Ipsum offerret.

Fratres dilecti, unâ voce vos admonemus. Tempus

breve est. Dominus venit. Vigilate, sobrii estote. State firmi in communione sanctorum in quâ vobis Deus locum concessit. Studete fide coadunari Christo in sanctissimo Corporis Ejus et Sanguinis Sacramento. Firma tenete Symbola, et purum illum Cultum atque Ordinem, quem gratiâ Dei a primitivâ Ecclesiâ hæreditarium vos possidetis. Cavete ne discessiones faciatis præter doctrinam quam accepistis. Orate et sectamini Unitatem invicem et inter omnes fideles in Jesu Christo. Et Dominus misericors perficiat vos, et conservet integrum corpus, animam et spiritum vestrum in Adventum Domini Nostri Jesu Christi. Amen.

 C. T. Cantuar. Archiepiscopus, et Metropolitanus, et totius Angliæ Primas.

 M. G. Armagh. Archiepiscopus, et Metropolitanus, et totius Hiberniæ Primas.

 R. C. Dublin. Archiepiscopus, et Metropolitanus, et Hiberniæ Primas.

 A. C. London. Episcopus.

 Robert Eden, Moray, Ross, Caithness. Episcopus, et Scoticæ Ecclesiæ Primas, &c. &c.

ΕΓΚΥΚΛΙΟΣ ΕΠΙΣΤΟΛΗ.

Ἐπισκόπων ἐν Ἀγγλίᾳ συνηθροισμένων, ἐν ἡμέραις 24—27 μηνὸς Σεπτεμβρίου, ἔτει 1867.

Τοῖς πιστοῖς ἐν Χριστῷ Ἰησοῦ, Πρεσβυτέροις, Διακόνοις καὶ λαϊκοῖς τῆς τοῦ Χριστοῦ Ἐκκλησίας, συγκοινωνοῖς τοῦ Ἀγγλικοῦ μέρους τῆς Καθολικῆς Ἐκκλησίας, χαίρειν ἐν Κυρίῳ.

Ἡμεῖς οἱ ὑπογράψαντες Ἐπίσκοποι, τῇ ἀγαθῇ τοῦ Θεοῦ προνοίᾳ ὁμοθυμαδὸν ἐπισυνηγμένοι, κοινῶν προσευχῶν ἕνεκα καὶ συμβουλεύσεως, ἐν τῷ τῆς Καντουαρίας Ἀρχιεπισκόπου παλατίῳ Λαμβηθανῷ, δεόμεθα ὑπὲρ ὑμῶν ἵνα λάβητε χάριν, ἔλεος, καὶ εἰρήνην ἀπὸ Θεοῦ

Πατρος, καὶ τοῦ Κυρίου ἡμῶν καὶ Σωτῆρος Ἰησου Χριστοῦ.

Εὐχαριστοῦμεν τῷ Θεῷ, ἀδελφοὶ ἀγαπητοὶ, ὑπὲρ τῆς πίστεως ὑμῶν ἐν Κυρίῳ ἡμῶν Ἰησοῦ Χριστῷ, καὶ ὑπὲρ τῆς ἀγάπης εἰς τοὺς ἁγίους, ἥτις ἐπερίσσευσεν ἐν ὑμῖν, καὶ ὑπὲρ τῆς Χριστοῦ ἐπιγνώσεως, ἣ δι' ὑμῶν ἐξήχηται ἐν τοῖς ἀνδρειοτάτοις τῆς οἰκουμένης ἔθνεσιν· καὶ ἑνὶ στόματι δεήσεις ποιούμεθα πρὸς τὸν Θεὸν καὶ Πατέρα, ἵνα τῇ τοῦ Ἁγίου Πνεύματος δυνάμει σθενώσῃ ἡμᾶς τῇ ἰσχύι Αὐτοῦ, εἰς τὸ ἐπανορθῶσαι τὰ παραπίπτοντα, καὶ τὰ λείποντα ἀναπληρῶσαι, καὶ ἐπεκτείνεσθαι εἰς ὑψηλότερα ἀγάπης μέτρα καὶ ζήλου ἐν τῷ λατρεύειν αὐτῷ, καὶ ἐν τῷ γνωρίζειν τὸ ὄνομα αὐτοῦ· καὶ προσευχόμεθα ἵνα ἐν τῷ δεκτῷ αὐτοῦ καιρῷ ἀποδῷ τῇ ὅλῃ Αὐτοῦ ἐκκλησίᾳ τὸ μακαριστὸν χάρισμα τῆς ἑνότητος ἐν τῇ ἀληθείᾳ.

Καὶ νῦν, ἀδελφοὶ, παρακαλοῦμεν ὑμᾶς ἐν ἀγάπῃ, ἵνα τηρῆτε ὁλόκληρον καὶ ἀδιάφθορον τὴν ἅπαξ παραδοθεῖσαν τοῖς ἁγίοις πίστιν, καθὼς αὐτὴν παρειλήφατε ἀπὸ τοῦ Κυρίου Ἰησοῦ. Ἐρωτῶμεν ὑμᾶς ἵνα γρηγορῆτε καὶ προσεύχησθε, καὶ ἀγωνίζησθε εὐκαρδίως μεθ' ἡμῶν κατὰ τῶν πανουργιῶν καὶ μεθοδειῶν, δι' ὧν ἡ πίστις τὸ πρὶν καὶ ἐν τῷ νῦν παρόντι χρόνῳ πορθεῖται.

Παρακαλοῦμεν ὑμᾶς ἵνα ἀσφαλῶς κρατῆτε, ὡς βέβαιον Θεοῦ λόγον, πάσας τὰς κανονικὰς γραφὰς τῆς Παλαιᾶς καὶ τῆς Καινῆς Διαθήκης, καὶ ἵνα, σπουδαίως ἐρευνῶντες ταῦτα τὰ λόγια τοῦ Θεοῦ, ζητῆτε περισσοτέρως γνῶναι τὸν Κύριον καὶ Σωτῆρα Ἰησοῦν Χριστόν, Θεὸν ἀληθινὸν καὶ ἄνθρωπον ἀληθινὸν, ᾧ πάντοτε προσκυνεῖν δεῖ καὶ λατρεύειν, ὃν αἱ γραφαὶ ἡμῖν ἀνακαλύπτουσιν, καὶ τὸ θέλημα τοῦ Θεοῦ, τὸ ἐν αὐταῖς φανερούμενον.

Ἅμα δὲ ὑμῖν, ἀδελφοὶ, διαμαρτυρόμεθα, φυλάξατε ἑαυτοὺς καὶ τοὺς ὑμετέρους ἀπὸ τῶν ἀεὶ αὐξανομένων ἐθελοθρησκειῶν καὶ ἐπιβλημάτων, δι' ὧν ἡ τοῦ Θεοῦ ἀλήθεια ἐν τοῖς ὑστέροις τούτοις χρόνοις παραπέπλασται, ἄλλως τε καὶ μάλιστα διὰ τῆς ἀντιποιήσεως μοναρχίας οἰκουμενικῆς, κατακυριευούσης τοῦ κλήρου τοῦ Θεοῦ, ἧς ἀξιοῦται παρά τισιν ἡ Ῥώμης καθέδρα· ἔτι δὲ διὰ τῆς ἐνεργοῦ ὑπεράρσεως τῆς μακαρίας Παρθένου Μαρίας εἰς τόπον Μεσίτου, ἀντὶ τοῦ Υἱοῦ αὐτῆς αὐτοθέου, καὶ διὰ προσευχῶν αὐτῇ προσφερομένων ὡς ἐντυγχανούσῃ ὑπὲρ ἀνθρώπων παρὰ Θεῷ. Προσέχετε ἀπὸ τοιούτων, εἰδότες ὅτι τὴν τιμὴν ἑαυτοῦ οὐχ ἑτέρῳ δίδωσιν ὁ ζηλωτὴς Θεός.

Ἐποικοδομεῖσθε οὖν, ἀγαπητοί, ἐπὶ τῇ ἁγιωτάτῃ ὑμῶν πίστει· αὐξάνεσθε ἐν χάριτι καὶ γνώσει καὶ ἀγάπῃ τοῦ Κυρίου ἡμῶν Ἰησοῦ Χριστοῦ. Καταδείξατε ἐνώπιον πάντων, διὰ τῆς πίστεως, αὐταπαρνήσεως, ἁγνείας, καὶ εὐσεβοῦς ἀναστροφῆς, ἅμα δὲ διὰ τῶν ὑμετέρων κόπων ὑπὲρ τῶν λαῶν ἐν οἷς ὁ Θεὸς ὑμᾶς εἰς τοσοῦτον εὖρος διαπεφύτευκε, καὶ διὰ τοῦ κηρύγματος τοῦ εὐαγγελίου τοῖς ἀπίστοις καὶ τοῖς ἔθνεσιν, ὅτι τῷ ὄντι ἐστὲ δοῦλοι Ἐκείνου, ὃς ἀπέθανεν ὑπὲρ ἡμῶν, ἵνα καταλλάξῃ ἡμῖν τὸν Πατέρα, καὶ ἵνα θυσίαν Ἑαυτὸν ἀνενέγκῃ ὑπὲρ τῶν ἁμαρτιῶν ὅλου τοῦ κόσμου.

Ἀδελφοὶ ἀγαπητοί, μιᾷ φωνῇ νουθετοῦμεν ὑμᾶς· ὁ καιρὸς συνεσταλμένος· ὁ Κύριος ἔρχεται· γρηγορεῖτε, νήφετε. Στήκετε ἑδραῖοι ἐν τῇ κοινωνίᾳ τῶν ἁγίων, ἐν ᾗ Θεὸς ὑμῖν μερίδα κεχάρισται· ζητεῖτε ἐν πίστει ἑνοῦσθαι τῷ Χριστῷ ἐν τῷ εὐλογημένῳ μυστηρίῳ τοῦ σώματος Αὐτοῦ καὶ αἵματος. Κατέχετε στερεῶς τὰ Σύμβολα, καὶ τὴν καθαρὰν θρησκείαν καὶ τάξιν, ἣν χάριτι Θεοῦ κεκληρονομήκατε ἀπὸ τῆς ἀρχῆθεν ἐκκλησίας. Βλέπετε μὴ διχοστασίας ποιῆτε κατὰ τῆς διδαχῆς ἣν ἐμάθετε. Ἐρωτᾶτε καὶ διώκετε ἑνότητα ἐν ἑαυτοῖς, καὶ ἐν πᾶσι τοῖς πιστοῖς ἐν Χριστῷ Ἰησοῦ· καὶ ὁ χρηστὸς Κύριος τελειώσαι ὑμᾶς, καὶ τηρήσαι ὑμῶν τὸ σῶμα, τὴν ψυχήν, καὶ τὸ πνεῦμα, εἰς τὴν παρουσίαν τοῦ Κυρίου Ἰησοῦ. Ἀμήν.

C. T. CANTUAR. ἀρχιεπίσκοπος, καὶ μητροπολίτης, καὶ πρῶτος ὅλης τῆς Ἀγγλίας.

M. G. ARMAGH. ἀρχιεπίσκοπος, καὶ μητροπολίτης, καὶ πρῶτος ὅλης τῆς Ἰβερνίας.

R. C. DUBLIN. ἀρχιεπίσκοπος, καὶ μητροπολίτης, καὶ πρῶτος Ἰβερνίας.

A. C. LONDON. ἐπίσκοπος.

C. R. WINTON. ἐπίσκοπος.

κ.τ.λ.

No. IX. (See page 17.)

The Formal Resolutions of the Conference of Sept. 24–27, 1867.

INTRODUCTION.

"We, Bishops of Christ's Holy Catholic Church in visible Communion with the United Church of England and Ireland, professing the Faith delivered to us in Holy Scripture, maintained by the Primitive Church and by the Fathers of the English Reformation, now assembled, by the good providence of God, at the Archiepiscopal Palace of Lambeth, under the presidency of the Primate of all England, desire —*First*, to give hearty thanks to Almighty God for having thus brought us together for common counsels and united worship; *Secondly*, we desire to express the deep sorrow with which we view the divided condition of the flock of Christ throughout the world, ardently longing for the fulfilment of the prayer of our Lord, 'That all may be one, as Thou, Father, art in Me, and I in Thee, that they also may be one in us, that the world may believe that Thou hast sent Me;' and, *Lastly*, we do here solemnly record our conviction that unity will be most effectually promoted by maintaining the Faith in its purity and integrity—as taught in the Holy Scriptures, held by the Primitive Church, summed up in the Creeds, and affirmed by the undisputed General Councils,—and by drawing each of us closer to our common Lord, by giving ourselves to much prayer and intercession, by the cultivation of a spirit of charity, and a love of the Lord's appearing."

Resolution I.—"That it appears to us expedient, for the purpose of maintaining brotherly intercommunion, that all cases of establishment of new Sees, and appointment of new Bishops, be notified to all

Archbishops and Metropolitans, and all presiding Bishops of the Anglican Communion."

Resolution II.—" That, having regard to the conditions under which intercommunion between members of the Church passing from one distant Diocese to another may be duly maintained, we hereby declare it desirable,—

" (1) That forms of Letters Commendatory on behalf of Clergymen visiting other Dioceses be drawn up and agreed upon ;

" (2) That a form of Letters Commendatory for lay members of the Church be in like manner prepared ;

" (3) That his Grace the Lord Archbishop of Canterbury be pleased to undertake the preparation of such forms."

Resolution III.—" That a Committee be appointed to draw up a Pastoral Address to all members of the Church of Christ in communion with the Anglican Branch of the Church Catholic, to be agreed upon by the assembled Bishops, and to be published as soon as possible after the last sitting of the Conference."

Resolution IV.—" That, in the opinion of this Conference, Unity in Faith and Discipline will be best maintained among the several branches of the Anglican Communion by due and canonical subordination of the Synods of the several branches to the higher authority of a Synod or Synods above them."

Resolution V.—" That a Committee of seven members (with power to add to their number, and to obtain the assistance of men learned in Ecclesiastical and Canon Law) be appointed to inquire into and report upon the subject of the relations and functions of such Synods, and that such Report be forwarded to his Grace the Lord Archbishop of Canterbury, with a request that, if possible, it may be communicated to any adjourned meeting of this Conference."

Resolution VI.—" That, in the judgment of the Bishops now assembled, the whole Anglican Communion is deeply injured by the present condition of the Church in Natal ; and that a Committee be now appointed at this General Meeting to report on the best mode by which the Church may be delivered from the continuance of this scandal, and the true faith maintained. That such Report be forwarded to his Grace the Lord Archbishop of Canterbury, with the request that he will be pleased to transmit the same to all the Bishops of the Anglican Communion, and to ask for their judgment thereupon."

Resolution VII.—" That we who are here present do acquiesce in the Resolution of the Convocation of Canterbury, passed on June 29, 1866, relating to the Diocese of Natal, to wit—

"'If it be decided that a new Bishop should be consecrated,—As to the proper steps to be taken by the members of the Church in the province of Natal for obtaining a new Bishop, it is the opinion of this House,—*first*, that a formal instrument, declaratory of the doctrine and discipline of the Church of South Africa should be prepared, which every Bishop, Priest, and Deacon to be appointed to office should be required to subscribe ; *secondly*, that a godly and well-learned man should be chosen by the clergy, with the assent of the lay-communicants of the Church ; and, *thirdly*, that he should be presented for consecration, either to the Archbishop of Canterbury,—if the aforesaid instrument should declare the doctrine and discipline of Christ as received by the United Church of England and Ireland,—or to the Bishops of the Church of South Africa, according as hereafter may be judged to be most advisable and convenient.'"

Resolution VIII.—" That, in order to the binding of the Churches of our Colonial Empire and the Missionary Churches beyond them in the closest union with the Mother-Church, it is necessary that they receive and maintain without alteration the standards of Faith and Doctrine as now in use in that Church. That, nevertheless, each Province should have the right to make such adaptations and additions to the services of the Church as its peculiar circumstances may require. *Provided*, that no change or addition be made inconsistent with the spirit and principles of the Book of Common Prayer, and that all such changes be liable to revision by any Synod of the Anglican Communion in which the said Province shall be represented."

Resolution IX.—" That the Committee appointed by Resolution V., with the addition of the names of the Bishops of London, St. David's, and Oxford, and all the Colonial Bishops, be instructed to consider the constitution of a voluntary spiritual tribunal, to which questions of doctrine may be carried by appeal from the tribunals for the exercise of discipline in each Province of the Colonial Church, and that their report be forwarded to his Grace the Lord Archbishop of Canterbury, who is requested to communicate it to an adjourned meeting of this Conference."

Resolution X.—" That the resolutions submitted to this Conference relative to the discipline to be exercised by Metropolitans, the Court of Metropolitans, the scheme for conducting the Election of Bishops, when not otherwise provided for, the declaration of submission to the Regulation of Synods, and the question of what Legislation should be proposed for the Colonial Churches, be referred to the Committee specified in the preceding Resolution."

Resolution XI.—" That a special committee be appointed to consider the Resolutions relative to the notification of proposed Missionary Bishoprics, and the Subordination of Missionaries."

Resolution XII.—" That the question of the bounds of the jurisdiction of different Bishops, when any question may have arisen in regard to them, the question as to the obedience of Chaplains of the United Church of England and Ireland on the Continent, and the Resolution submitted to the Conference relative to their return and admission into Home Dioceses, be referred to the Committee specified in the preceding Resolution."

Resolution XIII.—" That we desire to render our hearty thanks to Almighty God for the blessings vouchsafed to us in and by this Conference; and we desire to express our hope that this our meeting may hereafter be followed by other meetings to be conducted in the same spirit of brotherly love."

No. X. (See page 18.)

Correspondence with the Dean of Westminster respecting the use of Westminster Abbey in connection with the Conference of 1867.

1. *The Dean of Westminster to the Archbishop of Canterbury.*

DEANERY, WESTMINSTER,
September 21, 1867.

MY DEAR LORD ARCHBISHOP,

I have been honoured with a communication from your Grace, through the Bishop of London, requesting the use of Westminster Abbey for a special service to be held for the English, American, and Scottish Bishops now assembled in England, to be held, as I understood, on September 28.

On all occasions it is my earnest desire to render the Abbey and the precincts of Westminster available for purposes of general utility and edification, and this desire is increased when the request comes from your Grace.

You will kindly allow me to state the difficulty

which I feel in the present instance. I have endeavoured to act in such matters on the rule of granting the use of the Abbey to such purposes, and such only, as are either co-extensive with the Church of England, or have a definite object of usefulness or charity, apart from party or polemical considerations.

Your Grace will, I am sure, see that, however much your Grace's intentions would have brought the proposed Conference at Lambeth within this sphere, in fact, it can hardly be so considered. The absence of the Primate and the larger part of the Bishops of the Northern Province—not to speak of the Bishops of India and Australia, and of other important Colonial or Missionary Sees—must, even irrespectively of other indications, cause it to present a partial aspect of the English Church; whilst the appearance of other prelates not belonging to our Church, places it on a different footing from the institutions which are confined to the Church of England. And, further, the absence of any fixed information as to the objects to be discussed and promoted by the Conference, leaves me, in common with all who stand outside, in uncertainty as to what would be the proposals or measures which would receive, by implication, the sanction given by the use of the Abbey—a sanction which, in the case of a church so venerable and national in its character, ought, I conceive, to be lent only to public objects of well-defined or acknowledged beneficence.

These are the grounds why I hesitate to take upon myself the responsibility suggested. But, when stating this difficulty, I feel so strongly the value of the friendly intercourse to promote which has been the chief intention of your Grace, and of, I doubt not, many of the prelates who have concurred in this Conference; and I am so desirous that the Abbey should be made to minister to the edification of large sections of our Church, even when not representing the whole, and of those outside our own immediate pale (especially our brethren from America), who are willing to co-operate with us in all things lawful and good—that I would gladly, if possible, join in advancing such a purpose.

It has occurred to me, that, as the service indicated by your Grace is to be held after the Conference is finished, the Abbey might be granted for it, without any relation to the Conference itself; but either for some specific object, such as the Society for the Propagation of the Gospel, or for other Home or Foreign Missions of unquestioned importance, or else (in those general terms which, as I apprehend, express your Grace's wishes) for the promotion of brotherly goodwill and mutual edification amongst all members of the Anglican Communion.

Under these circumstances, and on this understanding, which I should wish to be made as public as the announcement of the service itself, I should have great pleasure in the permitting the use of the Abbey for such a service, to be held in the morning or afternoon of September 28th (as may be deemed most convenient), and I trust that, if this meets your Grace's wishes, your Grace will undertake to preach on the occasion.

I beg to remain, my dear Lord Archbishop,

Yours faithfully and respectfully,

A. P. STANLEY.

2. *The Archbishop of Canterbury to the Dean of Westminster.*

ADDINGTON PARK, CROYDON,
September 25, 1867.

MY DEAR DEAN,

I laid your note before the Conference yesterday, but it will probably not close its sittings on Friday evening, as there is reason to believe that committees will be appointed to report at a future date. Under these circumstances, it is obvious, from the tenor of your letter, that the Abbey is not open to us. I regret, therefore, that we shall not be able to avail ourselves of your kind offer, under the specified conditions.

Believe me, my dear Dean,
Yours very truly,
C. T. Cantuar.

3. *The Dean of Westminster to the Archbishop of Canterbury.*

Deanery, Westminster,
September 27, 1867.

My dear Lord Archbishop,

I have to acknowledge, with thanks, your Grace's letter of the 25th, and to express my regret that your Grace and the Bishops assembled should have felt themselves precluded from accepting my proposal—in reply to your Grace's request—to meet in the Abbey for "some specific object of charity or usefulness," or for the purpose of promoting brotherly goodwill and mutual edification amongst all members of the Anglican Communion.

I beg, however, that you will assure the prelates assembled, especially those of our American brethren, for whose sake, as I stated in my former letter, I especially proposed to grant the use of the Abbey as before mentioned; that if they, or any of them should wish to attend the services in the Abbey on Sunday next (at 10 a.m. or at 3 p.m.) every accommodation and welcome shall be afforded.

I beg to remain, my dear Lord Archbishop,
Yours faithfully and respectfully,
A. P. Stanley.

4. *The Dean of Westminster to the Bishop of Vermont, Presiding Bishop of the American Church.*

DEANERY, WESTMINSTER,
October 1, 1867.

MY DEAR LORD BISHOP,

Understanding that there has been some misapprehension on the part of the American bishops as to their invitation to a service in Westminster Abbey, I beg that you will do me the favour of communicating the following statement, in as public a way as you may think fit, to your Episcopal brethren.

It was impossible for me, as guardian of a building like the Abbey, which belongs to the whole Church and people of England, to take the responsibility of giving its sanction to a meeting which included only a portion of the English bishops, and of which the objects were undefined, the issues unknown, and the discussions secret. But I was so anxious to show every courtesy to the bishops from the United States, that, chiefly on their own account, as I particularly specified in my letter to the Archbishop of Canterbury, I so far deviated from the usual rules which guide the services in the Abbey as to propose the use of the Abbey for a service which should gather them there, either for some specific object of usefulness or charity or for the general promotion of goodwill and edification amongst all members of the Anglican Communion. I was encouraged the more to make this offer by the pledge that I had received that no questions exciting party differences should be introduced into the meetings, and I was therefore in hopes that his Grace would have felt himself able to accept a proposal which I had reason to believe would be gratifying to our American brethren.

The proposal was, however, declined; and I must therefore, through you, beg to express my regret that such an opportunity was lost of cultivating those feelings of amity between the two countries which are at all times so welcome.

The circumstances of the severe domestic affliction which has recently befallen us, whilst they prevented me from showing that hospitality which I should otherwise have offered to you, make me doubly anxious that, in a country from which we have received expressions of such sincere sympathy, there should be no misunderstanding as to the cordial desire that I entertain to welcome Americans on all occasions to our joint national sanctuary.

I trust that on some future occasion I may take the opportunity of renewing personally my assurance of the pleasure which it will ever give me to receive the citizens of a nation in which we must always feel peculiar interest.

I beg to remain,

Yours faithfully,

A. P. STANLEY.

No. XI. (See page 18.)

Sermon of Bishop Fulford, of Montreal, preached in Lambeth Parish Church on September 28, 1867.

Bishop Fulford's sermon was not published, but the following compressed report of it appeared in the *Guardian* of October 2, 1867, p. 1058 :—

"The Bishop of Montreal selected as his text, Psalm iv. 6. 'There be many that say, who will shew us any good?' The Bishop observed:

"If no public notice had been given of the fact, it might be perceived from the presence of so many of those Bishops who had been attending the meeting lately held in Lambeth Palace, that there was a special connection of the service of the day with the meeting. The business before the Conference was not entirely closed, because there were some committees appointed to carry out certain details and principles, especially in connection with the Colonial Church, and they would have to make their report at an adjourned meeting. But that, however, which concerned the whole community had been discussed, and a very important and solemn pastoral letter had been adopted, and signed unanimously by every member of the conference, to be sent out to the whole world. It was thought fitting that, as the Bishops had met in such large numbers, they should close their conference with a special service, and the celebration of the Holy Communion. He (the Bishop of Montreal) had undertaken to occupy the office on that occasion, at the request of the Archbishop of Canterbury, at very short notice, but he should endeavour to discharge the duty imposed upon him to the best of his ability. No one felt more fully than he did the importance of the meeting they had held, both as to what they had done and said, and what they had left undone and unsaid. And no one was more deeply sensible than himself of how much they owed to the Christian courage and large-heartedness which had enabled the Archbishop to make this great venture, and of his gentle, manly conduct and courtesy, in presiding over so large a gathering, and in bringing it to so successful an issue. How many persons had said, 'Who will shew us any good?' But, notwithstanding the sneers of the scornful, between seventy and eighty Bishops, holding Office in the Church of Christ, and representing the Anglican branch (in former years represented as confined to the British Isles), had come together at the Archbishop's invitation, so that every portion of the Church in every quarter of the globe had one representative or many representatives present. Some had come 10,000 or 12,000 miles to be present, and if they had done nothing more than give physical testimony to their oneness of faith and resolve upon that solemn pastoral, they would have done more for the unity of the Church than had been accomplished for the last 100 years. The Conference, however, had not confined its attention to that important document; many other matters had received earnest attention; and in the interchange of thought from minds of such different constitution, trained in so many different schools, moulded by such varying circumstances, living in such diverse positions, and influenced by such various surroundings, they had learnt to know and to love each other: the lesson has been of incalculable importance, and he thanked God for the great benefit which had thus been conferred upon all of them. Invitations to attend had been issued to 144 Bishops; many were utterly unable to accept it, and only a very small portion of them were not anxious to attend. All of these bishoprics had derived their existence and succession from the See of Canterbury, and between sixty and seventy were the result of the progress of the last few years. As regarded Canada, he had only to look back for sixteen years, when that province certainly possessed Bishops and a small number of missionaries, but the Church had no system of united action, and no concentrated method of order and government. But there was a meeting held at Quebec, such as the present gathering had been, and from it had sprung a regular system of synodical action, which was now in full vigour and power, and regularly constituted, and which progressed harmoniously, so that there was every reason to consider the Church in Canada as an established branch of Christ's holy Catholic Church. Then, again, in the United States, which had been so ably and so worthily represented at this Conference, he could but remember with feelings of gratitude the last General Convention of the Episcopal Church which he was privileged to attend. It was gathered together immediately after the country had been torn by internal dissensions, and when the whole social system had been rent by political disturbances. It was feared that the South would not again join the North; that political differences and party jealousy would prevent reunion; but God's providence ruled otherwise, and it was a most imposing sight, and one he could never forget, when the Bishops of the South took their accustomed places as before that unhappy war;—yes, that sight caused tears to flow down many a manly cheek, and when the aged prelates who presided, called aloud for a thanksgiving, their voices rose together even as one, shouting *Gloria in excelsis Deo.* And so with our own branch of the Church at home, it may have its trials and difficulties, but it was becoming day by day more instinct with energy and zeal. What ever threatening aspects might hover over her, she was yet a great and unspeakable blessing to the nation; she was great through herself and through her children; but she would be the greatest of all if she remained true to her noble mission and faithful to her Lord, the great Head of the Church; and thus he trusted that both in its present and future influences, the Conference just concluded might be fraught with increasing blessings to her and to her faithful children."

No. XII. (See page 19.)

REPORTS OF COMMITTEES APPOINTED BY THE CONFERENCE OF 1867.

A.—*Report of the Committee appointed under Resolution V., by the Conference of Bishops of the Anglican Communion, held at Lambeth Palace, September 24–27th, 1867.*[1]

The subject of the functions and relations of the several Synods, on which the Committee is appointed to report, appears to them to be necessarily connected with questions as to the constitution of these bodies. The following Report, therefore, embraces the whole subject of Synods. In discussing it, your Committee deems it necessary to deal with the question in the abstract, without reference to existing laws and usages in the several branches of the Anglican Communion, and to lay down general principles, the adoption or application of which must depend on circumstances, such, for example, as the laws which any Church may have inherited or already established.

---

[1] Resolution IV.—" That, in the opinion of this Conference, Unity in Faith and Discipline will be best maintained among the several branches of the Anglican Communion by due and canonical subordination of the Synods of the several branches to the higher authority of a Synod or Synods above them."

Resolution V.—" That a Committee of seven members (with power to add to their number, and to obtain the assistance of men learned in Ecclesiastical and Canon Law) be appointed to inquire into and report upon the subject of the relations and functions of such Synods, and that such Report be forwarded to his Grace the Lord Archbishop of Canterbury, with a request that, if possible, it may be communicated to any adjourned meeting of this Conference."

I.—In the organisation of Synodal order for the government of the Church, the Diocesan Synod appears to be the primary and simplest form of such organisation.

By the Diocesan Synod the co-operation of all members of the body is obtained in Church action ; and that acceptance of Church rules is secured, which, in the absence of other law, usage, or enactment, gives to these rules the force of laws " binding on those who, expressly or by implication, have consented to them."[1]

For this reason, wherever the Church is not established by law, it is, in the judgment of your Committee, essential to order and good government that the Diocese should be organised by a Synod.

Your Committee consider that it is not at variance with the ancient principles of the Church, that both Clergy and Laity should attend the Diocesan Synod, and that it is expedient that the Synod should consist of the Bishop and Clergy of the Diocese, with Representatives of the Laity.

The constitution of the Diocesan Synod may be determined either by rules for that branch of the Church established by the Synod of the Province, or by general consent in the Diocese itself, its rules being sanctioned afterwards by the Provincial Synod

Your Committee, however, recommend that the following general rules should be adopted ; viz., that the Bishop, Clergy, and Laity should sit together, the Bishop presiding ; that votes should be taken by orders, whenever demanded ; and that the concurrent assent of Bishop, Clergy, and Laity should be necessary to the validity of all acts of the Synod.

They consider that the Clerical members of the Synod should be those Clergy who are recognized by the Bishop, according to the rules of the Church

---

[1] Judgment of Judicial Committee of Privy Council in case of Long *v.* Bishop of Capetown. 1 Moore, P. C. C., N.S., 461.

in that Diocese, as being under his jurisdiction. Whether in large Dioceses, when the Clergy are very numerous, they might appear by representation, is a difficult question, and one on which your Committee are not prepared to express an opinion.

The Lay Representatives in the Synod ought, in the judgment of your Committee, to be Male Communicants of at least one year's standing in the Diocese, and of the full age of twenty-one. It should be required that the electors should be Members of the Church in that Diocese, and belong to the parish in which they claim to vote. It appears desirable that the regular meetings of the Synod should be fixed and periodical; but that the right of convening special meetings whenever they may be required should be reserved to the Bishop.

The office of the Diocesan Synod is, generally, to make regulations, not repugnant to those of higher Synods, for the order and good government of the Church within the Diocese, and to promulgate the decisions of the Provincial Synod.

II.—The Provincial Synod—or, as it is called in New Zealand, the General Synod, and in the United States the General Convention—is formed, whenever it does not exist already by law and usage, through the voluntary association of Dioceses for united legislation and common action. The Provincial Synod not only provides a method for securing unity amongst the Dioceses which are thus associated, but also forms the link between these Dioceses and other Churches of the Anglican Communion.

Without questioning the right of the Bishops of any Province to meet in Synod by themselves, and without affirming that the presence of others is essential to a Provincial Synod, your Committee recommend that, whenever no law or usage to the contrary already exists, it should consist of the Bishops of the Province, and of Representatives both of the Clergy and of the Laity in each Diocese.

Your Committee need not define the method in which a Provincial Synod may be first constituted, but they assume that its constitution and rules will be determined by the concurrence of the several Dioceses duly represented.

Your Committee consider that it must be left to each Province to decide whether, and under what circumstances, the Bishops, Clergy, and Laity in a Provincial Synod should sit and discuss questions in the same chamber or separately ; but, in the judgment of the Committee, the votes should in either case be taken by orders ; and the concurrent assent of Bishops, Clergy, and Laity should be necessary for any legislative action, wherever the Clergy and Laity form part of the constitution of a Provincial Synod ; such powers and functions not involving legislation being reserved as belong to the Bishops by virtue of their office.

The number, qualification, and mode of election of the Clerical and Lay Representatives from each Diocese must be determined by the Synods in the several Provinces.

It is the office of the Provincial Synod, generally, to exercise, within the limits of the Province, powers in regard to Provincial questions similar to those which the Diocesan Synod exercises, within the Diocese, in regard to Diocesan questions.

As to the relation between these two Synods, your Committee are of opinion that the Diocese is bound to accept positive enactments of a Provincial Synod in which it is duly represented, and that no Diocesan regulations have force, if contrary to the decisions of a higher Synod ; but that, in order to prevent any collision or misunderstanding, the spheres of action of the several Synods should be defined on the following principle, viz., That the Provincial Synod should deal with questions of common interest to the whole Province, and with those which affect the communion of the Dioceses with one another and with the rest of the Church; whilst the Diocesan Synod should be left free to dispose of matters of local interest, and to manage the affairs of the Diocese.

From this principle your Committee draws the following conclusions:—

1. All alterations in the Services of the Church, required by circumstances in the Province, should be made or authorized by the Provincial Synod, and not merely by the Diocesan.

2. The rule of discipline for the Clergy of the Province should be framed by the Provincial Synod.

3. Rules for the trial of Clergy should be made by the Provincial Synod; but, in default of such action on the part of that Synod, the Diocesan Synod should establish provisional rules for this purpose. The Provincial Tribunal of Appeal should be established by the Provincial Synod.

4. In questions relating to Patronage, the tenure of Church property, Parochial divisions, arrangements, officers, &c., there should be joint action of the Diocese and the Province; the former making such regulations as may be best suited to develop local resources, the latter providing against the admission of any principle inexpedient for the common interests of the Church.

5. The erection of a new Diocese within the limits of an existing Diocese should proceed by general rules established by the Provincial Synod.

6. The question of the election of a Bishop it is unnecessary here to consider, as it is submitted to another Committee.

III.—The question of a higher Synod of the Anglican Communion, and of the relation which the inferior Synods should hold towards it, whenever it might assemble, is one, your Committee are aware, of much greater difficulty than any of those which have been previously considered.

The fact, however, that a Conference of Bishops of the whole Anglican Communion has already met together, is of itself an indication of the need which is generally felt of united counsel in a sphere more extensive than that of a Provincial Synod. Indeed, the Resolutions under which this Committee was appointed contemplate the possibility at least of some Synod being established superior to the Provincial. It is also implied in Resolution VIII. of this Conference, that some such Assembly may be required, in order to preserve Colonial and Missionary Churches in close union with the Church of England, since it is provided that all changes in the Services of the Church made by one of their Provincial Synods should "be liable to revision by any Synod of the Anglican Communion in which the said Province should be represented."

The objections that may be urged against the united action of Churches which are more or less free to act independently, and other Churches whose constitution is fixed, not only by ancient ecclesiastical laws and usages, but by the law of the State, are obvious; but it appears to your Committee that the action of this Conference has proved that the difficulties which are anticipated are not insuperable, and suggests the method by which they may be overcome. Under present circumstances, indeed, no Assembly that might be convened would be competent to enact canons of binding ecclesiastical authority on these different bodies, or to frame definitions of faith which it would be obligatory on the Churches of the Anglican Communion to accept. It would be necessary, therefore, in the judgment of your Committee, to avoid all terms respecting this Assembly that might imply authority of this nature, and to call it a Congress, if even the term Council should be considered open to objection. Its decisions could only possess the authority which might be derived from the moral weight of such united counsels and judgments, and from the voluntary acceptance of its conclusions by any of the Churches there represented.

Your Committee consider that his Grace the Archbishop of Canterbury, as occupying the See from which the Colonial and American Churches derive their succession, should be the convener of such an Assembly. That it should differ from the present Conference in being attended by both Clerical and Lay Representatives of the several Churches, as consultees and advisers, each Diocese being allowed to send, besides its Bishop, a presbyter and a lay member of the Church, if they should desire to be thus represented; and further, in the proceedings being more formal and, in part at least, public. The question when for the first time, and at what periods, this Congress or Council should be called, your Committee deem it more respectful to leave for the consideration of his Grace the Archbishop of Canterbury and of the present Conference.

G. A. NEW ZEALAND, *Chairman.*
H. GRAHAMSTOWN, *Secretary.*

B.—*Report of the Committee appointed under Resolution IX. of the Lambeth Conference, on the Constitution of a voluntary spiritual Tribunal, to which questions of Doctrine may be carried by Appeal from the Tribunals for the exercise of discipline in each Province of the Colonial Church.*[1]

After full consideration of objections that have been urged against the establishment of any such Tribunal as that contemplated by this Resolution, your Committee are of opinion that these objections are not sufficient to outweigh the arguments in its favour, and that most of the objections will be found inapplicable to the particular form of Tribunal which the Committee recommend.

Your Committee consider that such a Tribunal is required in order to prevent the dissatisfaction which would arise if important questions were finally decided by those Colonial Churches, the circumstances of which render it impossible for them to form a sufficient Tribunal of last resort.

It would also tend to secure unity in matters of Faith, and uniformity in matters of Discipline, where Doctrine may be involved.

For these reasons your Committee recommend that such a Tribunal be established ; and from the desire

---

[1] Resolution IX.—"That the Committee appointed by Resolution V., with the addition of the names of the Bishops of London, St. David's, and Oxford, and all the Colonial Bishops, be instructed to consider the constitution of a voluntary spiritual Tribunal, to which questions of doctrine may be carried by appeal from the Tribunals for the exercise of discipline in each Province of the Colonial Church, and that their report be forwarded to his Grace the Lord Archbishop of Canterbury, who is requested to communicate it to an adjourned meeting of this Conference."

expressed by several branches of the Colonial Church, that this should be one of the results of this Conference, they believe that it will be generally accepted by those for whose benefit it is designed.

At the same time, they are sensible of the great difficulty of forming such a Tribunal, and of the necessity of proceeding with caution, lest it should interfere with the liberties of the Colonial Churches, or should have any appearance of collision with the Courts established by law, either here or in Her Majesty's foreign possessions.

Your Committee now proceed to lay before the Conference their conclusions as to the functions and constitution of the proposed Tribunal.

They are of opinion that it should not take cognizance of any case which shall not have been referred to it by some branch of the Anglican Communion which has consented to its constitution. Thus it would not interfere either with those Churches in which provision is made by the State for the exercise of discipline, or with the liberty and rights of ecclesiastical Provinces. These would be free to accept or to decline the appeal thus offered to them, and to withdraw afterwards their acceptance of the Tribunal, if they should so desire.[1]

Your Committee consider that this Tribunal of Appeal should take into consideration all the facts of the case as sent up to it in writing from the inferior Tribunal; that the Appeal, however, should not be on the facts, but only on the points of Doctrine and Discipline involved in them.

That during the Appeal the sentence of the Provincial Tribunal should continue in force, so far as it

---

[1] The decisions of such a Tribunal would be of the same nature as those of "arbitrators, whose jurisdiction rests entirely upon the agreement of the parties." (Judgment of Judicial Committee of the Privy Council in case of Long *v.* Bishop of Capetown, 1 Moore, P. C. C., N.S. 462.)

affects the present exercise of spiritual functions by the accused.

That the judgments of the Tribunal of Appeal should be delivered in the form of a decision that the teaching or practice of the accused party is (or is not) permissible.

That the Tribunal should use as the standards of faith and doctrine by which its decisions shall be governed, those which are now in use in the United Church of England and Ireland ; and that as to all matters not defined in such formularies, the judgments should be framed on any conclusions which shall be hereafter agreed to at any Council or Congress of the whole Anglican Communion: Provided always, that no such conclusion be contradictory to any now existing standard or formulary of the Church of England ; and provided further, that the Synod of that Province of the Church from which the Appeal shall be sent, shall not have refused to accept such conclusion.

Your Committee further recommend, subject to any regulations that may be made at any future Conference of the Anglican Communion :—

That, as it is a Tribunal for decisions in matters of faith, Archbishops and Bishops only should be judges, his Grace the Lord Archbishop of Canterbury being the President.

That each Province in the Colonial Church should have the right of electing two members of the Tribunal ; and that all the Dioceses of the Colonial Church not associated into Provinces should collectively have the right of electing two. That each Province of the United Church of England and Ireland should be requested to elect two members, but that the Province of Canterbury should elect three, in the event of his Grace the Archbishop not acting as President. That the Episcopal Church in Scotland should have the right of electing two. And (as it appears probable that the Protestant Episcopal

Church in the United States would avail itself of such a Tribunal) that Church should have the right of electing five members.

In the judgment of the Committee, the Bishops of the several Churches should elect those who shall represent them on this Tribunal.

That, so soon after January 1, 1869, as any ten names shall have been forwarded to the Archbishop of Canterbury as having been elected, the Tribunal should be deemed to be constituted.

That of the members thus elected, seven should form a quorum for the transaction of business, but a smaller number should have power to adjourn from time to time.

That the members of the Tribunal should continue in office, unless their seat be vacated by death, resignation, or removal by the electing body; but that, in the event of any Bishop of the Colonial or American Church notifying to the electing body that he is unable or declines to attend at any sitting of the Tribunal to which he may be summoned, it should be lawful for the body by which he was elected to appoint, instead of him, any Bishop of the Anglican Communion other than one of those already elected.

That, in the event of the Archbishop of Canterbury for the time being declining or being unable to act as President, it should be lawful for his Grace, if he should see fit, to nominate any other member of the Tribunal to act as President in his room; and in the event of no such appointment being made by him, that it should be lawful for the Tribunal at its first meeting to elect one of its members as President.

That the summons for the sitting of the Tribunal should be issued within thirty days from the time of the notice of Appeal being delivered by the agent of the Appellant to the proper officer of the Tribunal.

That the action of the Tribunal should not be

impeded by the absence from it of any of those who are at liberty to sit in it, provided there be a quorum.

That, before the assembling of the Tribunal for the hearing of an Appeal, the President should nominate as Assessors three theologians and three persons learned in the law, who should be present at the trial, and should answer any questions as to theological learning and law put to them by the Tribunal through its President in writing, and who should be at liberty to tender in writing to the Tribunal through its President their opinion upon any point of theological learning or law which may arise, and that the Tribunal should be bound to consider such opinion before coming to its decision.

That parties before the Tribunal may be represented by any counsel they may select, whether theologians or persons learned in the law.

That the rules of procedure of the said Tribunal, except as here provided for, should, as far as possible, be those of the higher Courts of Law, and that any necessary alterations in such rules should be made by the Tribunal itself.

That no sentence should be passed without the assent thereto of two-thirds of the Judges present during the trial.

That, at the time of delivering judgment, each member of the Tribunal who has been present during the trial should give his decision in writing, and may read, or cause to be read, openly in Court his decision, and the reasons for it; and that the judgment of the prescribed majority should be the judgment of the Tribunal.

F. MONTREAL, *Chairman.*
H. GRAHAMSTOWN, *Secretary.*

C.—*On the Courts of Metropolitans, and the Trial of a Bishop or Metropolitan.*[1]

I. Your Committee consider that the constitution of the Provincial Tribunal for Appeals from the decisions of Diocesan Tribunals should be determined, whenever it is not fixed by law, by the Synod of the Province; but it is expedient, in their judgment, that its rules should be assimilated, as far as circumstances will admit, to those of the proposed tribunal of Appeal in England.

II. In the case of charges against a Bishop, they suggest the following as general principles:—

That each Province should determine by rules made in its own Synod the offences for which a Bishop may be presented for trial, and who should be promoters of the charge.

That the charge should be presented to the Metropolitan.

That it appears doubtful whether a preliminary inquiry is expedient, provided that sufficient precautions are taken that no frivolous charges should be entertained.

That the Metropolitan should summon to the hearing of the cause all the Bishops of the Province (except the accused), who should sit as judges, not merely as assessors.

---

[1] Resolution X.—" That the Resolutions submitted to this Conference relative to the discipline to be exercised by the Metropolitans, the Court of Metropolitans, the scheme for conducting the Election of Bishops, when not otherwise provided for, the declaration of submission to the Regulation of Synods, and the question of what Legislation should be proposed for the Colonial Churches, be referred to the Committee specified in the preceding Resolution."

That no trial should take place, except before two-thirds of the Bishops of the Province, provided that there be never fewer than three Bishops present, including the Metropolitan.

That if three Bishops of the Province should be unable to attend, it should be lawful for the Metropolitan to call in one or more Bishops not of the Province.

That it is desirable that, whenever it may be practicable, there should be Assessors, as recommended by this Committee for the higher Tribunal of Appeal.

That, in case of the non-appearance of the accused after sufficient citations, the trial may go forward as if he were present, or he may be punished for contumacy, according as the Province may prescribe.

That there should be no sentence except by the judgment of two-thirds of the Tribunal, or by three judges, whichever should be the greater number; the assent of the Metropolitan not being necessary to the sentence.

That the general rules of procedure should be framed by the Synod of the Province; but should be, as far as possible, similar to those recommended by this Committee for the proposed Tribunal of Appeal.

That an appeal to the higher Tribunal recommended by this Committee should be allowed when the case is one of doctrine, or discipline involving doctrine, if notice of such appeal be given within   days from the delivery of sentence; and that, in all cases, proper provision should be made for a new trial on sufficient reason being shown.

That there should be no contract not to appeal to Civil Courts; but that sufficient provision should be made by the Declaration of Submission (to be considered in another Report) that the sentence of the Spiritual Tribunals may be effective.

That a Metropolitan should be tried in the same manner as any other Bishop—the senior Bishop, in that case, acting in the place of the Metropolitan.

F. MONTREAL, *Chairman.*
H. GRAHAMSTOWN, *Secretary.*

D.—*Scheme for conducting the Election of Bishops, when not otherwise provided for.*

Your Committee have to consider the proper mode for conducting the election of a Bishop, whenever it is not provided for by an existing law, and without reference to any question that might arise as to the temporalities connected with the See.

It is evident that there are two parties whose concurrent action is necessary in such an appointment —viz., the Clergy and Laity of the Diocese, and the Bishops of the Province by whom the person elected as Bishop is consecrated.

Your Committee are of opinion that, in accordance with the ancient usages of the Church, the election as a general rule should be made by the Diocese, and that the Bishops of the Province should confirm the election. They consider, however, that it is consistent with this principle that the Diocese should nominate two or more persons, of whom the Bishops of the Province should select one; or that the Diocese should delegate to any person or body the power of choosing a Bishop for the vacant See, it being understood that the Diocese must accept such choice as final.

The principle of the concurrent action of the two parties concerned would also be preserved if the Bishops of the Province should nominate two or more persons, from whom the Diocese should elect one.

In the election by the Diocese it appears to your Committee that the right of selecting the person who shall be their Bishop belongs to the Clergy, the Laity having the right of accepting or rejecting the person so chosen. But it is expedient, in their judgment, that the election should always be made by the Diocesan Synod, wherever one is established, and in accordance with the rules of that Synod. In those Dioceses in which there is no Diocesan Synod, they recommend that, for the election of a Bishop, a Convention should be summoned by the Dean, senior Archdeacon, or senior Presbyter of the Diocese; that this Convention should consist of all Presbyters and of lay-representatives, who should be male communicants of at least twenty-one years of age; that these representatives should be elected by each parish or congregation, in such manner as should be determined by the convener; that the person who should obtain the majority of votes of the Clergy, and also of those of the lay-representatives present at the Convention, should be accounted to be elected to the Bishopric; that this election should not be vitiated by the absence of any of the parties summoned, or by the failure of any congregation or parish to elect a lay-representative; that any question as to the validity of the election to the vacant See should be submitted, prior to the Consecration, to the Consecrating Bishops, whose decision should be final; and that after the consecration of a Bishop no objection should be entertained.

They further recommend that, where the Diocese is included in a Province, the confirmation of an election should be by the Metropolitan and a majority of the Bishops of the Province; but where the Diocese is extra-Provincial, that the confirmation should rest with the Archbishops of Canterbury and York and the Bishop of London; that the power of confirmation should be absolute—the Bishops having the right to refuse to confirm the election, without assigning any reason for their refusal.

All further rules necessary for conducting the election should, in the opinion of your Committee, be made by the Synod of the Province.

F. MONTREAL, *Chairman.*
H. GRAHAMSTOWN, *Secretary.*

E.—*On Declaration of Submission to Regulations of Synod.*

Your Committee recommend that, in all branches of the Church, the government of which is not determined by law, a Declaration should be made by those who hold office therein. They consider that a Declaration is necessary, in order to define the conditions of the consensual compact, and that it should be framed so as to secure submission to all synodical action in its legitimate sphere, and to the decisions of the constituted Tribunals.

They recommend the following declaration to be made, before the Metropolitan, or some person duly appointed by him, by all Bishops elect, either before their consecration or, if already consecrated, before exercising any Episcopal functions in their diocese :—

"I *A. B.*, chosen Bishop of the Church and See of   , do promise that I will teach and maintain the doctrine and discipline of the United Church of England and Ireland, as acknowledged and received by the Province of   , and I also do declare that I consent to be bound by all the rules and regulations which have heretofore been made or which may from time to time be made, by the Synod of the Diocese of   , and the Provincial Synod of   , or either of them; and, in consideration of being appointed Bishop of the said Church or See of   , I hereby undertake immediately to resign the said appointment, together with all the rights and emoluments appertaining thereto, if sentence requiring such resignation should at any time be passed upon me, after due examination had, by the Tribunal acknowledged by the Synod of the said Province for the trial of a Bishop ; saving all rights of Appeal allowed by the said Synod,"

They recommend that the following Declaration be made (in addition to the Declaration required by the rules of that Province or Diocese as to doctrine and worship) by persons to be admitted to holy orders, and by Clergymen to be admitted to the cure of souls, or to any other office of trust in the Church.

" I, *A. B.*, do declare that I consent to be bound by all the rules and regulations which have heretofore been made, or which may from time to time be made, by the Synod of the Diocese of   , and the Provincial Synod of   , or either of them ; [and in consideration of being appointed   , I hereby undertake immediately to resign the said appointment, together with all the rights and emoluments appertaining thereto, if sentence requiring such resignation should at any time be passed upon me, after due examination had, by the Tribunal appointed by the Synods of the aforesaid Province and Diocese for the trial of a Clergyman ; saving all rights of Appeal allowed by the said Synod]."

(The part in brackets to be omitted when there is no appointment to a cure of souls, or office of trust.)

Your Committee consider that it must be left to the Province or Diocese to decide whether laymen who are admitted to any office or position of trust should be required to sign a Declaration of the same nature.

G. A. NEW ZEALAND, *Chairman.*
H. GRAHAMSTOWN, *Secretary.*

F.—*On Provinces and Subordination to Metropolitans.*

On this subject your Committee beg to report as follows :—

They are of opinion that the association or federation of Dioceses within certain territorial limits, commonly called an Ecclesiastical Province, is not only in accordance with the ancient laws and usages of the Christian Church, but is essential to its complete organization.

Such an association is of the highest advantage for united action, for the exercise of discipline, for the confirmation of the election of Bishops, and generally to enable the Church to adapt its laws to the circumstances of the countries in which it is planted.

It is expedient, in the judgment of your Committee, that these ecclesiastical divisions should, as far as possible, follow the civil divisions of these countries.

Of the Bishops of these Dioceses thus associated, one, in conformity with ancient usage, ought to be Metropolitan or Primus, the functions and powers of the Metropolitan being determined by synodical action in the Province, except so far as Metropolitical powers are defined by undisputed General Councils of the Church.

It seems to your Committee most in accordance

with primitive usage that the Metropolitical See should be fixed, but they do not deem this to be essential. It appears expedient that the Provincial Synod should have the power of changing, when necessary, the site of the Metropolitical See.

Your Committee do not consider it necessary that the election to the Metropolitical See should be conducted differently from the election to other vacant sees; since the Bishops of the Province possess the right of confirming or refusing to confirm any election.

Your Committee strongly recommend that all those Dioceses which are not as yet gathered into Provinces should, as soon as possible, form part of some Provincial organization. The particular mode of effecting this in each case must be determined by those who are concerned.

It is sufficient for your Committee to point out that the steps to be taken for effecting this change are twofold, since the relations of the Dioceses in Provincial organisation, when complete, are formed on the one hand by the subordination of the Bishops of the Province to a Metropolitan, and on the other by the association of the Dioceses in Provincial action. Any alteration of existing arrangements would require, therefore, in the opinion of your Committee, the concurrent action of the Diocese which is to be gathered into a Province with other neighbouring Dioceses, and of his Grace the Archbishop of Canterbury, to whom the Bishops of the Dioceses that at present are extra-provincial have taken the oath of canonical obedience. In the case of the limits of an existing Province being altered, the consent of the Synod of that Province would be required for the alteration.

F. MONTREAL, *Chairman.*
H. GRAHAMSTOWN, *Secretary.*

G.—*Report of the Committee appointed under Resolution XI. of the Lambeth Conference.*[1]

Your Committee report that, after full consideration of the questions referred to them by the Conference, they have adopted the following Resolutions :—

I. That every branch of the Church is entitled to found a Missionary Bishopric.

II. That it is desirable that each branch of the Church should act upon rules agreed upon beforehand by the Synod or other Church Council of the said branch.

III. That each Missionary Bishopric should be deemed to be attached to one branch of the Church, and that all rules for the election of a Missionary Bishop, and for the formation of a Diocese or Dioceses out of the Missionary District, should be made by the Synod or other Church Council of such branch of the Church.

IV. That notice of the erection of any Missionary Bishopric, and the choice and consecration of the Bishop, should be notified to all Archbishops and Metropolitans, and all Presiding Bishops, of the Anglican Communion.

V. That in appointing a Missionary Bishop, the district within which he is to exercise his Mission should be defined as far as possible ; and that no other Bishop should be sent within the same district,

---

Resolution XI. — "That a Special Committee be appointed to consider the Resolutions relative to the notification of proposed Missionary Bishoprics, and the subordination of Missionaries."

without previous communication with that branch of the Church which gave mission for the work.

VI. That, while peculiar cases may occur in Missionary work, owing to difference of race and language, in which it may be desirable that more than one Bishop should exercise episcopal functions within the same district, the Committee consider that such cases should be regarded as exceptions, justified only by special circumstances.

VII. That, with respect to the special case of Continental Chaplaincies, the Committee suggest to the Conference the consideration of some ecclesiastical arrangement by which the various congregations of the Anglican Communion may be under one authority, whether of the English or American Church.

VIII. That the conditions on which a Missionary Bishopric should be brought within a Provincial organisation should be:—

1. The request of the Missionary Bishop, addressed both to the Church from which he received mission and to the Province which he wishes to join.

2. The consent of the Church from which he received mission, that consent being given by the Metropolitan or Presiding Bishop.

3. The consent of the Province he wishes to join, that consent being given by the Provincial Synod.

IX. That the status, jurisdiction, and designation of the Bishop thus received into a system of Provincial organisation should be determined by the Synod of the Province to which his Bishopric shall be then attached.

X. That, as a general rule, it is expedient that such Missionary Bishopric should be attached to the nearest Province; but that in certain cases it may be necessary that some more remote Province should be selected.

Bishop Tozer's Mission is a case to which the

Committee desire to draw the attention of the Conference, as being one in which, for the present, Provincial organization would seem to be impracticable, from the isolation of the district in which Bishop Tozer exercises his episcopal functions, and its remoteness from the Province of South Africa.

XI. That Missionary Bishops and their Clergy should be bound generally to the Canons of Doctrine and Discipline of the Church from which their mission is derived, or to which they may have been united, and that all alterations in matters of discipline be communicated to the authorities of that Church.

XII. That when a Missionary Church shall be received into the organisation of a Provincial Synod, the said Church should be bound by the acts of that body; but that, in order to effect this, the Missionary Church should be granted a power of representation, or of vote by proxy, in such Synod.

XIII. That, as a general rule, in conformity with Church order, all Missionaries and Chaplains residing or engaged in the exercise of ministerial duty within the Diocese or District of a Colonial or Missionary Bishop, should be licensed by, and be subject to the authority of, the said Bishop.

XIV. That every Clergyman removing from one Colonial or Missionary Diocese or District into another Diocese ought to carry with him Letters Testimonial from the Colonial or Missionary Bishop whose Diocese or District he is leaving.

XV. That no person admitted to Holy Orders by the Bishop of any Diocese in England or Ireland, who shall afterwards have been serving under the jurisdiction of any Scottish, Colonial, or Foreign Bishop, should be received into any of the Home Dioceses, without producing letters Dimissory or Commendatory from the Scottish, Colonial, or Foreign Bishop in whose Diocese he has been serving.

XVI. The attention of this Committee has been

called to the clause in the Paper of Arrangements for the Conference, headed "Subordination of Missionaries." The Committee have failed to understand what is meant by the words "instructions from those in authority at home," but they can recommend no scheme which interferes with the canonical relation which subsists between a Bishop and his clergy.

   W. J. GIBRALTAR, *Chairman.*
   WILLIAM GEORGE TOZER,
      Missionary Bishop, *Secretary.*

H.—*Report of the Committee appointed under Resolution VI. of the Lambeth Conference.*[1]

By the Resolution of the Lambeth Conference two questions were referred to the Committee:—

I. How the Church may be delivered from a continuance of the scandal now existing in Natal?

II. How the true faith may be maintained?

I. On the first question, the Committee recommend that an Address be made to the Colonial

---

[1] Resolution VI.—"That, in the judgment of the Bishops now assembled, the whole Anglican Communion is deeply injured by the present condition of the Church in Natal: and that a Committee be now appointed at this General Meeting to report on the best mode by which the Church may be delivered from a continuance of this scandal, and the true faith maintained. That such Report shall be forwarded to his Grace the Lord Archbishop of Canterbury, with the request that he will be pleased to transmit the same to all the Bishops of the Anglican Communion, and to ask for their judgment thereupon."

Bishoprics Council, calling their attention to the fact that they are paying an annual stipend to a Bishop lying under the imputation of heretical teaching, and praying them to take the best legal opinion as to there being any, and if so what, mode of laying these allegations before some competent court, and if any mode be pointed out, then to proceed accordingly for the removal of this scandal.

The Committee also recommend that the Address to the Colonial Bishoprics Council be prefaced with the following statement :—

"That, whilst we accept the spiritual validity of the sentence of deposition pronounced by the Metropolitan and Bishops of the South African Church upon Dr. Colenso, we consider it of the utmost moment for removing the existing scandal from the English Communion that there should be pronounced by some competent English court such a legal sentence on the errors of the said Dr. Colenso as would warrant the Colonial Bishoprics Council in ceasing to pay his stipend, and would justify an appeal to the Crown to cancel his Letters Patent."

II. On the second question :

"How the true faith may be maintained in Natal?"

The Committee submit the following Report :—

That they did not consider themselves instructed by the Conference, and therefore did not consider themselves competent, to inquire into the whole case ; but that their conclusions are based upon the following facts :—

1. That in the year 1863, *forty-one* Bishops concurred in an Address to Bishop Colenso, urging him to resign his Bishopric.

2. That in the year 1863, some of the publications of Dr. Colenso, viz.—" The Pentateuch and Book of Joshua critically examined," Parts I. and II., were condemned by the Convocation of the Province of Canterbury."

3. That the Bishop of Capetown, by virtue of his

Letters Patent as Metropolitan, might have visited Dr. Colenso with summary jurisdiction, and might have taken out of his hands the management of the Diocese of Natal.

4. That the Bishop of Capetown, instead of proceeding summarily, instituted judicial proceedings, having reason to believe himself to be competent to do so.

That he summoned Dr. Colenso before himself and suffragans.

That Dr. Colenso appeared by his proctor.

That his defence was heard and judged to be insufficient to purge him from the heresy.

That, after sentence was pronounced, Dr. Colenso was offered an appeal to the Archbishop of Canterbury, as provided in the Metropolitan's Letters Patent.

5. That this Act of the African Church was approved—

By the Convocation of Canterbury;

By the Convocation of York;

By the General Convention of the Episcopal Church in the United States, in 1865;

By the Episcopal Synod of the Church in Scotland;

By the Provincial Synod of the Church in Canada, in the year 1865;

And, finally, the spiritual validity of the sentence of deposition was accepted by *fifty-six* Bishops on the occasion of the Lambeth Conference.

Judging, therefore, that the See is spiritually vacant; and learning, by the evidence brought before them, that there are many members of the Church who are unable to accept the ministrations of Dr. Colenso, the Committee deem it to be the duty of the Metropolitan and other Bishops of South Africa to proceed, upon the election of the Clergy and Laity in Natal, to consecate one to discharge those spiritual functions of which these members of the Church are now in want.

In forwarding their Report to his Grace the Lord Archbishop of Canterbury, as instructed by the Resolution of the Conference, the Committee request his Grace to communicate the same to the adjourned meeting of the Conference, to be holden at Lambeth on the tenth day of the present month.

December 9th, 1867.

G. A. NEW ZEALAND,
Convener.

J.—*Form of Letters Dimissory for the Clergy.*

To the Right Reverend the Bishops and Reverend the Clergy, and to the faithful in Christ of the Diocese of A. We, B, by Divine permission Bishop of C, send greeting in the Lord.

We commend to your brotherly kindness by these our letters, D, E, Priest (or Deacon) of our Diocese, beseeching you to receive him in the Lord as a brother sound in the Faith, of a well-ordered and Religious Life, and worthy of all Christian Fellowship, and to render him any assistance of which he may stand in need; and so we bid you farewell in Christ our Lord

Witness our hand.

A, *Bishop.*
B, *Secretary.*

No. XIII. (See page 19.)

Resolutions of the Adjourned Conference, Dec. 10, 1867.

Resolution I.—" That this adjourned meeting of the Conference receives the Report (No. I.) of the Committee now presented, and directs the publication thereof, commending it to the careful consideration of the Bishops of the Anglican Communion, as containing the result of the deliberations of that Committee; and returns the members of the same its thanks for the care with which they have considered the various important questions referred to them."

(The same Resolution was passed with reference to Reports II., III., IV., V., VI., VII.)

Resolution II.—" That the Report (No. VIII.) of the Committee appointed under Resolution VI., laid before this meeting by his Grace the Archbishop of Canterbury be received and printed; that the thanks of this Meeting be given to the Committee for their labours; and that his Grace be requested to communicate the Report to the Council of the Colonial Bishoprics Fund."

Resolution III.—" That his Grace be requested, if applied to by the House of Bishops in the Episcopal Church in the United States of America, to allow a copy of the Records of the Conference to be made for them, and to be lodged in the hands of such officer as shall be designated by the House of Bishops to receive it, for reference by Bishops only, but not for publication."

Resolution IV.—" That his Grace the Archbishop of Canterbury be requested to convey to the Church in Russia an expression of the sympathy of the Anglican Communion with that Church, in the loss which it has sustained by the death of his Eminence Philarete, the venerable Metropolitan of Moscow."

Resolution V.—" That the thanks of this Conference be given to the Bishop of Grahamstown for the valuable services which he has rendered as Secretary to many of the Committees appointed by the Conference."

Resolution VI.—" That the thanks of this Conference be given to Philip Wright, Esq., and to Isambard Brunel, Esq., Barrister-at-Law, for their aid as

Assistant Secretaries to the Committees; and especially to the latter for his valuable assistance in all matters that required legal advice."

Resolution VII.—" That we cannot close this Conference without conveying our hearty thanks to his Grace the Archbishop of Canterbury, both for convening this meeting, and for the mode in which he has presided over its deliberations."

Besides the preceding Resolutions,—

The President reported that he had been authorised to annex the following signatures to the Encyclical Letter :—

>A. T. CICESTR.
>AUCKLAND, BATH AND WELLS.
>ROBERT DOWN AND CONNOR.
>WILLIAM DERRY.
>EDWARD NEWFOUNDLAND.
>J. FREDERICTON.
>T. E. ST. HELENA.

2. The following Bishops were appointed as a Sub-Committee, for the purpose of drawing up a Bill, in accordance with a Report submitted by the Committee appointed under Resolution IX. of the previous meeting :—

>BISHOP OF LONDON.
>   "   OXFORD.
>   "   LINCOLN.
>   "   ELY.
>   "   LICHFIELD (Elect).
>   "   MONTREAL.
>   "   GRAHAMSTOWN.
>BISHOP TROWER.

3. His Grace the Archbishop of Canterbury laid on the table a form of Letters Dimissory,[1] which he had prepared, in accordance with Resolution II. of the last session of the Lambeth Conference.

---

[1] J. page 136.

4. The Bishop of Illinois, at the request of the Conference, stated that the Meeting of the Triennial General Convention of the Protestant Episcopal Church in the United States would be held on the first Wednesday of October next, in the City of New York; and, in behalf of the Church in the United States, offered an affectionate invitation to the Bishops of the Conference to be present on that occasion; and also expressed the hope that the different branches of the Anglican Communion would depute one or more Bishops as Representatives of the Mother and Colonial Churches, to be present on that occasion, assuring all that might accept this invitation of cordial welcome and affectionate brotherhood.

5. At the request of the Conference, the Bishop of Lichfield (Elect) undertook the office of Corresponding Secretary for the Bishops of the Anglican Communion.

His Grace the President then pronounced the Benediction, and the Conference was closed.

No. XIV. (See page 21.)

Addresses from the Canadian and West Indian Houses of Bishops. 1872 and 1873.

1. To his Grace the President and their Lordships the Bishops of the Upper House of Convocation of Canterbury—

We, the Bishops of the Ecclesiastical Province of Canada, availing ourselves of the opportunity afforded by the meeting of a special Provincial Synod, desire that the following Address, touching the Lambeth

Conference, be forwarded to his Grace, the President, and to the Prolocutor of the Lower House of Convocation of the Province of Canterbury.

We, the Bishops aforesaid, encouraged by the successful results of the Address presented to his Grace the late Archbishop of Canterbury, by the Provincial Synod of Canada, whereby the Lambeth Conference was convened, humbly and earnestly petition that the Convocation of Canterbury will take such action as may seem most expedient to unite with us in requesting the Archbishop of Canterbury to summon a second meeting of the Conference.

We are persuaded that such meeting will be most efficacious in uniting the scattered branches of the Anglican Communion, and in promoting the extension of the Kingdom of Christ throughout the world; and we therefore pray that it may be again convened at the earliest day that may suit the convenience of the Archbishop of Canterbury.

A. MONTREAL (Metropolitan).
J. T. ONTARIO.
J. W. QUEBEC.
A. H. TORONTO.
J. HURON.

Montreal, Dec. 13, 1872.

2. "The West Indian Bishops [assembled at Georgetown, Demerara, in 1873] join in the request lately made to the Archbishop of Canterbury by the Bishops of the Canadian Province, that he would summon another meeting of the Bishops of the Anglican Communion throughout the world at as early a date as may seem to his Grace practicable and expedient."

No. XV. (See page 21.)

Correspondence between Bishops of the Protestant Episcopal Church in the United States and the Archbishop of Canterbury. 1874 and 1875.

1. *The Archbishop of Canterbury to Bishop Kerfoot, of Pittsburgh.*

ADDINGTON PARK, CROYDON, *Aug.* 21, 1874.

MY DEAR BISHOP,

Before you leave England, I wish to say to you that the subject of another gathering of Bishops of our Communion at Lambeth has been much talked of lately. If the House of Bishops of your Church were to express their wishes on this subject, it might help me in bringing the matter before my brethren of this country when we meet in January of next year.

Trusting that God will bless you in your journey and on your return to your work,

I am, your faithful Brother,

A. C. CANTUAR.

2. *The Bishop of Pittsburgh to the Archbishop of Canterbury.*

HOUSE OF BISHOPS, NEW YORK, *Nov.* 3, 1874.

MY DEAR LORD,

I had the pleasure not long since of writing to you from this House, to say that the request to your Grace to invite another Lambeth Conference had been signed by forty-three of the forty-six Bishops in attendance. I then said that I would write again fully when the engagements of the General Convention allowed me to do so.

The matter was introduced by me into this House early in our session, so that the Lord Bishop of Lichfield, who was with us for the first week of the Convention, might speak to the Bishops on the subject. He did this with great discretion and effect in our House, and also in the House of Deputies. While the Bishops generally were very favourably disposed towards the proposal (and your Grace's note to me of August 25th very much promoted this inclination), some of them wished that any action of the Bishops should be preceded by some expression from the clerical and lay deputies that would prevent any thought that the Bishops were acting for themselves alone, and not also for and with the clergy and laity. .... It was deemed by all the Bishops to be sufficient, and for several reasons best, that we should express our wish and convey our request to your Grace in the form in which it has by this time reached you through the Bishop of Lichfield. The Bishop of New York and myself prepared the paper, and received the signatures of the Bishops individually. As some of the signatures may not be readily legible, I enclose a printed list of the names of the signers.

It clearly appeared in the consultations of the deputies, and even of the Bishops, that there were not a few misconceptions about the Conference of 1867. This, I think, was due, in large measure, to the misrepresentation of its character and management in the memoir of the late Bishop Hopkins. . . . Bishop Hopkins himself would not, I am sure, have approved of the sketch of the Lambeth Conference given by his biographer. But its effects were seen, and I hope counteracted, in the discussions.

In the consultation of the Bishops, the wish was several times expressed that the arrangements for a

Conference in 1876 should be such as to manifest that the variety of the topics admitted, and the time allowed, should be such as would seem to justify a Convocation of our Bishops from all over the world. There was no wish to annex terms or conditions to our request to your Grace. The suggestions already made by the Canadian Synod (whose action on this subject was recited in our House of Bishops) covers most or all of this ground.[1] As our consultations went on, it seemed to be devolved on me, by general consent, to make to you this informal communication about such wishes. Two or three Bishops gave them to me in writing; some others in unwritten words. The thoughts were that the Bishops attending the Conference might propose for discussion such questions as each one should deem right; and that the sessions should be continued long enough to allow of the needful Conferences. Those of us who were at Lambeth seven years ago knew quite well that such were the real character and spirit of that Conference; but that it being then an enterprise and experiment at once novel and anxious, precautions were rightly taken and limitations wisely observed that persons at a distance could not fully or fairly comprehend. The invitation was even then given in advance to the Bishops to suggest topics; and many of us did this, and I believe every such topic was introduced.

I made such answers to the inquiries of some of my brethren, adding that, of course, as then, so whenever we should meet again, no topic should be introduced which must elicit discussions on the State relations of the Church of England. All the Bishops here at once recognise this as the right rule. I said this was the only real limitation I witnessed seven years ago. I ventured to anticipate that on this point every reasonable wish would be satisfied in the future Conference.

---

[1] See below, page 148.

In thus writing at, I hope, not a needless length to your Grace, I think that I quite fulfil the promises made to some of my American brethren, who united heartily in the request sent to you, and I hope that I also convey such intimations as will entirely meet your own views in your anticipation of any such Conference. I may also add that the careful consideration given to the whole scheme here of late only confirms our convictions of the wisdom and usefulness of the renewal of the Conference of 1867. I am, my dear Lord Archbishop, your Grace's very faithful and affectionate brother.

JOHN B. KERFOOT,
Bishop of Pittsburgh.

3. *The following is the formal Resolution referred to in the foregoing letter.*

The undersigned Bishops of the Protestant Episcopal Church in the United States, having had the pleasure of listening to the statements of the Right Reverend the Lord Bishop of Lichfield, of the Right Reverend the Lord Bishop of Montreal and Metropolitan, of the Right Reverend the Lord Bishop of Kingston, Jamaica, and of the Right Reverend the Lord Bishop of Quebec in reference to the benefits to the whole Anglican Communion to be derived from the holding of another Conference of the Bishops thereof, do most cordially express in their individual capacity their interest in the subject, and their hope that his Grace the Archbishop of Canterbury will find it consistent with his views of duty to take steps towards the assembling of such a Conference.

[The signatures of forty-two Bishops, including the presiding Bishop, are appended.]

4. *The Archbishop of Canterbury to the Bishop of Pittsburgh.*

LAMBETH PALACE, S.W.,
April 27, 1875.

[PRIVATE.]

MY DEAR BISHOP,

As I promised, I brought the question of a second Lambeth Conference and your kind letter before the Bishops of the Southern Province, who met lately in Convocation.

The holding of such a Conference in the autumn of next year is rendered impossible, if not by other causes, by the fact that I find that 1876 is the year in which I must (D.V.) hold my visitation in the autumn, and deliver my charge, and you will understand the impossibility of my undertaking at that time the additional work necessarily involved on so important an occasion as the reassembling of the Lambeth Conference.

We cannot, therefore, look forward to the Conference taking place earlier than 1877, which will be ten years from the time of the first meeting. But, as we know that your Convention meets in the autumn of that year, it appears to us that the Lambeth Conference might well be in the spring of 1877, thus leaving time for our American brethren to return home before this Convention.

I think I ought to add that there was a general impression that, before steps were taken for gathering Bishops from all parts of the world, we ought distinctly to understand what the subjects are on which discussion is desirable. There was a general feeling that matters of doctrine which are already settled by our formularies could not be re-opened, and matters of discipline must be left to the authorities of each separate Church. There remains, therefore, only such general questions as relate to the intercourse of the various branches of our Church, and that brotherly conference which was on former occasions found so valuable.

I write this private letter, as I think you may wish to know the feelings of the English Bishops on this important subject with as little delay as possible, and I hope before long to be able to return a formal answer to the document signed by the Bishops of the American Episcopal Church.

      Believe me to be, my dear Bishop,
         Very sincerely yours,

            A. C. CANTUAR.

5. *To the Right Rev. the Bishops of the Protestant Episcopal Church of the United States of America.*

        LAMBETH PALACE, S.E.,
            June 7, 1875.

RIGHT REV. AND DEAR BRETHREN,

I have laid before my brethren of the Province of Canterbury your letter on the subject of holding a second Lambeth Conference, and I have had communication on the same subject with the Archbishop of York, as representing the Bishops of the Northern Province.

We entertain a grateful sense of the advantages of that brotherly intercourse which the last Lambeth Conference tended to encourage, and we should look forward with much pleasure to another meeting of the same kind.

I am, however, instructed by my brethren to bring before you the two following considerations, respecting which I should be glad to have your opinion before taking any further steps in this matter.

  1. It seems to my brethren and myself that such a

Conference could not with advantage be held till the tenth year after the last meeting. I am aware that this would bring us to the year 1877, in which, as I understand, your general convention holds its triennial meeting; but the autumn of 1876, which has been mentioned by the Bishop of Lichfield as a suitable time, will, so far as I can foresee, be entirely occupied by my visitation of the Archdiocese of Canterbury, and it is the opinion of those whom I have consulted that the most convenient time would be the summer of 1877, say, in the month of July, which time would enable our brethren of the United States to return home for the meeting of their own Convention.

2. I have also been requested to bring before you the following point. You will at once see that I ought not to take the step of inviting so large a body of Bishops to leave the scene of their labours in their distant Dioceses without being able to state to them somewhat explicitly what the practical results are which are expected to be derived from the Conference.

It appears to us that, respecting matters of doctrine, no change can be proposed or discussed, and that no authoritative explanation of doctrine ought to be taken in hand. Each Church is naturally guided in the interpretation of its formularies by its recognised authorities. Again, respecting matters of discipline, each Church has its own appointed Courts for the administration of its ecclesiastical law, with which, of course, such a meeting of Bishops as is proposed claims no power to interfere. The present state of the Christian Church makes men more than usually sensitive as to any appearance even of a claim on the part of any one branch of the Church to interfere with the decisions or administrations of another. Each is considered qualified to regulate its own separate affairs, while all are united in the maintenance of the one faith. Therefore, if the Conference meets, it will be necessary to exclude all questions which might happen to trench on the complete independence of the several branches of the Church.

The propriety of the Bishops meeting in Conference must depend, I conceive, upon this—whether there appear a sufficient number of subjects relating to the brotherly intercourse of the various Branches of the Anglican Communion, on which a conference of the chief Ministers of the several Churches would be likely to throw light.

I should be greatly obliged for any communication which you may be disposed to send to me, during the next six months, as to your views on the general desirableness of our meeting under such circumstances as I have described. I will take care, before the close of the present year, to lay before my brethren in England any statement I receive as to the particular questions which you think it desirable for the Bishops of the Anglican Communion to consider.

This would enable us to come to a decision respecting the Conference, and make any arrangements that may be required.

I remain,
Your faithful brother and servant in Christ,
A. C. CANTUAR.

No. XVI. (See page 22.)

Memorandum of the Canadian House of Bishops. 1874.

Suggestions of the Canadian House of Bishops made to the Bishop of Lichfield concerning the Lambeth Conference.

1. As to the period of its meeting—

We would suggest that 1876 would be a period very convenient and welcome to the Church in Canada.

2. As to the duration of the Conference—

We are of opinion that there should be a continuous Session of one month, four days in each week being days of session ; or,

That there should be at least two weeks of Session, with an interval between the first and last week.

3. As to the matter to be discussed—

We feel that it is most desirable that the Reports of Committees laid before the Conference of 1867 should be carefully considered, with the exception of Report No. 8.

4. We think that it would be very convenient to the Bishops invited to the Congress that an opportunity should be given them of suggesting beforehand any subject which they may wish to have considered.

5. We feel that, if his Grace should be pleased to grant the Bishops an opportunity of assembling in Conference, it would be extremely desirable that his decision on the above matters should be embodied in the Circular of Invitation.

Signed, on behalf of the Bishops of the Province of Canada,

A. MONTREAL, Metropolitan.

No. XVII. (See page 24.)

Action of the Convocations of Canterbury and York with reference to the proposed Second Lambeth Conference.

The Memorials from the Canadian and West Indian Bishops (quoted above, No. XVI., page 148), were on April 29, 1874, referred by the Upper House of the Convocation of Canterbury to a Joint Committee of fifteen members, who, on July 10, 1874, presented a report in the shape of the following four Resolutions :—

1.. "That the relation of his Grace the Lord Archbishop of Canterbury to the other Bishops of the Anglican Communion be that of Primate among Archbishops, Primates, Metropolitans, and Bishops."

2. "That in accordance with the Memorial of the Bishops of the Ecclesiastical Province of Canada, and the resolution of the Bishops of the West Indian Dioceses, his Grace the Lord Archbishop of Canterbury be requested to convene a General Conference of the Bishops of the Anglican Communion to carry on the work begun by the Lambeth Conference in 1867.

3. "That the Reports of Committees presented at the adjourned Session of the Lambeth Conference in 1867, but not adopted or even discussed, be taken into consideration at the Second Conference."

4. "That the Committee recommend that his Grace be respectfully requested to convene the second meeting of the Lambeth Conference for the year 1876."

"G. A. LICHFIELD, Chairman."

The Report was received by the Upper House, and communicated to the Lower House, July 10, 1874.—(*See Chronicle of Convocation, pp.* 437–439.)

The Upper House of Canterbury Convocation had also resolved, on April 29, 1874, to invite an expression of opinion from the Convocation of York, and that Convocation, on February 26, 1875, passed the following resolution :—

"That this Synod, in reply to a communication from the Province of Canterbury, asking for an expression of opinion upon three resolutions respecting certain memorials received from the Ecclesiastical Province of Canada, and from the Bishops of the West Indian Dioceses, prays that his Grace the President will convey to his Grace the Archbishop of Canterbury the wish of this Synod that all necessary steps may be taken for the assembling of a second Conference at Lambeth, but would desire to leave all other questions involved in these resolutions to be decided as may seem best to the Archbishops and the bench of Bishops."

No. XVIII. (See page 24.)

Circular Letter of Inquiry addressed by the Archbishop of Canterbury to all the Anglican Bishops, March 28, 1876.

LAMBETH PALACE, *March* 28, 1876.

RIGHT REVEREND BROTHER,

A wish has been expressed by many Bishops of the Protestant Episcopal Church in the United States of America, by the Bishops of the Canadian Dominion, and by the West Indian Bishops, that a second Conference of our brethren should be held at Lambeth.

Before I decide upon the important step of inviting the Bishops of our Communion throughout the world to assemble at Lambeth, I have thought it right, after consultation with the Bishops of England, to give all our brethren an opportunity of expressing their opinion upon the expediency of convening such a Conference at this time, and upon the choice of the subjects which ought to engage its attention, if it be convened.

I therefore beg leave to intimate to you our readiness to hold a Conference at Lambeth in or about the month of July, 1878, if it shall seem expedient, after the opinions of all our brethren have been ascertained; and I need scarcely assure you that your advice is earnestly desired, and will be respectfully considered. May I ask, for our guidance, whether you are willing, and are likely to be able, to attend the Conference yourself?

Those who were present at Lambeth in 1867 thankfully acknowledged that, through the blessing of Almighty God, the Bishops of the various branches of the Anglican Communion were drawn together in closer bonds of brotherly love and sympathy.

The help and comfort which are due from the branches of Christ's Church to each other are more readily rendered, and more fully each is made acquainted with the wants of the rest. In this time of religious activity and increased intercourse between all parts of the world, there is greater need than ever of mutual counsel amongst the Bishops of our widely-extended Communion.

The Bishops of England, therefore, earnestly ask you to join with them in prayer that we may all be guided to a wise decision on this important matter, and if it should be resolved to hold the Conference, that its deliberations may issue in greater peace, and strength, and energy to the whole Church of Christ.

Anxiously awaiting your answer,

I remain,

Your faithful Brother and Servant in Christ,

A. C. CANTUAR.

The Right Reverend the Bishop of . . . . .

"*Covering letter*" *to the Metropolitans and Presiding Bishops.*

LAMBETH PALACE, S.E., *March* 28, 1876.

MY DEAR BISHOP,

After consultation with my Brethren the Bishops of England, including the Archbishop of York, I beg leave to address you as   of [1] and request you to circulate among the Bishops of your branch of the Church the enclosed documents, having reference to a second Lambeth Conference.

I shall feel obliged by your favouring us at your earliest convenience with your own views on the questions now submitted to your consideration.

I remain, your faithful brother and servant in Christ,

A. C. CANTUAR.

No. XIX. (See page 25.)

Letter of Invitation to the Conference of 1878.

LAMBETH PALACE, *July* 10, 1877.

RIGHT REVEREND AND DEAR BROTHER,

It is proposed to hold a Conference of Bishops of the Anglican Communion at this place, beginning on Tuesday, the second day of July, Eighteen hundred and Seventy-eight.

The Conference, it is proposed, shall extend over four weeks; the first week of four Sessions to be devoted to discussions, in Conference, of the subjects submitted for deliberation; the second and third weeks to the consideration of these subjects in Committees; and the fourth week to final discussions in Conference, and to the close of the Meeting.

---

[1] *e.g.*, Metropolitan of Canada.

The subjects selected for discussion are the following :—

1. The best mode of maintaining Union among the various Churches of the Anglican Communion.
2. Voluntary Boards of Arbitration for Churches to which such an arrangement may be applicable.
3. The relations to each other of Missionary Bishops and of Missionaries in various branches of the Anglican Communion acting in the same country.
4. The position of Anglican Chaplains and Chaplaincies on the Continent of Europe and elsewhere.
5. Modern forms of infidelity, and the best means of dealing with them.
6. The condition, progress, and needs of the various Churches of the Anglican Communion.

I shall feel greatly obliged if, at your early convenience, you will inform me whether we may have the pleasure of expecting your presence at the Conference.

I am, Right Reverend and dear brother, yours faithfully in Christ,

A. C. CANTUAR.

No. XX. (See page 29).

Sermon preached by the Archbishop of York, in Lambeth Palace Chapel, on Tuesday, July 2nd, 1878.

"But when Peter was come to Antioch, I withstood him to the face, because he was to be blamed."—*Gal.* ii. 11.

This is the first rupture amongst those who were to spread the knowledge of Christ throughout the world. An Apostle withstood an Apostle to the face, because he was to be blamed.[1] We all remember the facts. No direction had been left by the Lord as to the treatment of the Gentiles that should believe. Did their road to the Kingdom of Heaven conduct through the Temple? Were the Gentiles that believed to observe the law of Moses? If not, what advantage had the chosen people over the scum and off-scouring of the earth?

These questions, of vital moment, and now imperiously demanding a solution, were left open by the divine Founder of the Church; they were to be decided by the light of the Holy Spirit, working in the Church itself. Decided they were, and set at rest for ever. But the process of doubt and struggle may be to us the most seasonable subject of reflection. May that Holy Spirit, who has taught and guided the Church from the first, be with us all this day, meditating on this significant place of Holy Writ. Amen.

It was long before the Church would accept the plain meaning of this passage. Was it possible, then, that two such lights of the earth could fall apart in strife, and this about a matter of faith? What would the outside world say against the truth of God—nay, what *did* it say before the spectacle of such a strife? If the founders of the Church can thus diverge, what is the doctrine of the Church worth?[2] Thus they mocked; and the Fathers, hard pressed, adopted the theory of Origen, that this dispute was simulated, was nothing but a scene got up between the two Apostles, who had made up their minds in concert, about the position of the Gentiles, in order that a strong lesson of submission might be taught to the Judaising Christians in the person of Peter himself. It is strange that such a theory, in which an accusa-

---

[1] Rather "he was condemned;" whether this means "condemned by the very facts," or "condemned by some assembly or body of Christians" does not appear; the former is probable.

[2] Hieron., "Ep. ad Galat.," Pref.

tion of base deceit on the part of both is substituted for one of timidity on the part of one, should have been able to attract even Jerome; against whom Augustine rose up, and following the precedent, "withstood him to the face" for attributing to these Apostles a trick which would shake our faith in the Holy Scriptures themselves; since these hold up the quarrel as a reality, and not as a piece of acting.

It was indeed a quarrel. On some visit to Antioch, not, as I venture to think, after, but before, the decision of the Council of Jerusalem on this question, St. Peter, by eating and drinking in communion with the Gentiles recognised their conversion and their position as members of the Church. But then came some from Jerusalem, where the feeling was strong that the law should be observed. A fresh dispute sprang up. Peter desired to avoid offence to his own people, from Jerusalem, so he withdrew from the Gentile converts. It was a heavy censure; it was a bad example. Barnabas himself was entangled in this "hypocrisy." A great crisis of the Church had come, and such a desertion cut St. Paul to the heart. His anger was great. The wrong had been public, and so should the rebuke be. It does not appear that he reasoned with Peter in private. On some public occasion he withstood and rebuked him. Not the law, but Christ, could save. Why should Peter, who had once set himself free from the law, bind its chains again upon other people? If salvation was to be by the law, then Christ was dead in vain. We have no report of this dispute; but, whatever may be thought of the method of treatment, it is likely that the course taken by St. Paul did much to clear the ground in that momentous controversy. Barnabas, it is plain, must have retracted; and as for Peter, if I am right in supposing that this event preceded the Council at Jerusalem, we know how he regarded the Gentiles. God "put no difference between us and them, purifying their hearts by faith."

The grace of God, which raises men's hearts by degrees into conformity with the Divine image, does not suddenly destroy the old nature. St. Peter is still the same impulsive man who could now confess the Christ, and now, when troubles came, deny Him; who could follow him bravely into danger, yet be overcome by the gossiping remark of a girl that met him by chance. We must not try this case by the standard of Anglo-Saxon consistency; we sometimes perhaps run the risk of purchasing too dearly that favourite virtue, at the price of zeal and ardour. We are not naturally indulgent towards that impulsive nature, which the great Apostle, more Jewish in this than the Jews, derived from his race. Anxious to please, and to be in sympathy with those about him, he rejoiced at first in the Gentile freedom; until those came about him who were full of prejudice for their venerable law, its severe conditions of communion, its austere separation. Let us neither praise nor blame; let us only say, Grace has not yet wrought her perfect work in this Apostle's heart.

Nor has the other great Apostle yet learned all that the school of grace can teach him. Face to face, before the whole Church, he rebukes and humbles a brother, whom Christ had honoured, who had laboured much, and turned many from darkness to light. He quotes it as a proof of his independence amongst the Apostles, not without complacency. All this is consistent with his bold and resolute nature, which marched straight to its object, and refused to swerve, either out of respect of persons or out of fear. His steadfast resolution, that Christ should be all in all, came from above; his manner of compassing it bears clear marks of his old nature. That blessed change under the power of grace can be perhaps more fully studied in St. Paul's career than anywhere else in Church history; the strong, loving, fierce, harsh nature,—you see the faults transformed to virtues, the angles rounded off, the strong will made obedient to the bit and bridle of love; and yet it is the same man still. You recognise the old features of the portrait, but it is transfigured by a preternatural light. Again, we will not praise nor blame; we will rather recognise the power of the mighty Spirit of God; which could use for His purposes the timid impulse of one man and the impatient zeal of another, for building up the House of God; and at the same time could take in hand the timid and the impatient natures alike, and give courage to the one and softness to the other, thus building at one time the great House of God and carving delicately each living stone of which the House is compacted.

I need not expose before you, Right Reverend Fathers, the theory of Apostolic history which has been built chiefly on this passage. That a permanent quarrel and schism arose from this time between the two Apostles, lasting to the very end; that the history of the Apostolic age is the tale of this great struggle between the Apostle who would maintain and the Apostle who would abolish the Mosaic law, with the efforts made from time to time to make peace between them; these positions have been maintained by Baur and others, with great ingenuity, with wonderful exaggeration. Every page of the Gospels is supposed to bear marks of the struggle: Acts and Epistles are full of it. Modern criticism is as fanciful at times as those simple folk that peopled every wood with fays and sprites, looked for a dryad under every leaf and a nymph in every brook, and made out in the ordinary noises of the forest the voice of the god Pan. Common sense will not find anything in the Gospels that amounts even to a trace of this contention. Such a rupture could not have happened without leaving great marks everywhere. There are none. Luke, the friend of St. Paul, records in his Gospel things that tend to St. Peter's honour, which the other Gospels do not quote. Silas, the companion of Paul, was also the friend and companion of Peter. (1 Pet.

v. 12.) Lastly, when Peter writes his First Epistle to the Churches of Asia Minor, which Paul had founded, he says not a word to disparage the teaching of their founder: he says, "that this is the true grace of God, wherein ye stand." None of these things is consistent with the theory of a feud and hatred between these two chief pillars of the Church. Critics magnify divergent opinions into schisms; a scratch into a gaping wound. Had those two noble natures gone asunder, in lasting wrath, every page of Church history would have borne loud witness to the greatness of their sin.

It is very common for us to look up out of our welter of troubles, our sects, and schisms, and disputations, and to see far back in the first ages nothing but peace; a united Church, offering its harmonious, universal praise, a well-drilled army, marching in obedience to a single will, a code of faith which *always, everywhere, all* the faithful heard, and without questioning believed. But as the student draws near, the objects grow more distinct, the mists disperse, the shadows separate, and fall into their places; and the rose-flush of the dawn ceases to conceal the true colours of that primeval region. Then we come to see something very different from our preconceptions, and learn, what is indeed gladness to learn, that upon the whole, in the old time as in the new, the Holy Spirit sent of the Lord has wrought in the Church in the same manner. He was a Spirit of light and life and comfort to the souls of men; but then, as now, the men were enlightened, not transformed. And the glory of God's great work lay in this—not that the powers, wishes, and passions of the actors were petrified into a lifeless uniformity, and the superseding life from heaven took their place: but rather that, using as His instruments men so weak and perverse, He built with them the Church of God. To me, I do confess, it is a comfort to know that the Church in the first age grew by the same principles as it grows by in the nineteenth; that the very divisions amongst us have their counterparts in the age of the Apostles, and that our disputes, like theirs, may be but permitted struggles and aberrations of us who are acting out God's great commands, and that all the while He is making perfect the circle of His purpose, and accomplishing His Kingdom. The Evangelists were not four scribes, inditing with servile hands a manifesto for the new kingdom of heaven: they were men full of the Holy Ghost, whose task came upon them in the course of God's work, imposed by the march of events, yet not less truly by the voice of God, by whom the events were ordered. Are the Gospels less dear to you and me, from our knowing that oral preaching must have preceded them, that other histories and treatises must have been written, of greater and of less importance, of which the inspired Evangelists had knowledge? That they wrote at last on account of the spreading of the Church, and the gradual dispersion of the Jews, and the approaching doom of the Holy City? The Gospels are four green branches on the growing stem of the Church; are they therefore less divine to us who believe that the growth of the Church was divine? Beneath that growing tree the thorny branches of the old ceremonial law withered, gradually, and there were disputes like this one between Paul and Peter, as to how and when the dead boughs should be cleared away. But the question has been wisely settled: it disturbs us no more, albeit the settlement was gradual and not without strife. The Church has grown, as all things seem to grow, by the life within her striving to perfect itself amidst opposing forces. So grows the acorn, pushing its weak shoots through hard ground, and its strength and dignity are not less that once the swinish jaws narrowly missed devouring the mast, and the swinish foot did actually trample it into the clay. So grew the liberties of the English people: are they less dear to us because they have been threatened, and at times eclipsed in the past? So grow the mind and spirit of a man, passing through trials and efforts, even through falls, to the ripeness of a resolute, tolerant, patient, helpful age. So grew the Church of Christ; and her life is not less real, less secure, if she has passed sometimes through fears and fightings, and the deep waters of the proud have seemed to go even over her life. At one time Athanasius has had to stand against a world; at another a Hildebrand imperils the Church by making it the supreme Kingdom amongst the earthly kingdoms. Worldly motives are said to have tainted the reformation of religion in this country; and it is true. So much the greater is our reason for blessing God, that the sweet honeycomb has come from the lion's carcase; that amid the strifes and selfishness of kings, and the ignorance of peoples, the truth passed safely. So even now the Church is growing, and God dwelling in her gives the increase. We seem in deadly peril: there is unbelief on one side, and on the other that deadening system which would hand over the conscience to the priest, and the priest to a mediæval theology, hostile to knowledge and incapable of change. "The waves of the sea are mighty, and rage horribly, but yet the Lord that dwelleth on high is mightier."

Yet there is one more lesson which the study of the past might bring us. By the vehemence of past disputes, nay by the bitter hatred that they have brought in, one might think that men had lost faith in the power of the Holy Ghost to keep safe the ark of God upon the stormy waters. To "withstand to the face" has been the 'common remedy for emergencies. It may be permitted us reverently to doubt whether the pulse of divine life in the Church has been hastened by one beat, by the violence of the zealous, who have thought well to be angry for the cause of God. Through strife, but not by strife, the Church has passed upon her way. And we,

Right Reverend Fathers, meeting a second time in conference upon the interests of that branch of the Church, which springing from this little island, has so spread over the earth that the sun never sets upon her daughter Churches, we will never admit a doubt that God is with us still. Struggle and conflict, and even partial failure shall not convince us that God has left us; they are the heritage of the Church from the beginning. The faces that we miss, and they are many, are of those that have passed to rest; but the very words remind us that for us there is not rest. And whilst we are resolved to hold fast the faith committed to us, we may endeavour in one point to go beyond our fathers: the candour and the charity that springs from a firm trust in the truth, these should be our aim and special study. More than one writer has been pleased to point out that in the first century were three periods in which three Apostles, Peter, Paul, and John, predominated in succession: and they think they can trace the same succession in the larger field of Church history, so that the Petrine period ends at the Reformation, and the Pauline succeeds it, whilst the time of St. John is supposed to be beginning. There is something fanciful in this arrangement. Yet pardon the fancy for the truth that underlies it. And when Peter falters, impulsive, and is inconsistent with himself, and Paul withstands him to the face, let the third Apostle enter on the scene, and remind us that we can afford to use the largest charity whilst we hold still the firmest trust. His contribution to the eternal diapason of the Church's faith and love shall be this: 'Whosoever shall confess that Jesus is the Son of God, God dwelleth in him, and he in God. .... And this commandment have we from him, That he who loveth God love his brother also.' (1 John iv. 15, 21.)

No. XXI. (See page 32.)

Letter of the Bishops attending the Lambeth Conference of 1878, including the Reports adopted by the Conference.

CONTENTS.

Introductory ... *page*	164
Report of Committee on "The best mode of maintaining Union among the various Churches of the Anglican Communion" ...	164
Report of Committee on "Voluntary Boards of Arbitration for Churches to which such an arrangement may be applicable" ...	171
Report of Committee on "The relation to each other of Missionary Bishops and of Missionaries of various branches of the Anglican Communion, acting in the same country" ...	174
Report of Committee on "The position of Anglican Chaplains and Chaplaincies on the Continent of Europe and elsewhere"...	179
Report of Committee appointed to receive questions submitted to them, in writing, by Bishops desiring the advice of the Conference on difficulties or problems they have met with in their several Dioceses, and to report thereon ...	180
Conclusion ...	186
Notes ...	

LETTER.

TO THE FAITHFUL IN CHRIST JESUS, GREETING—

We, Archbishops, Bishops Metropolitan, and other Bishops of the Holy Catholic Church, in full communion with the Church of England, one hundred in number, all exercising superintendence over Dioceses, or lawfully commissioned to exercise Episcopal functions therein, assembled, many of us from the most distant parts of the earth, at Lambeth Palace, in the year of our Lord 1878, under the presidency of the most reverend Archibald Campbell, by Divine Providence Archbishop of Canterbury, Primate of all England; after receiving, in the private Chapel of the said Palace, the blessed Sacrament of the Lord's Body and Blood, and after having united in prayer for the guidance of the Holy Spirit, have taken into our consideration various definite questions submitted to us affecting the condition of the Church in divers parts of the world,

We have made these questions the subject of serious deliberation for many days, and we now commend to the faithful the conclusions which have been adopted.

Report of Committee on the best mode of maintaining union among the various Churches of the Anglican Communion.

1.—In considering the best mode of maintaining union among the various Churches of our Communion, the Committee, first of all, recognise, with deep thankfulness to Almighty God, the essential and evident unity in which the Church of England and the Churches in visible communion with her have always been bound together.¹ United under One Divine Head in the fellowship of the One Catholic and Apostolic Church, holding the One Faith revealed in Holy Writ, defined in the Creeds, and maintained by the Primitive Church, receiving the same Canonical Scriptures of the Old and New Testaments as containing all things necessary to salvation—these Churches teach the same Word of God, partake of the same divinely-ordained Sacraments, through the ministry of the same Apostolic orders, and worship one God and Father through the same Lord Jesus Christ, by the same Holy and Divine Spirit, Who is given to those that believe, to guide them into all truth.

2.—Together with this unity, however, there has existed among these Churches that variety of custom, discipline, and form of worship which necessarily results from the exercise by each "particular or national Church" of its right " to ordain, change, and abolish ceremonies or rites of the Church ordained only by man's authority, so that all things be done to edifying." We gladly acknowledge that there is at present no real ground for anxiety on account of this diversity; but the desire has of late been largely felt and expressed, that some practical and efficient methods should be adopted, in order to guard against possible sources of disunion in the future, and at the same time further to manifest and cherish that true and substantial agreement which exists among these increasingly numerous Churches.

3.—The method which first naturally suggests itself is that which, originating with the inspired Apostles long served to hold all the Churches of Christ in one undivided and visible communion. The assembling, however, of a true General Council, such as the Church of England has always declared her readiness to resort to, is, in the present condition of Christen-

---

¹ Note A, p. 187.

dom, unhappily but obviously impossible. The difficulties attending the assembling of a Synod of all the Anglican Churches, though different in character and less serious in nature, seem to us nevertheless too great to allow of our recommending it for present adoption.

4.—The experiment, now twice tried, of a Conference of Bishops called together by the Archbishop of Canterbury, and meeting under his presidency, offers at least the hope that the problem, hitherto unsolved, of combining together for consultation representatives of Churches so differently situated and administered, may find, in the providential course of events, its own solution.[1] Your Committee would, on this point, venture to suggest that such Conferences, called together from time to time by the Archbishop of Canterbury, at the request of, or in consultation with, the Bishops of our Communion, might with advantage be invested in future with somewhat larger liberty as to the initiation and selection of subjects for discussion. For example, a Committee might be constituted, such as should represent, more or less completely, the several Churches of the Anglican Communion; and to this Committee it might be entrusted to draw up, after receiving communications from the Bishops, a scheme of subjects to be discussed.

5.—Meanwhile, there are certain principles of Church order which, your Committee consider, ought to be distinctly recognized and set forth, as of great importance for the maintenance of union among the Churches of our Communion.

(1.) First, that the duly-certified action of every national or particular Church, and of each ecclesiastical Province (or Diocese not included in a Province), in the exercise of its own discipline, should be

---

[1] Note B, p 188.

respected by all the other Churches, and by their individual members.

(2.) Secondly, that when a Diocese, or territorial sphere of administration, has been constituted by the authority of any Church or Province of this Communion within its own limits, no Bishop or other Clergyman of any other Church should exercise his functions within that Diocese without the consent of the Bishop thereof.[1]

(3.) Thirdly, that no Bishop should authorize to officiate in his Diocese a clergyman coming from another Church or Province, unless such Clergyman present letters testimonial, countersigned by the Bishop of the Diocese from which he comes; such letters to be, as nearly as possible, in the form adopted by such Church or Province in the case of the transfer of a clergyman from one Diocese to another.

Passing to details, your Committee would call attention to the following points :—

1.—*Of Church Organization.*

6.—Inasmuch as the sufficient and effective organization of the several parts of the Church tends to promote the unity of the whole, your Committee would, with this view, repeat the recommendation in the sixth report of the first Lambeth Conference,[2] that those Dioceses which still remain isolated should, as circumstances may allow, associate themselves into a Province or Provinces, in accordance with the ancient laws and usages of the Catholic Church.

---

[1] This does not refer to questions respecting missionary Bishops and foreign chaplaincies, which have been entrusted to other Committees.

[2] Note C, p. 191.

II.—*Of Common Work.*

7.—Believing that the unity of our Churches will be especially manifested and strengthened by their uniting together in common work, your Committee would call attention to the great value of such co-operation wherever the opportunity shall present itself; as, for example, in founding and maintaining, in the missionary fields, schools for the training of a native ministry, such as that which is now contemplated in Shanghai, and, generally, as far as may be possible, in prosecuting missionary work, such as that which the Churches in England and Scotland are maintaining together in Kaffraria.

III.—*Of Commendatory Letters.*

8—(1.) This Committee would renew the recommendation of the first Lambeth Conference, that letters commendatory should be given by their own Bishops to clergymen visiting for a time other Churches than those to which they belong.

(2). They would urge yet more emphatically the importance of letters commendatory being given by their own clergymen to members of their flocks going from one country to another. And they consider it desirable that the clergy should urge on such persons the duty of promptly presenting these letters, and should carefully instruct them as to the oneness of the Church in its Apostolical constitution under its varying organization and conditions.

It may not, perhaps, be considered foreign to this subject to suggest here the importance of impressing upon our people the extent and geographical distribution of our Churches, and of reminding them that there is now hardly any part of the world where members of our Communion may not find a Church one with their own in faith, order, and worship.

IV.—*Of circulating Information as to the Churches.*

9.—It appears that the want has been much felt of some centre of communication among the Churches in England, Ireland, Scotland, America, India, the Colonies, and elsewhere, through which ecclesiastical documents of importance might be mutually circulated, and in which copies of them might be retained for reference. Your Committee would suggest that the Society for Promoting Christian Knowledge might be requested to maintain a department for this purpose, supported by special contributions; and also that provision might be made for the more general dissemination in each Church of information respecting the acts and current history of all the rest. They recommend that the Reports and other proceedings of this Conference, which it may think fit to publish, should be communicated through this channel. They further think it desirable that the official acts, and other published documents of each representative body of this Communion, should be interchanged among the respective Bishops and the officers of such bodies.

V.—*Of a Day of Intercession.*

10.—Remembering the blessing promised to united intercession, and believing that such intercession ever tends to deepen and strengthen that unity of His Church for which Our Lord earnestly pleaded in His great intercessory prayer, your Committee trust that this Conference will give the weight of its recommendation to the observance throughout the Churches of this Communion of a season of prayer for the unity of Christendom. This recommendation has been, to some extent, anticipated by the practice adopted of late years of setting apart a Day of Intercession for Missions. Your Committee would by no means wish to interfere with an observance which appears to have been widely accepted, and signally blessed of God. But, as our Divine Lord has so closely connected the unity of His followers with the world's belief in His own Mission from the Father, it seems to us that intercessions for the enlargement of His Kingdom may well be joined with earnest prayer that all who profess faith in Him may be one flock under one Shepherd. With respect to the day, your Committee have been informed that the Festival of St. Andrew, hitherto observed as the Day of Intercession for Missions, is found to be unsuitable to the circumstances of the Church in many parts of the world. They, therefore, venture to suggest that, after the present year, the time selected should be the Tuesday before Ascension Day (being a Rogation Day), or any of the seven days after that Tuesday; and they hope that all the Bishops of the several Churches will commend this observance to their respective Dioceses.

VI.—*Of Diversities in Worship.*

11.—Your Committee, believing that, next to oneness in "the Faith once delivered to the saints," communion in worship is the link which most firmly binds together bodies of Christian men, and remembering that the book of Common Prayer, retained as it is, with some modifications, by all our Churches, has been one principal bond of union among them, desire to call attention to the fact that such communion in worship may be endangered by excessive diversities of ritual. They believe that the internal unity of the several Churches will help greatly to the union of these one with another. And, while they consider that such large elasticity in the forms of worship is desirable as will give wide scope to all legitimate expressions of devotional feeling, they would appeal, on the other hand, to the Apostolic precept that "all things be done unto edifying," and to the Catholic principle that order and obedience, even at the sacrifice of personal preferences and tastes, lie at the foundation of Christian unity, and are even essential to the successful maintenance of the Faith.

12.—They cannot leave this subject without expressing an earnest hope that Churchmen of all views, however varying, will recognise the duty of submitting themselves, for conscience sake, in matters ritual and ceremonial, to the authoritative judgments of that particular or national Church in which, by God's Providence, they may be placed; and that they will abstain from all that tends to estrangement or irritation, and will rather daily and fervently pray that the Holy Spirit may guide every member of the Church to "think and do always such things as be rightful," and that He may unite us all in that brotherly charity which is "the very bond of peace and of all virtues."

Report of Committee on Voluntary Boards of Arbitration for Churches to which such an arrangement may be applicable.

1.—Your Committee beg to submit the following Report:—

2.—The necessity for considering the subject which is entrusted to your Committee—namely, Voluntary Boards of Arbitration for Churches to which such an arrangement may be applicable—has arisen from the fact that there is no appeal from the Ecclesiastical Tribunals in the Colonial Churches to any of the ordinary Ecclesiastical Courts of England, or to the Judicial Committee of the Privy Council, when advising Her Majesty on appeals from Ecclesiastical Courts. No questions relating to the exercise of discipline in a Colonial Church can come before the Judicial Committee of the Privy Council, except on appeal from Civil Courts in the colony, exercising jurisdiction in matters affecting property or civil rights. The subject, therefore, before your Committee is not the constitution or jurisdiction of Provincial or Diocesan tribunals, but whether there should be some external tribunals or " Voluntary Boards of Arbitration " to which an appeal or reference ought to be made ; how such Boards, when necessary, should be constituted ; and under what circumstances they should be approached.

3.—Your Committee, having taken into consideration the whole question, especially with reference to the action of some of the Colonial Churches since 1867, when a Report bearing upon this subject was prepared by a Committee of the Lambeth Conference held in that year, would make the following general recommendations :—

4.—I. (*a*) Every Ecclesiastical Province, which has constituted for the exercise of discipline over its clergy a tribunal for receiving appeals from its Diocesan Courts, should be held responsible for its own decisions in the exercise of such discipline ; and your Committee are not prepared to recommend that there should be any one central tribunal of appeal from such Provincial tribunals.

5.—(*b*) If any Province is desirous that its tribunals of appeal should have power to obtain, in matters of doctrine, or of discipline involving a question of doctrine, the opinion of some council of reference before pronouncing sentence, your Committee consider that the conditions of such reference must be determined by the Province itself ; but that the opinion of the council should be given on a consideration of the facts of the case, sent up to it in writing by the tribunal of appeal, and not merely on an abstract question of doctrine.

6.—(*c*) In Dioceses which have not yet been combined into a Province, or which may be geographically incapable of being so combined, your Committee recommend that appeals should lie from the Diocesan Courts to the Archbishop of Canterbury, to be heard by his Grace with such assistance as he may deem best. The circumstances of each Diocese must determine how such consensual jurisdiction could be enforced.

7.—II. As regards the very grave question of the trial of a Bishop, inasmuch as any tribunal, constituted for this purpose by a Province, is necessarily a tribunal of first instance, it would, in the opinion of your Committee, be expedient that, when any such provisions can be introduced by voluntary compact into the constitutions or canons of any Church, the following conditions should be observed :—

8.—(*a*) When any Bishop shall have been sentenced by the tribunal constituted for the trial of a Bishop in any Ecclesiastical Province, if no Bishop of the Province, other than the accused, shall dissent from the judgment, there should be no appeal, provided that the case be heard by not fewer than five Bishops, who shall be unanimous in their judgment.

9.—(*b*) If, in consequence of the small number of Bishops in a Province, or from any other sufficient cause, a tribunal of five comprovincial Bishops cannot be formed, your Committee would suggest that the Province should provide for the enlargement of the tribunal by the addition of Bishops from a neighbouring Province.

10.—(*c*) In the event of the Provincial tribunal not fulfilling the conditions indicated in paragraph 8 of this Report, your Committee would suggest that, whenever an external tribunal of appeal is not provided in the Canons of that Province, it should be in the power of the accused Bishop, if condemned, to require the Provincial tribunal to refer the case to at least five Metropolitans or chief Bishops of the Anglican Communion to be named in the said

Canons, of whom the Archbishop of Canterbury should be one ; and that, if any three of these shall require that the case, or any portion of it, shall be re-heard or reviewed, it should be so re-heard or reviewed.

11.—(*d*) In cases in which an Ecclesiastical Province desires to have a tribunal of appeal from its Provincial tribunal for trying a Bishop, your Committee consider that such tribunal should consist of not less than five Bishops of the Churches of the Anglican Communion, under the presidency of the Archbishop of Canterbury, if his Grace will consent thereto, with the assistance of laymen learned in the law.

Report of Committee on the relation to each other of Missionary Bishops and of Missionaries of various branches of the Anglican Communion acting in the same country.

1.—Your Committee beg to submit the following Report :—

I.

2.—Your Committee have had before them the question of providing Books of Common Prayer for converts from heathenism, suitable to the special wants of various countries; and they recommend as follows :—

3.—They think it very important that such books should not be introduced or multiplied without proper authority; and, since grave inconvenience might follow the use of different Prayer Books in the same district, in English and American Missions, they recommend that, whenever it is possible, one Prayer Book only should be in use.

4.—It is expedient that Books of Common Prayer, suitable to the needs of native congregations in heathen countries, should be framed : that the principles embodied in such books should be identical with the principles embodied in the Book of Common Prayer; and that the deviations from the Book of Common Prayer in point of form should only be such as are required by the circumstances of particular churches.

5.—In the case of heathen countries not under English or American rule, any such book should be approved by a Board consisting of the Bishop or Bishops under whose authority the book is intended to be used, and of certain clergymen, not less than three where possible, from the diocese or dioceses, or district, and should then be communicated by such Bishop or Bishops, or by the Metropolitan of the province to which any such Bishop belongs, to a Board in England, consisting of the Archbishops of England and Ireland, the Bishop of London, the Primus of the Scottish Episcopal Church, together with two Bishops and four clergymen selected by them, and also to a Board appointed by the General Convention of the Protestant Episcopal Church in the United States of America.

6.—No such book should be held to have been authorised for use in public worship unless it have received the sanction of these two Boards.

7.—In any Diocese of a country under English rule all such new books, being modifications or versions of the Book of Common Prayer, should be submitted, after approval by local authority, to the Board in England only.

II.

8.—Your Committee have considered the case of Missions in countries not under English or American rule, and they recommend as follows :—

9.—In cases where two Bishops of the Anglican Communion are ministering in the same country, as in China, Japan, and Western Africa at the present time, your Committee are of opinion that under existing circumstances each Bishop should have control of his own clergy, and their converts and congregations.

10.—The various Bishops in the same country should endeavour, as members of the same Communion, to keep up brotherly intercourse with each other on the subject of their Missionary work.

11.—In countries not under English or American rule, the English or American Church would not ordinarily undertake to establish Dioceses with strictly-defined territorial limits; although either Church might indicate the district in which it was intended that the Missionary Bishop should labour.

12.—Bishops in the same country should take care not to interfere in any manner with the congregations or converts of each other.

13.—It is most undesirable that either Church should for the future send a Bishop or Missionaries to a town or district already occupied by a Bishop of another branch of the Anglican Communion.

14.—When it is intended to send forth any new Missionary Bishop, notification of such an intention should be sent beforehand to the Archbishop of Canterbury, to the Presiding Bishop of the Protestant Episcopal Church in the United States of America, and to the Metropolitan of any Province near which the Missionary Bishop is to minister.

III.

15.—Your Committee have had before them a communication from the Bishop of Calcutta, dated June 4th, 1878, containing Resolutions of the Bishops of India and Ceylon, also a letter from Bishop Caldwell, dated June 1st, 1878, on the subject of the relation of Bishops abroad to the Missionaries in their Dioceses or districts.

16.—The questions raised by the Bishop of Calcutta's communication relate to the power and authority of the Bishop in respect of giving and withdrawing the licences, 1st, of the clergy under his charge; 2nd, of lay readers and catechists; also to the rights of the Bishop in reference to changes in the management, order of service, and place of worship of any congregation.

17.—As regards the licensing of the clergy, it is admitted generally that every Missionary clergyman, whether appointed by a society or otherwise, should receive the licence of the Bishop in whose Diocese he is to labour; but your Committee are of opinion that, in case of refusal to give a licence to a clergyman, the Bishop should, if the clergyman desire it, state the reasons of his refusal, and transmit them to the Metropolitan, who should have power to decide upon their sufficiency; such reasons should also be accessible to the person whose licence is in question. Where there is no Metropolitan, the reasons should be transmitted to the Archbishop of Canterbury, who should decide in like manner.

18.—As regards the withdrawal of a licence, your Committee find that in some Provinces the mode of proceeding for revocation has been fixed by canon, and the jurisdiction thus created has been established by consent. For these places it is not necessary to make any recommendations. Where no such jurisdiction exists, your Committee recommend that the Bishop should in no case proceed to the revocation of a clergyman's licence without affording him the opportunity of showing cause against it, and that if the Bishop shall afterwards proceed to revoke the licence, he should, if the clergyman desire it, state the reasons for his decision to such clergyman, and also to the Metropolitan, who should have power to sanction or disallow the revocation. In cases where there is no Metropolitan, the Archbishop of Canterbury should be regarded as the Metropolitan for this purpose. No such revocation should take place, except for grave ecclesiastical offences.

19.—The Bishop would probably find it desirable, where the clergyman is connected with one of the great Missionary societies, to communicate with the society, or its local representatives, before taking steps for revocation of a licence.

20.—With regard to lay agents, your Committee consider it desirable that such as are employed in more important spiritual functions should have the licence, or other express sanction of the Bishop; and that other laymen employed in Missionary work should be considered to have the implied sanction of the Bishop, and should not continue to be so employed, if the Bishop see fit, for a grave reason, to forbid them.

21.—The authority of the Bishop in appointing places for public worship has been always admitted in the Church. Every place in which the Holy Communion is regularly celebrated should have the sanction of the Bishop.

22.—Your Committee have been asked for an opinion as to Subordinate, Co-ordinate, or Suffragan Bishops in India, to minister to native congregations, within the limits of another Diocese. Your Committee think that there are manifest objections to the appointment of a Bishop to minister to certain congregations within the Diocese of another Bishop, and wholly independent of him. Your Committee think that, for the present, the appointment of Assistant Bishops, whether European or native, subordinate to the Bishop of the Diocese, would meet the special needs of India in this matter, and would offer the best security for order and peace.

Report of Committee on the position of Anglican Chaplains and Chaplaincies on the Continent of Europe and elsewhere.

1.—Your Committee have to report that they have agreed to the following recommendations :—

2.—I. That it is highly desirable that Anglican congregations, on the Continent of Europe and elsewhere, should be distinctly urged not to admit the stated ministrations of any clergyman without the written licence or permission of the Bishop of the Anglican Communion who is duly authorised to grant it ; and that the occasional assistance of strangers should not be invited or permitted without some satisfactory evidence of their ordination and character as clergymen.

3.—II. That it is desirable, as a general rule, that two chapels shall not be established where one is sufficient for the members of both Churches, American and English ; also that where there is only one church or chapel the members of both Churches should be represented on the Committee, if any.

4.—III. That it be suggested to the Societies which partly support Continental Chaplaincies, that; in places where English and American churchmen reside or visit, and especially where Americans outnumber the English, it may be desirable to appoint a properly-accredited clergyman of the American Church.

5.—IV. That your Committee, having carefully considered a Memorial addressed to the Archbishops and Bishops of the Church of England by four Priests and certain other members of " the Spanish and Portuguese Reformed Episcopal Church," praying for the consecration of a Bishop, cannot but express their hearty sympathy with the Memorialists in the difficulties of their position ; and, having heard a statement on the subject of the proposed extension of the Episcopate to Mexico by the American Church, they venture to suggest that, when a Bishop shall have been consecrated by the American Church for Mexico, he might be induced to visit Spain and Portugal, and render such assistance at this stage of the movement as may seem to him practicable and advisable.

Report of Committee appointed to receive questions submitted to them, in writing, by Bishops desiring the advice of the Conference on difficulties or problems they have met with in their several Dioceses, and to report thereon.

Attention has been called to the following subjects by questions submitted to your Committee:—

A.

1.—The position which the Anglican Church should assume towards the "Old Catholics" and towards other persons on the Continent of Europe who have renounced their allegiance to the Church of Rome, and who are desirous of forming some connection with the Anglican Church, either English or American.

2.—Applications for intercommunion between themselves and the Anglican Church from persons connected with the Armenian and other Christian communities in the East.

3.—The position of Moravian ministers within the territorial limits of Dioceses of the Anglican Communion.

B.

1.—The West Indian Dioceses.
    (*a*) Their proposed Provincial organization.
    (*b*) The position of their Diaconate.
2.—The Church of Haiti.

C.
Local peculiarities regarding the Laws of Marriage.

D.
A Board of Reference for matters connected with Foreign Missions.

E.
Difficulties arising in the Church of England from the revival of obsolete forms of Ritual, and from erroneous teaching on the subject of Confession.

A.

The fact that a solemn protest is raised in so many Churches and Christian communities throughout the world against the usurpations of the See of Rome, and against the novel doctrines promulgated by its authority, is a subject for thankfulness to Almighty God. All sympathy is due from the Anglican Church to the Churches and individuals protesting against these errors, and labouring, it may be, under special difficulties, from the assaults of unbelief as well as from the pretensions of Rome.

We acknowledge but one Mediator between God and men—the Man Christ Jesus, Who is over all, God blessed for ever. We reject, as contrary to the Scriptures and to Catholic truth, any doctrine which would set up other mediators in His place, or which would take away from the Divine Majesty of the fulness of the Godhead which dwelleth in Him, and which gave an infinite value to the spotless Sacrifice which He offered, once for all, on the Cross for the sins of the whole world.

It is therefore our duty to warn the faithful that the act done by the Bishop of Rome, in the Vatican Council, in the year 1870—whereby he asserted a supremacy over all men in matters both of faith and morals, on the ground of an assumed infallibility—was an invasion of the attributes of the Lord Jesus Christ.

The principles on which the Church of England has reformed itself are well known. We proclaim the sufficiency and supremacy of the Holy Scriptures as the ultimate rule of faith, and commend to our people the diligent study of the same. We confess our faith in the words of the ancient Catholic creeds. We retain the Apostolic order of Bishops, Priests, and Deacons. We assert the just liberties of particular or national Churches. We provide our people, in their own tongue, with a Book of Common Prayer and Offices for the administration of the Sacraments, in accordance with the best and most ancient types of Christian faith and worship. These documents are before the world, and can be known and read of all men. We gladly welcome every effort for reform upon the model of the Primitive Church. We do not demand a rigid uniformity; we deprecate needless divisions; but to those who are drawn to us in the endeavour to free themselves from the yoke of error and superstition we are ready to offer all help, and such privileges as may be acceptable to them and are consistent with the maintenance of our own principles as enunciated in our formularies.

Your Committee recommend that questions of the class now submitted to them be dealt with in this spirit. For the consideration, however, of any definite cases in which advice and assistance may, from time to time, be sought, your Committee recommend that the Archbishops of England and Ireland, with the Bishop of London, the Primus of the Scottish Episcopal Church, and the Presiding Bishop of the Protestant Episcopal Church in the United States of America, the Bishop superintending the congregations of the same upon the Continent of Europe, and the Bishop of Gibraltar, together with such other Bishops as they may associate with themselves, be requested to advise upon such cases as circumstances may require.

With regard to the special questions now raised respecting Moravian Orders,[1] the above-mentioned prelates are recommended to associate with themselves such learned persons as they may deem eminently qualified to assist them by their knowledge of the historical difficulties involved.

B.

1.—(*a*) With respect to the West Indian Dioceses, assuming such Dioceses to desire to be combined into a Province, your Committee advise that the formal consent of the Diocesan Representative Synods, if free (as regards their relation to the State) to give such consent, be first obtained.

The Bishops of the several Dioceses would then forward such formal consent, or expressed desire, to the Archbishop of Canterbury, requesting him to give his sanction to the formation of the Province.

Whether the General Synod of the Province should consist of the Bishops, with representatives of the

---

[1] The special questions submitted were the following :—

"1. If a Moravian presbyter or deacon desires to be received into the Anglican Ministry, ought I to (*a*) ordain him absolutely ; (*b*) reordain him conditionally ; (*c*) accept his orders as valid, and simply give him mission in the Anglican Church?

"2. Can I canonically and regularly commission a Bishop of the Unitas Fratrum in my Diocese either to confirm or to ordain for me, or to do both Episcopal acts according to the Anglican ritual?

"3. Am I justified, if called on, to confirm children, or ordain presbyters or deacons, or do both for the Moravians, in their churches, and according to their ritual?

"4. May Anglican presbyters and deacons, with their Bishop's sanction, officiate and minister the sacraments in Moravian churches, according to their ritual, and invite Moravian presbyters or deacons to execute the functions appertaining to their office in Anglican churches, and according to Anglican ritual?"

clergy and laity of the respective Dioceses, or should consist of the Bishops of the Province only; and, in the latter case, what limitation should be imposed on the powers of such purely Episcopal Synod, is a question which ought to be left to the Diocesan Synods to decide, with the approval of the Archbishop of Canterbury.

If the West Indian Dioceses be formed into a Province, it seems desirable that a Metropolitan should be, in the first instance, elected from and by the Bishops of the West Indian Dioceses.

(*b*) The questions[1] submitted respecting the peculiar circumstances of the West Indian Diaconate appear to your Committee, upon full consideration, to be such as can be adequately decided only in Diocesan or Provincial Synods.

2.—Your Committee desire to express their satisfaction on learning that a Church in connexion with the Anglican Communion has been planted in the island of Haiti; that a Bishop has been consecrated thereto by Bishops of the Protestant Episcopal Church in the United States of America, and the Bishop of Kingston, Jamaica; and that successful efforts are being made for the training of a native Ministry; and your Committee trust that God's blessing may rest upon the Bishop, Priests, and Deacons, and all other members of this Church.

---

[1] These questions raised the following points :—

1. The desirableness, or otherwise, of recognising a Diaconate which, in certain cases, shall be practically permanent, instead of regarding the Diaconate as the invariable step to the Presbyterate.

2. The desirableness, or otherwise, of permitting Deacons to engage in such secular callings as are not inconsistent with the due and edifying discharge of sacred functions.

3. What modifications, if any, should be allowed as regards the intellectual qualifications and tests to be required of, and imposed on, such laymen as desire to become Deacons without relinquishing their secular vocation.

C.

With regard to those questions in connexion with the Laws of Marriage which have been submitted to them, your Committee, while fully recognising the difficulties in which various branches of the Church have been placed by the action of local Legislatures, are of opinion that steps should be taken by each branch of the Church, according to its own discretion, to maintain the sanctity of marriage, agreeably to the principles set forth in the Word of God, as the Church of Christ hath hitherto received the same.

D.

With respect to what has been submitted to us on the subject of Foreign Missions, your Committee are of opinion that it is desirable to appoint a Board of Reference, to advise upon questions brought before it either by Diocesan or Missionary Bishops or by Missionary Societies. Your Committee are further of opinion that the details of the formation and constitution of such Board ought to be referred to the Archbishops of England and Ireland, the Bishop of London, the Primus of the Scottish Episcopal Church, the Presiding Bishop of the Protestant Episcopal Church in the United States of America, with the Bishop superintending the congregations of the same upon the Continent of Europe, and such other Bishops as they may associate with themselves, who should communicate with the authorities of the various Colonial Churches, and with the existing Missionary Organisations of the Anglican Communion.

E.

Considering unhappy disputes on questions of ritual, whereby divers congregations in the Church of England and elsewhere have been seriously disquieted, your Committee desire to affirm the principle that no alteration from long-accustomed ritual should be made contrary to the admonition of the Bishop of the Diocese.

Further, having in view certain novel practices and teachings on the subject of Confession, your Committee desire to affirm that in the matter of Confession the Churches of the Anglican Communion hold fast those principles which are set forth in the Holy Scriptures, which were professed by the Primitive Church, and which were re-affirmed at the English Reformation; and it is their deliberate opinion that no minister of the Church is authorised to require from those who may resort to him to open their grief a particular or detailed enumeration of all their sins, or to require private confession previous to receiving the Holy Communion, or to enjoin or even encourage the practice of habitual confession to a Priest, or to teach that such practice of habitual confession, or the being subject to what has been termed the direction of a Priest, is a condition of attaining to the highest spiritual life. At the same time your Committee are not to be understood as desiring to limit in any way the provision made in the Book of Common Prayer for the relief of troubled consciences.

These are the Reports of the Conference, and the practical conclusions at which we have arrived. Some of these conclusions have reference to the special circumstances of different branches of the One Church of Christ, according to peculiarities of their various Missionary work for the heathen, or their labours amongst their own people; some embody principles which apply to all branches of the Church Universal. They are all limited in their scope to those subjects which have been distinctly brought before the assembled Bishops. We invite to them the attention of the various Synods and other governing powers in the several Churches, and of all the faithful in Christ Jesus throughout the world.

We do not claim to be lords over God's heritage, but we commend the results of this our Conference to the reason and conscience of our brethren as enlightened by the Holy Spirit of God, praying that all throughout the world who call upon the name of our Lord Jesus Christ may be of one mind, may be united in one fellowship, may hold fast the Faith once delivered to the saints, and worship their one Lord in the spirit of purity and love.

Signed, on behalf of the Conference,

A. C. CANTUAR.

C. J. GLOUCESTER AND BRISTOL,
Secretary of the Conference.

HENRY, BISHOP OF EDINBURGH,
Secretary of Committees.

I. BRUNEL, Chancellor of the Diocese of Ely,
Assistant Secretary.

NOTE A (page 165).

The Churches thus united are, at this time, the Church of England and the Churches planted by her in India, the Colonies, and elsewhere, most of which Churches are associated into distinct Provinces[1]; the Church of Ireland; the Episcopal

---

[1] There are six Provinces, viz.:—
India, with six Dioceses.
Canada, with nine Dioceses.
Rupertsland, with four Dioceses.
South Africa, with eight Dioceses.
Australia, with twelve Dioceses.
New Zealand, with seven Dioceses.
And there are twenty Dioceses not yet associated in Provinces.

Church in Scotland; the Protestant Episcopal Church in the United States of America, with its Missionary Branches; and the Church in Haiti. Among the external evidences of the unity of these Churches, none is more significant than that which frequently occurs—the uniting of Bishops of different Churches, *e.g.*, of English, Scottish, and American Bishops, in that most important function by which the Episcopal succession is continued. On more than one occasion, also, the Church in Scotland has consecrated a Bishop in behalf of the Church of England, when legal difficulties have impeded the consecration in England.

NOTE B (page 166).

One of the results of the first Lambeth Conference was the appointment of a Committee to prepare a Bill for placing on a more satisfactory footing the status in England of clergy ordained by Bishops of Colonial and other Churches outside the Church in England.

A Bill to effect this object was introduced by Lord Blachford into Parliament in the Session of 1873, and became law in the Session of 1874, under the name of "The Colonial Clergy Act, 1874." (37 & 38 Vict., cap. 77.)

The Act does not apply to the clergy of the Episcopal Church in Scotland. The legal disabilities of the Scottish clergy were removed, and their position defined, by the Act 27 & 28 Vict., cap 94.

With this exception, the Act of 1874 deals with the status of all clergy ordained by Bishops other than Bishops of Dioceses in England and Ireland. It proceeds upon the assumption that all clergymen so ordained may be admitted to exercise their functions in the Church of England; but that the Bishops of that Church have a right, in respect of these clergy, to discretionary powers, analogous to those which they have in the case of ordination.

The following are the provisions of the Act which affect the clergy ordained by Bishops other than those of (1) Dioceses in England; or (2) The Church of Ireland; or (3) The Episcopal Church in Scotland.

"Section 3.—Except as hereinafter mentioned, no person who has been or shall be ordained Priest or Deacon, as the case may be, by any Bishop other than a Bishop of a Diocese in one of the Churches aforesaid shall, unless he shall hold or have previously held preferment or a curacy in England, officiate as such Priest or Deacon in any church or chapel in England, without written permission from the Archbishop of the Province in which he proposes to officiate, and without also making and subscribing so much of the declaration contained in 'The Clerical Subscription Act, 1865,' as follows—that is to say:

"'I assent to the Thirty-nine Articles of Religion, and to the Book of Common Prayer, and of the Ordering of Bishops, Priests, and Deacons. I believe the doctrine of the Church of England as therein set forth to be agreeable to the Word of God; and in public prayer and administration of the sacraments, I, whilst ministering in England, will use the form in the said Book prescribed and none other, except so far as shall be ordered by lawful authority.'

"Section 4.—Except as hereinafter mentioned, no person who has been or shall be ordained Priest or Deacon, as the case may be, by any Bishop other than a Bishop of a Diocese in one of the Churches aforesaid, shall be entitled as such Priest or Deacon to be admitted or instituted to any benefice or other ecclesiastical preferment in England, or to act as Curate therein, without the previous consent in writing of the Bishop of the Diocese in which such preferment or curacy may be situate.

"Section 5.—Any person holding ecclesiastical preferment, or acting as Curate in any Diocese in England under the provisions of this Act, may, with the written consent of the Bishop of such Diocese, request the Archbishop of the Province to give him a licence in writing under his hand and seal in the following form—that is to say:—

"'To the Rev. *A. B.*,

"'We, *C.*, by Divine Providence Archbishop of *D.*, do hereby give you, the said *A. B.*, authority to exercise your office of Priest (*or* Deacon) according to the provisions of an Act of the thirty-seventh and thirty-eighth years of her present Majesty, intituled "An Act respecting Colonial and certain other Clergy."

"'Given under our hand and seal on the day of

"'*C.* (L.S.) *D.*'

And if the Archbishop shall think fit to issue such licence, the same shall be registered in the registry of the Province, and the person receiving the licence shall thenceforth possess all such rights and advantages, and be subject to all such duties and liabilities, as he would have possessed and been subject to if he had been ordained by the Bishop of a Diocese in England: Provided that no such licence shall be issued to any person who has not held ecclesiastical preferment or acted as Curate for a period or periods exceeding in the aggregate two years."

The Act also contains the following provision as to the Consecration of Bishops:—

"Section 12.—It shall be lawful for the Archbishop of Canterbury or the Archbishop of York, for the time being, in consecrating any person to the office of a Bishop, for the purpose of exercising Episcopal functions elsewhere than in England, to dispense, if he think fit, with the oath of due obedience to the Archbishop."

NOTE C (page 167).

The following extract from the Report refers to this subject :—" Your Committee strongly recommend that all those Dioceses which are not as yet gathered into Provinces should, as soon as possible, form part of some Provincial organization. The particular mode of effecting this in each case must be determined by those who are concerned."

The Committee would also call attention to the concluding paragraph of the same Report :—

" In the case of the limits of an existing Province being altered, the consent of the Synod of that Province would be required for the alteration."

No. XXII. (See page 32.)

Latin and Greek Versions of the Bishops' Letter of 1878.

EPISTOLA CENTUM EPISCOPORUM

IN ANGLIA CONGREGATORUM, IN PALATIO LAMBETHANO, MENSE JULIO,

ANNO SALUTIS MDCCCLXXVIII.

Fidelibus in Christo salutem in Domino.

Nos Archiepiscopi, Metropolitani, aliique Episcopi Sanctæ Catholicæ Ecclesiæ, centum numero, cum Ecclesiâ Anglicanâ plenariè communicantes, universi super Diœceses jurisdictionem Episcopalem exercitantes, vel ad Episcopalia munia in eis obeunda legitimè delegati, multi nostrûm ex remotissimis orbis terrarum regionibus, congregati in Palatio Lambethano, anno salutis MDCCCLXXVIII. præsidente Reverendissimo Præsule Archibaldo Campbell, Divinâ Providentiâ Archiepiscopo Cantuariensi, totius Angliæ Primate, participes facti, in dicti Palatii sacello, Sacrosanctorum Mysteriorum Corporis et Sanguinis Domini Nostri Jesu Christi, et orationibus adunati ad Spiritûs Sancti directionem impetrandam, de variis præfinitis quæstionibus consilium inivimus cœtui nostro propositis, ad statum Ecclesiæ pertinentibus per diversas mundi partes diffusæ.

His quæstionibus seriò deliberandis complures dies impendimus, jamque determinationes earum a nobis approbatas fidelibus in Christo commendamus.[1]

Quæ sit optima ratio pensitantes unitatis conservandæ inter varias nostræ Communionis Ecclesias, primùm omnium Deo Omnipotenti gratias agentes quàm maximas, manifestam unitatem agnoscimus, quâ Ecclesia Anglicana, et Ecclesiæ cum illâ visibiliter communicantes, jugiter connexæ permanserunt.

Conjunctæ invicem sub Uno Divino Capite, Jesu Christo, in unius Catholicæ et Apostolicæ Ecclesiæ societate, firmiter tenentes unam Fidem, in Verbo Dei revelatam, Symbolis definitam, et a Primitivâ Ecclesiâ constanter conservatam, easdem Canonicas Scripturas Veteris et Novi Testamenti recipientes, utpote omnia continentes ad salutem sempiternam necessaria, hæ nostræ Ecclesiæ eundem Dei Sermonem prædicant, eorundem Sacramentorum, divinitus institutorum, per eorundem ordinum Apostolicorum ministerium dispensatorum, participes sunt,

---

[1] In hâc Latinâ interpretatione eorum capitulorum præcipuè delectum fecimus quæ ad Ecclesiam Universalem attinere quodammodo videbantur. In Anglico autem archetypo Relationes Delegationum (*Reports of Committees*), a Cœtu comprobatæ, plenariæ reperiuntur.

et Eundem Deum et Patrem venerantur, per Eundem Dominum Jesum Christum, in Eodem Spiritu Sancto super omnibus fidelibus effuso ad ducendos eos in omnem veritatem.

Verùm enimverò cum hâc unitate consociata nunquam non extitit ea consuetudinum, disciplinæ et rituum varietas, quæ ab illâ prærogativâ enasci solet, quam quævis Ecclesia particularis, sive nationalis, jure sibi vindicat ; scilicet constituendi, immutandi, atque abrogandi cærimonias vel ritus Ecclesiasticos, humanâ tantum auctoritate ordinatos, modò omnia ad ædificationem fiant.

Libenter quidem profitemur, nullam reverà etiamnum sollicitudinis causam in hâc diversitate reperiri. Constat autem, votum aliquorum animis nuper conceptum vocibus quoque passim significatum fuisse, hoc præsertim intuitu, ut rationes quædam actæ efficaces a nobis adhibeantur, ad occasiones discordim præcidendas, et ad illam genuinam et essentialeu unitatem, quæ nostras Ecclesias indies supercrescentes complectitur, manifestandam amplius atque fovendam.

Primùm quidem hujus concordiæ tuendæ illa in mentem venit ratio quæ inde ab Apostolis ipsis divinitùs inspiratis originem ducens, Ecclesiis omnibus in eâdem individuâ et visibili unitate continendis diu inserviit. Hodierna autem rei Christianæ ea est conditio, infausta quidem sed manifesta, ut Concilium verè Œcumenicum, ad quod Ecclesia Anglicana se paratam esse convenire semper professa est, convocari non possit. Difficultates quidem quæ impedimento sunt quominus Synodus ex omnibus Anglicanis Ecclesiis conflata congregetur, re diversæ et minus graves, nimiæ tamen nobis videntur, quàm ut illa ratio unitatis conservandæ a nobis commendetur.

Aliud autem experimentum, secundâ jam vice factum, congregatio scilicet Episcoporum ab Archiepiscopo Cantuariensi convocatorum, et Eo præsidente deliberantium spem saltem suppeditat, quæstionem, quæ hactenus insolubilis videbatur, rerum vicissitudine divinitus ordinatâ sponte solutum iri, ita ut Procuratores Ecclesiarum, situ et administratione diversarum, consultandi invicem causâ, in unum cœtum coalescant.

Persuasum est nobis, ad unitatem in fide semel sanctis traditâ proximè accedere divini cultûs communionem, eamque societates Christianas firmissimo nexu copulare : et probè recordantes Librum Precum Communium, ab omnibus nostris Ecclesiis, aliquatenus variatum, retineri, et eximium unitatis vinculum extitisse, fratres nostros admonendos censemus, divini cultûs communionem immoderatis rituum diversitatibus in discrimen posse adduci. Intrinsecam Ecclesiarum variarum unitatem custodiendæ earum concordiæ adjumentum allaturam esse validissimum confidimus. Et dum liberè profitemur, amplam quandam rituum Ecclesiasticorum flexibilitatem esse exoptandam, quippe quæ latum quasi campum patefaciat legitimis piorum affectuum significationibus, nihilominus ad Apostolicum præceptum provocamus, " Omnia ad ædificationem fiant," et ad illam Ecclesiæ Catholicæ legem principalem, rectum ordinem commendantis atque obedientiam, etsi cum privatorum sensuum et propensionum abnegatione conjungantur, tanquam subsidia Christianæ Unitatis fundamentalia, imò etiam ad fidem ipsam efficaciter conservandam necessaria.

Nolumus huic argumento finem imponere, quin spem nostram serio testificemur, omnes Ecclesiæ fideles agnituros fore, utcunque studiis in varia inclinantes, universos oportere subjici, conscientiæ ergo, in rebus ad ritus et cærimonias attinentibus, judiciis illis auctoritatem obtinentibus, quæ ab illâ Ecclesiâ particulari vel nationali promulgata sint, sub cujus tutelâ, Dei providentiâ, sint constituti ; et sibi sedulò temperaturos ab omni qualicunque alienationis vel exacerbationis occasione; et quotidie Deum enixè obsecraturos, ut omnia Ecclesiæ membra a

Spiritu Sancto dirigantur ad quæcunque recta sint excogitanda atque exequenda ; et ut nos universi in illâ fraternâ dilectione, quæ pacis est ipsissimum vinculum et omnium virtutum, adunare dignetur.

* * * *

Gratias agimus Deo Omnipotenti maximas, eò quod protestationes solennes a tot Ecclesiis et societatibus Christianis per orbem terrarum profectæ sint contra sedis Romanæ usurpationes, et contra novicia dogmata ejus auctoritate promulgata.

Affectuum benevolorum significatio debetur ab Ecclesiâ Anglicanâ universis, sive Ecclesiis, sive singulis, contra hos errores protestantibus, quippe qui difficultatibus forsitan laborent specialibus, quum propter Incredulitatis incursiones, tum vero propter Romanæ sedis arrogantiam.

Nos confitemur Unum tantum "Mediatorem Dei et hominum, Hominem Jesum Christum," "Qui est super omnia Deus in sæcula." Nos repudiamus, utpote Scripturis Sacris et Catholicæ veritati adversantem, qualemcunque doctrinam alios mediatores Ejus vice constituentem, vel aliquatenus detrahentem ab Illius Divinâ Majestate, et a plenitudine Deitatis in Illo inhabitantis, quæ immaculato illo Sacrificio, semel ab Eo in Cruce propter omnium hominum peccata oblato, infinitum pretium impertita est.

Commonendi igitur sunt a nobis fideles, facinus illud a Romano Episcopo patratum, in Concilio Vaticano, anno MDCCCLXX., quo sibi supereminentiam super omnes homines in rebus fidei et morum vindicavit, arrogatæ sibi Infallibilitatis prætextu, attributorum Ipsius Domini Nostri Jesu Christi manifestam fuisse invasionem.

Innotuerunt omnibus regulæ illæ fundamentales, juxta quas Ecclesia Anglicana seipsam reformavit. Nos Sanctas Scripturas sufficientem et supremam fidei regulam esse declaramus, et omnibus nostris diligenter scrutandas proponimus. Nos fidem nostram ipsis Symbolorum antiquorum vocibus profitemur. Nos Apostolicum ordinem Episcoporum, Presbyterorum et Diaconorum retinemus. Ecclesiarum particularium sive nationalium libertates legitimas asserimus. Nos Librum Communium Precationum, necnon Administrationis Sacramentorum, populis nostris in manus damus, vernaculo eorum sermone compositum, et juxta optima et antiquissima fidei et divini cultûs exemplaria adornatum. Orbi universo patefacta sunt hæc nostra documenta ; sciuntur et leguntur ab omnibus.

Libenter igitur amplectimur universos sese reformandi studiosos ad amussim Ecclesiæ primitivæ. Rigidam Uniformitatem non flagitamus ; supervacaneas dissensiones deprecamur. Omnibus ad nos allectis, dum jugum erroris et superstitionis excutere moliuntur, commodare operam nostrum parati sumus, et talia eis subministrare privilegia, qualia ipsis possint esse gratiosa, et nostris ipsorum institutis et formulis Ecclesiasticis consentanea.

*　　　*　　　*　　　*

Sed hæc hâctenus. Quod ad quæstiones attinet nobis propositas quæ leges Matrimonii tangunt, dum ex animo agnoscimus angustias, ad quas nonnullæ nostræ Ecclesiæ a popularium suorum legum lationibus redactæ sunt, censemus quoque officium esse uniuscujusque Ecclesiæ operam dare, ut sanctitati Matrimonii custodiendæ consulatur, secundum mandata in Dei Verbo præscripta, et quemadmodum ab Ecclesiâ Christi hâctenus sunt recepta.

Rixas quasdam luctuosas de rituum Ecclesiasticorum quæstionibus, considerantes, quibus nonnullæ nostræ congregationes graviter perturbatæ sunt nos affirmamus, nihil in diu usitatâ cærimoniarum consuetudine, contra Episcopi admonitionem, debere innovari.

Denique, nonnullas novitates, quum in agendo tum in docendo, quod ad Confessionem attinet, contemplantes, nos declaramus Anglicanæ Communionis

Ecclesias firmiter eas leges tenere, quæ in hanc rem in Sacris Scripturis sunt promulgatæ, primitivæ Ecclesiæ professione sancitæ, et ab Anglicanâ Reformatione instauratæ. Et nos consultò censemus, nulli Ecclesiæ Ministro licere, ab iis, qui ad eum se recipiunt, doloris aperiendi gratiâ, omnium sigillatim peccatorum minutam enumerationem exquirere; vel privatam confessionem iis imperare, ante Sacrosanctæ Eucharistiæ participationem; vel præscribere, vel etiam commendare, confessionis consuetudinariæ coram sacerdote exercitationem; vel docere talem exercitationem, vel sacerdoti subjectionem, directionis, ut aiunt, causâ, conditiones esse necessarias, ad sublimissimam vitam spiritualem attingendam. Nihilominus non in animo habemus quoquam modo terminos imponere subsidiis, quæ in Libro nostro Precum Publicarum, ad conscientiarum sollicitarum sublevationem, providè subministrantur.

Hæ sunt determinationes quæstionum nobis propositarum, quatenus Ecclesiæ Universalis vel Ecclesiarum nostrarum conditionem attingere videbantur.

Ad hæc inspicienda varias Ecclesiarum Synodos, aliosque in eis Ecclesiis auctoritatem exercitantes, et universos denique Christi fideles, per orbem terrarum invitamus. Dominationem in cleris non affectamus: sed has determinationes, a cœtu nostro approbatas, rationi et conscientiæ fratrum nostrorum, utpote a Spiritu Sancto illuminatorum, commendamus, enixè Deum apprecantes, ut omnes ubique gentium Domini Nostri Jesu Christi Nomen invocantes, unâ mente consocientur, in unâ Communione conjungantur, unam fidem semel sanctis traditam firmiter complectantur, et unum Suum Dominum in uno puritatis et dilectionis spiritu venerentur. Amen.

Subscripsi, in nomine Cœtûs Lambethani,

   ARCHIBALDUS CAMPBELL,
    Archiepiscopus Cantuariensis.

ΕΠΙΣΤΟΛΗ ἙΚΑΤΟΝ ΕΠΙΣΚΟΠΩΝ

Ἐν Ἀγγλίᾳ συνηθροισμένων, ἐν Παλατίῳ Λαμβηθανῷ, μηνὶ Ἰουλίῳ, ἔτει ͵αωοή (1878).

Τοῖς πιστοῖς ἐν Χριστῷ Ἰησοῦ χαίρειν ἐν Κυρίῳ.

Ἡμεῖς Ἀρχιεπίσκοποι, Μητροπολῖται, καὶ ἄλλοι ἐπίσκοποι τῆς ἁγίας Καθολικῆς Ἐκκλησίας, συγκοινωνοῦντες ὁλοκλήρως τῇ Ἀγγλικανῇ Ἐκκλησίᾳ, ἑκατὸν ὄντες τὸν ἀριθμὸν, ἅπαντες ἐπισκοπὴν παροικιῶν ἐπιτηδεύοντες, ἢ νομίμως ἐπισκοπικὰ τέλη ἐν αὐταῖς ἐπιτετραμμένοι, συνελθόντες, πολλοὶ ἐξ ἡμῶν ἀπὸ τῶν μακροτάτων τῆς οἰκουμένης κλιμάτων, ἐν τῷ Παλατίῳ Λαμβηθανῷ, ἔτει τῆς τοῦ Κυρίου ἐνσαρκώσεως ͵αωοή (1878), προεδρεύοντος σεβασμιωτάτου Ἀρχιβάλδου Κάμπβελλ, τῇ θείᾳ προνοίᾳ Ἀρχιεπισκόπου Καντουαρίας, Ἐπισκόπων ὅλης Ἀγγλίας πρωτοθρόνου, μετειληφότες, ἐν τῷ ναῷ τοῦ εἰρημένου παλατίου, τῶν ἁγίων μυστηρίων τοῦ σώματος καὶ τοῦ αἵματος τοῦ Κυρίου, καὶ προσευχαῖς ἡνωμένοι ὑπὲρ τῆς τοῦ ἁγίου Πνεύματος χειραγωγίας, ἐξέτασιν πεποιήκαμεν διαφόρων ζητημάτων ἡμῖν προβεβλημένων, ἀνηκόντων εἰς τὴν τῆς Ἐκκλησίας σχέσιν ἐν διαφόροις τοῦ κόσμου μέρεσιν.

Περὶ τούτων τῶν ζητημάτων σπουδαίως διὰ πλειόνων ἡμερῶν συμβεβουλευκότες, παρατιθέμεθα τανῦν τοῖς πιστοῖς τὰ συμπεράσματα ἡμῖν ὑπὲρ αὐτῶν δεδογμένα.[1]

Ἐνθυμούμενοι τὴν ἐπιτηδειοτάτην μέθοδον πρὸς τὴν τήρησιν τῆς ἑνότητος τῶν διαφόρων τῆς ἡμετέρας κοινωνίας ἐκκλησιῶν, πρώτιστα πάντων ἀναγνωρίζομεν, μετ᾽ ἐγκαρδίου εὐχαριστίας τῷ Παντοκράτορι Θεῷ, τὴν οὐσιώδη καὶ ἐναργῆ ἑνότητα, ἐν ᾗ ἡ Ἀγγλικανὴ Ἐκκλη-

---

[1] Ἐν ταύτῃ τῇ μεταφράσει, τῶν κεφαλαίων ἐκλογὴν πεποιήκαμεν, τῶν μάλιστα τῇ καθόλου Ἐκκλησίᾳ προσηκόντων· ἐν δὲ τῷ Ἀγγλικῷ τῆς Ἐπιστολῆς ἀρχετύπῳ αἱ τῶν ἐπιτρόπων· τοῦ συμβουλίου ἐκθέσεις (*Reports of Committees*), ἀπὸ τοῦ Συμβουλίου δοκιμασθεῖσαι, ὁλοτελεῖς εὑρίσκονται.

σία, καὶ αἱ ἐκκλησίαι μετ' αὐτῆς ὁρατῶς συγκοινωνοῦσαι, διατελοῦσι συνημμέναι. Ἡνωμέναι ὑπὸ μιᾶς θείας Κεφαλῆς, Ἰησοῦ Χριστοῦ, ἐν τῇ κοινωνίᾳ τῆς μιᾶς Καθολικῆς Ἐκκλησίας, κατέχουσαι τὴν μίαν πίστιν, ἐν ταῖς ἁγίαις Γραφαῖς ἀποκεκαλυμμένην, ἐν τοῖς Συμβόλοις ὡρισμένην, καὶ ὑπὸ τῆς ἀρχῆθεν Ἐκκλησίας κεκρατημένην, δεχόμεναι τὰς αὐτὰς κανονικὰς Γραφὰς τῆς παλαιᾶς καὶ τῆς καινῆς Διαθήκης, ὡς τὰ πάντα πρὸς σωτηρίαν ἀναγκαῖα περιεχούσας, αὗται αἱ ἡμέτεραι Ἐκκλησίαι τὸν αὐτὸν τοῦ Θεοῦ λόγον κηρύσσουσι, τῶν αὐτῶν θεόθεν διατεταγμένων μυστηρίων μεταλαμβάνουσι διὰ τῆς ὑπηρεσίας τῶν αὐτῶν ἀποστολικῶν βαθμῶν, καὶ προσκυνοῦσι τῷ αὐτῷ Θεῷ καὶ Πατέρι, διὰ τοῦ αὐτοῦ Κυρίου Ἰησοῦ Χριστοῦ, ἐν τῷ αὐτῷ ἁγίῳ καὶ θείῳ Πνεύματι, πᾶσι τοῖς πιστεύουσιν ἐπιχορηγουμένῳ, πρὸς τὸ ὁδηγεῖν αὐτοὺς εἰς πᾶσαν τὴν ἀλήθειαν.

Ἀμέσως μὲν οὖν μετὰ ταύτης τῆς ἑνότητος, ὑπῆρξεν ἐν ἡμετέραις ἐκκλησίαις ἐκείνη συνηθείας, διατάξεως, καὶ λειτουργίας διαφορά, ἥτις ἀναγκαίως ἐκφύεται ἐξ ἀσκήσεως τῆς ἐξουσίας, τῆς ἑκάστῃ μερικῇ ἢ ἐθνικῇ ἐκκλησίᾳ προσηκούσης, τοῦ διατάσσειν, παραχαράσσειν, καὶ ἀκυροῦν θεσμοὺς καὶ τελετὰς ἐκκλησιαστικάς, ὑπ' ἀνθρωπίνης ἐξουσίας διατεταγμένας, μόνον ὥστε πάντα πρὸς οἰκοδομὴν γίγνεσθαι.

Ἀσμένως μὲν ὁμολογοῦμεν μηδεμίαν εἰσέτι εὑρίσκεσθαι μερίμνης αἰτίαν, διὰ ταύτην τὴν διαφωνίαν. Ὅμως μέντοι ἐπιπόθησίς τις νεωστὶ ἐπιπολὺ αἰσθήσει καὶ λόγῳ πεφανέρωται, ὡς ἐννοητέα καὶ προσαπτέα εἴη ὄργανά τινα, πρὸς τὸ ἐκκόπτειν, εἰ τύχοι, ἀφορμὰς διχοστασίας, καὶ πρὸς τὴν λαμπροτέραν ἀπόδειξιν καὶ αὔξησιν τῆς ἀληθινῆς καὶ οὐσιώδους ὁμονοίας ἐν ἡμετέραις ἐκκλησίαις ὑπαρχούσης.

Τὸ πρῶτον μὲν εἰς νοῦν ἀνερχόμενον ὄργανον τοιαύτης ἑνώσεως εὐλόγως ἂν εἴη ἐκεῖνο, ὅπερ, ἀρχὴν ἔχον ἀπὸ τῶν θεοφόρων ἀποστόλων, συνέζευξεν ἁπάσας τὰς Χριστοῦ ἐκκλησίας ἐν μιᾷ ἀδιαιρέτῳ καὶ ὁρατῇ κοινωνίᾳ. Ἀλλὰ μὲν οὖν ἡ συνάθροισις ἀληθινῶς οἰκουμενικῆς Συνόδου, πρὸς ὁποίαν ἡ Ἀγγλικανὴ Ἐκκλησία πάντοτε ἐπηγγέλλετο ἑτοίμη εἶναι συνέρχεσθαι, ἐν τῇ σημερινῇ τοῦ Χριστιανισμοῦ καταστάσει, δυστυχῶς μὲν, ἄλλα φανερῶς, πέφυκεν ἀμήχανος. Αἱ μὲν ἀπορίαι, αἵτινες παρακολουθήσειαν ἂν τῇ συνελεύσει συνόδου ἐκ πασῶν τῶν ἀγγλικανῶν ἐκκλησιῶν συγκεκροτημένης, καίπερ ἀνόμοιοι καὶ μετριώτεραι τῶν εἰρημένων, ὅμως μέντοι εἰσὶ βαρύτεραι ἢ συγχωρῆσαι ταύτης τῆς μεθόδου, ἐν τῷ νῦν χρόνῳ, συναίνεσιν. Ἀλλ' ἡ πεῖρα, δὶς γεγονυῖα, συμβουλίου ἐπισκόπων, ἀπὸ τοῦ Καντουαρίας Ἀρχιεπισκόπου συγκεκλημένων, καὶ ὑπ' αὐτοῦ προεδρεύοντος συνηθροισμένων, ἐλπίδα ἡμῖν παρέχει αὐτομάτου λύσεως προβλήματος μέχρι τοῦ νῦν ἀλύτου, δηλονότι συναθροίσεως καὶ συμβουλεύσεως τοποτηρητῶν ἐκκλησιῶν τῇ τε θέσει καὶ τῇ διοικήσει διαφερουσῶν.

Ἐγγύτατα μετὰ τὴν ἑνότητα ἐν τῇ πίστει, τῇ τοῖς ἁγίοις ἅπαξ παραδοθείσῃ, πεπεισμένοι ἐσμὲν τὴν θρησκείας κοινωνίαν ἰσχυρότατον εἶναι σύνδεσμον πρὸς τὴν σύναψιν τῶν χριστιανικῶν ἑταιριῶν· καὶ καλῶς μεμνημένοι ὅτι τὸ ἡμέτερον τῶν δημοσίων προσευχῶν βιβλίον, μετά τινων οἵων δήποτε ἀλλοιώσεων ἐν πάσαις ἡμετέραις ἐκκλησίαις κατεχόμενον, ἐξαίρετόν τι ἑνότητος γέγονε φυλακτήριον, νουθετεῖν ἀξιοῦμεν τοὺς ἡμεδαποὺς, ὅτι αὕτη ἡ θρησκείας κοινωνία κινδυνεύοι ἂν λυμαίνεσθαι δι' ὑπερβολικῶν ἱερουργίας παραλλάξεων. Ἡ ἐσωτερικὴ μὲν τῶν ἐκκλησιῶν ἑνότης ταύτῃ τῇ θρησκείας κοινωνίᾳ, καθὼς πεποίθαμεν, ὑπηρετήσει· ἀλλ' ὅμως, (καίπερ ἐννοοῦντες ὅτι τοία τις ἀμφιλαφὴς λειτουργικῶν τελετῶν ἐλευθερία αἱρετή ἐστιν, οἵα πάσαις ταῖς νομίμαις θρησκευτικῶν αἰσθημάτων ἀποδείξεσιν εὐρυχωρίαν ἂν χαρίσαιτο,) τὴν ἀποστολικὴν παραγγελίαν ἐπικαλούμεθα, "πάντα πρὸς οἰκοδομὴν γιγνέσθω," καὶ τὸν καθολικὸν κανόνα ἐπιμαρτυρόμεθα, τὸν διορίζοντα εὐταξίαν καὶ πειθαρχίαν, καίπερ μετ' αὐταπαρνήσεως ἰδίων προσκλίσεων καὶ αἰσθήσεων ἀποδιδομένας, ὡς χριστιανικῆς ἑνότητος θεμέλια, καὶ ὡς ἀναγκαίας πρὸς αὐτῆς τῆς πίστεως νικηφόρον ὑπεράσπισιν. Τοιγαροῦν οὐ παυσόμεθα τοιαῦτα νουθετοῦντες πρὶν ἐκφωνῆσαι ἐκτενῶς τὴν ἐλπίδα, ὅτι πάντα τῶν ἡμετέρων ἐκκλησιῶν τέκνα, ὁποίαις τισὶν οὖν θεωρίαις διαφέροντα, μέλλουσιν ὁμολογεῖν τὸ καθῆκον τοῦ ὑποτάσσεσθαι, διὰ τὴν συνείδησιν, ἐν θεσμοῖς καὶ τελεταῖς θρησκευτικαῖς, ταῖς ἐξουσιαστικαῖς κρίσεσιν τῆς μερικῆς ἢ ἐθνικῆς ἐκκλησίας, ὑφ' ἧς θείᾳ προνοίᾳ τυγχάνωσι κατῳκισμένα· καὶ ὅτι ἀφέξονται παντὸς πράγματος εἰς ἀλλοτρίωσιν ἢ ἐρεθισμὸν τείνοντος, καὶ ὑσήμερον θερμῶς προσεύξονται, ἵνα τὸ ἅγιον Πνεῦμα πάντα τῆς ἐκκλησίας μέλη ὁδηγῇ εἰς τὸ λογίζεσθαι καὶ ἐργάζεσθαι πάντοτε ἃ δεῖ, καὶ ἡμᾶς πάντας συνάπτῃ τῇ φιλαδελφικῇ ἐκείνῃ ἀγάπῃ, ἥτις ἐστὶν αὐτὸς εἰρήνης καὶ πασῶν ἀρετῶν σύνδεσμος.

* * * *

Εὐχαριστοῦμεν τῷ Παντοκράτορι Θεῷ, ὅτι σεμνοπρεπής τις διαμαρτυρία ἐξήχηται ἀπὸ πάνυ πολλῶν ἐκκλησιῶν, καὶ ἀπὸ κοινοτήτων χριστιανῶν καθ' ὅλον τὸν κόσμον, κατὰ τῶν τῆς Ῥωμαίας καθέδρας πλεονεκτημάτων, καὶ κατὰ τῶν νεωτερικῶν δογμάτων, ὑπ' ἐξουσίας αὐτῆς διωρισμένων.

Ἡ Ἀγγλικανὴ Ἐκκλησία ὀφείλει πᾶσαν συμπάθειαν ἐκκλησίαις κοινῇ, καὶ χριστιανοῖς ἰδίᾳ, διαμαρτυρομένοις κατὰ τούτων πλανημάτων, καὶ στενοχωρουμένοις, εἰ τύχοι, ὑπ' ἀποριῶν ἐξάλλων, διὰ τῶν τῆς ἀπιστίας προσβολῶν, ἅμα καὶ διὰ τῶν τῆς Ῥώμης ἐπιχειρημάτων.

Ἡμεῖς ὁμολογοῦμεν ἕνα μόνον Μεσίτην θεοῦ καὶ ἀνθρώπων, Ἄνθρωπον Ἰησοῦν Χριστόν, ὅς ἐστιν ἐπὶ πάντων Θεὸς εὐλογητὸς εἰς τοὺς αἰῶνας. Ἀπωθούμεθα, ὡς ἐναντίον ταῖς Γραφαῖς καὶ τῇ καθολικῇ ἀληθείᾳ, πᾶν ὁτιοῦν δόγμα, ὅπερ καθιστάναι ἄλλους μεσίτας ἀντ' Ἐκείνου τολμήσειεν ἄν, ἢ ἀφαιρεῖν ὁτιοῦν ἀπὸ τῆς θείας μεγαλειότητος τοῦ πληρώματος τῆς θεότητος ἐν Αὐτῷ κατοικοῦντος, καὶ τιμὴν ἄπειρον παρέχοντος τῇ ἀμώμῳ ἐκείνῃ θυσίᾳ, τῇ ἅπαξ ὑπ' Αὐτοῦ ὑπὲρ τοῦ ὅλου τοῦ κόσμου ἁμαρτιῶν ἐπὶ σταυροῦ προσενεχθείσης.

Χρεωστοῦμεν οὖν νουθετεῖν τοὺς πιστούς, τὸ ἔργον ὃ κατείργασται ὁ τῆς Ῥώμης ἐπίσκοπος ἔτει 1870 ἐν τῇ Βατικανῇ συνόδῳ, δι' οὗ ὑπεροχῆς ἀντεποιήσατο ὑπὲρ πάντων ἀνθρώπων, τήν τε πίστιν καὶ τὰ ἤθη, ἐπὶ προσχήματι ἀπλανησίας ἑαυτῷ ἐφαρπασθείσης, ἐπέμβασιν γεγονέναι τῶν ἀξιωμάτων τῷ Κυρίῳ Ἰησοῦ Χριστῷ προσηκόντων.

Γνώριμοι πᾶσίν εἰσιν οἱ κανόνες, καθ᾽ οὓς ἡ Ἀγγλικανὴ Ἐκκλησία ἑαυτὴν μετερρύθμισεν. Ἀνακηρύττομεν τὴν αὐτάρκειαν καὶ τὴν ὑπεροχὴν τῶν ἱερῶν Γραφῶν, ὡς ὁριστικὴν πίστεως στάθμην, καὶ τῷ ἡμετέρῳ λαῷ παραγγέλλομεν σπουδαίαν αὐτῶν μελέτην· τὴν πίστιν ἡμῶν ταῖς τῶν ἀρχαίων Συμβόλων φωναῖς ὁμολογοῦμεν· τὸ ἀποστολικὸν τάγμα Ἐπισκόπων, Πρεσβυτέρων καὶ Διακόνων κατέχομεν· τὴν ἔννομον ἐλευθερίαν μερικῶν ἢ ἐθνικῶν ἐκκλησιῶν διαβεβαιούμεθα· τῷ λαῷ ἡμῶν ἐγχειρίζομεν, ἐν τῇ ἐγχωρίῳ αὐτοῦ διαλέκτῳ, βιβλίον προσευχῶν δημοσίων καὶ τελετῶν, καὶ τῶν μυστηρίων ἱερουργίας, κατὰ τὰ ἄριστα καὶ παλαιότατα χριστιανικῆς πίστεως καὶ λατρείας ἀρχέτυπα.

Ταῦτα τὰ ἡμῶν μαρτυρήματα ἐνώπιον τῆς οἰκουμένης ἀναπτύσσεται, γιγνωσκόμενα καὶ ἀναγιγνωσκόμενα ὑπὸ πάντων ἀνθρώπων.

Ἀσμένως οὖν ἀσπαζόμεθα πᾶσαν πεῖραν μεταρρυθμίσεως κατὰ τὸ παράδειγμα τῆς ἀρχαίας ἐκκλησίας· στερεὰν ταὐτότητα οὐκ ἀπαιτοῦμεν· ἀνωφελεῖς διχοστασία παραιτούμεθα· πᾶσιν τοῖς πρὸς ἡμᾶς ἐφελκομένοις ἐν τῷ ἐπιχειρεῖν ἑαυτοὺς ἐλευθερῶσαι ἀπὸ ζυγοῦ πλάνης καὶ δεισιδαιμονίας πᾶσαν βοήθειαν προθύμως προτείνομεν, καὶ οἷα ἑαυτοῖς προνόμια εἴη ἀρεστά, καὶ ἡμετέροις κανόσιν, τοῖς ἐν ἡμετέραις διατυπώσεσιν ὡρισμένοις, σύμφωνα, ἐθελόντως προκομίζομεν.

* * * *

Περὶ τῶν ζητημάτων ἡμῖν παρατεθέντων ὑπὲρ τῶν τοῦ Γάμου νόμων ἐμφανίζομεν, ὅτι τὰς ἀπορίας ἐπιγιγνώσκοντες, ἐν αἷς ἔνιαι ἐκκλησίαι ἐμπλέκονται, διὰ τῶν θεσμῶν τῆς τοπικῆς νομοθεσίας, νομίζομεν ὅτι δεῖ πᾶσαν ἐκκλησίαν, κατὰ τὴν ἑαυτῆς γνώμην, τὴν τοῦ Γάμου ἁγιωσύνην διαφυλάττειν, κατὰ τὰ ἐν τῷ ῥήματι τοῦ Θεοῦ ὁρισθέντα, καὶ καθὰ ἡ τοῦ Χριστοῦ Ἐκκλησία μέχρι τοῦ νῦν ταῦτα δέδεκται.

Ἀναθεωροῦντες τοὺς λυγροὺς διαλογισμούς, περὶ τελετῶν ἐκκλησιαστικῶν, δι᾽ ὧν ἔνια τῶν ἡμετέρων πλήθη χαλεπῶς τεθορύβηνται, διαβεβαιούμεθα τὸν κανόνα, ὁρίζοντα μηδὲν δεῖν νεωτερίζειν, ἐν τῇ εἰθισμένῃ θρησκείας διατάξει, κατὰ τῆς τοῦ ἐπισκόπου νουθεσίας.

Λοιπὸν ἐνθυμούμενοι καινοτομίας τινὰς, τῇ τε πράξει καὶ τῇ διδαχῇ, περὶ τῆς ἐξομολογήσεως, διϊσχυριζόμεθα, τὰς τῆς Ἀγγλικανῆς κοινωνίας Ἐκκλησίας κρατεῖν βεβαίως τοὺς κανόνας περὶ τῆς ἐξομολογήσεως ἐν ταῖς ἁγίαις Γραφαῖς ἀποδεδειγμένους, καὶ ὑπὸ τῆς ἀρχαίας Ἐκκλησίας συνωμολογημένους, καὶ ἐν τῇ Ἀγγλικῇ Μεταρρυθμίσει ἀνακεκαινωμένους· καὶ ἐσκεμμένως ἐγνώκαμεν, μηδενὶ τῆς ἐκκλησίας ὑπηρέτῃ ἐξεῖναι ἀπαιτεῖν ἐκ τῶν πρὸς αὐτὸν φοιτώντων, διὰ τὴν τῆς αὐτῶν λύπης ἀνάπτυξιν, ἁπασῶν τῶν ἁμαρτιῶν κατὰ μέρος ἑκάστων ἐξαρίθμησιν, ἢ ἰδίαν ἐξομολόγησιν ἐκβασανίζειν, πρὸ τῆς ἁγίας εὐχαριστίας μεταλήψεως, ἢ ἐπιτάσσειν ἢ καὶ παραινεῖν τὴν τῆς συνήθους τῷ ἱερεῖ ἐξομολογήσεως ἐπιτήδευσιν, ἢ διδάσκειν ὅτι τοία ἐπιτήδευσις, ἢ τὸ ὑποτάσσεσθαι τῇ οὑτωσὶ καλουμένῃ ἱερέως χειραγωγίᾳ, ἀναγκαῖά ἐστι προπαιδεύματα πρὸς τὴν τῆς ἀνωτάτης πνευματικῆς ζωῆς ἐπίβασιν. Ὅμως μέντοι οὐδαμῶς ἐννοοῦμεν ἐπιτέμνειν τὴν ἐν τῇ βίβλῳ τῶν δημοσίων προσευχῶν, πρὸς τὸν βεβαρημένων συνειδήσεων ἐπικουφισμὸν, ἐπιχορηγίαν προνενοημένην.

Ταῦτά ἐστι τὰ συμπεράσματα εἰς ἃ κατηντήκαμεν, περὶ τῶν ἡμῖν προβεβλημένων ζητημάτων, ἐν οἷς τὰ πάντων τῆς Καθολικῆς Ἐκκλησίας τέκνων ἁπτόμενα ταῖς συνόδοις ἐκκλησιῶν, καὶ ταῖς ἐξουσίαις καθ' ἑκάστην κυβερνητικαῖς, καὶ πᾶσιν ἁπλῶς τοῖς πιστοῖς ἐν Χριστῷ Ἰησοῦ φιλοφρόνως σαφηνίζομεν.

Οὐκ ἀντιποιούμεθα τοῦ κατακυριεύειν ἐν κλήροις, ἀλλὰ ταῦτα τῷ ἡμετέρῳ συμβουλίῳ ἀρέσαντα συνίσταμεν τῷ λογισμῷ καὶ τῇ συνειδήσει τῶν ἀδελφῶν, ὡς ὑπὸ τοῦ ἁγίου Πνεύματος πεφωτισμένων, ἐκτενῶς Θεῷ προσευχόμενοι, ἵνα πάντες οἱ τὸ ὄνομα τοῦ Κυρίου ἐπικαλούμενοι, μιᾷ γνώμῃ καὶ μιᾷ κοινωνίᾳ ἡνωμένοι, τὴν πίστιν τὴν ἅπαξ τοῖς ἁγίοις παραδοθεῖσαν βεβαίως κρατῶσιν, καὶ τῷ ἑνὶ αὐτῶν Κυρίῳ ἐν ἑνὶ ἀφθαρσίας καὶ ἀγάπης πνεύματι λατρεύωσιν. Ἀμήν.

Ὑπέγραψα ἐν τῷ ὀνόματι τοῦ συμβουλίου,

ΑΡΧΙΒΑΛΔΟΣ ΚΑΜΠΒΕΛΛ,
Ὁ Καντουαρίας Ἀρχιεπίσκοπος.

No. XXIII. (See page 26.)

OFFICIAL LIST OF THE BISHOPS PRESENT AT THE LAMBETH CONFERENCE OF 1878.

THE ARCHBISHOP OF CANTERBURY.
THE ARCHBISHOP OF YORK.
THE ARCHBISHOP OF ARMAGH.
THE ARCHBISHOP OF DUBLIN.

THE BISHOP OF LONDON.
THE BISHOP OF WINCHESTER.
THE BISHOP OF LLANDAFF.
THE BISHOP OF RIPON.
THE BISHOP OF NORWICH.
THE BISHOP OF BANGOR.
THE BISHOP OF GLOUCESTER AND BRISTOL
THE BISHOP OF CHESTER.
THE BISHOP OF ST. ALBAN'S.
THE BISHOP OF HEREFORD.
THE BISHOP OF PETERBOROUGH.
THE BISHOP OF LINCOLN.
THE BISHOP OF SALISBURY.
THE BISHOP OF CARLISLE.
THE BISHOP OF EXETER.
THE BISHOP OF BATH AND WELLS.
THE BISHOP OF OXFORD.
THE BISHOP OF MANCHESTER.
THE BISHOP OF CHICHESTER.
THE BISHOP OF ST. ASAPH.
THE BISHOP OF ELY.
THE BISHOP OF ST. DAVID'S.
THE BISHOP OF TRURO.
THE BISHOP OF ROCHESTER.
THE BISHOP OF LICHFIELD.
THE BISHOP OF SODOR AND MAN.

THE BISHOP OF MEATH.
THE BISHOP OF DOWN.
THE BISHOP OF KILLALOE.
THE BISHOP OF LIMERICK.
THE BISHOP OF DERRY.
THE BISHOP OF CASHEL.
THE BISHOP OF OSSORY.

Official List of Bishops Present, 1878.

The Bishop of Moray. *Primus.*
The Bishop of St. Andrew's.
The Bishop of Edinburgh.
The Bishop of Aberdeen.
The Bishop of Glasgow.
The Bishop of Brechin.
The Bishop of Argyll.

The Bishop of Delaware.
The Bishop of New York.
The Bishop of Ohio.
The Bishop of Pennsylvania.
The Bishop of Western New York.
The Bishop of Nebraska.
The Bishop of Pittsburgh.
The Bishop of Louisiana.
The Bishop of Missouri.
The Bishop of Long Island.
The Bishop of Albany.
The Bishop of Central Pennsylvania.
The Assistant Bishop of North Carolina.
The Bishop of New Jersey.
The Bishop of Wisconsin.
The Bishop of Iowa.
The Bishop of Colorado.

The Bishop of Haiti.
The Bishop of Shanghai.

The Bishop of Montreal, *Metropolitan.*
The Bishop of Fredericton.
The Bishop of Nova Scotia.
The Bishop of Ontario.
The Bishop of Huron.
The Bishop of Toronto.
The Bishop of Niagara.

The Bishop of Madras.
The Bishop of Colombo.
The Bishop of Bombay.

The Bishop of Guiana.
The Bishop of Kingston.
The Bishop of Antigua.
The Bishop of Barbados.
The Bishop of Nassau.

The Bishop of Sydney. *Metropolitan.*
The Bishop of Adelaide.
The Bishop of North Queensland.

THE BISHOP OF CHRISTCHURCH. *Metropolitan.*
THE BISHOP OF DUNEDIN.

THE BISHOP OF GIBRALTAR.

THE BISHOP OF CAPETOWN. *Metropolitan.*
THE BISHOP OF ST. HELENA.
THE BISHOP OF MARITZBURGH.
THE BISHOP OF BLOEMFONTEIN.
THE BISHOP OF PRETORIA.

THE BISHOP OF RUPERTSLAND. *Metropolitan.*
THE BISHOP OF BRITISH COLUMBIA.
THE BISHOP OF SASKATCHEWAN.

THE BISHOP OF THE FALKLAND ISLANDS.

THE BISHOP SUFFRAGAN OF DOVER.
THE BISHOP SUFFRAGAN OF GUILDFORD.
THE BISHOP SUFFRAGAN OF NOTTINGHAM.

BISHOP PERRY.
BISHOP MCDOUGALL.
BISHOP RYAN.
BISHOP CLAUGHTON.

Officers of the Conference.

THE BISHOP OF GLOUCESTER AND BRISTOL, *Secretary of the Conference.*

THE BISHOP OF EDINBURGH, *Secretary of Committees.*

ISAMBARD BRUNEL, D.C.L., (Chancellor of the Diocese of Ely, *Assistant Secretary.*

No. XXIV. (See page 29.)

Order of Bishops in the Processions at Lambeth Palace and in St. Paul's Cathedral in 1878.

The following is an official list, as prepared for the Processions on July 2 and July 27, 1878. The order had to be materially changed on the occasion of the actual services, by the absence, at the moment, of

Bishops who had been expected, but the same principle of arrangement was in each case followed. The Archbishop of Canterbury had the Archbishop of York and the Bishop of London on his right and left hand, and was preceded by the Metropolitans of the Irish, Scottish, and Colonial Provinces. The Bishops from the United States walked, as guests, abreast of the English Diocesans. The other Bishops were arranged, two and two, according to date of consecration. The processions moved, as usual, in reverse order, the junior Bishops first, the Archbishops last.

Archbishop of York.	Archbishop of Canterbury.	Bishop of London.
	,, Armagh.	
	,, Dublin.	
Bishop of Delaware.	Primus of Scottish Episcopal Church.	,, Winchester.
,, New York.	Bishop of Sydney.	,, Llandaff.
,, Ohio.	,, Christchurch, New Zealand.	,, Ripon.
,, Pennsylvania.	,, Montreal.	,, Bangor.
,, Western New York.	,, Capetown.	,, { Gloucester & Bristol.
,, Nebraska.	,, Rupert's Land.	,, Chester.
Bishop of Pittsburgh.		Bishop of St. Alban's.
,, Louisiana.		,, Hereford.
,, Missouri.		,, Peterborough.
,, Long Island.		,, Lincoln.
,, Albany.		,, Salisbury.
,, Central Pennsylvania.		,, Carlisle.
Assistant Bishop of North Carolina.		,, Exeter.
Bishop of New Jersey.		,, Bath and Wells.
,, Wisconsin.		,, Oxford.
,, Iowa.		,, Manchester.
,, Colorado.		,, Chichester.
,, St. Asaph.		,, Ely.
,, St. David's.		,, Rochester.
,, Truro.		,, Lichfield.
,, Sodor and Man.		,, Dover.
,, Guildford.		,, Nottingham.
Bishop Perry.		,, Killaloe.
,, M'Dougall.	Bishop Ryan.	
Bishop of Meath.		,, Claughton.

And the other Bishops according to their date of consecration.

No. XXV. (See page 33.)

Sermon preached by Bishop Stevens, of Pennsylvania, in St. Paul's Cathedral, on Saturday, July 27th, 1878.

"And I, if I be lifted up from the earth, will draw all men unto Me."—*St. John* xii. 32.

Most Rev. Fathers and Brethren Beloved—

It is with unfeigned diffidence that I stand before you this morning.

Deeply as I appreciate the honour of having been selected as your preacher, still more deeply am I burdened with a sense of the responsibility which rests upon me as your mouthpiece on this great occasion. Not that I am commissioned to speak your views, or declare what we have said or done, but I am your mouthpiece as guiding your thoughts in this closing hour, and summing them up in words appropriate to the valedictory of this remarkable Conference. May the Holy Ghost so illumine my mind that I may think only those things which are right, and so touch my lips that I shall speak only that which shall be for the glory of the Triune God!

I shall not attempt to review the doings of the Conference now brought to an end. Within this present month, and within the Library of Lambeth Palace, has been made a history, the record of which will constitute one of the most illuminated chapters in the annals of the Holy Catholic Church. Never before have so many English-speaking Bishops met together. Never before have all branches of the

Anglican Communion been so fully represented in an ecclesiastical assembly. Such a gathering converges to itself the eyes of the thinking world, and such a gathering must radiate from itself a power for weal or woe that shall reach to far-distant ages. The history of that Conference is made. The result of that Conference will be fully known only when the record of eternity shall be revealed. We met as standard-bearers of the Cross of Christ. That fact has been the prominent one in all our deliberations, and we separate to go back to our dioceses, more impressed than ever that it is in and through an uplifted Christ—faithfully held up and fully displayed, that our work can be accomplished, and all men—men of all races, all climes, all countries—be drawn to the feet of the Crucified and to the Church, which is His Body. In this precious truth we have found not only a bond of personal union, but of real unity throughout the wide-spreading branches of our Holy Church.

Our little diversities, personal and national, as to non-essentials of faith and the accessories of worship, look very small before the great essentials in which we all agree. We feel that we all rest on the same corner and foundation stones laid in Zion, even Christ and His Apostles, and the eternal and distinctive verities of faith revealed in God's Holy Word.

This sacred *depositum* intrusted to the Church as the keeper and witness of the faith once delivered to the saints, embodied in the creeds of Christendom, endorsed by the undisputed General Councils, and maintained and defended by the *consensus* of the undivided Church in the writings of the early Fathers, is the blessed heritage of us all, and binds us together in the oneness and unity of a living organism, operating through diverse members and by diverse functions, yet all holding to the one Divine Head—nourished by the one Divine Blood, breathing the one Divine Breath of Life.

Another fact, which has grown out of the more faithful lifting up of the Lord Jesus Christ, and which this Conference has brought prominently out, is the increase of spiritual life and work in all the branches of the Anglican Church. The reports of the Bishops from every quarter testify to this pleasing fact. Not only is this increase seen in a more widely-spread and deeper-toned personal piety, but also in the gratifying increase of reverence for holy things and places, in the more life-inspiring renderings of our beautiful Liturgy, in the more frequent celebrations of the Holy Communion, and in the multifarious forms of Church work springing up in all our dioceses and missionary jurisdictions.

It is further seen in the bringing into effective and judicious use agencies for the cultivation of personal holiness, and the better reaching of the sick and the poor, and for the wider extension of Church privileges, which have either never been used before, or which have long been disused, because abused to purposes of superstition and error. We feel, and I think rightly, that whatever has been done or used in other ages, or by other communions, which has been productive of good, even though tainted with the evils of the age, or the communion using them, ought not on that account to be set aside ; but rather should be reclaimed from wrong-doing, and by wise and authoritative adaptation be made to serve the right and the true in faith and worship. Hence implements of spiritual tillage, hitherto neglected or suspected, have been remodelled and rightly utilised.

Methods of Church work, which were once looked upon with distrust, have been prudently adjusted to our own needs and times. Our Blessed Lord gave to His Church that same power of self-adjustment which in a higher and holier way He showed in His own conduct when on earth. He gave it marvellous flexibility of circumference, combined with central fixedness and unchangeableness—flexibility, so as to conform to all the outlines of human needs, just as He has made the great ocean to flow as readily into the little cove beside the fisherman's hut as into the magnificent bays which harbour the navies of the world; and fixedness, so that the substantial body of truth shall never be changed, just as He holds the same great ocean in the hollow of His Hand. The multiplied agencies which the Church has set in motion in the last half-century illustrate what I mean as to adjustment of the Church to the demands of modern society.

Specially I may mention the introduction of lay-helpers, both men and women, into the active service of the Church. The fact proves that the Church is reviving from her languid state, when it was too much the fashion to regard the clergy as the Church, and rather to frown upon lay effort as trenching upon clerical prerogative. It was this spirit which lost to the Church of England the fruit of that great uprising of zeal under the Wesleys and Whitfield, which, had it been recognised and utilised, and taught to work in Churchly channels, as it now would be, would have rooted the Church of England tenfold more in the hearts of the toiling classes, and kept them from drifting away into fragmentary divisions; would have welded together social elements which would admirably supplement each other; and would have made the disestablishment and denationalisation of the Church of England utterly impossible.

The introduction of the lay element into the councils of the Church, whether diocesan or Convocational, is a grave question, because, in some cases, encumbered with serious difficulties. Therefore each national Church must deal with it as a national question, and settle it as shall best subserve its national interests. But the patent fact is, that the bringing in of the laity as a constituent part of the various working assemblies of the Church has in the United States and in many of the Colonial provinces and dioceses been of the highest value to the cause of our holy faith. Intrust the laity with responsibility, and you secure their confidence. Make them a part of your deliberate counsels, and they will educate themselves to discharge aright the duties of their position. Let them realise that the Church leans upon their wisdom as well as upon their purse, and they will show that strong common sense, knowledge, and discretion which shall make them as powerful allies in Church legislation as they now are in Church work.

It is true that with this increase of vitality has been an increase of abnormal life, running out into excesses, both in doctrine and in ritual. In a Church made up of imperfect beings, with all possible tastes, temperaments, and idiosyncrasies, such evils cannot well be avoided. Our Blessed Lord told us in His parables that this would be the case. St. Paul distinctly declared to the Corinthians that "there must be also heresies among you, that they which are approved may be made manifest among you," thus not merely recognizing in His day, and in Apostolic Churches, the existence of this Church life running out into wrong channels of thought and action, but giving as a reason for its permissive existence, that the Lord used these heresies and these sects as a means of testing and manifesting the true,—making the true more clearly true by placing alongside of it its stimulating error.

Nor has the Church of Christ ever been free from these errors, and the words of our Lord in the parable of the Tares and Wheat, "Let both grow together until the harvest," and then saying that that harvest was the end of the world, indicates with certainty that these heresies, and this schismatic spirit, will continue the earthly lifetime of the Church. Lamentable indeed are these displays, splitting off from the Church into open schism, on the one hand, or raising up factions, turbulent and menacing, within the bounds of the Church, on the other.

These evils can only be partially held in check or corrected by any legal or technical decisions of civil or ecclesiastical courts, for in some instances they have fostered more scandals than they have allayed. The real remedy lies in another direction. It is to draw men to a common centre by preaching a great central and unifying truth. That great central truth is that which is both centred and sphered in an unlifted Christ. When men are drawn to His person, His service, and His salvation, you have a basis for that real unity which alone meets the conditions of our Lord's intercessory prayer—" That they all may be one, as Thou Father art in me, and I in Thee." Not organically one, but one in the harmony of an interior life derived from a common source, sustained by a common faith, and having a common end and aim.

When the pure strength of Evangelical truth welling up in life-giving freshness in the Word of God shall flow more freely through the channels of Apostolic order and sacramental ordinances; when this Evangelical spirit, to which the Church of England owed its revival of life and activity in the last century, shall avail itself more of churchly agencies, and address itself more to working along Church lines, with the same zeal with which it has so well addressed itself to the maintenance and defence of doctrine, and shall thus make the clergy and the parishes alive with new-born zeal and love, showing by their own example that they are as earnest, as sincere, as self-sacrificing, as sound in the faith and as loyal to the Church as those whom they condemn—then will the spirit of lawlessness, and erroneous and strange doctrine, and the sickly imitations of a foreign communion be met and answered by a purer faith, a more Christ-like zeal, a more obedient reverence to the powers that be as ordained of God, and a higher and holier aim—namely, the advancement, not of self nor of party, but the honour and glory of the uplifted Christ.

Looking in another direction, we find the Church confronted by critical scepticism and scientific doubt, which aim to break down the bulwarks of her faith and raze her walls of salvation to the ground. But while we survey this frowning evil, let us not be unduly alarmed, or make too hasty concessions, but be vigilant and wise in meeting it on broad and sound grounds. Holding to the Bible as our sole rule of faith and practice, we must maintain the supremacy of the Bible by placing it in its right position; and that is, that it is a perfectly completed book. The Bible of to-day is the Bible of all the centuries of the Christian era, and will be of all the centuries to come. As it came from Him, it can neither be added to nor taken from without incurring the anathema of its Author. But the science which opposes this Bible is but the science of to-day. It was not the science of the last century; it will not be of the century to come. These sciences, of whatever name, are variable and uncertain. Not one is on a fixed and immovable basis. Not one that may not be altered, or set aside by some new discovery, or by some new generalization. It will be time enough to say whether these sciences and the Bible do agree when the perfected circle of science shall be placed on the perfected circle of the Holy Scriptures. Then only can we rightly measure each, and when that time comes it will be found that the circumference of science and the circumference of revelation have one and the same periphery, because they have one and the same Divine Centre, the same one living and true God. In the Apostles' day there were "oppositions of science falsely so-called." In every age since then the same assaults have been renewed, but the Bible has calmly held on its way. It waits patiently for confirmation as the ages roll on, and each advance of true science does bring it more into accord with revelation. What the clergy have to do is not to attempt to put on Saul's armour and go forth to fight what they would call a Philistine science with something that they have not proved and cannot wield, but to take the smooth stones out of the brook of Scripture, and in the name of the Uplifted One so hurl them that even giant defiers of the Israel of God shall fall before the simple truth, slung by the humblest shepherd of the flock. This preaching is now, as in Paul's day, to the Jew a stumbling-block, and to the Greek foolishness, but it is still what it was then, and what it will ever be, Christ the power of God and the wisdom of God. When the Apostles preached this uplifted Christ, they did it not in the words which man's wisdom teacheth, lest the Cross of Christ should be made of none effect, but with that simple plainness of men fully imbued with the truth which they heralded, and telling it out in the fulness and directness of that earnestness which all will feel who realize that they are bought with a price, even the precious blood of the uplifted Jesus.

Looking in still another direction, we find the Church in the midst of social evils which threaten alike the well-being of the Church and of the State. Can the Church deal with these manifold economical questions which at times so seriously agitate the whole framework of human society? Yes. The uplifting of Christ will do it. The most important factor in the world's history was the coming down into it of Christ our Lord. His incarnation is the axle on which turn all the wheels of human life. Any science of sociology which leaves Him out as its central and controlling power is, like a science of the solar system without the sun, erroneous at its centre and erroneous at its circumference. It is the presence of Christ in the world that has given birth to all the philanthopies of the world—is banishing its most crying evils and bringing in all that is refining and elevating in mind and heart and life. This being so, and no student of history can truly deny it, it follows that all that is needed to meet and remove the social evils of our time is the clear, true, and forceful setting forth of Christ as the Light and Life of men. For just in proportion as they bask in His light and breathe the breath of His life will they become Christlike in mind and heart, and the prevalence of the mind of Christ and the love of Christ will change the moral and social aspect of the world.

Finally, God has set before the Church of this age an open door into the regions beyond and bidden her go in and possess the land. Never, it may truly be said, has the Church been so thoroughly equipped as now for missionary work. Geographical exploration and commercial adventure have opened up to us long unknown and almost mythical regions. Ethnology and philology have brought the varying languages and races of men into better classification. Technical art and science have put into our hands implements and skill for reforming and enlarging all the industrial pursuits of men. Thus these auxiliary forces become in the progress of time almost apostles of Christianity.

A higher and truer education in heathen lands must result in breaking down the old errors based on ignorance and superstitions. Science is already at work through manifold ways, undermining and sapping the Oriental religions—Buddhism, Brahminism, Confucianism, Lamaism — and preparing the way for their downfall. It has not been until within a few years that we have really understood the doctrines, usages, and inner power of the dominating religions of Asia. We have known their general features, but have mostly grouped them all together in one idolatrous mass of hopeless superstition and cruel orgies, and as such have levelled our theological artillery relentlessly against them. Now, however, through the labours of men who seem to have been specially raised up for the purpose, the eight great religions of the world into which Max Müller reduces the many schemes of human worship have been studied and analysed, and their sacred books carefully translated, annotated, and compared with our own, so that almost a new science—the science of comparative religion—has been created by the diligent and painstaking men who have made careful surveys of these Oriental religions, and enabled us to weigh, measure, and examine systems of belief which hold more than one-half the human race in their moulding power. Thus Christianity is fast acquiring all those outside forces necessary to give to it a world-wide equipment for its world-wide conquest. And when the evangelistic forces of the Church shall go forth in their full power, it will be with a momentum hitherto unknown, enabling her to do in a day the work of a year, and in a year the work of centuries, until, through these vastly-augmented agencies, blessed and utilised by the Holy Ghost, it shall be literally true as the prophet has declared, " a nation shall be born in a day."

Brethren, beloved, this is the great work which is intrusted to us in an especial manner, to proclaim in all the quarters of the world where our lot is cast an uplifted Jesus. We are to lift Him up by exalting the Divine Scripture, in which He is enshrined; by exalting the sacrament which shows forth this uplifting until He come; by exalting the ministry appointed by Christ Himself to be His heralds and teachers; by exalting the Church, which is His mystical Body,—exalting all these things, not by exalting them above Him, of Whom and to Whom they all testify; but because they are all means and aids for getting a better, clearer, and more life-giving view of the uplifted Jesus.

All attempt to put anything between the soul of the sinner and the uplifted Christ, or to raise anything to the same level with Him, is derogatory to His honour and contrary to His Word. To what purpose would the bitten Israelite have been told to look at the serpent of brass lifted up by Moses in the wilderness if anything had been placed by Moses or the elders of Israel between the eyes of the sufferer and the object to which he was directed to look? Or if alongside of that serpent of brass had been placed other objects to which equal efficacy was attributed, and thus confused his mind and deflected his faith?

This lifting up of Christ in all the aspects of His offices as Prophet, Priest, and King can be done by us only as we are taught by the Holy Ghost, for it is His office to take of the things of Christ and to show them unto men. Dear brethren, if there is one thought more than another which presses upon me at this time, in reference especially to the work committed to us as Bishops in the Church of God, it is that we need a fresh baptism of the Holy Spirit and fresh outpouring into our hearts of the love-power of the uplifted Jesus. If even Apostles, the three years' daily companions of our blessed Lord when He dwelt among men, had no power to preach the Cross of Christ until the Holy Spirit came upon them, surely we need to be sprinkled from on high, that Pentecostal grace may not merely light upon our heads in tongue-like flames but that, like the precious ointment upon the head of Aaron that went down to the skirts of his garments, the unction that the Holy Spirit only can bestow may flow over our whole being, sanctifying our lives, enlightening our minds, giving grace to our lips, and wisdom to our acts, and power to our administration, so that it may be said of each of us as of the first martyr, St. Stephen, " He was a man full of faith and of the Holy Ghost."

Our ministry of the Word and our office as Bishops can only be duly and wisely discharged in and through the power and guidance of the Holy Ghost. Let us never forget that this is the source of all ministerial strength and grace and influence. Our constant and wrestling prayer should be that we may daily increase in that Holy Spirit more and more until we come unto His everlasting kingdom.

Let us also, dear brethren, endeavour to induce the clergy to be more diligent and distinct in setting forth this uplifted Christ as the great sunlike truth of our salvation. The real remedy for the troubles within our own Church is not by repressive, or by restrictive, or by punitive legislation; is not by courts of law, civil or ecclesiastical; is not by bandying criminous and contemptuous words, and organising parties in battle array under standards and principles foreign to the spirit of the Gospels, but it is a more faithful setting forth of Christ.

But I must stop, though many and weighty topics rise in my mind, created by the occasion.

The day has arrived when this assembly of Anglican Bishops will separate. But before we separate, our hearts are to be re-knit together by participation in that blessed Sacrament which, while it binds each to each, binds all as one to the heart of our common Lord. From that altar we shall go away northward to the Arctic Circle, southward to Australia, eastward to China, westward to the United States, never to meet together as a body here below. Of the seventy-six Bishops gathered at the last Lambeth Conference in 1867, thirty are dead. Death has reaped out of that assembly a rich harvest, and garnered up some of the wisest, the noblest, the holiest men, who ever bore the burden of the Episcopate. They rest together in the Paradise of God.

This thought cannot but give a tone of solemnity to this sacred hour; yet along with this under-tone of sorrow rises up our souls' *Te Deum* that we have been permitted to meet as brethren, to confer so long and so lovingly together, and to part with that profound respect and affection which intercourse has engendered and which love has cemented.

Speaking as an American Bishop, and in behalf of American Bishops, I feel warranted in saying that we desire thus publicly to acknowledge the manifold courtesies and civilities which have been so markedly bestowed upon us—that we appreciate and shall ever remember the unwearied kindness and loving words of our brethren of the English bench, and of all others who made up this Conference.

We have learned here lessons of wisdom and zeal which will influence all our future. We go back richer than we came, for we return with the wealth of new friendships, new plans of usefulness, new aspirations after higher results, and the treasured memories of Church life and home life into which, as into a garden of spices, we have been so lovingly invited. Our admiration of the Church of England has been greatly increased. As we have walked around its walls, grey with antiquity, and marked well its bulwarks, scarred, but not weakened, by the conflicts of the Christian centuries; as we have associated with those who bear Episcopal rule in this Zion, and with the band of learned and self-sacrificing clergy who work therein, and with the intelligent and zealous and liberal laity that form the noble body of the faithful—as we have surveyed all these we may have seen here and there things that are strange to us, points that we should have altered, defects, as we might term them, that needed correction, the filling up of some crevice here, and the stripping off of some of the old ivy there; but after all we should be forced to exclaim, "Beautiful for situation, the joy of the whole earth is this City of our God: Her foundations are on the everlasting hills. The Lord is in the midst of her; she shall not be moved. God shall help her, and that right early." As I behold the grand spectacle which the Anglican Church now presents—bristling with its multiplied agencies and vigorous with re-enkindled life and earnestness, and contrast it with the impotence of its assailers and the envy of its rivals, I recall the magnificent vision of Milton, in which he describes the rising power and glory of the Commonwealth; and substituting the word "Church" for the word "nation," I seem to find in it a description of the present aspect of the spiritual commonwealth of dear old England. "Methinks," says the blind bard, "I see in my mind, a noble and puissant Church, rousing herself like a strong man after sleep, and shaking her invincible locks; methinks I see her as an eagle, renewing her mighty youth, and kindling her undazzled eyes at the full midday beam, purging and unscaling her long-abused sight at the fountain itself of heavenly radiance; while the whole noise of timorous and flocking birds, with those also that love the twilight, flutter about amazed at what she means," and, I may add, confounded at her revived greatness. And so we say, with one mouth and one heart, to the dear mother of us all, the Church of England, "Peace be within thy walls, and plenteousness within thy palaces. For my brethren and companions' sake, I will wish thee prosperity."

The next time, dear brethren, that we meet together will be before the Great White Throne. Such a thought warns us that we must be watching, waiting, working, until the day of death comes; and when that shall come, may we each, through faith in the atoning blood of the uplifted Jesus, pass in through the gate into the celestial city, and hear from the lips of Him who sitteth upon the throne, "Well done, good and faithful servant, enter thou into the joy of thy Lord."

No. XXVI.

Prayer for the Conference.

O LORD God Almighty, Father of Lights and Fountain of all Wisdom : we humbly beseech Thee that Thy Holy Spirit may lead into all truth Thy servants the Bishops now [to be] gathered together in Thy Name. Grant them Grace to think and do such things as shall tend most to Thy Glory and the good of Thy Holy Church : direct and prosper, we pray Thee, all their consultations, and further them with Thy continual help, that, the true Catholic and Apostolic Faith once delivered to the Saints being maintained, Thy Church may serve Thee in righteousness of living and in all godly quietness through Jesus Christ our Lord. *Amen.*

No. XXVII.

Papers issued to the Bishops before the first Services or Meetings in connection with the Conference of 1888.

(1) PROGRAMME.

The following are the official arrangements with respect to the forthcoming Lambeth Conference.

SATURDAY, JUNE 30th.

3.0 p.m. * Service in Canterbury Cathedral.

MONDAY, JULY 2nd.

7.0 p.m. * Service in Westminster Abbey, with Sermon by the Archbishop of Canterbury.

> [Bishops and Chaplains attending this Service will enter the Abbey through Dean's Yard, by the Jerusalem Chamber entrance.]

TUESDAY, JULY 3rd.

11.0 a.m. * Holy Communion in Lambeth Palace Chapel, with Sermon by the Bishop of Minnesota, deputed by the Presiding Bishop of the Protestant Episcopal Church in the United States.

1.30 p.m.—4.45 p.m.

First Session of the Conference in Lambeth Palace Library—

(A) Opening Address by the Archbishop of Canterbury.

(B) Discussion of Subject (No. II.)—"*Definite teaching of the Faith to various classes and the means thereto.*"

> To be introduced by the Bishops of London, Maine, and Carlisle.

Wednesday, July 4th.

10.45 a.m.   Litany in Lambeth Palace Chapel.

11.0 a.m.—1.30 p.m.

Discussion of Subject (No. III.)—"*The Anglican Communion in relation to the Eastern Churches, to the Scandinavian and other Reformed Churches, to the old Catholics and others.*"

> To be introduced by the Archbishop of Dublin, the Bishops of Winchester, Gibraltar, Lichfield, Jamaica, and Bishop Blyth.

2.0 p.m.—4.45 p.m.

Discussion of Subject (No. IV.)—"*Polygamy of Heathen Converts.—Divorce.*"

> To be introduced by the Bishops of Durham, Chester, Zululand, The Niger, Maryland, and Bombay.

Thursday, July 5th.

10.45 a.m.   Litany in Lambeth Palace Chapel.

11.0 a.m.—1.30 p.m.

Discussion of Subject (No. V.)—"*Authoritative Standards of Doctrine and Worship.*"

> To be introduced by the Bishops of Sydney, Aberdeen, Western New York, Salisbury, and Albany.

2.0 p.m.—4.45 p.m.

Discussion of Subject (No. VI.)—"*Mutual relations of Dioceses and Branches of the Anglican Communion.*"

> To be introduced by the Bishops of Capetown, Brechin, and Derry.

Friday, July 6th.

10.45 a.m.   Litany in Lambeth Palace Chapel.

11.0 a.m.—1.30 p.m., and 2.0 p.m.—4.45 p.m.

Discussion of Subject (No. I.)—"*The Church's*

practical work in relation to (A) *Intemperance.* (B) *Purity.* (C) *Care of Emigrants.* (D) *Socialism.*"

> To be introduced by (A) the Bishops of London and New York; (B) the Bishops of Durham and Calcutta; (C) the Bishops of Liverpool, North Queensland, and Quebec; (D) the Bishops of Manchester and Mississippi.

MONDAY, JULY 9th, to SATURDAY, JULY 21st.

Meetings of the various Committees appointed during the first week's Sessions.

MONDAY, JULY 23rd, to FRIDAY, JULY 27th.

Sessions of Conference in Lambeth Palace Library to receive and consider the Reports of the various Committees. Litany, each day, in Chapel, at 10.45, except on Wednesday, July 25th (S. James' Day), when there will be a celebration of Holy Communion at 10.0 a.m.

SATURDAY, JULY 28th.

11 a.m. * Concluding Service in St. Paul's Cathedral, with Sermon by the Archbishop of York.

At the services marked thus (*) the Bishops present are requested to attend in their Episcopal Robes. It is requested that each Bishop present at the services in Westminster Abbey and St. Paul's Cathedral may be attended by one Chaplain (or Acting Chaplain) who will take a place in the procession. The arrangements at Canterbury and at Lambeth Palace will not admit of the attendance of any Chaplains. If such Bishops (and Chaplains) as can conveniently do so would go already robed to Westminster Abbey and St. Paul's, it would relieve the necessary pressure upon the space available for robing. In the case of the Lambeth Palace service, rooms will be set apart for robing and unrobing—as Episcopal Robes will not be worn during the Conference Debates. Pastoral Staves will in no case be carried except by the Diocesans in whose Cathedrals the services are held.

The rule found necessary at the former Conferences will be again adopted—that should any petitions or memorials be presented to the Conference, they be placed without discussion in the hands of the President ; and that it be understood that no answer can in any case be returned.

EDW: CANTUAR.

C. J. GLOUCESTER & BRISTOL,
Episcopal Secretary.

RANDALL T. DAVIDSON,
(Dean of Windsor.) *General Secretary*:

B. F. SMITH,
(Archdeacon of Maidstone.) *Assistant Secretary*.

June 23*rd,* 1888.

---

(2)   LAMBETH CONFERENCE, 1888.

The following arrangements have now been made in connection with the forthcoming Lambeth Conference :—

1. In the debates of the opening week the formal motion proposed will in each case be for the appointment of a Committee to consider the particular subject, and to report in the closing week of the Conference.

2. Certain Bishops conversant with the particular subjects have been invited to open the several dis-

cussions, but time will as far as possible be afforded for the speeches of others who may wish to take part in the opening debates.

3. It is requested that the names of Bishops who may be regarded as specially qualified to serve on the different Committees, may be handed to the secretaries, either before or during the opening debates, for the President's consideration before the Committees are nominated.

4. The invited speakers are requested, in opening the discussions, to express their views by means of speeches, not written papers, and it is particularly hoped that no speech will exceed fifteen minutes in duration, opportunity for fuller treatment of the subjects being afforded in the discussions and reports of the Committees.

5. A verbatim report of all the speeches will, as before, be taken, and the transcript will be preserved at Lambeth. No part of the debates will be open to the public.

6. The rule found necessary at the former Conferences will be again adopted—that, should any petitions or memorials be presented to the Conference, they be placed without discussion in the hands of the President; and that it be understood that no answers can, in any case, be returned.

7. It is requested that each Bishop attending the Services in Westminster Abbey and St. Paul's Cathedral may be attended by one Chaplain (or Acting Chaplain), who will take a place in the procession. The arrangements at Canterbury and at Lambeth Palace will not admit of the attendance of any Chaplains.

EDW. CANTUAR.

June 9th, 1888.

(3)

In reply to enquiries from several Bishops as to whether the red ("Convocation") chimere should be worn by the Bishops attending the Lambeth Conference Services, the Archbishop of Canterbury has recommended that, for the sake of uniformity and convenience, the dress worn by all the Bishops should be the ordinary Episcopal Habit—black chimere with lawn rochet and D.D. hood. Chaplains to wear cassock, surplice, hood and scarf.

LAMBETH PALACE,
25th June, 1888.

No. XXVIII. (See page 41.)

Sermon preached by the Archbishop of Canterbury, in Westminster Abbey, on Monday Evening, July 2, 1888.

"All the body fitly framed and knit together through that which every joint supplieth."—EPH. iv. 16.

THE well-known words—so rich, so worthy, might seem a motto for this Abbey in its glorious age. But they are fitter to describe this Assembly in its perfect modernness. They are the Christian view of the facts of the Church's growth—facts seen from within. The structural progress of the organism is what the Apostle notes.

The consequent changes in the surrounding world are no less notable. Her materials of beauty and strength, added to the new, are in a way subtracted from the old. Shaped and glorified and quickened they are replaced at the service of the old. For the

Church is not a dead Temple quarried out of living rock and leaving a chasm behind. It is still in the world. A living Temple into which a half-dead world is to be absorbed.

The world has abundant vitality to resent the process. Hence, not only old persecutions, but all antagonism, all dislike—save that large amount which is drawn on us by our own inconsistencies.

Some thinking people still find it doubtful whether the world will ever be absorbed by Christianity, as Christ and the writers of the New Testament evidently conceive that it will be.

But there was a time when greater thinkers still would have held any theory of the unity of Man, to be brought about by any cause whatever, irrational and unnatural, an evident contradiction of all such design as could be attributed to nature.

For instance, in the long and beautiful fragment which remains to us of the Sixth Book of Cicero's greatest work—his treatise " Of the Republic,"—he sketches the physical features of the distribution of man on the globe. From the Milky Way he marks in vision the few, the narrow, and the scattered "patches" of the earth which were habitable—the waste, impassable tracts which severed the races of mankind—the invincible impossibility of serviceable communications. It is from these laws and certainties of nature, that he draws the lofty, melancholy moral of the worthless narrowness of human fame. " The Southern Zone bears absolutely no relation to the condition of Europe. Even Europe has very little nterest in the eyes of the humane world of Italy."

This was the judgment of a mind open to all the considerations which had hitherto suggested themselves in thought and literature. Yet a few years later a society was summoned into existence whose earliest call was to be " Fishers of Men," to gather together in one "the children of God who were scattered abroad."

The Statesman expressly affirms it to be "unimaginable that the mightiest Name from lands of civilisation and culture should pass the eternal barriers of Caucasus or be wafted over Ganges." A few years later the Apostle was writing of "One Name to which every knee would bow."

To the Christian it was in the nature of things that scattered humanity should be welded into one mass, and the uniting attraction be the human Name of Jesus. The Oneness of Humanity is the essence of the Faith. The One Body not yet "fitly framed together," but, as the Apostle literally wrote, "framing itself together," as by an hourly process, is the Ideal to which all work, all energies should be directed. This includes and involves every impulse, every labour of the Church. This is the sum of her self-offering to the Glory of the Father.

The Church looks very far forward and very far behind. Missions, which in all the pressure of their necessity are upon us now, are but one step. The consolidating and compacting of what has been long converted is a parallel, a continuous, a greater work. Missions have known long pauses in their progress—how long was that which followed the conversion of England—centuries in which unchristian races lay about Christendom and threatened its existence. If Missions are vital, the conservation of Christianity within our populations and the confederation of Christian populations are no less of a necessity for the Kingdom of God, and manifestly no less a difficulty.

It has been pretended that the development of the Anglican communion springs rather from the extension of our race than from the energy of our faith. It would indeed be difficult to outrun the race-wave which now sweeps all shores. Yet there are bounteous archipelagos, populous tropic wildernesses, primæval churches in peril among the heathen, where the English or American missioner's is the only household which belongs to our race. And were it otherwise, the mission spirit is at least now eminently characteristic of the blood. Southern Europe had been drawn out earlier, through its natural contact with the East, and the struggles at home kept our efforts low. With the Reformation came one touch to our national conscience. Our Elizabethan mariners dedicating continents to Christ, witness in some measure to a consciousness that Gospel and Church were gifts to be imparted. Yet it ought to sting us to think that it is but a century since England found in her heart to give her America a bishop; but a century since our convict ships landed their terrible freight in Australia, with no more spiritual comforters than the musketeers. Alas! it is not ninety years since we first began to repay the precious earthly things of either Africa or Asia with a share in our spiritual things. Would that it were more possible than it is to identify the extension of our race with that of our faith. Yet signs do still follow the footsteps of them that believe; and new churches are forming new nations even as we were formed. Higher ideas of the basis of society, of the marriage union, of family life, of self-restraint, of truthfulness, not only lift the individual but form the people. A recognised commercial morality, an even administration of justice, a conscience in dealing with subject races, public action on principles not merely selfish, the devotion of lives to benevolent causes, are things found under Christian Governments, and scarcely looked for elsewhere. Independent witnesses avow these to be direct results of Christian faith, and the growth of national character through these, far more than numbers of adherents, or prevalence of observances, assures us that the Church is still the nurse of nations.

We know the need of caution—how we may enervate native churches by nursing them too long or wreck them by launching them too soon; we know that diversity of development according to the genius of the races is essential to their vitality ; we know isolation may peril unity, and independence risk disintegration ; still we know how Church life fostered our own early nationality, how the recovery of a national Church awoke all the force and fire of our national spirit, and we long to see many dormant peoples born to the world, by being born to Christ.

Surely we draw near to the threshold of an era in which the fulfilment of such hopes will come. What the Roman vision saw as wild wastes round a few centres of light, are now old empires. Those empires are small regions compared with the wastes into which the overflowing peoples stream onward, miles in a day ; those overflowing peoples are few compared with the dark races which once were thought born for slavery either in their old homes or their new—few compared with the labour-populations that surge up on many shores, or even with the utterly new-born half-races owned and disowned both by East and West. Will not all these follow the old lines of history ? Will not these be empires to which what we have called colossal will be pigmy ? And the Church of Christ, if she has a mission to any, has a mission to all. What tremendous issues ! If she meets them, the Church history of the past is a mere preface to the volume.

Or think of the countries where Commerce, taking the field at once with capital and labour at command, founds harbours and marts great and fair as the old world's. Step by step with their creation, their redemption, we think, may keep pace. Where resources, where energies are practically unlimited the spirit, we think, will not fail. Nor does it. But side by side with all, arise the old world's problems in all their pain and perplexity. The old world's quarrels are perpetuated, when their origins, which gave them some sad dignity, are forgotten and grown meaningless. If spreading churches glory to be part and parcel with us, and we with them, we pray them at least to forget English divisions, and to be at such unity among themselves that rays from their circle may be focussed here.

Two such enterprises might seem vocation enough —to form peoples that are no peoples into the one people of God—and to weld into affectionate religion the new-born communities of commerce. But there is a third worthy to rank with the other two—namely, to win to the cross the fully-organised civilisations of remote antiquity which are saturated with religious feeling. Of those primæval religions the root conviction is one of three. Either self-sacrifice on the part of God is inconceivable; or the Incarnation of a God is in quest of a higher or lower pleasure; or else there is no personality in heaven or earth which is worth the keeping. Were it not worth all we are or have if we could contribute aught to dispel such dire glooms and substitute the certainties that there is no sacrifice which God has not made for man; that the Incarnation means an eternity of love for all humanity; that we shall for ever be ourselves, yet rising from glory to glory.

Within the bosom of Christendom itself lie problems no less strange. While distant difficulties call only for faithful activity on the part of our own churches, the nearest questions are the hardest, the nearest duties most dim and indistinct. There is the inevitable reformation—or inevitable decline in the faith—of some western populations. There is the revival of languid and oppressed churches in things that belong to divine knowledge, morals, spiritual diligence. Some churches are in danger of absorption; some have "fought" and "almost devoured one another;" some rival even Israel itself in dispersion and in tenacity; in some the clerical order includes the most enlightened and the rudest of the community; in some, a yearning to undeceive the people of gross superstitions is crushed by a forbidding fear of yielding up outworks which seem like a fence of Faith. Intrude we may not: yet we can still less refuse to touch such burdens with a finger, and look on prayerless and unsympathising.

The ages lengthen out apace. The work of Christ is not accomplished. The world judges by results. That matters not if it be the Master's will that His chariot drive heavily; that the salvation of the Gentiles linger, and the unity of man tarry. But do we think it is so? or are we conscious of causes purely human, of wills and factions that despise peace?

Yet the movement is onward though the pace is halting. Tremblingly yet rejoicingly we do believe that new charities blossom from our differences. The attitude of an opponent now is almost always an attitude of respect. The asperities of the present are almost milder than the forbearance of the past. Affection between advocates of mutually destructive views is no unreal or unwonted thing. If rougher tests of progress are of value, much more so is the prevalence of a spirit which makes characteristic diversities not merely tend towards truce, but lean longingly towards unity. For this, beyond question, is the working of the Spirit of Christ.

If we look back now for causes which have promoted this growing unity of spirit, we find it in the activity of those forces which rescue, which teach, which guide, which comfort, which raise, which feed, which warm. Whatever outside of Christianity does these works, does Christ's work.

The forces which are set forth in Christ's two Sacraments and in the two Apostolic rites of Confirmation and Ordination are these. They are the forces that cleanse, and bind together; that strengthen, and organize for growth. On the contrary the spirit of Regulation—the intrusive meddling spirit which travesties the spirit of Order—whether it exhibit itself in minute prescription or minute litigation—

the spirit (to speak plainly) of so many Councils since the earliest, has been often the apple of discord, and often the germ of schisms.

I. The energy which within the Church has in our times revived the courage and increased the activity of our peoples, which has added continents and islands to the conquests of the faith; the attraction which has held together many elements of division, and even welded them into strong instruments of work, has been found again and again to reside in those *Strong Centres* which Apostles designed for this very function of assigning work to all, and stimulating the zeal of all. Natural analogies are perhaps not mere resemblances, but the same laws of God. In our own national history at any rate, and in the history of the Churches, we find ourselves well warned to keep our Christian groupings wide enough, and our centres strong enough. Strong by position to traverse, to learn from, to influence each rank and class by turns; strong in councils of men, sufficiently versed in the world's thought and experience, habitually taught by devotional lives to refer daily questions to eternal principles; faithful to administer and to apply far reaching organizations for the benefit of the bodies and minds and spirits of men. Through this strong system, however short of its ideal, still an ideal influence has been exercised within Christian society, and by that society on all surrounding powers.

The very errors that have been made have tested it. When every petty city of Africa had its bishop and the doctrine of episcopacy was strongest, the effectiveness of the episcopate was lowest. A Cyprian had no difficulty in obtaining their unanimous vote, a vote contrary to Scripture principle, Church tradition, and the subsequent ruling of the Catholic word—a vote that heretical or schismatical baptism was void.

Vigour and character were not in hand for so many posts of leaders. Poly-episcopacy ceased to be episcopacy when the diocese became so small a unit. When every civil district in Phrygia and Galatia became a see, failing such an imperial will as Cyprian's to unite them, their controversies became, according to St. Paul's forecast, internecine. The like multiplication in Italy converted churches into cliques, and delivered Italy over to the one strong see, and Europe followed the leading country.

Half a century with us has seen seven colonial sees grow to seventy, and so vast still is their area, that another half-century will not be too long to work out the sub-division. Yet the old policy of England must be nowhere forgotten, that sub-division should cease before dioceses become too small for the influence of each to radiate through all, before the administration anywhere becomes so narrow as to represent only local patriotism.

II. Yet strong central forces are not all that is required to prevent a merely larger congregationalism from supplanting the catholic system. Much has been said, done, tested, which shows that these times demand supplementary organizations. We should lack either courage or intelligence if we did not admit it. The three-fold ministry is complete in itself for its own great ends. The seals of its origin are patent. But outside those ends are many functions to which it is not adapted. The long attempt to adapt it brings out the inadequacy. From the Apostolic text of the Epistles down to the last Parochial Report of any well worked district we see how much energy and blessing lives in other orders in the Church. There is a vast reservoir of devotion truly ministerial, which cannot possibly discharge itself through that triple channel. We have on a small scale the partial Dedication of lay-reading, school-teaching, visiting, " Church-work," as it is called, at large. Very precious are these. All of them practical uses of Spiritual Gifts. Nothing less. But it is confessed that the whole Anglican group is weak in the life of sisterhoods, and brotherhoods, and "armies," as, when well trained, they may be not unfitly called. The self-devotion of such auxiliaries, as they elsewhere exist, is not less, but more, absorbing than that of the ministry itself. One church there is which candour places beyond praise for the ceaseless multitudinous self-surrender of men to energetic life-work, without fee or reward, without property or domestic life. They multiply infinitely the effectiveness of the ministry. Say that that Church is careless of pure doctrine or ignorant of Scripture Truth; that makes the facts still more marked for us, if Truth suggests sacrifice for the Truth, or for the souls that want the Truth. Here with us they would be, not as of old foreign influences set against the organization of diocese and parish, but as already in these beginnings dependent on both, and part of both, and their main work the carrying of the Gospel into unreached places. What is the reason that they are missing? Have abuses created an eternal prejudice against the thing abused? Have we no confidence in our own safeguards? Have we cut down the oak to kill the ivy? Or are the centres we spoke of not now strong enough to take additional strain? Or is there force, but no material for it to lay hold upon?

Or may we think there is indeed a gradual deepening of spiritual yearnings, a gradual leavening of spiritual men into readiness to reply, "Here I am; send me," when the voice is heard from the throne, "Whom shall we send, and who will go for us?"

I incline from some signs, even from the safeguards themselves, to think this is the account of our position. There are flecks of glory along our horizon, and they surely are lights of dawn, not relics of sunset.

But the beginning must be in some real, definite spritual conquest. Let such a trained band complete the virtual Christianisation of a town or district here, or among our fellow-subjects in India, or work the conversion of such an untouched land as the Corea, and a new impulse would strike every home and foreign mission. Men would wonder then not at the smallness, but the largeness of what had been done hitherto with such slight forces. They would wonder still more that Church life had rolled on so many days without auxiliaries, almost without voluntary forces.

III. " Some spiritual conquest," I said. The word "spiritual" must be the keynote of all we do, say, think about the Church's daily new-born work. The spirit makes itself a body to dwell in. All needed material help would wait upon a spiritual outburst as ever of old.

"Ye are built up a spiritual house." Spiritual yet built. Built but remaining spiritual.

Prophets and Apostles foresaw all worldly material brought and built into it. Yet it was to remain spiritual. When it ceases to be so it is no more the building which will bear the Trial and the Fire.

We know well that spiritual life may be real without apostolic form. Only we seem to see that, even in its most beautiful and manifold manifestations, it cannot without that form propagate itself indefinitely. Time after time spiritual varieties surrender their separate life and merge into the completer existence.

On the other hand, we know well, that there may be apostolic form without spiritual life, and that like any other form that lacks life, its end is to break up and supply pabulum for lower forms of life.

Our own humble, hopeful confidence, lies in the possession of apostolic form with fervent spiritual charity and living faith. The form is secured. Our every-day vigilance must be for the spiritual animation, the spiritual "increase of every part in that which every joint supplieth."

An unworldly church, an unworldly clergy, means not a poor church or poverty-stricken clergy. A poor, unprovided, dependent clergy is scarcely able to be an unworldly one, and certainly cannot betoken an unworldly laity. A laity which breaks the bread of its ministers into smaller and smaller fragments, and has none of the divine will to multiply, works no miracle and has no honour.

Unworldliness is not emptiness of garners, but the right and noble use of garners filled by God. An unworldly clergy is not a clergy without a world, but one which knows the world, uses and teaches man how to use the world for God until it brings at last the whole world home to God.

Never more necessary than now to use the world as not abusing it. To abuse it gracefully is the temptation of the age—and to gild the abuse with philanthropy. The philanthropy of the Gospel without its philotheism is popular. But its philanthropy will never live without its philotheism, any more than the form of a church will live without the spirit.

To say "Christianity is not a Theology" is in one sense true, because Christianity is a Life. But it would be just as true to say Christianity is not a History, or Christianity is not a worship. But you cannot have the Life without the Worship, without the History, or without the Theology. The spiritual life is the Life of God. As material life has its science of Biology, so has spiritual life its science of Theology. Without Theology, Christian Life will have no intellectual, no spiritual expression, as without Worship it will have no emotional expression, without History no continuous development. Intellectual expression is necessary to the Propagation and so to the Permanence of the Faith. To know it is the profession of the clergyman, and the most living interest of the cultured layman.

Let us, the whole world over, where the common speech is spoken, the common prayer prayed, the

Scripture open, keep touch with each other, firm, inseparable—find all the points of contact that we can honestly with them that are in a way separate; yet not risk our greater unity for the sake of smaller ones.

To me it seems no fancy—it is none I trust to you —that the triple voice we have caught to-night is the very harmony that swells on our inner ear from roof and aisle and sanctuary. Here where the historic past "lives in the living present;" here, where greatest, best, and sweetest are honoured so in death that in a parable their shadow may fall on some of us; here, where in never pausing procession sweep onward Parliaments of Law, Councils of Faith, Divine Orators, princely marriages, funerals with sorrow of nations, commemorations, consecrations, coronations—the Jubilee with its beloved Queen, its lost Emperor; here, where Edward the Confessor bids Englishmen and English tribes never forget that the ideal State is the Church, and the ideal Church is the State, here, methinks, we well may lay to heart this threefold voice.

Strong central forces: how infinitely greater their operation and their impulse, than if distributed into the most symmetric minor nuclei. Their very power to attract, to move, to lift, to quicken, is their own concentredness.

Again. How we learn from this great Abbey the value of organizations that lie off the direct line of action. It is the grandest organic centre, yet it stands detached, favouring, labouring for every good cause, yet freely on its own account. Differing even in plan and structure radically from every sanctuary in the land, it is the symbol of all those forces which work not subordinated but in alliance. It confirms by separateness.

Once more. No soul was ever lowered by the sight of this wondrous fabric into material thoughts. No man ever failed to see, read, hear its witnesses to things spiritual. From mysterious triforium to roadside porch "the stone cries out of the wall, and the beam of the timber answers it; 'Put not your trust in man, nor in any child of man.' 'Come up here, and I will show thee things that must be hereafter.'"

And is not this the very auditory that is tuned to the key of this house of power and holiness. From zones which the Roman Seer declared could never help or heed each other come the chiefs of the Church to consult in one love for the welfare of all men,—how they may "make all men see" the intellectual, the spiritual light of the world, and the perfect law of liberty. Lightly borne across barriers which he said "No Name could ever overleap," they come with no strength no pretension of their own; but in the strength of One Name to which every knee shall bow, a strength perfected in our weakness.

May we catch the inspiration of the hour, the place, the Name. Then may we work out our work; strengthen our centres of force; throw out organisations which will penetrate society, poor and great; flood every corner of our house with spiritual light; have nothing cold and "no part dark,"—"the whole body full of light" and of warm blood. This is the very hope set before us, that we "may grow into Him in all things, which is the Head—even Christ."

No. XXIX. (See page 42.)

Sermon preached by Bishop Whipple, of Minnesota, in Lambeth Palace Chapel, on Tuesday, July 3, 1888.

MOST Reverend and Right Reverend Brethren,— No assembly is fraught with such awful responsibility to God as a council of the Bishops of His Church.

Since the Holy Spirit presided in the first council of Jerusalem, faithful souls have looked with deep interest to the deliberations of those whom Christ has made the shepherds of His flock, and to whom He gave His promise, "Lo, I am with you always to the end of the world." The responsibility is greater when division has marred the beauty of the Lamb's Bride. Our words and acts will surely hasten or (which God forbid) retard the reunion of Christendom. Feeling the grave responsibility which is imposed on me to-day, my heart cries out as did the prophet's, "I am a child and cannot speak." Pray for me, venerable brethren, that God may help me to obey His word—"Whatsoever I command, that shalt thou speak." I would kneel with you at our Master's feet and pray that "the Holy Spirit may guide us in all truth." We meet as the representatives of national Churches; each with its own peculiar responsibility to God for the souls intrusted to its care; each with all the rights of a national Church, to adapt itself to the varying conditions of human society; and each bound to preserve the order, the faith, the sacraments, and the worship of the Catholic Church, for which it is a trustee. As we kneel by the table of our common Lord we remember separated brothers. Division has multiplied division until infidelity sneers at Christianity as an effete superstition, and the modern Sadducee, more bold than his Jewish brother, denies the existence of God. Millions for whom Christ died have not so much as heard that there is a Saviour. It will heal no division to say, Who is at fault? The sin of schism does not lie at one door. If one has sinned by self-will, the other has sinned as deeply by lack of charity and love. The way to reunion looks difficult. To man it is impossible. No human eirenicon can bridge the gulf of separation. There are unkind words to be taken back, alienations to be healed, and heart-burnings to be forgiven. When we are blind,

God can make a way. When "the God of Peace" rules in all Christian hearts, our Lord's prayer will be answered—" That they all may be one, as Thou, Father, art in Me, and I in Thee that they all may be one in Us, that the world may believe that thou hast sent Me." No one branch of the Church is absolutely by itself alone the Catholic Church; all branches need reunion in order to the completeness of the Church. There are blessed signs that the Holy Spirit is quickening Christian hearts to seek for unity. We all know that this divided Christianity cannot conquer the world. At a time when every form of error and sin is banded together to oppose the kingdom of Christ, the world needs the witness of a united Church. Men must hear again the voice which peals through the lapse of centuries bearing witness to "the faith once delivered to the saints," or else for many souls there will be only rationalism and unbelief—while this sad, weary world, so full of sin and sorrow, is pleading for help, it is a wrong to Christ and to the souls for whom He died that His children should be separated in rival folds. As baptized into Christ we are brothers. Notwithstanding the hedges of human opinions which men have builded in the garden of the Lord, all who look for salvation alone through faith in Jesus Christ do hold the great verities of Divine faith. The opinions which separate us are not necessary to be believed in order to salvation. The truths in which we agree are parts of the Catholic faith. The Holy Spirit has passed over these human barriers, and set his seal to the labours of separated brethren in Christ, and rewarded them in the salvation of many precious souls. The grace of the Lord Jesus Christ and the renewing and sanctifying influences of the Holy Ghost are the same in the peasant in the cottage and in the emperor on the throne. They share with us in the long line of confessors and martyrs for Christ. We would not rob them of one sheaf which they have gathered in the garner of the Lord. We rejoice that Churches with a like historic lineage with us are seeking reunion, Churches whose faith has been dimmed by coldness or clouded by errors are being quickened into new life from the Incarnate Son of God.

Our hearts go out in loving sympathy to the Old Catholics of Europe and America, whose names always will be linked with Selwyn, Wilberforce, and Wordsworth, Whittingham, Kerfoot, and Brown, in defence of the faith. It is with deep sorrow that we remember that the Church of Rome has separated herself from the teaching of the primitive Church by additions to the faith once delivered to the saints, and by claiming for its Bishop prerogatives which belong only to the Divine Head of the Church. While we honour the devotion and zeal of her missionary heroes, and rejoice at the good work of multitudes of her children, we lament that lack of charity which anathematises disciples of Christ who have carried the Gospel to the ends of the earth.

We bless God's Holy Name for the fraternal work which has been carried on under the guidance of the see of Canterbury, and which we trust will lead ancient Churches to a deeper personal faith in Jesus Christ.

We are sad that some of our kinsmen in Christ, children of one mother, have forsaken her ways. God can over-rule even this sorrow, so that it shall fall out to the furtherance of the Gospel. They must take with them precious memories of the love and the faith of the mother whom they have forsaken, and of the liberty wherewith the truth in Christ has made her children free—under God these may be a link in the chain of His providence to the restoration of unity. It is a singular providence that at this period of the world's history, when marvellous discoveries have united the people of divers tongues in common interests, He has placed the

Anglo-Saxon race in the forefront of the nations. They are carrying civilisation to the ends of the earth. They are bringing liberty to the oppressed, elevating the down-trodden, and are giving to all these divers tongues and kindreds their customs, traditions, and laws. I reverently believe that the Anglo-Saxon Church has been preserved by God's Providence (if her children will accept this Mission) to heal the divisions of Christendom, and lead on in His work to be done in the eventide of the world. She holds the truths which underlie the possibility of re-union, the validity of all Christian baptism in the Name of the Father, the Son, and the Holy Ghost. She administers the two sacraments of Christ as of perpetual obligation, and makes faith in Jesus Christ, as contained in the Catholic Creed, a condition of Christian fellowship. The Anglo-Saxon Church does not perplex men with theories and shibboleths which many a poor Ephraimite cannot speak—she believes in God the Father Almighty, Maker of heaven and earth, and in Jesus Christ, His only Son, and in the Holy Ghost, three Persons and one God, but she does not weaken faith in the Triune God by human speculations about the Trinity in Unity. She believes that the sacred Scriptures were written by inspiration of God, but she has no theory about inspiration. She holds up the Atonement of Christ as the only hope of a lost world; but she has no philosophy about the Atonement. She teaches that it is through the Holy Ghost that men are united to Christ. She ministers the sacraments appointed by Christ as His channels of grace; but she has no theory to explain the manner of Christ's presence to penitent believing souls. She does not explain what God has not explained, but celebrates these Divine mysteries, as they were held and celebrated for one thousand years after our Lord ascended into heaven, before there was any East or West arrayed against each other in the Church of God. Surely we may and ought to be first to hold up the olive-branch of peace over strife, and say, "Sirs, ye are brethren."

In so grave a matter as the restoration of organic unity, we may not surrender anything which is of Divine authority, or accept terms of communion which are contrary to God's Word. We cannot recognise any usurpation of the rights and prerogatives of national Churches which have a common ancestry, lest we "heal the hurt of the daughter of my people slightly," and say " peace where there is no peace;" but we do say that all which is temporary and of human choice or preference we will forego from our love to our own kinsmen in Christ.

The Church of the Reconciliation will be an historical and Catholic Church in its ministry, its faith, and its sacraments. It will inherit the promises of its Divine Lord. It will preserve all which is Catholic and Divine. It will adopt and use all instrumentalities of any existing organisation which will aid it in doing the Lord's work. It will put away all which is individual, narrow, and sectarian. It will concede to all who hold the faith all the liberty wherewith Christ hath made His children free.

Missions.—In the presence of brethren who bear in their bodies the marks of the Lord Jesus, I hardly know how to clothe in words my thoughts as I speak of Missions. The providence of God has broken down impenetrable barriers—the doors of hermit nations have been opened; commerce has bound men in common interests, and so prepared "a highway for our God"—Japan, India, China, Africa, Polynesia, amid the solitudes of the icy north, and in the lands of tropic suns, world-wide there are signs of the coming of the kingdom of Jesus Christ. The veil which has so long blinded the eyes of the ancient people, our Lord's kinsmen according to the flesh, is being taken away. We bless God for the good example of martyrs like Patteson, Mackenzie, Parker, Hannington, and others, who have laid down their lives for the Lord Jesus. We rejoice that our branch of the Church has been counted worthy to add to the names of those who "came out of great tribulation, and have washed their robes and made them white in the blood of the Lamb." "A great and effectual door is opened." There is no country on the earth where we may not carry the Gospel. The wealth of the world is largely in Christian hands. The Church only needs faith to grasp the opportunity to do the work.

In the presence of fields so white for the harvest, we must ask, "Lord what wilt Thou have me to do?"

1. There must be unceasing, prevailing intercessory prayer for those whom we send out to heathen lands. The hearts of all Christian nations were turned with anxious solicitude to that brave servant of God and his country in Khartoum. Shall we feel less for the servants of Christ who have given up home and country to suffer and it may be to die for Him? Some of us remember that when Missions were destroyed, when clouds were all around us, and the very ground drifted from under our feet, that we were made brave to work and wait for the salvation of God by the prayers which went up to God for us. When "prayers were made without ceasing of the Church unto God," the fast-closed doors of the prison were opened for the Apostle. It will be so again.

2. There must be the entire consecration of all unto Christ. The wisdom of Paul and the eloquence of Apollos may plant, but "God alone giveth the increase." If success comes, if "the rod of the priesthood bud and blossom and bear fruit," it must be "laid up in the ark of God." He will not give His glory to another. The work is Christ's. "We are ambassadors for Him." "I have chosen you and ordained you that ye should go and bring forth fruit."

3. They who would win souls must have a ripe knowledge of the sacred Scriptures. "They were written by inspiration of God .... that the man of God may be perfect, thoroughly furnished unto all good works." Our orders may be unquestioned, our doctrine perfect in every line and feature, but we shall not reach the hearts of men unless we preach Christ out of an experimental knowledge of the truths of Divine Revelation. There is but one Book which can bring light to homes of sorrow, one light to scatter clouds and darkness, one message to lead wandering folk unto God. This blessed Book will be to every weary soldier and lonely missionary what it was to Livingstone dying alone in Africa, or to Captain Gardiner dead on the desolate shores of Patagonia, whose finger pointed to the words, "The blood of Jesus Christ cleanseth from all sin."

4. We must love all whom Christ loves. We may have the gift of teaching, we may understand all mysteries, we may have all knowledge, we may bestow all our goods to the poor, we may even give our bodies to be burned, but without that love which comes alone from Christ, we shall be "as sounding brass and a tinkling cymbal." With St. Paul we must say, "Whereinsoever Christ is preached I do rejoice, and will rejoice."

5. Above all gifts we need the baptism of the Holy Ghost. When *this* consecration comes there will be no cry of an empty treasury. We shall no longer be weary with the bleating of lost sheep, to whom we have to say, I have no means and no shepherd to send you.

Christian Work.—We rejoice at every sign that Christians realise that wealth is a sacred trust, for which they shall give an account. We rejoice more that they are giving that personal service which is a law of His Kingdom. Men and women of culture and gentle birth are going into the abodes of sickness and sorrow to comfort stricken homes and lead sinful folk to the Saviour. Brotherhoods, sisterhoods, and deaconesses are multiplying. Never was there greater need for their holy work. Many of our own baptized children have drifted away from all faith. To thousands God is a name, the Bible a tradition, faith an opinion, and heaven and hell fables. But that which gives us the deepest sadness and makes all Christian work more difficult is that so many of those to whom the people look for example have given up the Bible, the Lord's Day, the house of God, and Christian faith. Alas! they are telling these weary toilers whose lives are clouded by anxiety and sorrow that there is no hereafter. "They know not what they do." They are sowing to the wind and will reap the whirlwind. May God show them the danger before it is too late. The loss of faith is the loss of everything; without it morality becomes prudence or imprudence. When the tie which bends man to God is broken all other ties snap asunder. No nation has survived the loss of its religion. We are appalled at the mad cry of anarchy which tramples all which we hold dear for time and eternity under its feet. We cannot look into its face without seeing the lineaments of that man of sin who "opposeth and exalteth himself above all that is called God and worshipped." Antichrist is he who usurps the place of Christ. "He is antichrist who denieth the Father and the Son." Our hearts go out in pity for those whose mechanical ideas of the universe may be a revolt from a mechanical theology which has lost sight of the Fatherhood of God. We stand where two ways meet. We shall take care of the people or the people will take care of us. The people are the rulers; the power of the future is in their hands. Limit their horizon to this life, let penury, sickness, and sorrow change the man to a wolf, let him know no God and Father Who hears his cry, no Saviour to help, no brother to bind up his wounds, let there be on the one side wealth and luxury and wanton waste, and on the other side poverty, misery, and despair—there will be, as there has been, a cry for blood. We wonder why men pass by the Church to found clubs and brotherhoods and orders. They will have them, and they ought to have them, until the Church is in its Divine love what its Founder designed it to be—the brotherhood in Christ of the children of our God and Father. What the world needs to-day is not alms, not hospitals, not homes of mercy alone. It needs the spirit and the power of the love of Christ. It needs the voice, the ear, the hand, and the heart of Christ seen in and working in His children. No powers of government, no *prestige* of social position, no prerogatives of Churchly authority can meet the issues of this hour; we have waited already too long. Brotherhood men will have, and it will be the brotherhood of the commune, or brotherhood in Christ as the children of our God and Father. Infidelity answers no questions, heals no wounds, fulfils no hopes. The Gospel will do, is doing, to-day what it has done through all the ages, leading men out of sin and darkness and despair to the liberty of sons of God.

In a day of division and unrest there will be many questions which perplex earnest souls. Some will dwell on the subjective side of the faith, others will think most of its manifestations in the life. These questions will affect organisation for Christian work, public worship, and find expression in the ritual of the Church. There is no room for differences if Christ be first, Christ be last, and Christ in everything. The ritual of the Church must be the expression of her life. It must symbolise her faith; it must be subject to her authority. As the years go by worship will be more beautiful. The "garments of the king's daughter may be of wrought gold," and she "clothed in raiment of needlework," but "she will have a name that she liveth and is dead," unless her "fine linen is the righteousness of the saints." Lastly, to none is this council so dear as to those whose lives are spent in the darkness of heathenism, or who have gone out to new lands to lay foundations for the work of the Church of God. In loneliness, with deferred hopes, neglected by brethren, your only refuge to cry as a child to God, it is a joy for you to feel the beating of a brother's heart, and hear the music of a brother's voice, and kneel with brothers at the dear old trysting-place, the table of our Lord. Let us consecrate all we have and are to Him, let us remember loved ones far away, let us gather all the work we have so long garnered in our hearts and lay it at His feet. We shall not have met in vain if out of the love learned of Him we give each to other, and to all fellow-labourers for Him, a brother's love, a brother's sympathy, and a brother's prayers. I do not know how to clothe in words the thronging memories which cluster around us in this holy place, what searchings of heart, what cries to God, what communions with Christ, what consolations of the Holy Spirit have been witnessed in this sacred place. I cannot call over the long roll of saints, confessors, and martyrs, whose "names are written in the Lamb's Book of Life." Two names will be remembered to-day by us all. One, that gentle Archbishop Longley, who in the greatness of his love saw with a prophet's eye the Mission of the Church, and planned these conferences that our hearts might beat as one in the battle of the last time. The other, the wisest of counsellors and the most loving of brethren, the great-hearted Archbishop Tait, whose dying legacy to his brethren was "love one another." They have finished their course and entered into rest. A little more work, a few more trials, and we, too, shall finish our course. We are not two companies, the militant and triumphant are one. We are the advance and rear of one host travelling to the Canaan of God's rest. God grant that we, too, may so follow Christ that we may have an abundant entrance to His eternal kingdom.

No. XXX. (See page 45.)

Address to the Queen. Signed by the Bishops present at the Third Lambeth Conference, July, 1888.

May it please Your Majesty,

We, Archbishops and Bishops, gathered together at Lambeth from every part of Your Majesty's Dominions, from the United States of America, and from Mission Fields in all quarters of the World, desire respectfully to convey to Your Majesty an assurance of the earnest prayer which we offer to Almighty God, through our Lord and Saviour Jesus Christ, that health, peace, and prosperity may rest upon Your Majesty, and upon every Member of Your Royal House.

Met as we are, in the Providence of God, to consider how we may best promote among men an increase of the Christian Faith, of brotherly kindness, of honesty and pureness of life, and of reverence for all that is good, we would express to Your Majesty our grateful sense of the debt which we owe to the beneficent influence of Your Majesty's Court and Home during the fifty years of a great and glorious reign.

In thanking God for the rapid and continuous extension of the Anglican Church in Your Majesty's

Kingdom and Empire, and in the vast Continent of America, we cannot forget the constant evidence which has been given of Your Majesty's earnest sympathy with all efforts to promote whatsoever things are true and pure and of good report, or tend to advance among the nations of the earth the Kingdom of our Lord and Saviour Jesus Christ.

We are well assured that Your Majesty unites with us in thanksgivings to Almighty God for the progress already vouchsafed to His Church on earth, and in continued prayer for the Divine blessing.

Edw. Cantuar.
W. Ebor.
R. Armagh.
Plunket Dublin.
F. Londin.
J. Fredericton.
Edward R. Calcutta.
R. Rupertsland.
W. P. Guiana.
W. W. Capetown.
Alfred Sydney.
J. B. Dunelm.
J. Hereford.
H. A. Neely (Maine).
H. Carlisle.
C. P. Meath.
Jno. Moosonee.
William Stevens Perry, Bishop of Iowa.
E. H. Winton.
W. Basil St. Davids.
Allan B. Grahamstown.
George H. North Queensland.
J. M. Rangoon.
R. Llandaff.
W. C. Peterborough.
G. Columbia.
Maurice S. Huron.
John Mitchinson, Bp.
William Derry & Raphoe.
Chas. M. Clogher.
H. B. Whipple, Bishop of Minnesota.
L. G. Bombay.
R. S. Colombo.
E. Dover.
C. J. Gloucester and Bristol.
E. Lincoln.
J. M. Trav. and Cochin.
Wm. B. Killaloe.
A. Colchester.
John Sarum.
J. J. Penrith.
Alfred Marlborough.
Alwyne Ely.
E. G. Sierra Leone.
Robert S. Cork.
Samuel Kilmore.
G. F. Popham Blyth, Bishop in Jerusalem and the East.
Cyprian Saskatchewan and Calgary.
J. C. Bangor.
E. Jamaica.
Andrew Burn Nelson, N.Z.
E. H. Exon.

F. Nova Scotia.
Edw. Bickersteth, Bishop in Japan.
Charles P. Scott, Bishop in North China.
C. W. Gibraltar.
J. Manchester.
W. T. T. Brisbane.
Edward C. Waiapu.
W. D. Lichfield.
C. J. Branch, Bishop Coadj. Antigua.
W. Kenneth Maritzburg.
William Hobart Hare, Bishop of S. Dakota.
H. Barbados.
S. T. Dunedin.
W. W. Antigua.
G. W. Adelaide.
Cortlandt Whitehead, Pittsburgh.
O. W. Whitaker, Bishop of Pennsylvania.
T. B. Lyman, Bishop of N. Carolina.
B. Wistar Morris, Bishop of Oregon.
W. E. McLaren, Bishop of Chicago.
John T. Spalding, Bishop of Colorado.
John Scarborough, Bishop of New Jersey.
W. G. Rulison, Assistant Bishop, Central Pennsylvania.
S. A. Crowther, Bishop of Niger Territory.
Benj. H. Paddock, Bishop of Massachusetts.
Alexander Burgess, Bishop of Quincy.
C. A. Smythies, Bishop of the Universities' Mission to Central Africa.
A. G. Aberdeen and Orkney.
Alex. Bishop of Argyll and the Isles.
J. Edenburgen.

John A. Paddock, Bishop of Washington Territory.
Charles Perry (Bishop).
A. W. Roffen.
Hugh W. Brechin, Primus.
Bishop Coad. of London, for N. and C. Europe.
W. Cestr.
C. H. Bromby, Bishop.
Maurice N. Cashel.
F. Cramer Roberts, Assistant Bishop of Manchester.
F. H. Leicester.
D. B. Knickerbacker, Bishop of Indiana, U.S.A.
H. B. Pretoria.
E. Algoma.
James, Bishop of Moray and Ross.
E. R. Newcastle.
Charles Niagara.
H. Tully, Coadjutor of Fredericton.
Charles Limerick.
Arthur Toronto.
Arthur C. Bath and Wells.
Wm. D. Walker, Bishop of North Dakota.
J. W. Quebec.
R. Cicestr.
George F. Seymour, Bishop of Springfield, U.S.A.
Waite H. Falkland Islands.
William Garden, Bishop of Auckland, N.Z.
G. M. Singapore & Sarawak.
Thomas A. Starkey, Bishop of Newark.
E. R. Tufnell, Bishop.
George H. Truron.
George Southwell.
Adelbert, Bishop of Qu'Appelle.
Wm. Croswell Doane, Bishop of Albany.
H. C. Potter, Bishop of New York.
R. C. Bedford.

Bransby, Bishop of S. John, Kaff.
Wm. Walsham Wakefield.
R. Caledonia.
A. W. New Westminster.
Hugh Miller Thompson, Bishop of Mississippi.
Alfred Honolulu.
William Paret, Bishop of Maryland.

Douglas, Bishop for Zululand.
Dan. J. Tuttle, Bishop of Missouri.
Llewellyn Newfoundland.
W. B. Ripon.
William P. Ossory.
J. T. Ontario.
J. St. Asaph.
Hy. N. Pierce, Arkansas.
E. Nottingham.

27th July, 1888.

The following is Her Majesty's answer to the above Address, forwarded by the Secretary of State to his Grace the Archbishop of Canterbury, " for communication to the Most Reverend and right Reverend Prelates who signed the address:"—

" I have received with much gratification the address of the recent meeting held at Lambeth, of Archbishops and Bishops of the Church of England, and of Churches in communion therewith in various parts of my dominions, in the United States of America, and in other foreign countries, on the subject of the continuous extension of such Churches throughout the course of my reign.

" I thank you heartily for your expressions of good will towards my Throne and person.

"You may be assured that it will ever be my anxious desire to promote all measures which may tend to maintain and extend the spirit of true religion, and I earnestly pray that Almighty God may bless your labours for an increase of Christian faith and of the virtues which it inspires in all quarters of the world.

"VICTORIA, R.I."

No. XXXI.

LIST OF THE BISHOPS ATTENDING THE LAMBETH CONFERENCE OF 1888.

[With the exception of Metropolitans and others entitled to special precedence, the Bishops are arranged, in the following list, according to the date of their consecration.]

ARCHBISHOP OF CANTERBURY	25th April, 1877.
ARCHBISHOP OF YORK	15th December, 1861.
ARCHBISHOP OF ARMAGH	1st May, 1849.
ARCHBISHOP OF DUBLIN	10th December, 1876.
BISHOP OF GUIANA	24th August, 1842.
BISHOP OF FREDERICTON	4th May, 1845.
BISHOP OF RUPERTSLAND	24th June, 1865.
BISHOP OF BRECHIN	28th October, 1871.
BISHOP OF CAPETOWN	17th May, 1874.
BISHOP OF CALCUTTA	30th November, 1876.
BISHOP OF SYDNEY	1st January, 1884.
BISHOP OF LONDON	21st December, 1869.
BISHOP OF DURHAM	25th April, 1879.
BISHOP OF WINCHESTER	29th March, 1864.
BISHOP PERRY	29th June, 1847.
BISHOP OF ST. ANDREW'S	25th January, 1853.
BISHOP OF NORWICH	11th June, 1857.
BISHOP OF COLUMBIA	24th February, 1859.
BISHOP OF BANGOR	14th June, 1859.
BISHOP TUFNELL	14th June, 1859.
BISHOP OF MINNESOTA	13th October, 1859.
BISHOP OF ANTIGUA	17th May, 1860.
BISHOP OF ONTARIO	25th March, 1862.
BISHOP OF GLOUCESTER AND BRISTOL	25th March, 1863.
BISHOP OF QUEBEC	21st June, 1863.
BISHOP IN THE NIGER TERRITORY	29th June, 1864.
BISHOP BROMBY	29th June, 1864.

List of Bishops attending the Conference.

BISHOP OF WESTERN NEW YORK	4th January, 1865.
BISHOP OF TENNESSEE	11th October, 1865.
BISHOP OF LIMERICK	29th June, 1866.
BISHOP OF NELSON	24th August, 1866.
BISHOP OF MAINE	25th January, 1867.
BISHOP OF MISSOURI	1st May, 1867.
BISHOP OF ST. ALBANS	11th June, 1867.
BISHOP OF MORAY AND ROSS	24th August, 1867.
BISHOP OF DERRY	13th October, 1867.
BISHOP OF HEREFORD	24th June, 1868.
BISHOP OF PETERBOROUGH	15th November, 1868.
BISHOP OF OREGON	3rd December, 1868.
BISHOP OF MARITZBURG	25th January, 1869.
BISHOP OF ALBANY	2nd February, 1869.
BISHOP OF AUCKLAND	29th June, 1869.
BISHOP OF PENNSYLVANIA	13th October, 1869.
BISHOP OF CARLISLE	30th November, 1869.
BISHOP OF BATH AND WELLS	21st December, 1869.
BISHOP OF FALKLAND ISLANDS	21st December, 1869.
BISHOP OF ARKANSAS	25th January, 1870.
BISHOP OF DOVER	25th March, 1870.
BISHOP OF CHICHESTER	8th May, 1870.
BISHOP OF ST. ASAPH	8th May, 1870.
BISHOP WILKINSON	8th May, 1870.
BISHOP OF GRAHAMSTOWN	30th November, 1870.
BISHOP OF DUNEDIN	4th June, 1871.
BISHOP OF HONOLULU	2nd February, 1872.
BISHOP OF CASHEL	13th April, 1872.
BISHOP OF TRINIDAD	29th June, 1872.
BISHOP OF MOOSONEE	15th December, 1872.
BISHOP OF SOUTH DAKOTA	9th January, 1873.
BISHOP MITCHINSON	24th June, 1873.
BISHOP OF MASSACHUSETTS	17th September, 1873.
BISHOP OF NORTH CAROLINA	11th December, 1873.
BISHOP OF COLORADO	31st December, 1873.
BISHOP OF GIBRALTAR	1st February, 1874.
BISHOP OF ST. DAVID'S	24th August, 1874.
BISHOP OF MILWAUKEE	25th October, 1874.
BISHOP OF NEW JERSEY	2nd February, 1875.
BISHOP OF CORK	30th March, 1875
BISHOP OF CHICAGO	8th December, 1875.
BISHOP OF COLOMBO	28th December, 1875.
BISHOP OF BOMBAY	1st May, 1876.
BISHOP OF IOWA	10th September, 1876.
BISHOP OF MANCHESTER	22nd October, 1876.
BISHOP OF ROCHESTER	25th June, 1877.
BISHOP OF NOTTINGHAM	21st December, 1877.
BISHOP OF WAIAPU	1st January, 1878.
BISHOP OF PRETORIA	2nd February, 1878.
BISHOP OF NEWFOUNDLAND	1st May, 1878.
BISHOP OF QUINCY	15th May, 1878.
BISHOP OF SPRINGFIELD	11th June, 1878.

BISHOP OF LICHFIELD	24th June, 1878.
BISHOP CRAMER-ROBERTS	24th June, 1878.
BISHOP OF NORTH QUEENSLAND	24th June, 1878.
BISHOP OF OSSORY	29th September, 1878.
BISHOP OF TORONTO	1st May, 1879.
BISHOP OF WAKEFIELD	25th July, 1879.
BISHOP OF TRAVANCORE AND COCHIN	25th July, 1879.
BISHOP OF CALEDONIA	25th July, 1879.
BISHOP OF MICHIGAN	17th September, 1879.
BISHOP OF NEW WESTMINSTER	1st November, 1879.
BISHOP OF NEWARK	8th January, 1880.
BISHOP OF LIVERPOOL	11th June, 1880.
BISHOP OF JAMAICA	28th October, 1880.
BISHOP IN NORTH CHINA	28th October, 1880.
BISHOP IN ZULULAND	30th November, 1880.
BISHOP OF WASHINGTON TERRITORY	15th December, 1880.
BISHOP OF SINGAPORE AND SARAWAK	26th May, 1881.
BISHOP COADJUTOR OF FREDERICTON	10th July, 1881.
BISHOP OF PITTSBURGH	25th January, 1882.
BISHOP OF RANGOON	1st May, 1882.
BISHOP OF BARBADOS	1st May, 1882.
BISHOP OF COLCHESTER	24th June, 1882.
BISHOP OF ALGOMA	29th June, 1882.
BISHOP OF NEWCASTLE	25th July, 1882.
BISHOP COADJUTOR OF ANTIGUA	27th July, 1882.
BISHOP OF ADELAIDE	30th November, 1882.
BISHOP OF MISSISSIPPI	24th February, 1883.
BISHOP OF SIERRA LEONE	24th February, 1883.
BISHOP OF LLANDAFF	25th April, 1883.
BISHOP OF TRURO	25th April, 1883.
BISHOP OF ABERDEEN	1st May, 1883.
BISHOP OF ST. JOHN'S, KAFFRARIA	12th August, 1883.
BISHOP OF ARGYLL AND THE ISLES	24th August, 1883.
BISHOP OF INDIANA	14th October, 1883.
BISHOP OF NEW YORK	20th October, 1883
BISHOP IN CENTRAL AFRICA	30th November, 1883.
BISHOP OF HURON	30th November, 1883.
BISHOP OF NORTH DAKOTA	20th December, 1883.
BISHOP OF KILLALOE	24th February, 1884.
BISHOP OF KILMORE	25th April, 1884.
BISHOP OF CHESTER	25th April, 1884.
BISHOP OF SOUTHWELL	1st May, 1884.
BISHOP OF QU'APPELLE	24th June, 1884.
BISHOP OF RIPON	25th July, 1884.
ASST.-BISHOP OF CENTRAL PENNSYLVANIA	28th October, 1884.
BISHOP OF MARYLAND	8th January, 1885.
BISHOP OF LINCOLN	25th April, 1885.
BISHOP OF EXETER	25th April, 1885.
BISHOP OF NIAGARA	1st May, 1885.
BISHOP OF BRISBANE	11th June, 1885.
BISHOP OF MEATH	29th September, 1885.
BISHOP OF SALISBURY	28th October, 1885.

List of Bishops attending the Conference.

BISHOP OF ELY	2nd February, 1886.
BISHOP IN JAPAN	2nd February, 1886.
BISHOP OF NASSAU	24th February, 1886.
BISHOP OF CLOGHER	29th June, 1886.
BISHOP OF EDINBURGH	21st September, 1886.
BISHOP IN JERUSALEM AND THE EAST	23th March, 1887.
BISHOP OF SASKATCHEWAN AND CALGARY	7th August, 1887.
BISHOP OF SODOR AND MAN	24th August, 1887.
BISHOP OF MARLBOROUGH	24th February, 1888.
BISHOP OF SHREWSBURY	24th February, 1888.
BISHOP OF NOVA SCOTIA	25th April, 1888.
BISHOP OF PENRITH	22nd May, 1888.
BISHOP OF BEDFORD	15th July, 1888.
BISHOP OF LEICESTER	15th July, 1888.

No. XXXII.

LIST OF THE BISHOPS ATTENDING THE LAMBETH CONFERENCE OF 1888, ARRANGED ACCORDING TO PROVINCES.

ARCHBISHOP OF CANTERBURY (MOST REV. DR. BENSON).
BISHOP OF LONDON (RT. REV. DR. TEMPLE).
BISHOP OF WINCHESTER (RT. REV. DR. HAROLD BROWNE).
BISHOP OF NORWICH (RT. REV. AND HON. DR. PELHAM).
BISHOP OF BANGOR (RT. REV. DR. CAMPBELL).
BISHOP OF GLOUCESTER AND BRISTOL (RT. REV. DR. ELLICOTT).
BISHOP OF ST. ALBANS (RT. REV. DR. CLAUGHTON).
BISHOP OF HEREFORD (RT. REV. DR. ATLAY).
BISHOP OF PETERBOROUGH (RT. REV. DR. MAGEE).
BISHOP OF BATH AND WELLS (RT. REV. LORD A. HERVEY).
BISHOP OF CHICHESTER (RT. REV. DR. DURNFORD).
BISHOP OF ST. ASAPH (RT. REV. DR. HUGHES).
BISHOP OF ST. DAVIDS (RT. REV. DR. BASIL JONES).
BISHOP OF ROCHESTER (RT. REV. DR. THOROLD).
BISHOP OF LICHFIELD (RT. REV. DR. MACLAGAN).
BISHOP OF LLANDAFF (RT. REV. DR. LEWIS).
BISHOP OF TRURO (RT. REV. DR. WILKINSON).
BISHOP OF SOUTHWELL (RT. REV. DR. RIDDING).
BISHOP OF LINCOLN (RT. REV. DR. KING).
BISHOP OF EXETER (RT. REV. DR. E. H. BICKERSTETH).
BISHOP OF SALISBURY (RT. REV. DR. J. WORDSWORTH).
BISHOP OF ELY (RT. REV. LORD A. COMPTON).
BISHOP SUFFRAGAN OF DOVER (RT. REV. DR. PARRY).
BISHOP SUFFRAGAN OF NOTTINGHAM (RT. REV. DR. TROLLOPE).
BISHOP SUFFRAGAN OF COLCHESTER (RT. REV. DR. BLOMFIELD).
BISHOP SUFFRAGAN OF MARLBOROUGH (RT. REV. DR. EARLE).
BISHOP SUFFRAGAN OF SHREWSBURY (RT. REV. SIR L. STAMER)
BISHOP SUFFRAGAN OF BEDFORD (RT. REV. DR. BILLING).
BISHOP SUFFRAGAN OF LEICESTER (RT. REV. DR. THICKNESSE)
BISHOP PERRY.
BISHOP TUFNELL.
BISHOP BROMBY.
BISHOP WILKINSON.
BISHOP MITCHINSON.

ARCHBISHOP OF YORK (MOST REV. DR. THOMSON).
BISHOP OF DURHAM (RT. REV. DR. LIGHTFOOT).

List of Bishops attending the Conference.

BISHOP OF CARLISLE (RT. REV. DR. GOODWIN).
BISHOP OF MANCHESTER (RT. REV. DR. MOORHOUSE).
BISHOP OF WAKEFIELD (RT. REV. DR. WALSHAM HOW).
BISHOP OF LIVERPOOL (RT. REV. DR. RYLE).
BISHOP OF NEWCASTLE (RT. REV. DR. WILBERFORCE).
BISHOP OF CHESTER (RT. REV. DR. STUBBS).
BISHOP OF RIPON (RT. REV. DR. BOYD CARPENTER).
BISHOP OF SODOR AND MAN (RT. REV. DR. BARDSLEY).
BISHOP SUFFRAGAN OF PENRITH (RT. REV. DR. PULLEINE).
BISHOP CRAMER-ROBERTS.

ARCHBISHOP OF ARMAGH (MOST REV. DR. KNOX).
BISHOP OF MEATH (MOST REV. DR. REICHEL).

BISHOP OF DERRY (RT. REV. DR. ALEXANDER).
BISHOP OF KILMORE (RT. REV. DR. SHONE).
BISHOP OF CLOGHER (RT. REV. DR. STACK).

ARCHBISHOP OF DUBLIN (MOST REV. LORD PLUNKET).
BISHOP OF LIMERICK (RT. REV. DR. GRAVES).
BISHOP OF CASHEL (RT. REV. DR. DAY).
BISHOP OF CORK (RT. REV. DR. GREGG).
BISHOP OF OSSORY (RT. REV. DR. WALSH).
BISHOP OF KILLALOE (RT. REV. DR. CHESTER).

BISHOP OF BRECHIN (RT. REV. DR. JERMYN), *Primus*.
BISHOP OF ST. ANDREW'S (RT. REV. DR. C. WORDSWORTH).
BISHOP OF MORAY AND ROSS (RT. REV. DR. KELLY).
BISHOP OF ABERDEEN (RT. REV. AND HON. DR. DOUGLAS).
BISHOP OF ARGYLL AND THE ISLES (RT. REV. DR. HALDANE).
BISHOP OF EDINBURGH (RT. REV. DR. DOWDEN).

BISHOP OF MINNESOTA (RT. REV. DR. WHIPPLE).
BISHOP OF WESTERN NEW YORK (RT. REV. DR. COXE).
BISHOP OF TENNESSEE (RT. REV. DR. QUINTARD).
BISHOP OF MAINE (RT. REV. DR. NEELY).
BISHOP OF MISSOURIE (RT. REV. DR. TUTTLE).
BISHOP OF OREGON (RT. REV. DR. MORRIS).
BISHOP OF ALBANY (RT. REV. DR. DOANE).
BISHOP OF PENNSYLVANIA (RT. REV. DR. WHITAKER).
BISHOP OF ARKANSAS (RT. REV. DR. PIERCE).
BISHOP OF SOUTH DAKOTA (RT. REV. DR. HARE).
BISHOP OF MASSACHUSETTS (RT. REV. DR. PADDOCK).
BISHOP OF NORTH CAROLINA (RT. REV. DR. LYMAN).
BISHOP OF COLORADO (RT. REV. DR. SPALDING).
BISHOP OF MILWAUKEE (RT. REV. DR. WELLES).
BISHOP OF NEW JERSEY (RT. REV. DR. SCARBOROUGH).
BISHOP OF CHICAGO (RT REV. DR. MCLAREN).

BISHOP OF IOWA (RT. REV. DR. STEVENS-PARRY).
BISHOP OF QUINCY (RT. REV. DR. BURGESS).
BISHOP OF SPRINGFIELD (RT. REV. DR. SEYMOUR).
BISHOP OF MICHIGAN (RT. REV. DR. HARRIS).
BISHOP OF NEWARK (RT. REV. DR. STARKEY).
BISHOP OF WASHINGTON TERRITORY (RT. REV. DR. PADDOCK).
BISHOP OF PITTSBURGH (RT. REV. DR. WHITEHEAD).
BISHOP OF MISSISSIPPI (RT. REV. DR. THOMPSON).
BISHOP OF INDIANA (RT. REV. DR KNICKERBACKER).
BISHOP OF NEW YORK (RT. REV. DR. POTTER).
BISHOP OF NORTH DAKOTA (RT. REV. DR. WALKER).
ASST.-BISHOP OF CENTRAL PENNSYLVANIA (RT. REV. DR. RULISON).
BISHOP OF MARYLAND (RT. REV. DR. PARET).

BISHOP OF FREDERICTON (RT. REV. DR. MEDLEY), *Metropolitan*.
BISHOP OF ONTARIO (RT. REV. DR. LEWIS).
BISHOP OF QUEBEC (RT. REV. DR. WILLIAMS).
BISHOP OF TORONTO (RT. REV. DR. SWEATMAN).
BISHOP OF ALGOMA (RT. REV. DR. SULLIVAN).
BISHOP OF HURON (RT. REV. DR. BALDWIN).
BISHOP OF NIAGARA (RT. REV. DR. HAMILTON).
BISHOP OF NOVA SCOTIA (RT. REV. DR. COURTNEY).
BISHOP COADJUTOR OF FREDERICTON (RT. REV. DR. KINGDON).

BISHOP OF CALCUTTA (RT. REV. DR. JOHNSON), *Metropolitan*).
BISHOP OF COLOMBO (RT. REV. DR. COPLESTON).
BISHOP OF BOMBAY (RT. REV. DR. MYLNE).
BISHOP OF TRAVANCORE & COCHIN (RT. REV. DR. SPEECHLEY).
BISHOP OF RANGOON (RT. REV. DR. STRACHAN).

BISHOP OF GUIANA (RT. REV. DR. AUSTIN), *Metropolitan*.
BISHOP OF ANTIGUA (RT. REV. DR. JACKSON).
BISHOP OF TRINIDAD (RT. REV. DR. RAWLE).
BISHOP OF JAMAICA (RT. REV. DR. NUTTALL).
BISHOP OF BARBADOS (RT. REV. DR. BREE).
BISHOP OF NASSAU (RT. REV. DR. CHURTON).
BISHOP COADJUTOR OF ANTIGUA (RT. REV. DR. BRANCH).

BISHOP OF SYDNEY (RT. REV. DR. BARRY), *Metropolitan*.
BISHOP OF NORTH QUEENSLAND (RT. REV. DR. STANTON).
BISHOP OF ADELAIDE (RT. REV. DR. KENNION).
BISHOP OF BRISBANE (RT. REV. DR. WEBBER).

BISHOP OF NELSON (RT. REV. DR. SUTER).
BISHOP OF AUCKLAND (RT. REV. DR. COWIE).
BISHOP OF DUNEDIN (RT. REV. DR. NEVILLE)
BISHOP OF WAIAPU (RT. REV. DR. STUART).

List of Bishops attending the Conference.

BISHOP OF CAPETOWN (RT. REV. DR. W. W. JONES), *Metropolitan*.
BISHOP OF MARITZBURG (RT. REV. DR. MACRORIE).
BISHOP OF GRAHAMSTOWN (RT. REV. DR. WEBB).
BISHOP OF PRETORIA (RT. REV. DR. BOUSFIELD).
BISHOP OF ZULULAND (RT. REV. DR. MACKENZIE).
BISHOP OF ST. JOHN'S, KAFFRARIA (RT. REV. DR. KEY).

BISHOP OF RUPERTSLAND (RT. REV. DR. MACHRAY), *Metropolitan*.
BISHOP OF MOOSONEE (RT. REV. DR. HORDEN).
BISHOP OF QU'APPELLE (RT. REV. AND HON. DR. ANSON).
BISHOP OF SASKATCHEWAN & CALGARY (RT. REV. DR. PINKHAM).

BISHOP OF COLUMBIA (RT. REV. DR. HILLS).
MISSIONARY BISHOP IN THE NIGER TERRITORY (RT. REV. DR. CROWTHER).
BISHOP OF THE FALKLAND ISLANDS (RT. REV. DR. STIRLING).
BISHOP OF HONOLULU (RT. REV. DR WILLIS).
BISHOP OF GIBRALTAR (RT. REV. DR. SANDFORD).
BISHOP OF NEWFOUNDLAND (RT. REV. DR. LLEWELLYN JONES).
BISHOP OF CALEDONIA (RT. REV. DR. RIDLEY).
BISHOP OF NEW WESTMINSTER (RT. REV. DR. SILLITOE).
MISSIONARY BISHOP IN NORTH CHINA (RT. REV. DR. SCOTT).
BISHOP OF SINGAPORE AND SARAWAK (RT. REV. DR. HOSE).
BISHOP OF SIERRA LEONE (RT. REV. DR. INGHAM).
MISSIONARY BISHOP IN CENTRAL AFRICA (RT. REV. DR. SMYTHIES).
MISSIONARY BISHOP IN JAPAN (RT. REV. DR. E. BICKERSTETH).
BISHOP OF THE CHURCH OF ENGLAND IN JERUSALEM AND THE EAST (RT. REV. DR. BLYTH).

Officers of the Conference.

BISHOP OF GLOUCESTER AND BRISTOL (RT. REV. DR. ELLICOTT), *Episcopal Secretary*.

DEAN OF WINDSOR (VERY REV. R. T. DAVIDSON), *General Secretary*.

ARCHDEACON OF MAIDSTONE (VEN. B. F. SMITH), *Assistant Secretary*.

No. XXXIII. (See page 45.)

Encyclical Letter issued by the Bishops attending the third Lambeth Conference, July, 1888.

TO THE FAITHFUL IN CHRIST JESUS, GREETING—

WE, Archbishops, Bishops Metropolitan, and other Bishops of the Holy Catholic Church, in full communion with the Church of England, one hundred and forty-five in number, all having superintendence over Dioceses or lawfully commissioned to exercise Episcopal functions therein, assembled from divers parts of the earth, at Lambeth Palace, in the year of our Lord 1888, under the presidency of the Most Reverend Edward, by Divine Providence Archbishop of Canterbury, Primate of All England and Metropolitan, after receiving in the Chapel of the said Palace the Blessed Sacrament of the Lord's Body and Blood, and uniting in prayer for the guidance of the Holy Spirit, having taken into consideration various questions which have been submitted to us affecting the welfare of God's people and the condition of the Church in divers parts of the World,

We have made these matters the subject of careful and serious deliberation during the month past, both in general Conference and in Committees specially appointed to consider the several questions; and we now commend to the faithful the conclusions at which we have arrived.

We have appended to this letter two sets of documents, the one containing the formal Resolutions of the Conference, and the other the Reports of the several Committees. We desire you to bear in mind that the Conference is responsible for the first alone. The Reports of Committees can only be taken to represent the mind of the Conference in so far as they are reaffirmed or directly adopted in the Resolutions; but we have thought good to print these Reports, believing that they will offer fruitful matter for consideration.

In the first place we desire to speak of the moral and practical questions which have engaged the attention of the Conference; and in the forefront we would place the duty of the Church in the promotion of temperance and purity.

Temperance. Noble and self-denying efforts have been made for many years, within and without the Church, for the suppression of intemperance, and it is our earnest hope that these efforts will be increased manifold. The evil effects of this sin on the life of the Church and the nation can scarcely be exaggerated. But we are constrained to utter a caution against a false principle which threatens to creep in and vitiate much useful work. Highly valuable as we believe total abstinence to be as a means to an end, we desire to discountenance the language which condemns the use of wine as wrong in itself, independently of its effects on ourselves or on others, and we have expressed our disapproval of a reported practice (which seems to be due to some extent to the tacit assumption of this principle) of substituting some other liquid in the celebration of Holy Communion.

Purity. On the other hand Christian society is only now awakening to a sense of its active duty in the matter of purity; and we therefore desire to avail ourselves of an occasion which has brought together representatives of the Anglican Communion from distant parts of the world, to proclaim a crusade against that sin which is before all others a defilement of the body of Christ and a desecration of the temple of the Holy Spirit. We recall the earnest language of the Report: we believe that nothing short of general action by all Christian people will avail to arrest the evil: we call upon you to rally round the standard of a high and pure morality; and we appeal to all whom our voice may reach to assist us in raising the tone of public opinion, and in stamping out ignoble and corrupt traditions which are not only a dishonour to the Name of our Master Christ, but degrading to the dignity of a being created in the image of God.

Sanctity of Marriage. In vital connection with the promotion of purity is the maintenance of the sanctity of marriage, which is the centre of social morality. This is seriously compromised by facilities of Divorce which have been increased in recent years by legislation in some countries. We have therefore held it our duty to reaffirm emphatically the precept of Christ relating thereto, and to offer some advice which may guide the Clergy of our Communion in their attitude towards any infringement of the Master's rule.

Polygamy. The sanctity of marriage as a Christian obligation implies the faithful union of one man with one woman until the union is severed by death. The polygamous alliances of heathen races are allowed on all hands to be condemned by the law of Christ; but they present many difficult practical problems which have been solved in various ways in the past. We have carefully considered this question in the different lights thrown upon it from various parts of the mission-field. While we have refrained from offering advice on minor points, leaving these to be settled by the local authorities of the Church, we have laid down some broad lines on which alone we consider that the missionary may safely act. Our first care has been to maintain and protect the Christian conception of marriage, believing that any immediate and rapid successes which might otherwise have been secured in the mission-field would be dearly purchased by any lowering or confusion of this idea.

Observance of the Lord's Day. The due observance of Sunday as a day of rest, of worship, and of religious teaching, has a direct bearing on the moral well-being of the Christian community. We have observed of late a growing laxity which threatens to impair its sacred character. We strongly deprecate this tendency. We call upon the leisurely classes not selfishly to withdraw from others the opportunities of rest and of religion. We call upon master and employer jealously to guard the privileges of the servant and the workman. In "the Lord's Day" we have a priceless heritage. Whoever misuses it incurs a terrible responsibility.

Socialism. Intimately connected with these moral questions is the attitude of the Christian Church towards the social problems of the day. Excessive inequality in the distribution of this world's goods: vast accumulation and desperate poverty side by side: these suggest many anxious considerations to any thoughtful person, who is penetrated with the mind of Christ. No more important problems can well occupy the attention—whether of Clergy or Laity—than such as are connected with what is popularly called Socialism. To study schemes proposed for redressing the social balance, to welcome the good which may be found in the aims or operations of any, and to devise methods, whether by legislation or by social combinations, or in any other way, for a peaceful solution of the problems without violence or injustice, is one of the noblest pursuits which can engage the thoughts of those who strive to follow in the footsteps of Christ. Suggestions are offered in the Report which may assist in solving this problem.

Care of Emigrants. One class of persons more especially had a claim upon the consideration and sympathy of the Conference. In our emigrants we have a social link which binds the Churches of the British Islands to the Church of the United States, and to the Churches in the Colonies. No more pertinent question, therefore, could have been suggested for our deliberations than our duty towards this large body of our fellow-Christians. It is especially incumbent upon the Church to follow them with the eye of sympathy at every point in their passage from their old home to their new, to exercise a watchful care over them, and to protect them from the dangers, moral and spiritual, which beset their path. We have endeavoured to offer some suggestions, by following which this end may be attained.

Definite Teaching of the Faith. Recognising thus the primary importance of maintaining the moral precepts and discipline of the Gospel in all the relations of life and society, we proceed to the consideration of the means, within the reach and contemplation of the Churches, for inculcating the definite truths of the Faith, which are the basis of such moral teaching.

We cannot escape the conviction that this department of work requires great attention and much improvement. The religious teaching of the young is sadly deficient in depth and reality, especially in the matter of doctrine. This deficiency is not confined to any class of society, and the task of remedying the default is one which the Laity must be prepared to share with the Clergy. On parents it lies as a divine charge. Godfathers and Godmothers should be urged to fulfil the duty which they have undertaken for the children whose sponsors they have been, and to see that they are not left uninstructed, or inadequately prepared for Confirmation. The use of public catechising and regular preparation of candidates for Confirmation is capable of much development. The work done in Sunday Schools requires, as we believe, more constant supervision and more sustained interest than, in a great many cases, it receives from the Clergy. The instruction of Sunday-School teachers, and of the pupil-teachers in Elementary Schools, ought to be regarded as an indispensable part of the pastoral work of a Parish Priest; and the moral and practical lessons from the Bible ought to be enforced by constant reference to the sanctions, and to the illustrations of doctrine and discipline belonging to them, to be found in the same Holy Scripture. It would be possible, to a greater extent than is now done, to make sermons in church combine doctrinal and moral efficiency, and, by illustrating the rationale of divine service, lead on the congregations to the perception of the definite relations between worship, faith, and work—the lessons of the Prayer Book, the Catechism, and the Creeds.

It is not, however, with reference to the young alone, or to the recognised members of their own flock, that the Clergy have need to look carefully to the security of definiteness in teaching the faith.

The study of Holy Scripture is a great part of the mental discipline of the Christian, and the Bible itself is the main instrument in all teaching of religion.

Unhappily, in the present day, there is a widespread system of propagandism hostile to the reception of the Bible as a treasury of Divine knowledge, and throughout society, in all its ranks, misgivings, doubts, hostile criticisms, and sceptical estimates of doctrinal truths as based on Revelation, are very common.

The doubts which arise from the misapprehension of the due relations between Science and Revelation may be, and ought to be, treated with respect, and a sympathetic patience ; and, where minds have been disquieted by scientific discovery or assertion, great care should be taken not to extinguish the elements of faith, but rather to direct the thinker to the realisation of the fact that such discoveries elucidate the action of laws which, rightly conceived, tend to the higher appreciation of the glorious work of the Creator, upheld by the word of His power.

The dangers arising from the hostile or sceptical temper and attitude are increased by the difficulty of determining how far our teaching and the popular acceptance of it can be harmonised with a due consideration for the views on inspiration, and especially on the character of the discipline of the Old Testament dispensation, which, although they have never received definite sanction in the Church, have been long and widely prevalent.

We must recommend to the Clergy cautious and industrious treatment of these points of controversy, and most earnestly press upon them the importance of taking, as the central thought of their teaching, our Lord Jesus Christ, as the sacrifice for our sins, as the healer of our sinfulness; the source of all our spiritual life, and the revelation to our consciences of the law and motive of all moral virtue. To Him and to His work all the teachings of the Old Testament converge, and from Him all the teachings of the New Testament flow, in spirit, in force, and in form. The work of the Church is the application and extension of the blessings of the Incarnation, and her teaching the development of its doctrinal issues as contained in the Creeds of the Church.

Mutual Relations. Our discussion on the mutual relations of dioceses and branches of our Communion has brought out some points which we desire to commend to your consideration. It appears necessary to draw attention to the principles laid down in the Conference of 1878, and to urge that within our

Communion the duly-certified action of each Church or Province should be respected by the other Churches and their members; that no Bishop or Clergyman should exercise his functions within any regularly-constituted diocese without the consent of the Bishop of that diocese; and that no Bishop should authorise the action of any Clergyman coming from another diocese without proper letters testimonial. The neglect of these rules has led to some grievous scandals. The Bishops, on their part, are prepared to do their best to guard against such mischiefs, by adding private advice to the formal document in use, but the Clergy must resolve to exercise greater caution in signing testimonials; and those who require them must check all tendency to over-sensitiveness, when they find themselves subjected to inquiries as to character and identification, which, however unnecessary they may deem them in their own case, are certainly indispensable for securing such measure of safety as we require.

This caution applies with especial force to the Clergy ordained for Colonial work. We most heartily recognise the principle that those who have given the best years of their life to work abroad are entitled to great consideration when the time comes at which they want such rest or change of employment as may be found at home. But to lay down any general rules on this point is impossible.

One matter has been laid before us in a more formal way—the possibility of constituting a Council or Councils of reference to advise upon, or even to decide, questions laid before them by the authorities of the Provinces of the Colonial Church. As to this, we would counsel patient consideration and consultation, of such character as may eventually supersede the necessity for creating an authority which might, whether as a Council of advice, or in a function more closely resembling that of a Court, place us in circumstances prejudicial alike to order and to liberty of action.

Home Reunion. After anxious discussion we have resolved to content ourselves with laying down certain articles as a basis on which approach may be, by God's blessing, made towards Home Reunion. These articles, four in number, will be found in the appended Resolutions.

The attitude of the Anglican Communion towards the religious bodies now separated from it by unhappy divisions would appear to be this :—We hold ourselves in readiness to enter into brotherly conference with any of those who may desire intercommunion with us in a more or less perfect form. We lay down conditions on which such intercommunion is, in our opinion, and according to our conviction, possible. For, however we may long to embrace those now alienated from us, so that the ideal of the one flock under the one Shepherd may be realised, we must not be unfaithful stewards of the great deposit entrusted to us. We cannot desert our position either to faith or discipline. That concord would, in our judgment, be neither true nor desirable which should be produced by such surrender.

But we gladly and thankfully recognise the real religious work which is carried on by Christian bodies not of our Communion. We cannot close our eyes to the visible blessing which has been vouchsafed to their labours for Christ's sake. Let us not be misunderstood on this point. We are not insensible to the strong ties, the rooted convictions, which attach them to their present position. These we respect, as we wish that on our side our own principles and feelings may be respected. Competent observers, indeed, assert that not in England only, but in all parts of the Christian world, there is a real yearning for unity—that men's hearts are moved more than heretofore towards Christian fellowship. The Conference has shown in its discussions as well as its resolutions that it is deeply penetrated with this feeling. May the Spirit of love move on the troubled waters of religious differences.

Relation to the Scandinavian Church. Among the nations with whom English-speaking peoples are brought directly in contact are the Scandinavian races, who form an important element of the population in many of our dioceses. The attitude, therefore, which the Anglican Communion should take towards the Scandinavian Churches could not be a matter of indifference to this Conference. We have recommended that fuller knowledge should be sought and friendly intercourse interchanged until such time as matters may be ripe for a closer alliance without any sacrifice of principles which we hold to be essential.

To Old Catholics and Others. Nor, again, is it possible for members of the Anglican Communion to withhold their sympathies from those Continental movements towards reformation which, under the greatest difficulties, have proceeded mainly on the same lines as our own, retaining Episcopacy as an Apostolic ordinance. Though we believe that the time has not come for any direct alliance with any of these, and, though we deprecate any precipitance of action which would transgress primitive and established principles of jurisdiction, we believe that advances may be made without sacrifice of these, and we entertain the hope that the time may come when a more formal alliance with some at least of these bodies will be possible.

To the Eastern Churches. The Conference has expressed its earnest desire to confirm and to improve the friendly relations which now exist between the Churches of the East and the Anglican Communion. These Churches have well earned the sympathy of Christendom, for through long ages of persecution they have kept alive in many a dark place the light of the Gospel. If that light is here and there feeble or dim, there is all the more reason that we, as we have opportunity, should tend and cherish it; and we need not fear that our offices of brotherly charity, if offered in a right spirit, will not be accepted. We reflect with thankfulness that there exist no bars, such as are presented to communion with the Latins by the formulated sanction of the Infallibility of the Church residing in the person of the Supreme Pontiff, by the doctrine of the Immaculate Conception, and other dogmas imposed by the decrees of Papal Councils. The Church of Rome has always treated her Eastern sister wrongfully She intrudes her Bishops into the ancient Dioceses, and keeps up a system of active proselytism. The Eastern Church is reasonably outraged by these proceedings, wholly contrary as they are to Catholic principles ; and it behoves us of the Anglican Communion to take care that we do not offend in like manner.

Individuals craving fuller light and stronger spiritual life may, by remaining in the Church of their baptism, become centres of enlightenment to their own people.

But though all schemes of proselytising are to be avoided, it is only right that our real claims and position as a historical Church should be set before a people who are very distrustful of novelty, especially in religion, and who appreciate the history of Catholic antiquity. Help should be given towards the education of the Clergy, and, in more destitute communities, extended to schools for general instruction.

Authoritative Standards. The authoritative standards of doctrine and worship claim your careful attention in connexion with these subjects. It is of the utmost importance that our faith and practice should be represented, both to the ancient Churches and to the native and growing Churches in the mission-field, in a manner which shall neither give cause for offence nor restrict due liberty, nor present any stumbling-blocks in the way of complete communion.

In conformity with the practice of the former

Conferences we declare that we are united under our Divine Head in the fellowship of the one Catholic and Apostolic Church, holding the one faith revealed in Holy Writ, defined in the Creeds, maintained by the primitive Church, and affirmed by the undisputed Œcumenical Councils: as standards of doctrine and worship alike we recognise the Prayer Book with its Catechism, the Ordinal, and the Thirty-nine Articles, —the special heritage of the Church of England, and, to a greater or less extent, received by all the Churches of our Communion.

We desire that these standards should be set before the foreign Churches in their purity and simplicity. A certain liberty of treatment must be extended to the cases of native and growing Churches, on which it would be unreasonable to impose, as conditions of communion, the whole of the Thirty-nine Articles, coloured as they are in language and form by the peculiar circumstances under which they were originally drawn up. On the other hand, it would be impossible for us to share with them in the matter of Holy Orders, as in complete intercommunion, without satisfactory evidence that they hold substantially the same form of doctrine as ourselves. It ought not to be difficult, much less impossible, to formulate articles, in accordance with our own standards of doctrine and worship, the acceptance of which should be required of all ordained in such Churches.

We close this letter rendering our humble and hearty thanks to Almighty God for His great goodness towards us. We have been permitted to meet together in larger numbers than heretofore. Contributions of knowledge and experience have been poured into the common stock from all parts of the earth. We have realised, more fully than it was possible to realise before, the extent, the power, and the influence of the great Anglican Communion. We have felt its capacities, its opportunities, its privileges. In our common deliberations we have tested its essential oneness amidst all varieties of condition and development. Wherever there was diversity of opinion among us there was also harmony of spirit and unity of aim ; and we shall return to our several dioceses refreshed, strengthened, and inspired by the memories which we shall carry away.

But the sense of thanksgiving is closely linked with the obligation of duty. This fuller realisation of our privileges as Members of the Anglican Communion carries with it a heightened sense of our responsibilities which do not end with our own people or with the mission-field alone, but extend to all the Churches of God. The opportunities of an exceptional position call us to an exceptional work. It is our earnest prayer that all—Clergy and laity alike—may take God's manifest purpose to heart, and strive in their several stations to work it out in all its fulness.

With these parting words we commend the results at which we have arrived in this Conference to your careful consideration, praying that the Holy Spirit may direct your thoughts and lead you to all truth, and that our counsels may redound through your action to the glory of God and the increase of Christ's kingdom.

Signed, on behalf of the Conference,

EDW : CANTUAR :

C. J. GLOUCESTER & BRISTOL,
Episcopal Secretary.
RANDALL T. DAVIDSON,
Dean of Windsor,
General Secretary.
B. F. SMITH,
Archdeacon of Maidstone,
Assistant Secretary.

27*th July*, 1888.

No. XXXIV. (See page 45.)

RESOLUTIONS FORMALLY ADOPTED BY THE CONFERENCE OF 1888.

1. That this Conference, without pledging itself to all the statements and opinions embodied in the Report of the Committee on Intemperance, commends the Report to the consideration of the Church.

2. That the Bishops assembled in this Conference declare that the use of unfermented juice of the grape, or any liquid other than true wine diluted or undiluted, as the element in the administration of the cup in Holy Communion, is unwarranted by the example of Our Lord, and is an unauthorised departure from the custom of the Catholic Church.

3. That this Conference earnestly commends to all those into whose hands it may come the Report on the subject of Purity, as expressing the mind of the Conference on this great subject.[1]

   [[1] Carried unanimously.]

4. (A) That, inasmuch as Our Lord's words expressly forbid Divorce, except in the case of fornication or adultery, the Christian Church cannot recognise divorce in any other than the excepted case, or give any sanction to the marriage of any person who has been divorced contrary to this law, during the life of the other party.

(B) That under no circumstances ought the guilty party, in the case of a divorce for fornication or adultery, to be regarded, during the lifetime of the innocent party, as a fit recipient of the blessing of the Church on marriage.

(C) That, recognising the fact that there always has been a difference of opinion in the Church on the question whether Our Lord meant to forbid marriage to the innocent party in a divorce for adultery, the Conference recommends that the Clergy should not be instructed to refuse the Sacraments or other privileges of the Church to those who, under civil sanction, are thus married.

---

5. (A) That it is the opinion of this Conference that persons living in polygamy be not admitted to baptism, but that they be accepted as candidates and kept under Christian instruction until such time as they shall be in a position to accept the law of Christ.*

[* Carried by 83 votes to 21.]

(B) That the wives of polygamists may, in the opinion of this Conference, be admitted in some cases to baptism, but that it must be left to the local authorities of the Church to decide under what circumstances they may be baptized.*

[* Carried by 54 votes to 34.]

---

6. (A) That the principle of the religious observance of one day in seven, embodied in the Fourth Commandment, is of Divine obligation.

(B) That, from the time of our Lord's Resurrection, the first day of the week was observed by

Christians as a day of worship and rest, and, under the name of "The Lord's Day," gradually succeeded, as the great weekly festival of the Christian Church, to the sacred position of the Sabbath.

(C) That the observance of the Lord's Day, as a day of rest, of worship, and of religious teaching, has been a priceless blessing in all Christian lands in which it has been maintained.

(D) That the growing laxity in its observance threatens a great change in its sacred and beneficent character.

(E) That especially the increasing practice, on the part of some of the wealthy and leisurely classes, of making Sunday a day of secular amusement is most strongly to be deprecated.

(F) That the most careful regard should be had to the danger of any encroachment upon the rest which, on this day, is the right of servants as well as their masters, and of the working classes as well as their employers.

---

7. That this Conference receives the Report drawn up by the Committee on the subject of Socialism, and submits it to the consideration of the Churches of the Anglican Communion.

---

8. That this Conference receives the Report drawn up by the Committee on the subject of Emigration, and commends the suggestions embodied in it to the consideration of the Churches of the Anglican Communion.

---

9. (A) That this Conference receives the Report

drawn up by the Committee on the subject of the Mutual Relation of Dioceses and Branches of the Anglican Communion, and submits it to the consideration of the Church, as containing suggestions of much practical importance.

(B) That the Archbishop of Canterbury be requested to give his attention to the Appendix attached to the Report, with a view to action in the direction indicated, if, upon consideration, His Grace should think such action desirable.

10. That, inasmuch as the Book of Common Prayer is not the possession of one Diocese or Province, but of all, and that a revision in one portion of the Anglican Communion must therefore be extensively felt, this Conference is of opinion that no particular portion of the Church should undertake revision without seriously considering the possible effect of such action on other branches of the Church.

---

11. That, in the opinion of this Conference, the following Articles supply a basis on which approach may be by God's blessing made towards Home Reunion :—

   (A) The Holy Scriptures of the Old and New Testaments, as "containing all things necessary to salvation," and as being the rule and ultimate standard of faith.

   (B) The Apostles' Creed, as the Baptismal Symbol ; and the Nicene Creed, as the sufficient statement of the Christian faith.

   (C) The two Sacraments ordained by Christ Himself—Baptism and the Supper of the Lord—

ministered with unfailing use of Christ's words of Institution, and of the elements ordained by Him.

(D) The Historic Episcopate, locally adapted in the methods of its administration to the varying needs of the nations and peoples called of God into the Unity of His Church.

12. That this Conference earnestly requests the constituted authorities of the various branches of our Communion, acting, so far as may be, in concert with one another, to make it known that they hold themselves in readiness to enter into brotherly conference (such as that which has already been proposed by the Church in the United States of America) with the representatives of other Christian Communions in the English-speaking races, in order to consider what steps can be taken, either towards corporate Reunion, or towards such relations as may prepare the way for fuller organic unity hereafter.

13. That this Conference recommends as of great importance, in tending to bring about Reunion, the dissemination of information respecting the standards of doctrine and the formularies in use in the Anglican Church; and recommends that information be disseminated, on the other hand, respecting the authoritative standards of doctrine, worship, and government adopted by the other bodies of Christians into which the English-speaking races are divided.

14. That, in the opinion of this Conference, earnest efforts should be made to establish more friendly relations between the Scandinavian and Anglican Churches ; and that approaches

on the part of the Swedish Church, with a view to the mutual explanation of differences, be most gladly welcomed, in order to the ultimate establishment, if possible, of intercommunion on sound principles of ecclesiastical polity.

15. (A) That this Conference recognises with thankfulness the dignified and independent position of the Old Catholic Church of Holland, and looks to more frequent brotherly intercourse to remove many of the barriers which at present separate us.[1]

(B) That we regard it as a duty to promote friendly relations with the Old Catholic Community in Germany, and with the "Christian Catholic Church," in Switzerland, not only out of sympathy with them, but also in thankfulness to God Who has strengthened them to suffer for the truth under great discouragements, difficulties, and temptations; and that we offer them the privileges recommended by the Committee under the conditions specified in its Report.[1]

(C) That the sacrifices made by the Old Catholics in Austria, deserve our sympathy, and that we hope, when their organisation is sufficiently tried and complete, a more formal relation may be found possible.[1]

(D) That, with regard to the reformers in Italy, France, Spain, and Portugal, struggling to free themselves from the burden of unlawful terms of communion, we trust that they may be enabled to adopt such sound forms of doctrine and discipline, and to secure such Catholic organisation as will permit us to give them a fuller recognition [1]

(E) That, without desiring to interfere with the rights of Bishops of the Catholic Church to interpose in cases of extreme necessity, we deprecate any action that does not regard primitive and established principles of jurisdiction and the interests of the whole Anglican Communion.[1]

[[1] Resolutions (A) (B) (C) (D) (E) were carried *nemine contradicente*.]

16. That, having regard to the fact that the question of the relation of the Anglican Church to the *Unitas Fratrum*, or Moravians, was remitted by the last Lambeth Conference to a Committee, which has hitherto presented no Report on the subject, the Archbishop of Canterbury be requested to appoint a Committee of Bishops who shall be empowered to confer with learned theologians, and with the heads of the *Unitas Fratrum*, and shall report to His Grace before the end of the current year, and that His Grace be requested to take such action on their Report as he shall deem right.

17. That this Conference, rejoicing in the friendly communications which have passed between the Archbishops of Canterbury and other Anglican Bishops, and the Patriarchs of Constantinople and other Eastern Patriarchs and Bishops, desires to express its hope that the barriers to fuller communion may be, in course of time, removed by further intercourse and extended enlightment. The Conference commends this subject to the devout prayers of the faithful, and recommends that the counsels and efforts of our fellow-Christians should be directed to the encouragement of internal reformation in the Eastern Churches,

rather than to the drawing away from them of individual members of their Communion.

18. That the Archbishop of Canterbury be requested to take counsel with such persons as he may see fit to consult, with a view to ascertaining whether it is desirable to revise the English version of the Nicene Creed or of the *Quicunque Vult.**

[* Carried by 57 votes to 20.]

19. That, as regards newly-constituted Churches, especially in non-Christian lands, it should be a condition of the recognition of them as in complete intercommunion with us, and especially of their receiving from us Episcopal Succession, that we should first receive from them satisfactory evidence that they hold substantially the same doctrine as our own, and that their clergy subscribe Articles in accordance with the express statements of our own standards of doctrine and worship; but that they should not necessarily be bound to accept in their entirety the thirty-nine Articles of Religion.

No. XXXV. (See page 44.)
REPORTS OF COMMITTEES.

N.B.—*The following Reports must be taken as having the authority only of the Committees by whom they were respectively prepared and presented. The Committees were not in every case unanimous in adopting the Reports.*

The Conference, as a whole, is responsible only for the formal Resolutions agreed to after discussion, and printed above, pages 277 to 284.

No. 1.—INTEMPERANCE.

REPORT OF THE COMMITTEE[1] APPOINTED TO CONSIDER THE SUBJECT OF THE DUTY OF THE CHURCH WITH REGARD TO INTEMPERANCE.

It is not necessary to say much of the sinfulness of intemperance in itself, or of the widespread mischief that is caused by it. If it cannot be considered the most sinful of all sins, it is difficult to deny that it is the most mischievous. And wherever large masses of the population find it difficult to obtain work at all, and large masses can only obtain it at wages too low

---

[1] Names of the Members of the Committee:—
Bishop of London (*Chairman*).   Bishop of Rochester.
„   Colorado.   „   Saskatchewan.
„   Kilmore.   „   Sierra Leone.
„   Newcastle.   „   Sodor and Man.
„   The Niger.   „   Zululand.
„   Pennsylvania.

to sustain healthy life, the evils caused by intemperance press with heavier weight than ever they did before. The Church cannot be justified in witnessing this enormous amount of sin and misery without endeavouring to ascertain whether any special means can be discovered for effectually dealing with it, or whether it must be left to ordinary agencies used with more than ordinary zeal and persistency.

The experience of the last fifty years is strongly in favour of the use of the special means which have hitherto achieved whatever success has been achieved in stemming the strong current of this widely-prevailing sin. It may be true that, if the whole Church had been thoroughly alive to the extent and nature of the mischief, much might have been done by more earnest efforts, both of Clergy and Laity, in the ordinary course of the Church's work. But it is the perseverance and insistance of the Temperance Societies that has awakened the Church, and without these Societies we have no evidence to show that much or even anything would have been done to deal with the evil. The Temperance Societies have compelled the attention of the public at large, and have by so doing profoundly modified public opinion. There can be no doubt that drunkenness is now regarded with much more severe condemnation than before these Societies began their work, and the change is largely, if not entirely, due to them. The Temperance Societies have compelled the medical profession to study the subject with more care than before, and the result of this study has greatly influenced both their utterances and their practice. The science of medicine is so complex and difficult, and the practice of medicine has been so largely influenced by tradition, that any particular question, such as that of the influence of alcohol on the body, has to wait its turn for examination unless some strong reason forces it forward. But the urgency of the Temperance Societies drew the attention of the profession, and the result has justified that urgency. To the Temperance Societies is due the change in the practice of Insurance Offices. Fifty years ago it was their ordinary rule to require higher premiums from life-insurers who totally abstained from intoxicating liquors. It is now proved that the total abstainers live longer than other men. And this has been confirmed by the experience of the Benefit Societies among which those that make total abstinence a condition of membership are able to show a much smaller average of sickness than the others. And to all this is to be added the great and still-increasing effect of the Bands of Hope which though in some cases open to objection, are, nevertheless, every year adding largely to the number of pledged abstainers among adults, and bid fair before long entirely to change the public opinion of the classes that live by manual labour.

And it is natural that this should be so, for the sin, being one of the sins of the flesh, must be dealt with as indeed all such sins must be dealt with, mainly by flight from temptation. The special characteristic of all temptations of the flesh is the enormous difference in power between temptations close at hand and temptations at a distance. If a man is weak in this respect the one hope of his safety lies in keeping the temptation from him, and him from the temptation. There are no doubt many who have no need of this. But those who have fallen or are approaching a fall can, as a rule, be upheld in no other way. Now, this is precisely a work in which men can help each other, and in which that help can most effectually be given by an organisation formed for the purpose. Men can help each other by breaking through those customs of society which now surround men with incessant temptations in every transaction of life, by using their influence to diminish the enormous number of public-houses which now make every street and road a peril to the weak, by diligently investigating the effects of alcoholic drinks on the body, and disproving the assertion that alcohol is necessary (except in rare and special cases) to health or to vigorous action. But even more can men help the weak by sympathy with them in their struggle, and by doing all they can to make the struggle easier. A weak man is told to abstain altogether; and, easy as this is to many, to some it is exceedingly difficult, and the difficulty to these is greatly increased if they are to abstain quite alone, and thus, apparently, cut themselves off from the rest; if their abstinence is, in itself, to be a kind of stigma, and to brand them with a public exposure of their weakness. Such men need to be shielded and supported by the stronger, or the battle which is often hard enough in any case becomes too much for their strength.

Whatever may be said concerning what might have been done by other methods, it is undeniable that to organisations for the express purpose of dealing with intemperance, and to these organisations alone, must be attributed what has been done. And if any other method of doing the work is to claim precedence, it must first establish that claim by actual experience before it will be possible to take cognisance of it in determining the course that the authorities of the Church should recommend. The Temperance Societies are now doing the work, and there is at present no sign of any other mode of doing it being likely equally to succeed.

And after what has been said above it clearly follows that the main weapon to be used in this warfare is the practice of total abstinence from intoxicating liquors by those who desire to help their fellow-men. Nothing but this has the same hold of the weak or the tempted, give them the same encouragement to fight their battle in the only true way, wins their affections maintains their perseverance. Exhortations to total abstinence by those who do not themselves abstain are always comparatively feeble, sometimes irritating. The exhorter often fails to win even where perhaps he succeeds in convincing. The lesson that he teaches is that of moderation, which is an excellent lesson for the strong, but not the lesson which is needed by the weak. He may do something to prevent some from falling who now stand upright; he can do little to save those who are on the edge, or to rescue those who have fallen already.

The burden of the work must be borne by those who are willing to abstain entirely. But, on the other hand, it cannot be said that every one is bound to take up this particular burden as part of his service of Christ. Some are called to one form of devotion, some to another. There can be no question that every one who abstains, and makes it known that he abstains, for the sake of his weaker fellow-men, is giving them help, and in some cases more help than he knows, yet while men are all bound to help their fellows, they are not all bound to help them in the same manner or in the same degree or against the same enemies. All are bound to help the foreign mission work of the Church, but not all are bound to be missionaries. All are bound to help in spiritual work at home, but all are not called to the same spiritual work. All are bound to help the weak in their battle with intemperance, but not all to help them by total abstinence in their own persons.

It seems reasonable, however, to say that those who are brought much into contact with intemperance should arm themselves with this weapon of total abstinence in their own persons. It would be well that wherever this battle with intemperance is of exceptional importance, or forms for the time the first duty imposed on the Clergy, total abstinence should be the weapon employed. This applies not only to England, but still more to many places in other parts of the world where native races have to be rescued from previous habits of intemperance, or to be upheld in their struggle to resist temptations of this kind.

There is, however, much work to be done in this cause outside the direct battle with intemperance itself. And the Church cannot stand aloof from it.

It seems to belong to the Church to use its utmost influence to press on all Governments the duty of diminishing the enormous amount of temptation which at present hinders the work of elevating and civilising the masses. There can be no doubt that wise legislation might do a great deal in this direction. The diminution in the number of Public Houses, the shortening of the hours of sale, Sunday Closing, are instances of legislative measures that would probably be very beneficial. And a combination between Governments might wipe out the grievous stain which now rests on the countries that are counted foremost in the world—the stain of degrading and destroying the weaker races. It has pleased God to make the Christian nations stronger than any other —stronger than all others combined. But this strength brings with it a very solemn responsibility. And this solemn responsibility the Church ought incessantly to press on those who bear authority. It is grievous that it should be possible to say, with any most distant resemblance of truth, that it would be better for native races that Christian nations should never come into contact with them at all.

In conclusion, it is of importance to lay much stress on the essential condition of permanent success in this work, namely, that it should be taken up in a religious spirit as part of Christian devotion to the Lord. The work must be done in His Name for the sake of His children whom He has bought with His Blood. A brief success may be obtained by forgetting the religious character of the task, and thinking only of the misery which intemperance causes and of the degradation inherent in it. But the religious spirit alone will maintain the conflict steadily through the obstinate resistance that will have to be encountered, and in spite of the many disappointments and failures that will have to be borne.

It is, again, the religious spirit which can alone repress the fanaticism which sometimes makes the total abstainer talk of his abstinence as the one thing needful; which sometimes makes him uncharitable and presumptuous; which sometimes makes him think lightly of grievous sin, provided it be not the one sin which he condemns.

But taken up in a religious spirit this work has a double blessing. It is not only blessed in the victory over sin and evil, but blessed also, and perhaps still more, in the door which it opens for the whole Gospel to enter men's souls. The conscience of the mass of the people speaks more clearly on this point than, perhaps, on any other. The Minister of the Gospel who begins with this finds that a very large number are at once ready to accept his teaching, because he carries their consciences with him from the first. They have already learnt that intemperance is wrong, and they are ready to believe in the value of a Ministry which visibly and systematically wages war on it. And having learnt to trust and follow the Minister in this, they are far more ready to trust and follow him in all else. To be all things to all men, in order that he might save some, was St. Paul's rule. And as things now are in many parishes, and in many parts of the world, the same rule will be best kept by those Ministers of the Church who make a point of showing themselves thoroughly in earnest in this great battle.

Signed on behalf of the Committee,

F. LONDIN :

Chairman.

No. 2.—PURITY.

REPORT OF THE COMMITTEE[1] APPOINTED TO CONSIDER THE CHURCH'S PRACTICAL WORK IN RELATION TO THE SUBJECT OF PURITY.

IN submitting the following Report your Committee would observe that they have cast it in such a form that, if accepted, it may go forth as the utterance of the united Conference.

We speak as those who are deeply conscious of their responsibility before God for the words which they utter upon a subject of tremendous moment.

Knowing, as we do know, how sins of impurity are not only a grave public scandal, but are also festering beneath the surface, and eating into the life of multitudes in all classes and in all lands, we cannot keep silence, although we dare not utter all that we know.

We are constrained, as Bishops of the Church of God, to lift up the standard of a high and pure morality, and we call upon all, whether of our own Communion or not, in the name of God our common Father, to rally round the standard. Especially do we press upon those on whom lies the responsibility of the cure of souls, to face the question, and to ask

---

[1] Names of the Members of the Committee:—

Bishop of Durham (*Chairman*).	Bishop of North Dakota.
" Brechin.	" Shrewsbury.
" Calcutta.	" Toronto.
" Carlisle.	" Truro.
" Marlborough.	" Wakefield.
" Massachusetts.	

themselves what they are doing, or can do, to protect their flocks from the deadly ravages of sensual sin.

We believe that, although the public conscience is in some degree awakened, and the self-sacrificing efforts of those who have laboured to this end have not been wholly in vain, yet the awful magnitude of the evil is but imperfectly realised.

We are not blind to the danger of dealing publicly with the subject of impurity. We dread the effect, especially upon the young, of any increased familiarity with the details of sin. Notwithstanding we hold that the time has come when the Church must speak with no uncertain voice.

We solemnly declare that a life of purity is alone worthy of a being created in the image of God.

We declare that for Christians the obligation to purity rests upon the sanctity of the body, which is the "Temple of the Holy Ghost."

We declare that a life of chastity for the unmarried is not only possible, but is commanded by God.

We declare that there is no difference between man and woman in the sinfulness of sins of unchastity.

We declare that on the man, in his God-given strength of manhood, rests the main responsibility.

We declare that no one known to be living an immoral life ought to be received in Christian society.

We solemnly protest against all lowering of the sanctity of marriage.

We would remind all whom our voice may reach that the wrath of God, alike in Holy Scripture and in the history of the world, has been revealed against the nations which has transgressed the law of purity; and we solemnly record our conviction that, wherever marriage is dishonoured and sins of the flesh are lightly regarded, the home-life will be destroyed, and the nation itself will, sooner or later, decay and perish.

We, on our part, as Bishops of the Church of God, satisfied as to the gravity of this matter, and feeling that nothing short of general action on the part of all Christian people will avail to arrest the evil, determine to confer with the Clergy and faithful Laity of our several Dioceses as to the wisest steps to be taken for the accomplishment of the weighty enterprise to which God is calling us.

We believe that we may profitably deliberate upon such questions as the following:—

1. How best to bring about a general reformation of manners, and to enforce a higher moral tone in the matter of purity.

2. How especially to guard the sanctity of marriage and to create a healthier public opinion upon the subject, and, to this end, how best to make the celebration of Holy Matrimony as reverent and impressive as possible.

3. How most wisely to deal with this difficult and delicate question as regards our children, our homes, our schools, and other places of education.

4. How best to strengthen the hands of those who are striving in the Army, the Navy, and other public services, to create and maintain a high standard of purity.

5. How best to provide safeguards for those who, from inability to marry, or from other circumstances of their lives, are exposed to special temptation.

6. How best to bind together, and to encourage by the sense of union, all who desire to help, or to be helped, in the battle against impurity.

7. How best to purify art and literature, and to repress all that is immodest in language, manners, and dress.

8. How best to enforce or amend the laws framed to guard the innocent, to punish the guilty, to rescue the fallen, to suppress the haunts of vice, and to remove temptation from our thoroughfares.

We thank God for the readiness, and even enthusiasm, with which the movement in favour of purity has been welcomed by young men of every class.

There is a generosity and chivalry among the young which is seldom appealed to in vain; while large numbers are deeply thankful for every aid in the desperate battle against the sins of the flesh.

Once more, as witnesses for God, we would speak to all whom our voice may reach. "Be strong in the Lord, and in the power of His might." Live pure lives. Speak pure words. Think pure thoughts. Shun and abhor all that is not of perfect modesty. Guard with all jealousy the weak and the young. Above all pray for the sanctifying grace of the Holy Spirit of God, "that your whole spirit and soul and body may be preserved blameless unto the coming of our Lord Jesus Christ."

Signed on behalf of the Committee,

J. B DUNELM,
Chairman.

No. 3.—DIVORCE.

REPORT OF THE COMMITTEE [1] APPOINTED TO CONSIDER THE SUBJECT OF DIVORCE.

THE Committee appointed to consider the subject of "Divorce, and the question whether it may be practicable to offer any advice or suggestion which may help the Bishops and Clergy towards agreement in their action concerning it," reports as follows:—

They think it necessary to call attention to the fact that in very many Christian nations there is evidently a growing laxity of principle and of practice with regard to Divorce, and that in some countries strong attempts have been made to afford further facilities for it, with the result of weakening and lowering, both in law and in popular sentiment, the idea of the sanctity of marriage.

1. They therefore consider it important to declare that, inasmuch as our Lord's words expressly forbid Divorce, except in the case of fornication or adultery, the Christian Church cannot recognise Divorce in any other than the excepted case, or give any sanction to the marriage of any person who has been divorced contrary to this law, during the life of the other party.

2. They would add that under no circumstances ought the guilty party, in a case of Divorce for forni-

---

[1] Names of the Members of the Committee:—

Bishop of	Chester (*Chairman*).	Bishop of	Huron.
,,	Bombay.	,,	Maryland.
,,	Dover.	,,	Mississippi.
,	Durham.	,,	Quincy.
,,	Exeter.	,,	Singapore.

cation or adultery, to be regarded, during the lifetime of the innocent party, as a fit recipient of the blessing of the Church on marriage.

3. They recognise the fact that there always has been a difference of opinion in the Church on the question whether our Lord meant to forbid marriage to the innocent party in a Divorce for adultery: and they recommend that the Clergy should not be instructed to refuse the Sacraments or other privileges of the Church to those who, under civil sanction, are thus married.

4. But whereas doubt has been entertained whether our Lord meant to permit such marriage to the innocent party, the Committee are unwilling to suggest any precise instructions in this matter, and recommend that, where the laws of the land will permit, the determination should be left to the judgment of the Bishop of the Diocese, whether the Clergy would be justified in refraining from pronouncing the blessing of the Church on such unions.

Signed on behalf of the Committee,

W. CESTR:

Chairman.

No. 4.—POLYGAMY.

REPORT OF THE COMMITTEE[1] APPOINTED TO CONSIDER THE SUBJECT OF POLYGAMY OF HEATHEN CONVERTS.

YOUR Committee have approached the consideration of the subject submitted to them with an overwhelming sense of their responsibilities; inasmuch as the question intimately affects the sanctity of marriage, and therefore lies at the root of social morality.

After considering various representations which have been laid before them from divers quarters, they beg leave to report as follows:—

1. Your Committee desire to affirm distinctly that Polygamy is inconsistent with the law of Christ respecting marriage.

2. They cannot find that either the law of Christ or the usage of the early Church would permit the baptism of any man living in the practice of polygamy, even though the polygamous alliances should have been contracted before his conversion.

3. They are well aware that the change from polygamy to monogamy must frequently involve

---

[1] Names of the Members of the Committee:—

Bishop of Durham (*Chairman*). Bishop of the Niger.
„ Central Africa. Bishop Perry.
„ Chester. Bishop of Sierra Leone.
„ Exeter. „ South Dakota.
„ Guiana. „ Travancore.
„ London. „ Waiapu.
„ Meath. „ Zululand.
„ Missouri.

great difficulty and even hardship, but they are of opinion that it is not possible to lay down a precise rule to be observed under all circumstances in dealing with this difficulty.

They consequently think that the question of time and manner, which must depend largely on local circumstances, can only be determined by local authority.

4. Your Committee recommend that persons living in polygamy should, on their conversion, be accepted as candidates for Baptism, and kept under Christian instruction until such time as they shall be in a position to accept the law of Christ.

They consider it far better that Baptism should be withheld from such persons, while nevertheless they receive instruction in the truths of the Gospel, than that a measure should be sanctioned which would tend to lower the conception of the Christian law of marriage, and thus inflict an irreparable wound on the morality of the Christian Church in its most vital part.

5. The wives of polygamists may, in the opinion of the Committee, be admitted, in some cases, to Baptism; inasmuch as their position is materially different from that of the polygamist husband. In most countries where polygamy prevails they have no personal freedom to contract or dissolve a matrimonial alliance; and moreover they presumably do not violate the Christian precept which enjoins fidelity to one husband.

6. In carrying into effect the principles here laid down, with due regard to the dictates of love and justice, serious burdens will in some cases be imposed on the Churches, but no trouble, or cost, or self-sacrifice, ought to be spared to make any suffering which may be caused as light and easy to bear as possible.

7. Difficult questions of detail which may arise in following these recommendations must be left to the

decision of the local authorities of the Church, whether Diocesan or Provincial.

8. Throughout this Report polygamy has been taken to mean the union of one man with several wives; but among some tribes the union of one woman with several husbands is a recognised institution. It will be plain that no such union can be recognised by the Church.

9. It has been represented to your Committee that heathen marriages in many cases do not imply a mutual pledge of life-long fidelity; and instruction has been asked as to the mode of dealing with such cases on the conversion of the contracting parties, so as to impart a Christian character to the contract. The Committee think it best to leave the local authorities of the Church to determine in what way this end may be best attained; but they deprecate any course which would tend to impair the validity (within their own sphere) of contracts undertaken prior to conversion, so far as these contracts are not inconsistent with the law of Christ.

10. In laying down the principles which should rule the admission of Christian converts for the future, the Committee have no intention of passing any censure on those who have decided otherwise in the past; and they desire to leave to individual Bishops the responsibility of dealing with difficulties which may arise in any part of the mission-field from the adoption of a different line of action heretofore by those in authority.

J. B. DUNELM,
Chairman.

No. 5.—SUNDAY OBSERVANCE.

REPORT OF THE COMMITTEE[1] APPOINTED TO CONSIDER THE SUBJECT OF THE OBSERVANCE OF SUNDAY.

YOUR Committee have met and prayerfully considered the subject of the sanctity and observance of the Lord's Day, and have agreed to the following statements of their deliberate judgment on this momentous question, which they submit as their report:—

1. That the principle of the religious observance of one day in seven is of Divine and primeval obligation, and was afterwards embodied in the Fourth Commandment.
2. That from the time of our Lord's Resurrection the first day of the week was observed as a day of sacred joy by Christians, and was ere long adopted by the Church as the Christian Sabbath or "the Lord's Day."
3. That the observance of the Lord's Day as a day of rest, of worship, and of religious teaching, has been a priceless blessing in all Christian lands in which it has been maintained.
4. That the growing licence in its observance threatens a grave change in its sacred and beneficent character.

---

[1] Names of the Members of the Committee :—
Bishop of Exeter (*Chairman*).   Bishop of Indiana.
   ,,   Argyll.   ,, Liverpool.
   ,,   Brisbane.   ,, Wakefield.
   ,,   Cashel.   ,, Washington.

5. That especially the increasing practice on the part of some of the wealthy and leisurely classes of making the day a day of secular amusement is most strongly to be deprecated.
6. That the most careful regard should be had to the danger of any encroachment upon the rest which on this day is the right of servants as well as their masters, and of the working classes as well as their employers.

Signed on behalf of the Committee,

E. H. EXON.
Chairman.

No. 6.—SOCIALISM.

REPORT OF THE COMMITTEE[1] APPOINTED TO CONSIDER THE SUBJECT OF THE CHURCH'S PRACTICAL WORK IN RELATION TO SOCIALISM.

This Committee was directed to report "on the Church's practical work in relation to Socialism." It will be desirable therefore, in the first place, to ascertain, if possible, what is the meaning of Socialism. This, however, is not easy, as the word is used at present in very different senses. When Proudhon was asked, What is Socialism? he replied, "It is every aspiration towards the improvement of society." Laveleye remarks upon this answer, that "Proudhon's definition is too wide,—it omits two characteristics. In the first place, every socialistic doctrine aims at introducing greater equality into social conditions; and, secondly, it tries to realise those reforms by the action of the law or the State." So far, however, as this definition makes the interference of the State a necessary element of Socialism, it is not universally accepted. Schäffle, for instance, says:—"The alpha and omega of Socialism is the transformation of private competing capitals into a united collective capital;" and T. Kirkup, in a thoughtful article on Socialism in the last edition of the Encyclopædia

---

[1] Names of the Members of the Committee :—

Bishop of Manchester (*Chairman*).		Bishop of Mississippi.	
,,	Brisbane.	,,	Pittsburgh.
,,	Carlisle.	,,	Rochester.
,,	Derry.	,,	Sydney.
,,	Michigan.	,,	Wakefield.

Britannica, affirms that "the central aim of Socialism is to terminate the divorce of the workers from the natural sources of subsistence and of culture"; and, again, he says, "the essence of the theory consists in this—associated production, with a collective capital, with the view to an equitable distribution." Speaking broadly, then, and with reference to such definitions as the preceding, any scheme of social reconstruction may be called Socialism which aims at uniting labour and the instruments of labour (land and capital), whether by means of the State, or of the help of the rich, or of the voluntary co-operation of the poor.

Between Socialism, as thus defined, and Christianity, there is obviously no necessary contradiction. Christianity sets forth no theory of the distribution of the instruments or the products of labour; and if, therefore, some Socialists are found to be in opposition to the Christian religion, this must be due to the accidents and not to the essence of their social creed. Some Socialists are atheists, others advocate loose doctrines as to family ties; others, like the Anarchists, seek to realise their aims, so far as they have any, by undisguised murder and robbery; while, according to some, the very possession of private property is a usurpation and a wrong to the community. With such men the Christian Church can form no alliance. And yet at the same time with what they profess to be their central aim, the improvement of the material and moral condition of the poor, she must have the deepest sympathy. Their methods, indeed, are not hers. Spoliation or injustice in any form is abhorrent alike to her sentiment and belief. She has no faith in the inherent power of humanity to redeem itself from selfishness. She seeks to make men prosperous and wise and good, not by the force of laws or bayonets, but by the change of individual hearts, and the introduction of a new brotherhood in Christ.

Not the less, however, is she bound, following the teaching of her Master, to aid every wise endeavour which has for its object the material and moral welfare of the poor. Her Master taught her that all men are brethren, not because they share the same blood, but because they have a common Heavenly Father. He further taught her that if any of the members of this spiritual family were greater, richer, or better than the rest, they were bound to use their special means or ability in the service of the whole. "He that is greatest among you," He said, "shall be your servant,"—and that for a special reason, because each disciple was bound to imitate his Divine Master, "Who came not to be ministered unto, but to minister, and to give His life a ransom for many."

The Church's practical duty, then, towards Socialism must be determined by the answer to this question, will the union of labour and the instruments of labour tend to improve the material, mental, and moral condition of mankind? Experience seems to show that it will.

It may still, however, be a question, what is the wisest *method* of bringing about this union between labour and its instruments? Two principal schemes have been proposed :—

(1) That labourers shall be encouraged in habits of thrift, in order that with the property thus acquired they may purchase land, or shares in societies for co-operative production.

(2) That the State shall take possession of the whole land and capital of any country, with or without compensation to their former owners; that the property thus nationalised, shall be held in trust for the community by the State, the Commune, or associations of working men; that then the State, the Commune, or the association as the case may be, shall take measures for the preservation, increase, and employment of the common capital, requiring work from each man according to his ability, and bestowing property upon each man according to his needs, or the value of his labour. Minor modifications of this

scheme, tending to bring it into closer harmony with the existing state of society, have been proposed by some Socialistic teachers, but still it may be taken as a substantially correct representation of the ultimate aim of very many.

To this second method of uniting labour and its instruments the Committee would urge the following objections:—(1) If full compensation were given to the present holders of property the scheme could hardly be realised, while if full compensation were withheld it would become one of undisguised spoliation. (2) If Government were able to acquire just possession of the whole property of a community, it is difficult to see how the affairs of any great commercial undertaking could be conducted by the State or the Commune with the energy, economy, and sagacious foresight which are necessary to secure success. (3) If all men had to work under State or Communal inspection and compulsion, it would be difficult for them to retain freedom, the sense of parental responsibility, and those numerous traits of individuality which give richness to the human character.

The Committee strongly recommend the adoption of the first-named method. They believe that it will be well to encourage working men to become possessors of small farms, and of shares in societies for co-operative production in trade and agriculture. They are not unaware that these societies have frequently failed, but they believe that the opinion is not without its weight, that if due care be taken to secure efficient and trustworthy managers, to pay them an adequate salary, and to treat them with a generous confidence, there is no reason why such undertakings should not become successful, as indeed they commonly are now, when their management is in competent hands.

Two objections have been frequently advanced against this method of diminishing the present distress; 1st, that it is unjust to let any one but the labourer obtain possession of any part of the products of his labour; and, 2ndly, that no man of property or ability ought to seek personal profit from the employment of his special advantages, or ought even to be allowed to become the permanent owner of either land or capital.

The first objection is not tenable. The Committee hold that it is just (1) to pay high wages for exceptional ability; (2) to compensate for his abstinence the man who refrains from consuming his own share of the products of labour, and by so doing makes it possible to maintain and increase the capital of the community; (3) to allow any one to convert his savings into the form of capital or estate.

The second objection is really founded upon the general spirit of our Lord's teaching—viz., that greatness, ability, or wealth should be made the means of service to the poor and weak without special fee or reward. The Committee fully admit that this is the ideal set before us by our Divine Master, and that it is the end, towards which we should press, as quickly as the conquest of selfishness will allow us. But they hold that there is no surer cause of failure in practical affairs, than the effort to act on an ideal which has not yet been realised. If the Church is to act safely as well as sublimely, she must take the self-regarding motives with her on the long path by which she advances towards the perfect life of love. She must not assume the existence of what does not yet exist. She must not, like the Anarchists, destroy the whole existing framework of society for the sake of making experiments. Nay, more, she must not ignore the fact that self-regard is the necessary condition of self-preservation, and that her Master's law of moral conduct, that each shall love his neighbour as himself, implies a certain amount of self-regard. Competition is not injurious in itself, it only becomes so when it is unrestricted, when it takes no counsel of the dictates of brotherly love.

The Committee do not doubt that Government can do much to protect the class known as proletarians from the evil effects of unchecked competition. The English poor-law has long ago provided the bare necessaries of life for those who cannot otherwise obtain them; the institution of State Savings Banks has provided for the poor man a safe investment and moderate return for his savings. Acts of Parliament have required the builders and owners of houses to have regard for the health and comfort of their tenants, while the factory legislation of this country has effectually protected those labourers who cannot protect themselves. The Committee believe, further, that the State may justly and safely extend this protective action in several directions. It may legalise the formation of Boards of Arbitration, to avert the disastrous effects of strikes. It may assist in the formation and maintenance of technical schools. It may see that powers, already existing, under Sanitary Acts, are more effectually exercised. It may facilitate the acquisition by Municipalities of town lands. The State may even encourage a wider distribution of property by the abolition of entail, where it exists; and it may be questioned whether the system of taxation might not be varied in a sense more favourable to the claims of labourers than that which now exists.

But, after all, the best help is self-help. More even than increase of income, and security of deposit, thrift and self-restraint are the necessary elements of material prosperity. And in encouraging and strengthening such habits and feelings the Church's help is invaluable. By requiring some knowledge of economic science from her candidates for orders; by forming and fostering institutions for the provision of practical education and rational recreation; by establishing penny banks and workmen's guilds; above all, by inducing capitalists to admit their workmen to profit-sharing, and by teaching artisans how to make co-operative production successful she may do much to diminish discontent, and to increase the feeling of brotherly interest between class and class. The Clergy may enter into friendly relations with Socialists, attending, when possible, their club meetings, and trying to understand their aims and methods. At the same time it will contribute no little to draw together the various classes of society if the Clergy endeavour, in sermons and lectures, to to set forth the true principles of Society, showing how property is a trust to be administered for the good of humanity, and how much of what is good and true in Socialism is to be found in the precepts of Christ. The call to aid the weak, through works of what is ordinarily known as charity, has been, at all times, faithfully pressed by the Church of Christ, and has been met by a noble response, which has been the chief strength of works of beneficence in modern Society. But the matter is one, not merely of Charity, but of Social and Christian Duty. It is in this light that the Church has to proclaim it in these critical times, with some special boldness and earnestness. At the same time the word of warning should not be wanting. Mutual suspicion and the imputation of selfish and unworthy motives keep apart those who have, in fact, a common aim. Intestine strife and doctrines of spoliation destroy confidence, arrest trade, and will but increase misery.

The Committee believe that, in the present condition of thought and knowledge, they cannot wisely or profitably go further than they have done above in the way of detailed suggestion. There is less temptation to over-haste in forcing on social experiments, inasmuch as the history of the past shows convincingly that the principles of the Gospel contain germs from which Social renovation is surely, if slowly, developed by the continuous action of Christian thought and feeling upon every form of evil and suffering. If all will only labour, under the impulse of Christian love, for the highest benefit of each, we shall advance by the shortest possible path to that better and happier future for which our Master taught us to hope and pray.

Signed on behalf of the Committee,

J. MANCHESTER,
Chairman.

No. 7.—CARE OF EMIGRANTS.

REPORT OF THE COMMITTEE[1] APPOINTED TO CONSIDER THE CHURCH'S PRACTICAL WORK IN RELATION TO THE CARE OF EMIGRANTS.

IN considering the question of the practical work of the Church in relation to the Care of Emigrants, your Committee have limited their inquiries and the recommendations which they desire to submit to the judgment of the Conference, to those points which bear on the promotion of the religious and moral well-being of our emigrants. They are of opinion that the wider subject of encouraging and assisting emigration is outside the scope of their deliberations, and, even were this not the case, that it is far too large a question to be adequately dealt with in the time at their disposal.

I. In the first place, your Committee feel that they cannot too strongly emphasise the *vast importance of the subject* entrusted to them for consideration. They believe that the problem is one of the most urgent and pressing of the many problems with which the Church has to deal at the present day. And they cannot but think that before many years have passed away, the difficulties of dealing with the problem will

---

[1] Names of the Members of the Committee :—
Bishop of Llandaff (*Chairman*).   Bishop of North Dakota.
    „   Algoma.   „   North Queensland.
    „   Liverpool.   „   Pittsburgh.
    „   Maritzburg.   „   Quebec.
    „   Newark.   „   Rupertsland.
    „   Niagara.   „   Sodor and Man.

be immeasurably increased; and thus it becomes of paramount necessity that the machinery for coping with these difficulties should be organised and set in motion while the extent of emigration is such as to render this possible.

When once the machinery is in good working order, it will then be capable of almost indefinite extension, to meet the increasing demands upon its capacities.

(a) Foremost among the reasons which point to the importance of due provision being made for the spiritual care of our emigrants is this:—Those who leave the British Isles and go forth to seek their fortune in new lands, choose, for the most part, either the United States of America, or Canada, or some of the Colonies of Australia. Of these a very large number are *children of one or another Branch of the Anglican Communion*, and, as such, have a right to expect that the Anglican Church will duly minister to them in whatever part of the world their lot may be cast. An enormous responsibility lies upon the Church in this matter, and it is her duty, so far as in her lies, to prevent estrangement, or any loss of spiritual life in her children, through the accident of their removal from one Branch of the Anglican Church to another.

(b) The simple consideration of the *very large number of emigrants* who have left and who are still leaving British Ports, is a sufficient indication of the immense responsibility of the Church towards them. Since the year of the Battle of Waterloo (1815) the total number of emigrants leaving the United Kingdom has been 11,740,573. But a truer estimate of the great increase in later years is shown from the fact that, during the last ten years, since the Lambeth Conference of 1878, 3,519,660 out of the above-named 11 millions have left this country. This gives an average of 319,566 emigrants per annum (including British subjects and foreigners). The average is, however, now greatly exceeded every year, as the following figures will show:—

British and Irish Emigrants who have left British Ports in the last 10 years.	Total number of Emigrants, including British subjects and Foreigners, who have left British Ports in the last 10 years.
In 1878 ... 112,902	In 1878 ... 147,663
„ 1879 ... 164,274	„ 1879 ... 217,163
„ 1880 ... 227,542	„ 1880 ... 332,294
„ 1881 ... 243,002	„ 1881 ... 392,514
„ 1882 ... 279,366	„ 1882 ... 413,288
„ 1883 ... 320,118	„ 1883 ... 397,157
„ 1884 ... 242,179	„ 1884 ... 303,901
„ 1885 ... 207,644	„ 1885 ... 264,385
„ 1886 ... 232,900	„ 1886 ... 330,801
„ 1887 ... 281,487	„ 1887 ... 396,494
Total ... 2,311,414	Total ... 3,195,660
Average per Annum of British and Irish Emigrants. } 231,141	Average per Annum of all Emigrants } 319,566

By far the largest proportion of emigrants go to the United States. The percentage, in 1887, to the three chief fields of emigration, was as follows:—To the United States, 72 per cent.; to British North America, 11 per cent.; to the Australasian Colonies, 12 per cent.; to all other places, 5 per cent. The following table shows the distribution of the actual number of emigrants in 1887:—

Emigrants (British and Irish only) 1887.		Total Emigrants (British and Foreign) 1887.	
To the United States	201,526	To the United States	296,901
„ British North America	32,025	„ British North America	44,406
„ Australasia	34,183	„ Australasia	35,198
„ all other places	13,753	„ all other places	19,989
	281,487		396,494

Thus, very nearly three-fourths of the 396,494 people who left the United Kingdom last year were of British or Irish origin, whose spiritual interests the Church cannot properly disregard.

(*c*) A third reason for urging the importance of the care of our emigrants is the *danger to which they are exposed* between the time of their leaving their old home and the time when they are finally established in their new one.

The dangers on the voyage are by no means inconsiderable. The impossibility, when 500 or more emigrants are carried in one vessel, of separating the reckless and careless from those who are thoughtful and well-disposed, exposes the latter to great temptations. This is especially the case with young unmarried women. Then, again, the dangers are no less great at the port of arrival, where young persons, among strangers and surroundings which are new and unknown, are liable to fall a prey to the unscrupulous men and women who are ever on the watch, at such times, to take advantage of ignorance and innocence. And, perhaps, the greatest danger of all arises from the temptations to intemperance and other vices to which the emigrants are exposed on arrival at their new settlement.

(*d*) One more point remains to be mentioned under this head, and that is, the enormous *value of the opportunity* afforded by the softening influence which is brought about by the severance of the associations of home and early life, for awakening religious impressions in those who have hitherto been insensible to the Church's teaching, as well as for deepening the spiritual life of those who are true Christians. Wherever this opportunity is taken advantage of, the result is seen in the strengthening of the Church in the country to which the emigrant goes.

Having thus dwelt upon some of the chief reasons why the spiritual care of emigrants is of such

supreme importance, your Committee proceed to consider—
  What work has already been done in this direction.
  What work still remains to be done.

II. Work which has already been done.

Your Committee have pleasure in acknowledging what has already been accomplished in the establishment and continuance of moral and religious work among emigrants. The Society for Promoting Christian Knowledge has organised a plan which is working with much success, and which, when further developed, promises to be of the highest value to the Church. Your Committee desire to express their hearty sense of gratitude which is due for the admirable work carried on by that Society, which has always been at the head of all religious efforts on behalf of emigrants. They would also acknowledge with thankfulness the meritorious work which has been done by other Societies, especially at the Port of London, and notably that which has been undertaken by the St. Andrew's Waterside Mission.

Without being able to give a complete account of every attempt made to assist and benefit emigrants, it is gratifying to be able to point to the following efforts, which have been successfully carried out, and which have led to valuable results :—

(*a*) Chaplains have been appointed at all the ports of departure in the United Kingdom, whose duty it is to minister to emigrants; to arrange services for them, both before starting and on the voyage; to give them introductions to Clergymen abroad; and generally to arrange for their reception by the Church in the new country to which they are travelling.

(*b*) The Church in the United States of America has initiated a most important work, in having appointed Chaplains at New York, Baltimore, and Philadelphia, whose duty it is to give such spiritual aid as is possible to arriving immigrants, and to commend them further to the Church at their ultimate destination inland.

(*c*) Chaplains who accompany emigrants on the voyage, and who minister to them, and hold frequent services on board, have also been appointed on many vessels going to America, Australia, and New Zealand, and the Cape. The great value of having such Chaplains on board is evident, and this is especially the case on the long-voyage ships to Australia and the Cape. The financial burden of the remuneration of these Chaplains is borne by the S.P.C.K.

(*d*) In order to provide due protection for girls and single women emigrating, matrons (other than the regular Government Emigrant Matrons) have from time to time been appointed, who are required to look after their charges during the voyage and on arrival at their destination. The help derived from their protection and the moral influence of the matrons has been largely felt. In this branch of the work your Committee desire to acknowledge the valuable services rendered by the Girls' Friendly Society.

(*e*) Clergymen living in all parts of the world have consented to allow persons emigrating to be specially commended to them by letter, and they have given valuable assistance and advice to emigrants when first settling in a new country.

(*f*) The publication of some thousands of handbooks for the use of emigrants has in the past proved a valuable held to them. These books contain particulars about the various Colonies, and other matters likely to be of assistance. The recent establishment by the English Government of an "Emigrants' Information Office," where books, leaflets, and information may be had, is found to be of very great service.

(*g*) A large number of books (Bibles, Prayer-books, and other books of a religious or interesting nature) have been provided for the emigrants on their outward voyage. Many of these have been given away, and in this manner religious teaching and influence have been brought to bear upon them.

(*h*) Forms of Letters of Commendation for the use of emigrants have been issued in large numbers,[1] and it is most desirable that Clergymen should provide themselves with these letters. The Clergyman of the parish in which the intending emigrant resides should fill up such forms, and address to a Bishop or Clergyman of the Church abroad, where the emigrant intends to settle. Where these letters have been given, they have been proved to be of real value, as forming a link between home and foreign countries, and securing for the emigrant a welcome from the Church.

III. Work still remaining to be done.

Your Committee consider that, notwithstanding the praiseworthy efforts made and carried out, for the moral and spiritual welfare of emigrants, a very large and increasing amount of work lies before the Church, which calls for immediate, earnest and united action on the part of every branch of the Anglican Communion. They consider that this work may be attempted in two ways: (i.) as a development and improvement of existing organisations; and (ii.) as a new departure.

(A) Under the head of the *development of organisations* which already exist, your Committee would mention the following suggestions which seem to be of importance:—

(1) That the English Bishops should impress upon the Parochial Clergy, at Diocesan Conferences and on other occasions, the solemn duty (*a*) of providing that not one of their Parishioners be allowed to leave home without being provided with a Letter of Com-

---

[1] For a copy of this Form, see Schedule A.

mendation to the Church abroad, stating particularly whether they have been baptized and confirmed, or are communicants; (*b*) of informing intending emigrants that the Protestant Episcopal Church in the United States of America is the only Church in the United States which is in full communion with the Church of England.

(2) That it is expedient that letters should be sent from England (in addition to the above Commendatory Letters), to precede the emigrant on his journey out. These letters should be sent to the Bishop abroad, and should give notice of the intended arrival of the emigrant, adding such information with regard to character and qualifications as may be of assistance to the Bishop or Clergyman to whom the emigrant is commended.

(3) That the Bishops in the Colonies and in the United States of America be urged to press upon their Clergy the duty of prompt attention to such Commendatory Letters as may be presented to them from emigrants, either directly or through the Bishops.

(4) That the attention of the Church in the United States be called to the extreme desirability and need of at once increasing the number of immigrant Chaplains at New York and other ports, where at present the number of emigrants makes it impossible for the existing staff to minister adequately to those who arrive. At New York especially it would seem that these increased Church ministrations should be supplied with as little delay as possible.

(5) That, with the view of increasing the number of Chaplains who shall accompany emigrants on the voyage, the Clergy should be specially invited, when travelling to the Colonies, to take every opportunity of acting as Chaplains on board emigrant ships.[1]

---

[1] Full information as to the duties of such Chaplains, and of the remuneration which can in some cases be offered them, is obtainable from the S.P.C.K.

(6) That, in consideration of the great influence exercised upon emigrants by the Government Matron on board ship, it is important that care be taken in the selection of good Christian women for the office.

(B) Your Committee feel that the work which has already been attempted for the spiritual welfare of our emigrants has been carried out by the best methods, and therefore their recommendations for the future have been mainly devoted to the development and extension of existing organisations.

They would, however, suggest for consideration the following four *points of new departure*, as being, in their opinion, of paramount importance at the present time:—

(1) That the Church in Australasia and in Canada be urged to provide more adequate spiritual ministrations for immigrants at the ports of arrival, by the appointment of Chaplains whose whole time could, if necessary, be devoted to the work.

(2) That it is most desirable to establish homes for emigrants at the ports of departure and arrival, where those needing protection or care may be received.

(3) That the Archbishops of Canterbury and York and the Bishop of London be requested to prepare a Form of Prayer for Use at Sea, having regard to the special needs of emigrants.

(4) That it would be of great service if more frequent and regular interchange of reports of work done, and of the requirements in respect of emigrants, could take place between the Church in England and the Church in the United States and in the Colonies.

Your Committee cannot bring their report to a close without expressing their deep thankfulness to Almighty God for the measure of success which has hitherto attended the Church in her efforts on behalf of her emigrants, and an earnest prayer for the guidance and blessing of the Holy Spirit in the years to come.

Signed on behalf of the Committee,
R. LLANDAFF, *Chairman*.

Schedule A.

[FORM OF COMMENDATORY LETTER.]

....

Reverend and dear Sir,

I desire herewith to commend to your pastoral care and brotherly good offices.................................. from the Parish of...in the Diocese of.................................who is about to settle in...

And I certify that*...
....
....
....
....

Dated this...

* *Here state whether baptized, confirmed, or a Communicant.*

[S.P.C.K.]

No. 8.—MUTUAL RELATIONS.

REPORT OF THE COMMITTEE[1] APPOINTED TO CONSIDER THE SUBJECT OF THE MUTUAL RELATIONS OF THE DIOCESES AND BRANCHES OF THE ANGLICAN COMMUNION.

THE Committee feel that it would be impossible for them to deal in any complete and exhaustive manner with a subject so extensive as that which has been referred to them for consideration. They have therefore determined to confine their attention to such definite and practical points as have been brought under their notice, and as appear to them to be worthy of being made the subject of report.

I. The attention of the Committee has been directed to alleged neglect of certain important principles which were laid down by the Lambeth Conference of 1878. The principles are contained in the following quotations :—

    (1) First, that the duly-certified action of every national or particular Church, and of each ecclesiastical Province (or Diocese not included in a Province), in the exercise of its

---

[1] Names of the Members of the Committee :—
Bishop of Carlisle (*Chairman*). Bishop of Derry.
  " Adelaide.   " Jamaica.
  " Auckland.   " Manchester.
  " Brechin.   " Moray and Ross.
  " Calcutta.   " New Jersey.
  " Capetown.   " North China.
  " Central Pennsylvania. " Sierra Leone.
  " Chester.   " Tennessee.
  " Colombo.

own discipline, should be respected by all the other Churches, and by their individual members.

(2) Secondly, that when a Diocese, or territorial sphere of administration, has been constituted by the authority of any Church or Province of this Communion within its own limits, no Bishop or other Clergyman of any other Church should exercise his functions within that Diocese, without the consent of the Bishop thereof.

(3) Thirdly, that no Bishop should authorise to officiate in his Diocese a Clergyman coming from another Church or Province unless such Clergyman present letters testimonial, countersigned by the Bishop of the Diocese from which he comes, such letters to be as nearly as possible in the form adopted by such Church or Province in the case of the transfer of a Clergyman from one Diocese to another.

(See above, page 166-7.)

The Committee would urge that more attention should be paid by Metropolitans and Bishops, or persons temporarily administering the affairs of a Diocese, to the practical enforcement of the principles above enunciated; and they would add in particular the following recommendation — namely, that the Archbishop of Canterbury be respectfully requested to consider whether it be possible to devise and suggest any means whereby it may be made more easy to avoid the intrusion of unworthy or pretended Priests or Deacons into the various Dioceses of the Anglican Communion.

II. It has been brought under the notice of the Committee that difficulty has arisen with regard to the validity of orders derived from certain Bishops alleged to be schismatical. It would be exceedingly desirable that some definite and uniform course of action should be adopted by all Bishops of the Anglican Communion in dealing with persons holding such so-called orders.

The Committee are of opinion that, although much may have been said to the contrary, there are in reality no persons claiming Anglican Orders of doubtful character whose claims deserve serious consideration. With regard to Orders alleged to be derived, though irregularly, through the American Church, it may be sufficient to say that the whole transaction is disallowed and regarded as null and void by the American Episcopate. This fact, in the opinion of the Committee, may be taken as a sufficient guide to all Bishops of the Anglican Communion.

III. A question has been brought before the Committee, based upon a Report made to the General Synod of the Dioceses in Australia and Tasmania, on the subject of the title of Archbishop. The Committee have been asked to express an opinion as to the desirability of assigning the title of Archbishop to the Primate of Australia and Tasmania. The Committee feel that there is great difficulty in coming to a clear judgment upon a question which must, of necessity, to some extent depend for its answer upon local circumstances; but taking the question upon broad grounds, and looking to the general interests of the whole Church, the Committee have no hesitation in expressing their opinion that there are cases of important Provinces in which distinct advantages would result from adopting the ancient and honoured title of Archbishop. In the event of this course being adopted weighty questions might arise with regard to authority and precedence, but upon these questions the Committee think that it would be unwise to enter.

IV. The Committee have given anxious consideration to the question of the formation of a central Council of Reference, to which recourse may be had for advice on questions of doctrine and discipline by the tribunals of appeal of the various Provinces of the Anglican Communion.

With reference to this question, which has already been before the Conferences of 1867 and 1878, the Committee think that they cannot do better than call attention to what has actually been done in the case of Australia and Tasmania.

The following resolutions were adopted by the General Synod of Australia and Tasmania in 1872:—

> If, in the opinion of the Committee of Appeal of the General Synod of the Church of England in Australia and Tasmania, the matter of appeal concerns a question of doctrine, or discipline involving a question of doctrine, the Committee may, at its discretion, state a case for the opinion thereon of a body in England, to be called the Council of Reference. Such Council of Reference shall consist of the Archbishops of Canterbury and York, and the Bishop of London, together with four laymen learned in the law, the first four such laymen being Lord Hatherley, Lord Chelmsford, Lord Cairns, and Lord Penzance. The General Synod shall have power to fill up vacancies as they shall from time to time occur, but in the event of a vacancy or vacancies existing when a case shall be before the Council, the Archbishops and Bishop shall fill up the same for the purpose of disposing of that particular case. The opinion of the Council shall be binding on the Committee, and pending the obtaining of such an opinion, the appeal shall stand adjourned, with liberty to either of the parties to set the appeal down

to be disposed of upon the opinion when obtained. If from any cause it shall be impracticable to obtain an opinion from the Council of Reference within a time to be limited by the rules to be made under the resolutions, the Committee of its own motion may, or at the instance of either of the parties shall, determine the appeal; but in such case the concurrence of one of the two Bishops shall be requisite in any decision.

The Committee are of opinion that a plan of reference to a Council in England, framed upon such principles as those adopted by the General Synod of Australia and Tasmania, would probably meet the wants, should they arise, of other Provinces.

It has been brought to the attention of the Committee that, in some parts of the Anglican Communion, notably, in the Province of the West Indies, schemes somewhat different from that above described have been adopted. It is needless to say that the Committee do not desire to pass an opinion upon details, but only to indicate a general method of action.

V. The attention of the Committee has been further directed to the danger of important divergences with regard to matters of doctrine, as well as forms of worship, being introduced amongst the Anglican Churches by the possible assumption on the part of each Province or Diocese of the power of revising the Book of Common Prayer. Such divergences might be injurious to the Church at large, and would certainly interfere with the mutual relations of its different parts.

It is not within the province of the Committee to lay down rules as to the powers of the different branches of the Anglican Communion in this matter, or as to the line of action which they ought to follow. This remark applies with especial emphasis to the Episcopal Church of America, though the Committee cannot abstain from remarking with pleasure that recent changes made in the Book of Common Prayer by that Church have been rather in the direction of nearer approach to the English Book than of further departure from it. But with regard to the branches of the Church within the limits of her Majesty's dominions, the Committee cannot express too strongly the opinion which they entertain with regard to the danger of alteration in existing services. They do not deny in general that the Book of Common Prayer may be susceptible of improvement; this susceptibility may probably be predicated of all things human; though it must be remembered that it might be hard to find many improvements, which would be generally and heartily accepted as such. Neither do they wish to express an opinion unfavourable to efforts made to supplement the prayers and services of the Church by others which her needs demand. But the point which the Committte would chiefly urge is this—that the Book of Common Prayer is not the possession of one Diocese or Province, but of all; that a revision in one portion of the Anglican Communion must, therefore, be extensively felt, and that it is not just that any particular portion should undertake revision without consultation with other portions, and especially with the Church at home.

VI. There appears to be a notion current that Clergymen ordained for work in England, who go out to labour for a time in the Colonies, are regarded as more or less disqualified for subsequent preferment at home. The Committee regret that such a notion should be current, and they are of opinion that Clergymen who have been willing to give a portion of the best time of their lives to colonial work may be regarded as having special claims for consideration on their return home. The Committee are aware that the subject is not free from difficulties, and that it is impossible to lay down any general rule; but they have thought it right to give it a place in their Report, and that some benefit may arise from the course thus adopted.

These are all the matters which have been brought under the notice of the Committee, or which have been deemed of sufficient importance or of a suitable kind to be brought before the Conference. In concluding their Report the Committee would desire to express their sense of the extent and difficulty of the subject which has been entrusted to them, and of the modest character of their contribution to its treatment. But they believe that the wise and perhaps the only course of dealing with such a subject is not to attempt to lay down rules which shall solve all possible problems, but to discuss practical difficulties as they arise, in dependence upon the Holy Spirit of God and trusting that He who permits the difficulties will give grace and strength to overcome them.

Signed on behalf of the Committee,

H. CARLISLE,
Chairman.

APPENDIX TO REPORT OF COMMITTEE.
No. 8.

ANOTHER subject has been brought under the notice of the Committee, concerning which they have felt great doubt as to whether it can be regarded as coming within the terms of their reference. The subject, however, is so important, and the Committee have felt so desirous that it should be fairly brought before the Conference, that they have determined to introduce it in the form of an Appendix to their Report.

The question was raised in the first meeting of the Conference, whether it would not be desirable that some declaration should be made concerning the teaching of the English Church, and of those Churches which are in full communion with her.

There can be little doubt as to the existence of much ignorance and misunderstanding, not only as to what this teaching is, but also as to the ground upon which those Churches stand, and as to their relation to other Churches and Christian Societies. Such ignorance and misunderstanding can scarcely fail to interfere seriously with the results of their teaching.

It is true that the English Church possesses a body of teaching in the Book of Common Prayer, in the Catechism, and in the Thirty-nine Articles, to say nothing of the Book of Homilies. But these repositories of teaching, precious as they are, do not appear to the Committee to possess the qualities which ought to belong to a declaration, such as is contemplated in the remarks now made. What is wanted is a plain and brief summary of the definite doctrinal grounds upon which the Anglican Churches stand (somewhat, perhaps, after the manner of the earlier of the Thirty-nine Articles), together with a statement of their relation to other Churches and Christian Societies, and, perhaps, of other cognate matters upon which, on consideration of the whole subject, it might be considered desirable that some distinct utterance should be made. The summary should be such as the whole body of English-speaking Bishops could adopt ; it should, therefore, be free from all questions of doubtful controversy ; it should be a document which could be freely circulated as a manifesto of the Anglican Churches concerning their status and their teaching.

The proposal, undoubtedly, has its difficulties, as almost every important proposal has ; but we think that the difficulties might possibly be overcome ; and certainly all danger of mischief would be avoided, if the following plans were adopted :—

It is respectfully suggested :

(1) That a small committee of English Bishops be appointed by the Archbishop of Canterbury for the purpose of drafting such a declaration.

(2) That the Committee have power to consult, if they think fit, with any of their episcopal brethren, and also with eminent divines outside the episcopal body.

(3) That the draft declaration, having been provisionally settled by the Committee, be submitted to the Archbishop of Canterbury, with the request that his Grace will forward copies to each Metropolitan for the consideration of the Bishops in his Province, and that he will, in conjunction with the Archbishop of York, bring the declaration before the English Bishops.

[The term Metropolitan includes Primates of Provinces, the Primus of Scotland, and the Presiding Bishop of the Church of America.]

(4) That each Metropolitan be requested to return

a copy of the declaration, either approved, or with suggestions of amendment, within twelve months.

(5) That the Archbishop of Canterbury, be requested upon the return of the drafts to take such further steps as the circumstances in his judgment shall appear to warrant.

The Committee recommend that the declaration should be in the form of a series of statements or articles; each dealing with a different subject, and to be expressed in the simplest possible language.

The Committee feel that they would be going beyond their province if they attempted to dictate the subjects upon which statements should be framed: but in order more clearly to indicate the kind of declaration which they think the needs of the time demand, they venture to specify the following subjects which they believe might be profitably introduced:—

I. Of the Catholic Faith.
II. Of the Holy Scriptures.
III. Of the Sacraments.
IV. Of the Forms of Prayer and Liturgy in use in the Anglican Churches.
V. Of the relation of the Anglican Churches to the Church of Rome.
VI. Of the relation of the Anglican Churches to the Churches of the East.
VII. Of the relation of the Anglican Churches to other Christian Churches and Societies.
VIII. Of the relation of the teaching of the Church of Christ to human knowledge.

It is almost unnecessary to state that the Committee do not regard the above list as exhaustive; nor, on the other hand, do they desire to insist upon each and all of the suggested subjects as essential to the completeness of the proposed declaration.

Signed on behalf of the Committee,

H. CARLISLE,
Chairman.

No. 9.—HOME REUNION.

REPORT OF THE COMMITTEE[1] APPOINTED TO CONSIDER WHAT STEPS (IF ANY) CAN BE RIGHTLY TAKEN ON BEHALF OF THE ANGLICAN COMMUNION TOWARDS THE REUNION OF THE VARIOUS BODIES INTO WHICH THE CHRISTIANITY OF THE ENGLISH-SPEAKING RACES IS DIVIDED.

THE Committee was appointed to consider "what "steps (if any) can be rightly taken, on behalf of the "Anglican Communion, towards the Reunion of the "various bodies into which the Christianity of the "English-speaking races is divided."

I. On entering upon their duty they had at once brought to their notice evidence of a strong *consensus* of authoritative opinion, from various branches of the Anglican Communion, that the time for some action in this matter, under prayer for God's guidance through many acknowledged difficulties and dangers, has already come; and that the Conference—speaking, as it must speak, with the greatest weight of moral authority—should not separate without some such utterance as may further and direct such action.

---

[1] Names of the Members of the Committee :—

Bishop of Sydney (*Chairman*). Bishop of Minnesota.
   ,, Adelaide.   ,, Nelson.
   ,, Antigua (Coadjutor).   ,, New York.
   ,, Brechin.   ,, Ripon
   ,, Edinburgh.   ,, Rochester.
   ,, Hereford.   ,, Rupertsland.
   ,, Jamaica.   ,, St. Andrew's.
   ,, Lichfield.   ,, Wakefield.
   ,, Manchester.

In the Convocation of Canterbury the subject has been under discussion, at intervals, for nearly thirty years. In the year 1861 a resolution, on the motion of the Rev. Chancellor Massingberd, was carried *nem. con.* in the Lower House, praying the Bishops to commend the subject of "the Reunion of the divided members of Christ's Body" to the prayers of the faithful.

In 1870, at the instance of the Lower House, a Committee was appointed on Reunion, with power to confer with any similar Committee which might be appointed in the Northern Province. The Committee, in its Report, recommended the use of the special Prayer for Unity, appointed for the day of the Queen's Accession, and the consideration of the propriety of communication on the subject with the chief Nonconformist bodies; and these recommendations, after a singularly interesting debate were adopted by the House.

The Report contained the following passage :—
" The Committee do not recommend that we should set
" out with proposing alterations of our existing formu-
" laries of faith and worship, while they by no means
" deny that concessions might be admitted hereafter,
" as the consequence of negotiations carried on in a
" spirit of love and unity." It also suggested that on the day of the Queen's Accession "all classes of Nonconformists should be invited to institute similar prayers" for unity, and that the subject might be brought by Sermons before our own people.

In 1887 the subject was again taken up, and a Resolution carried, on the motion of Canon Medd, that " His Grace the President be requested to direct
" the appointment of a Committee of this House to
" consider, and from time to time to report upon, the
" relations between the Church and those who in this
" country are alienated from her Communion ; and
" generally to make suggestions as to means which
" might tend, by God's blessing, to the furtherance of

"the Reunion of all among our countrymen who "hold the essentials of the Christian faith." In the speech of the mover of the resolution special reference was made to the probability of the discussion of the subject at the Lambeth Conference.

In the Convocation of York, the Committee have reason to know that similar action has been taken; but, under pressure of time, they have been unable to obtain detailed information of the actual proceedings.

From various Synods of the Colonial Church similar, and even stronger, expressions of a desire to make some movement on the part of the Anglican Communion in this direction have been brought before the Committee. The General Synod of the Church in Australia and Tasmania, in 1886, "desired "to place on record its solemn sense of the evils of the "unhappy divisions among professing Christians, and, "through His Grace the Archbishop of Canterbury, "respectfully prayed the Conference of Bishops, to "be assembled at Lambeth in 1888, to consider in "what manner steps should be taken to promote "greater visible unity among those who hold the "same Creed." A Resolution was passed in almost the same words by the Diocesan Synod of Montreal; and similar Resolutions by the Provincial Synod of Rupertsland, and the General Synod of New Zealand. At the Session of the Provincial Synod of Canada in 1886, a Joint Committee was appointed, to confer with any similar Committees, which might be appointed by other Religious Bodies, on the terms upon which some honourable union might be arrived at.

But the most important and practical step has been taken by our brethren of the American Church in the General Convention of 1886, in accordance with the prayer of a petition signed by more than a thousand Clergy, including thirty-two Bishops. At that Convention a Committee of the House of Bishops presented a remarkable Report, which, after stating emphatically that the Church did "not seek to absorb "other Communions, but to co-operate with them on "the basis of a common Faith and Order, to dis"countenance schism, and to heal the wounds of the "Body of Christ"; and that she was prepared to make all reasonable concessions on "all things of "human ordering and of human choice," dwelt upon the duty of the Church to preserve, "as inherent "parts of the sacred deposit of Christian faith and "order committed by Christ and His Apostles to the "Church, and as therefore essential to the restoration "of unity," the following :—

"1. The Holy Scriptures of the Old and New Testament, as the Revealed Word of God.

"2. The Nicene Creed, as the sufficient statement of the Christian Faith.

"3. The two Sacraments—Baptism and the Supper of the Lord—ministered with unfailing use of Christ's words of institution, and the elements ordained by Him.

"4. The Historic Episcopate, locally adapted in the methods of its administration to the varying needs of the nations and peoples called of God into the Unity of His Church."

The Report concluded with the following words :—

"Furthermore, deeply grieved by the sad divisions which afflict the Christian Church in our own land, we hereby declare our desire and readiness, so soon as there shall be any authorised response to this Declaration, to enter into brotherly conference with all or any Christian bodies seeking the restoration of organic Unity of the Church, with a view to the earnest study of the conditions, under which so priceless a blessing might happily be brought to pass."

This Report was adopted by the House of Bishops, and communicated to the House of Clerical and Lay Deputies; and, at the instance of the latter House, it was resolved—

"That a Commission consisting of five Bishops

"five Clerical, and five Lay Deputies, be appointed, "who shall at their discretion communicate, to the "organised Christian Bodies of our country, the "Declaration set forth by the Bishops on the twentieth "day of October; and shall hold themselves ready "to enter into brotherly conference with all or any "Christian Bodies seeking the restoration of the "organic unity of the Church."

After consideration of these significant documents, and of memorials from certain Associations which have already done good service in this cause, it was decided by the Committee that they were more than justified in recommending to the Conference that some steps should be taken by it in the direction specified in the Resolution constituting the Committee.

II. In considering how this could best be done, it appeared to the Committee that the subject divided itself naturally into two parts; first, the basis on which the United Church might, in the future, safely rest; secondly, the conditions under which present negotiations for reunion, in view of existing circumstances, could be carried on.

The Committee with deep regret felt that, under present conditions, it was useless to consider the question of Reunion with our brethren of the Roman Church, being painfully aware that any proposal for reunion would be entertained by the authorities of that Church only on condition of a complete submission on our part to those claims of absolute authority, and the acceptance of those other errors, both in doctrine and in discipline, against which, in faithfulness to God's Holy Word, and to the true principles of His Church, we have been for three centuries bound to protest.

But, in regard to the first portion of the subject, the Committee were of opinion that with the chief of the Non-conforming Communions there would not only be less difficulty than is commonly supposed as to the basis of a common faith in the essentials of Christian doctrine, but that, even in respect of Church Government, many of the causes which had originally led to secession had been removed, and that both from deeper study and from larger historical experience, there was in the present day a greater disposition to value and to accept the ancient Church order. It did not, indeed, appear to them that the question before them, which was of the duty, if any, of the Anglican Communion in this matter, was to be absolutely determined by these considerations; but they seemed, nevertheless, to give important encouragement to the Church in the endeavour to do what might appear to be her duty in furthering this all-important matter.

Accordingly, after careful consideration, they determined to take as the basis of their deliberations on this part of the subject the chief articles embodied in the Report of the Committee of the House of Bishops in the American Church; and after discussion of each, they submit them to the wisdom of the Conference, with some modifications, as supplying the basis on which approach might be, under God's blessing, made towards Reunion:—

1. The Holy Scriptures of the Old and New Testaments, as "containing all things necessary to salvation," and as being the rule and ultimate standard of faith.
2. The Apostles' Creed, as the Baptisimal Symbol; and the Nicene Creed, as the sufficient statement of the Christian faith.
3. The two Sacraments ordained by Christ himself —Baptism and the Supper of the Lord—ministered with unfailing use of Christ's words of institution, and of the elements ordained by him.
4. The Historic Episcopate, locally adapted in the methods of its administration to the varying needs of

the nations and peoples called of God into the unity of His Church.

The Committee believe that upon some such basis as this, with large freedom of variation on secondary points of doctrine, worship, and discipline, and without interference with existing conditions of property and endowment, it might be possible, under God's gracious providence, for a United Church, including at least the chief of the Christian Communions of our people, to rest.

III. But they are aware that the main difficulty of the subject lies in the consideration of what practical steps can be taken towards such reunion under the actual religious conditions of the community at home and abroad—complicated, moreover, in England and Scotland by legal difficulties. It appears to them, moreover, clear, that on this subject the Conference can only express an opinion on general principles, and that definite action must be left to the constituted authorities, in each branch of our Communion, acting, as far as possible, in concert.

They therefore respectfully submit to the Conference the following Resolution :—

> "That the constituted authorities of the various "branches of our Communion, acting, so far "as may be, in concert with one another, "be earnestly requested to make it known "that they hold themselves in readiness to "enter into brotherly conference (such as "that which has already been proposed by "the Church in the United States of "America) with the representatives of other "chief Christian Communions in the "English-speaking races, in order to con-"sider what steps can be taken, either "towards corporate reunion, or towards such "relations as may prepare the way for fuller "organic unity hereafter."

IV. They cannot conclude their report without laying before the Conference the following suggestion, unanimously adopted by the Committee :—

> "That the Conference recommend as of great "importance, in tending to bring about Re-"union, the dissemination of information "respecting the standards of doctrine, and "the formularies in use in the Anglican "Church; and that information be dis-"seminated, on the other hand, respecting "the authoritative standards of doctrine, "worship, and government adopted by the "other bodies of Christians into which the "English-speaking races are divided."

They also desire—following in this respect the example of the Convocation of Canterbury—to pray the Conference to commend this matter of Reunion to the special prayers of all Christian people, both within and (so far as it may rightly do so) without our Communion, in preparation for the Conferences which have been suggested, and while such Conferences are going on; and they trust that the present Lambeth Conference may also see fit to issue, or to pray His Grace the President to issue, some pastoral letter to all Christian people, upon this all-important subject. For never certainly did the Church of Christ need more urgently the spirit of wisdom and of love, which He alone can bestow, who is "the Author and Giver of all good things."

Signed on behalf of the Committee,

ALFRED SYDNEY,
Chairman.

No. 10.

SCANDINAVIANS—OLD CATHOLICS.

REPORT OF THE COMMITTEE [1] APPOINTED TO CONSIDER THE RELATION OF THE ANGLICAN COMMUNION (A) TO THE SCANDINAVIAN AND OTHER REFORMED CHURCHES (B) TO THE OLD CATHOLICS AND OTHER REFORMING BODIES.

A.

YOUR Committee consider that, in view of the increasing number of Swedes and other Scandinavians now living in America and in the English Colonies, as well as for the furtherance of Christian Unity, earnest efforts should be made to establish more friendly relations between the Scandinavian and Anglican Churches.

In regard to the Swedish Church, your Committee are of opinion that, as its standards of doctrine are to a great extent in accord with our own, and its continuity as a national Church has never been broken, any approaches on its part should be most gladly welcomed with a view to mutual explanation of differences, and the ultimate establishment, if possible, of permanent intercommunion on sound principles of Ecclesiastical polity.

Greater difficulties are presented as regards com-

---

[1] Names of the Members of the Committee :—
　　Bishop of Winchester　　　　Bishop of Dunedin.
　　　　　　(*Chairman*).　　　　　,,　　Gibraltar.
　　Archbishop of Dublin.　　　　　,,　　Iowa.
　　Bishop of Albany.　　　　　　　,,　　Lichfield.
　　　　,,　　Cashel.　　　　　　　,,　　Lincoln.
　　　　,,　　Central Africa.　　　　,,　　North Carolina.
　　　　,,　　Cork.　　　　　　　　,,　　Salisbury.
　　　　,,　　Derry.　　　　　　　　,,　　Western New York.

munion with the Norwegian and Danish Churches by the constitution of their ministry; but there are grounds of hope, in the growing appreciation of Church order, that in the course of time these difficulties may be surmounted. It is much to be desired that a basis of union should be formed with a people who are distinguished by great devotional earnestness and uprightness of character.

B.

By the name Old Catholics we understand, in general terms, those members of foreign Churches who have been excommunicated on account of their refusal, for conscience' sake, to accept the novel doctrines promulgated by the authority of the Church of Rome, and who yet desire to maintain in its integrity the Catholic Faith, and to remain in full communion with the Catholic Church. As in the previous Conference, held in 1878,[1] we declare that " all sympathy is due from the Anglican Church to "the Churches and individuals protesting against "these errors"; and, " to those who are drawn to us "in the endeavour to free themselves from the yoke "of error and superstition we are ready to offer all "help and such privileges as may be acceptable to "them and are consistent with the maintenance of "our own principles, as enunciated in our formularies."

Ten years have passed since this declaration was issued, and we are now called to consider more in detail our relations to the different groups comprehended under this general title.

I.

First of all it is due to the ancient Church of Holland, which in practice accepts the title of Old

---

[1] Official Letter of 1878. Supra, page 181.

Catholic, to recognise the fact that it has uttered energetic protests against the novel dogmas of the Immaculate Conception of the Blessed Virgin Mary, and of the universal Bishopric and infallibility of the Bishop of Rome. It is to this Church that the community, usually termed Old Catholic, in the German Empire, owes in the providence of God the Episcopal succession. We recognise, with thankfulness, the dignified and independent position which the Church of Holland maintained for many years in almost absolute isolation. It has now broken through this isolation, as regards its neighbours on the Continent. As regards ourselves, the Church of Holland is found on inquiry to be in agreement with our Church in many points, and we believe that with more frequent brotherly intercourse many of the barriers which at present separate us might be removed.

II.

The Old Catholic community in Germany differs from the Church of Holland, in this respect, amongst others, that it does not retain possession of the ancient Sees. The Bishop of that community has wisely refrained from assuming a territorial title; we are not, however, without hope that the Old Catholic body may be, with the divine guidance and in God's good time, instrumental in restoring to that country the blessing of a united national Church. It may be noted that Bishop Reinkens, shortly after his consecration, was recognised as a Catholic Bishop by the civil power in Prussia, Baden, and Hesse.[1] He and the parochial Clergy under him have the right and duty, recognised by the State, of teaching the chil-

---

[1] The documents in question are printed at length in *Der Altkatholikismus*, published in 1887 by J. F. von Schulte, pp. 405, 415, 416. The Prussian Old Catholic law is to be found on pp. 44–46. Cf. pp. 549 foll. (Staatszuschuss für die Altkatholiken).

dren of their own confession in the public schools. They are also in undisturbed possession of a number of ancient churches and benefices, and receive for the present a subsidy granted by Parliament.

As regards the form of doctrine actually professed by this body, we believe that its return to the standards of the undivided Church is a distinct advance towards the reunion of Christendom. We learn that it formulates the fuller expression of its belief in catechisms and manuals of instruction, rather than in articles or confessions, because it desires to avoid any methods which might create or perpetuate divisions.

We cannot consider that it is in schism as regards the Roman Church, because to do so would be to concede the lawfulness of the imposition of new terms of communion, and of the extravagant assertions by the Papacy of ordinary and immediate jurisdiction in every Diocese. For ourselves we regard it as a duty to promote friendly relations with the Old Catholics of Germany, not only out of sympathy with them, but also in thankfulness to God, who has strengthened them to suffer for the truth under great discouragements, difficulties, and temptations. We owe them our intercessions, our support, and our brotherly counsel; and we have reason to believe that aid from individual members of our Church, may be most beneficially given towards the training of their future Clergy.

We see no reason why we should not admit their Clergy and faithful Laity to Holy Communion on the same conditions as our own Communicants, and we also acknowledge the readiness which they have shown to offer spiritual privileges to members of our own Church.

We regret that differences in our marriage laws, which we believe to be of great importance, compel us to state that we are obliged to debar from Holy Communion any person who may have contracted a marriage not sanctioned by the laws and canons of the Anglican Church. Nor could we, in justice to the Old Catholics, admit any one who would be debarred from communion among themselves.

III.

The "Christian Catholic Church" in Switzerland, which has adopted a title long used by the Church in that country, has a recognised civil position of much the same character as that possessed by the Old Catholics of Germany. We consider that it is a body now sufficiently established to receive the assurance of the same sympathy and the offer of the same privileges from ourselves.

IV.

The Old Catholic community in Austria has been recognised by the State as a distinct religious association, in accordance with the law of May 20th, 1874.[1] Its constitution provides for the presidency of a Bishop, but no election has as yet taken place, not from any indifference on the part of its members, but on account of the difficulty of securing the stipend required by law. In the mean time it has many of the rights secured by law to the German body. The Austrian Old Catholics have made great sacrifices, and deserve great sympathy from us; which we hope may be expressed in a practical manner. They have, we believe, an important future before them, if rightly guided. We cannot, however, regard the organisation in Austria as sufficiently tried and complete to warrant a more formal relation on our part at the present time.

V.

The same remark applies with even greater force to the smaller groups of brave and earnest men of the

---

[1] Von Schulte, *Der Altkatholikismus*, p. 435.

Latin races, driven under somewhat similar circumstances to associate themselves in separate congregations in Italy, France, Spain, and Portugal. We sympathise with their efforts to free themselves from the burden of unlawful terms of communion. We have reason to believe that there are many who think with them, but have not seen the way to follow the outward steps which they have taken. We trust that in time they may be enabled to adopt such sound forms of doctrine and discipline and to secure such Catholic organisation as will permit us to give them a fuller recognition. We desire, in our outlook into the future, to call to mind the well-known declaration of the Gallican Clergy of 1862,[1] and also the advances made by Archbishop Wake in correspondence with the Doctors of the Sorbonne,[2] towards establishing

---

[1] See Bossuet's *Défense de la Declaration du Clergé de France, &c.* 2 vols., 4to. Amsterdam, 1745, and Dupin's *Manuel du Droit public ecclésiastique français*, pp. 97–100, ed. 5. Paris: Henri Plon, 1860.

[2] Archbishop Wake wrote as follows to Mr. Beauvoir, on November 18th, 1718, in regard to this correspondence:—" If " we could once divide the Gallican Church [from the Roman], a " reformation in other matters would follow as a matter of " course. The scheme that seems to me most likely to prevail, " is, to agree in the independence (as to all matters of authority) " of every national Church on any others ; and in their right " to determine all matters that arise within themselves ; and, " for points of doctrine, to agree, as far as possible, in all " articles of any moment (as in effect we already do, or easily " may) ; and, for other matters, to allow a difference till God shall " bring us to a union in those also. One only thing should be " provided for, to purge out of the public offices of the Church " such things as hinder a perfect communion in the service of " the Church, that so, wherever any come from us to them or " from them to us, we may all join together in Prayers and the " Holy Sacraments with each other. In our Liturgy there is " nothing but what they allow, save the single rubric relating " to the Eucharist ; in theirs nothing but what they agree may " be laid aside, and yet the public offices be never the worse or " more imperfect for the want of it. Such a scheme as this I

a basis for intercommunion between the Churches of France and England. If some such principles could now be revived, we have reason to believe that they would be welcomed by many both in France and Italy, and they might again form the basis of hopeful negotiations.

In concluding this portion of our Report we feel it our duty to express the opinion that the consecration, by Bishops of our Communion, of a Bishop, to exercise his functions in a foreign country, within the limits of an ancient territorial jurisdiction and over the natives of that country, is a step of the gravest importance and fraught with enduring consequences, the issues of which cannot be foreseen. Whilst the right of Bishops of the Catholic Church to interpose under conditions of extreme necessity has always been acknowledged, we deprecate any action that does not carefully regard primitive and established principles of jurisdiction and the interests of the whole Anglican Communion.

VI.

Lastly, the Committee have been asked at the last moment to consider the subject of the orders of the United Brethren, commonly called the Moravians. At the last Conference a number of the Bishops "were recommended to associate with themselves "such learned persons as they might deem eminently "qualified to assist them by their knowledge of the

---

" take to be a more proper ground of peace at the begininng " than to go to more particulars."

The correspondence of Archbishop Wake with Mr. Beauvoir, Dr. Dupin, Dr. P. Piers Girardin, and others, is printed in the fourth Appendix to Dr. Maclaine's translation of Mosheim's *Church History*, vol. vi., pp. 126, foll., London, 1828. The above letter will be found in full on p. 172, and is quoted in Rev. G. G. Perry's *History of the English Church, third period,* p. 48, London, 1887.

Z

"historical difficulties involved."[1] These Bishops have not been able to act upon this recommendation, and no report is before the Conference. Your Committee, in the short time allowed them, have not found it possible to inquire into the details of this subject with such care as would enable them to propose to the Conference any sufficient basis for the expression of an authoritative opinion.

It must not, however, be overlooked that from time to time, up to the present day, very friendly relations have existed between Moravians and members of our Communion. In their greatest trials they have received from eminent English Bishops and Churchmen the sympathy and support due to a zealous body of Christians, imbued with a primitive spirit, and claiming to possess a valid Episcopate.

The labours of Moravian Missionaries are known to all the world. We should therefore welcome any clearer illustration of their history and actual status on the part of their own divines.

The subjects committed to the consideration of this Committee have embraced, as will be seen, a very wide range of interests, and we have reluctantly been compelled, on this account, to confine our Report almost entirely to the bodies specified in the terms of our commission.

Signed on behalf of the Committee,

E. HAROLD WINTON,

Chairman.

---

[1] Supra, page 183.

No. 11.—EASTERN CHURCHES.

REPORT OF THE COMMITTEE[1] APPOINTED TO CONSIDER THE RELATION OF THE ANGLICAN COMMUNION TO THE EASTERN CHURCHES.

YOUR Committee regard the friendly feelings manifested towards our Church by the Orthodox Eastern Communion as a matter for deep thankfulness. These feelings inspire the hope that at no distant time closer relations may be established between the two Churches. Your Committee, however, are of opinion that any hasty or ill-considered step in this direction would only retard the accomplishment of this hope. Our expectations of nearer fellowship are founded upon the friendly tone of the correspondence which the Archbishop of Canterbury and his predecessors have held from time to time with Patriarchs of the Orthodox Church, and upon the cordiality of the welcome given by the Heads of that Church to Anglican Bishops and Clergy, such as the Bishop of Gibraltar, who have travelled in the East. Additional grounds of hope are furnished by the visit of Archbishop[2] Lycurgus to England in 1870, by the conversation which passed between him and the present Bishop of Winchester at Ely, by the words which Archbishop

---

[1] Names of the Members of the Committee :—

Bishop of Winchester. (*Chairman*).	Bishop of Limerick.
Bishop Blyth.	,, Meath.
Bishop of Gibraltar.	,, Springfield.
,, Iowa.	,, Travancore.

[2] Lycurgus, late Archbishop of Syra and Tenos.

Lycurgus used at the conclusion of the second Conference held at Bonn;[1] and by the request which the Orthodox Patriarch of Jerusalem recently addressed to the Archbishop of Canterbury, that the Anglican Bishopric in Jerusalem should be re-constituted, and that the head-quarters of the Bishop should be placed in that city rather than at Beyrout or elsewhere.

We reflect with thankfulness that there exist no bars, such as are presented to communion with the Latins by the formulated assertion of the infallibility of the Church residing in the person of the Supreme Pontiff, by the doctrine of the Immaculate Conception, and other novel dogmas imposed by the decrees of later Councils.

We must congratulate the Christian world that, through the research of a Greek Metropolitan, literature has been lately enriched by the recovery of an ancient document which throws unexpected light upon the early development of ecclesiastical organisation.

It would not be right, however, to disguise from ourselves the hindrances which exist on either side. The first and most formidable of these is the disputed clause inserted in the Creed of Constantinople,

---

[1] At the end of the Conference at Ely (1870), Archbishop Lycurgus said :—

"When I return to Greece I will say that the Church of "England is not like other Protestant bodies. I will say that "it is a sound Catholic Church very like our own ; and I trust "that by friendly discussion union between the two Churches "may be brought about."

At the end of the Bonn Conference (1875), he said to Dr. Von Döllinger :—

"In the name of all those of my own communion I thank "you, Mr. President, for your marvellous efforts in the work of "reuniting the several Churches, of bringing together again "the so numerous divisions of the Rock of our Redeemer. "Our joy is full ; and there will be great joy in our homes "also. We earnestly pray God for His further blessing."

erroneously called the Nicene Creed, without any Conciliar authority, by the Latin Church. This clause, which has the prescription of centuries, and is capable of being explained in an orthodox sense, it may be very difficult to remove. Another barrier to full understanding between the Orthodox Eastern Church and ourselves would be the extreme importance attached by that Church to trine immersion in the rite of Baptism, which practice, however, there is nothing to prevent our Church from formally sanctioning. We, on the other hand, experience a somewhat similar difficulty as regards the Eastern rite of Confirmation, which we can hardly consider equivalent to ours, inasmuch as it omits the imposition of the Bishop's hands, and is usually conferred upon unconscious infants; yet we do not regard this as requiring members of the Orthodox Church to receive our Confirmation. It would be difficult for us to enter into more intimate relations with that Church so long as it retains the use of icons, the invocation of the Saints, and the cultus of the Blessed Virgin; although it is but fair to state that the Greeks, in sanctioning the use of pictorial representations for the purpose of promoting devotion, expressly disclaim the sin of idolatry, which they conceive would attach to the bowing down before sculptured or molten images. Moreover, the decrees of the second Council of Nicæa, sanctioning the use of icons, were framed in a spirit of reaction against the rationalising measures, as they were regarded, of the iconoclastic Emperors. The Greeks might be reminded that the decrees of that Council, having been deliberately rejected seven years afterwards by the Council of Frankfort, and not having been accepted by the Latin Church till after the lapse of two centuries, and then only under Papal influence, cannot be regarded as binding upon the Church.

Your Committee would impress upon their fellow-Christians the propriety of abstaining from all efforts to induce individual members of the Orthodox Eastern Church to leave their own communion. If some be dissatisfied with its teachings or usages, and find a lack of spiritual life in its worship, they should be advised not to leave the Church of their baptism, but by remaining in it to endeavour to become centres of life and light to their own people; more especially as the Orthodox Eastern Church has never committed itself to any theory that would make it impossible to reconsider and revise its standard and practice.

Your Committee think it desirable that the Heads of that communion should be supplied with some authoritative document setting forth the historical facts relating to our orders and our position in the Catholic Church; as much misconception appears still prevail on this subject. Your Committee feel that the position which England now occupies in Cyprus and in Egypt places in our hands exceptional opportunities of elevating the moral and spiritual life of our Eastern brethren. Especially may this be done by introducing or promoting higher education: any help given in this way we have reason to believe would be warmly welcomed. We rejoice to know that schools have lately been established at Constantinople and elsewhere for the purpose of supplying education to those who are in training for the ministry. In the more general diffusion of knowledge amongst the instructors of the people lies the best hope of that mutual understanding and esteem for which the Heads of the Orthodox Church have shown so much desire.

Your Committee cannot be expected to deal separately with the other Churches of the East, among which the Armenian appears to be the largest and most important. Approaches have been made to us from time to time by Bishops and other representatives of this communion, appealing for aid in support of educational projects for the instruction of their own people. The Armenian Church lies under the imputation of heresy. But it has always protested against this imputation, affirming the charge to have arisen from a misconception of its formularies. The departure from orthodoxy may, perhaps, have been more apparent than real; and the erroneous element in its creed appears now to be gradually losing its hold upon the moral and religious consciousness of the Armenian people.

In regard to other Eastern communities, such as the Coptic, Abyssinian, Syrian, and Chaldean, your Committee consider that our position in the East involves some obligations And if these communities have fallen into error, and show a lack of moral and spiritual life, we must recollect that but for them the light of Christianity in these countries would have been utterly extinguished, and that they have suffered for many centuries from cruel oppression and persecution. If we should have opportunity, our aim should be to improve their mental, moral, and religious condition, and to induce them to return to the unity of the faith without prejudice to their liberty. This we take to be the purpose of the Assyrian Mission set on foot by the late Archbishop of Canterbury, and continued by his successor.

In conclusion, we would could call attention to the fact that in the East advance is slow, and even in the West we find differences perpetuate themselves, owing to national peculiarities, hereditary prejudices, and other causes, in spite of real wish for unity. We think that Christians need to be cautioned against impatience in expecting quick results. Such impatience argues imperfect trust in the ultimate fulfilment of our Lord's prayer for His people that they "all may be ONE."

Signed on behalf of the Committee,

E. HAROLD WINTON,
Chairman.

No. 12.—AUTHORITATIVE STANDARDS.

REPORT OF THE COMMITTEE[1] APPOINTED TO CONSIDER THE SUBJECT OF AUTHORITATIVE STANDARDS OF DOCTRINE AND WORSHIP.

IN considering the subject of the Authoritative Standards of Doctrine and Worship, which are the primary means of securing internal union amongst ourselves, and of setting forth our Faith before the rest of Christendom, we acknowledge first of all, with deep thankfulness to Almighty God, the vital and growing unity of the great Communion to which we belong.

We acknowledge also with the same heartfelt thankfulness the increasing intercourse which is taking place between our own Churches and other Churches of Christendom, and the extension of our own Communion into many non-Christian countries, to which God has especially called us to minister by the diffusion of the English-speaking race throughout the world.

The consideration of the new conditions thus created seems to call for a careful statement of our own position in regard to authoritative standards of doctrine and worship.

---

[1] Names of the Members of the Committee :—

Bishop of Ely (*Chairman*).   Bishop of Meath.
    „ Aberdeen.   „ Nassau.
    „ Albany.   „ Qu'Appelle.
    „ Arkansas.   „ Rupertsland.
    „ Derry.   „ Salisbury.
    „ Dover.   „ St. David's.
    „ Edinburgh.   „ Sydney.
    „ Grahamstown.   „ Western New York.
Bishop in Japan.

This statement is divided into three parts :—first, as to standards of doctrine and worship which unite us with the great Body of the Church Universal; second, as to those which regulate our internal union or should be imposed upon Missionary Churches; third, as to a manual of doctrine for general use, but which should not be authoritative.

I.

We recognise before all things, and amidst all discouragements and divisions, the great bond of an essential unity which exists amongst all Christians who own the one Lord Jesus Christ as their Head and King, who accept the paramount authority of Holy Scripture, who confess the doctrine of the Nicene Faith, and who acknowledge one Baptism into the Name of the Blessed Trinity.

But we cannot regard this measure of unity as adequately fulfilling our Lord's prayer that His followers should be one, and we feel, therefore, that it is our duty to explain our own principles as regards standards of doctrine and worship, in the humble hope of preparing the way, so far as in us lies, for the reunion of Christendom.

We have a duty to the Church Universal; we have a duty also towards those who are now distinctly within our own Communion or who may hereafter be so closely allied to it as to form practically one body with ourselves.

As in former Conferences,[1] we declare that we continue "united under one divine Head in the fellowship of the one Catholic and Apostolic Church, holding the one faith revealed in Holy Writ, defined in the Creeds, maintained by the primitive Church," and "affirmed by the undisputed" Œcumenical " Councils."

---

[1] Supra, pp. 97 and 116.

In defining our own position more explicitly we recognise, with the general consent of the Fathers that the canonical books of the Old and New Testament "contain all things necessary to salvation," and are the rule and ultimate standard of all Christian doctrine.

In addition to the Creed commonly called the Nicene Creed, to which we have already referred, we, as a part of the Western Church, have a common inheritance in the "Apostles' Creed," confessed by us all in the Sacrament of Baptism. In like manner we accept the hymn *Quicunque vult*, whether or not recited in the public worship of our Churches, as resting upon certain warrant of Scripture, and as most useful, both at home and in our missions, in ascertaining and defining the fundamental mysteries of the Holy Trinity, and of the Incarnation of our Blessed Lord; and thus guarding believers from lapsing into heresy.

In relation to the doctrine of the Procession of the Holy Spirit, while we believe that there is no fundamental diversity of faith between the Churches of the East and West,[1] we recognise the historical fact that the clause *Filioque* makes no part of the Nicene Symbol as set forth by the authority of the undivided Church.

We are of opinion that, as opportunity arises, it would be well to revise the English version of the Nicene Creed and of the *Quicunque vult*.

We suggest to the Conference that the President be requested to appoint a Committee for this purpose.

---

[1] The Committee beg to refer, in illustration of this statement, to the important propositions, accepted by Members both of the Eastern and Western Churches, which were agreed to at the Reunion Conference held at Bonn, August 16th, 1875, under the Presidency of Dr. J. J. I. von Döllinger. See the *Report of the Proceedings, &c.*, with a Preface by Dr. Liddon.—Pickering: London, 1876, pp. 103, 104.

With regard to the authority of the Œcumenical Councils, our Communion has always recognised the decisions of the first four Councils on matters of faith, nor is there any point of dogma in which it disagrees with the teaching of the fifth and sixth.

The second Council of Nicæa commonly called the seventh Council is, however, not undisputed, and while we recognise the historical circumstances of the eight century, which naturally led to the strong protest against iconoclasm made there, it is our duty to assert that our Church has never accepted the teaching of that Council in reference to the veneration of sacred pictures.

II.

From the standards of doctrine of the Universal Church which the whole Anglican Communion has always accepted,[1] we now pass to those standards of doctrine and worship which are specially the heritage of the Church of England, and which are, to a greater or less extent, received by all her sister and daughter

---

[1] "Let Preachers take care that they never teach anything in a sermon which they wish to be religiously held and believed by the people, except what is in accord with the doctrine of the Old or New Testament, and what the Catholic Fathers and ancient Bishops have collected from the same doctrine."— *Canon of* 1571, *concerning Preachers.*

"Such person &c. * * shall not in anywise have authority or power to order, determine or adjudge any matter or cause to be heresie, but onely such as heretofore have been determined, ordered or adjudged to be heresie, by the authority of the Canonical Scriptures or by the first four general Councils or any of them, or by any other general Council wherein the same was declared heresie by the express and plain words of the said Canonical Scriptures, or such as hereafter shall be ordered judged or determined to be heresie, by the High Court of Parliament of this realm, with the assent of the Clergy in their Convocation ; anything in this Act contained to the contrary notwithstanding."

1 ELIZ. 1 § XXXVI.

Churches. These are the Prayer Book with its Catechism, the Ordinal, and the XXXIX. Articles of Religion.

All these are subscribed by our clergy at ordination or admission to office, but the XXXIX. Articles are not imposed upon any person as a condition of communion. With respect to the Prayer Book and Articles, we do not consider it an indispensable condition of inter-communion that they should be everywhere accepted in their original form, or that the interpretation put upon them by local courts or provincial tribunals should be received by every branch or province of the Anglican Communion. In illustration of this principle, we would refer to the differences from the English Order of the Administration of the Holy Communion which have long existed in the Scottish and American Churches, and to the facts that the XXXIX. Articles of Religion were only accepted in America in the year 1801 with some variations, and in Scotland in 1804, and that the Church of Ireland as well as the Church in America, has introduced some modifications into the Book of Common Prayer.

We, however, strongly deprecate any further material variation in the text of the existing Sacramental offices of the Church, or of the Ordinal, than is at present recognised among us, unless with the advice of some Conference or Council representing the whole Communion.

With regard to the daily offices and such further forms of service as the exigencies of different Churches or countries may demand, we feel that they may be safely left for the present to the action of the Bishops of each Province. We do not demand a rigid uniformity, but we desire to see the prevalence of a spirit of mutual and sympathetic concession, which will prevent the growth of substantial divergences between different portions of our communion. With regard to those Dioceses which are not yet united into Provinces, we recommend that the Bishop of the Diocese should not act in the way of revision of, or additions to, such offices without the advice of the Archbishop of Canterbury; or in the case of foreign Missionary jurisdictions of the American Church, without the advice of its Presiding Bishop.

With regard to the XXXIX. Articles of Religion we thank God for the wisdom which guided our fathers, in difficult times, in framing statements of doctrine, for the most part accurate in their language and reserved and moderate in their definitions. Even when speaking most strongly and under the pressure of great provocation, our Communion has generally refrained from anathemas upon opponents, and we desire in this to follow those who have preceded us in the faith. The omission of a few clauses in a few of the Articles would render the whole body free from any imputation of injustice or harshness toward those who differ from us. At the same time we feel that the Articles are not all of equal value, that they are not, and do not profess to be, a complete statement of Christian doctrine, and that, from the temporary and local circumstances under which they were composed, they do not always meet the requirements of Churches founded under wholly different conditions.

Some modification of these Articles may therefore naturally be expected on the part of newly-constituted Churches, and particularly in non-Christian lands. But we consider that it should be a condition of the recognition of such Churches as in complete intercommunion with our own, and especially of their receiving from us our episcopal succession, that we should first receive from them satisfactory evidence that they hold substantially the same type of doctrine with ourselves. More particularly we are of opinion that the Clergy of such Churches should accept articles in accordance with the positive statements of our own standards of doctrine and worship, particularly on the substance and rule of faith, on the state and redemption of man on the office of the

Church, and on the Sacraments and other special ordinances of our holy religion.

III.

In the foregoing resolutions we have confined ourselves to a consideration of existing authoritative formularies, and to such as may serve the like use under particular conditions. We are unable, after careful consideration of the subject, to recommend that any new declaration of doctrine should, at the present time, be put forth by authority. We are, however, of opinion that the time has come when an effort should be made to compose a manual for teachers which should contain a summary of the doctrine of the Church, as generally received among us. Such a manual would draw its statements of doctrine from authoritative documents already existing, but would exhibit them in a completer and more systematic form. It would, also, naturally include some explanation of the Services and ceremonies of the Church. The whole might be preceded by a historical sketch of the position and claims of our Communion.

Such a Manual would, we believe, be of great service both in maintaining the type of doctrine to which we have referred, and in enabling members of other Churches to form a just opinion of our doctrines and worship. We suggest that His Grace the President be requested to nominate three or more Bishops to undertake such a work, and, if it seem good to him and to the other Archbishops, Metropolitans, and presiding Bishops of the Church, that they give the work, when completed, the sanction of their imprimatur. We do not suggest that the Conference should be asked to undertake this work, or that it should be regarded as an authoritative standard of the Church.

Signed on behalf of the Committee,

ALWYNE ELY, *Chairman.*

XXXVI.

A Statement in regard to Ordinations or Consecrations performed by Dr. Cummins, or others claiming Ordination or Consecration from him, prepared by the presiding Bishop of the American Church, the Right Rev. John Williams, D.D., LL.D.

" Bishop Cummins was consecrated as Assistant-Bishop of Kentucky, November 15th, 1866. In the autumn of 1873, he abandoned the Church, and announced his intention of setting up for himself. On the 12th of December, 1873, the Bishop of Kentucky (Dr. Benjamin B. Smith) withdrew authority from him, and inhibited him from the exercise of Episcopal dutuies,[1] nder, and in terms of, Title I., Canon 15, Sec. 5.

Soon after this, probably on the day following, Bishop Cummins, assisted by four presbyters, went through some form of Consecration, by which he declared that the Rev. Charles E. Cheney, D.D., was elevated to the Episcopate.

We have considered that in this, so called, Consecration, four things must be taken into account—(1) the condition of the Consecrator; (2) the act itself; (3) the service used; and (4) the condition of the person said to be consecrated.

1.—Bishop Cummins had not been deposed, and therefore his act, however inconvenient, cannot, so far as he is concerned, be counted as having no force. He was, however, acting in the face of canonical obligations.

---

[1] An Assistant-Bishop shall perform such Episcopal duties, and exercise such Episcopal authority in the Diocese, as the Bishop shall assign to him.—Title I., Canon 15, Sec. 5.

2.—The Consecration itself is, clearly, utterly uncanonical, though, of course, not, *per se*, invalid.

3.—How far the Ordinal was used, whether any sufficient form was employed, we do not know. We do know, from open and clear declarations of avowed principles, that there was not even a pretence of ordaining and consecrating a Bishop in the meaning and intention of the Ordinal. We do not, of course, mean in this to affirm that a secretly[1] held and unexpressed intention *not* to do what the service purported to do, would invalidate the act. In this instance, the purpose *not* to do what the service purported to do was openly declared. Under such circumstances, if the Ordinal were used, the use of it was nothing short of a mockery.

4.—As to the condition of Dr. Cheney, he was at that time under sentence of deposition, which sentence had been canonically pronounced upon him years before by his Diocesan, the Bishop of Illinois (Dr.

---

[1] In referring to the intention of Bishop Cummins, the Bishops beg to be understood as not implying that an Officer of any Religious Body can invalidate his official act, by a lack of intention to use the Offices of that Body for the purposes for which they were authorised. This is a different case. Bishop Cummins had ceased to be an Officer of the Church in America. He was acting *for himself*. And he not only did not intend, but by his own statement *he intended not* to consecrate Dr. Cheney to the Episcopal Order. Proof of which is found in the subjoined extracts from his own sermon delivered on the occasion of the so-called consecration of Dr. Cheney.

"There is no evidence from Scripture that the Apostles
"established the Episcopate as an *order* in the Ministry distinct
"from and superior in rank to the Presbyterate. If there is to
"be found any trace of Episcopacy in the New Testament, it is
"only as an office exercised by one who was himself a fellow-
"presbyter, commissioned or set apart for the exercise of such
"powers as were rendered necessary by the exigencies of the
"Church, and for the promotion of its well-being by a system
"of general oversight and superintendence.

"What then is the true position of the Episcopate as it is
"retained in this reformed Episcopal Church, following Holy
"Scripture and the practice of the early Church?

Whitehouse). In regard to the capacity, so to speak, of a deposed presbyter to be elevated to the Episcopate (which was the crucial question touching Dr. Cheney), we found that in the well-known case of Timothy Aelurus, the Bishops of Cappadocia, writing to the Emperor Leo, asserted that Timothy was, as a deposed presbyter, incapable "*ad majorem currere dignitatem*" (Labbe and Cossart's Concilia, vol. iv., col. 956). We also found the Bishops of Galatia, writing to the same Emperor, that a deposed presbyter was incapable '*ad majorem gradum venire*" (ut sup., col. 970).

We could not but regard this view as entirely reasonable and just. For, hold as strongly as we may to the indelibility of Holy Orders, grant as fully as we may that acts done by one, who having been deposed from an office still continues to do acts pertaining *only to that office*, though they are irregular, may be valid; it surely does not follow, that such a person is capable of receiving additional power or of

---

"1. It is not a continuation of the Apostolate. Bishops are "not the successors of the Apostles. The Apostles of our Lord "could have no successors, as their office was of special "appointment by Christ Himself, endowed with miraculous "powers by the Holy Ghost, and could be filled only by those "who were 'eye-witnesses of the majesty,' and of the 'sufferings "of Jesus.' Their Office ceased with their lives, and Holy "Scripture contains not a suggestion indicating that others "could ever perpetuate their Office in the Church.

"2. The Episcopate is not the depository of the Faith, the "Divinely-constituted body to which are committed all gifts of "grace, as the sole channel through which they can be dis-"pensed. Holy Scripture warrants us in rejecting such teaching "as utterly antagonistic to the very spirit and essence of the "Gospel of the Son of God.

"3. The Episcopate is not an ordinance of Apostolic institu-"tion, but it was adopted by the post-Apostolic Church as the "development of the practice or custom first suggested by the "Apostles, in delegating to certain of their fellow-labourers "among the Presbyters the oversight or superintendence of the "Churches in certain districts temporarily."

2 A

being elevated to a higher grade in the ministry. The contrary conclusion would seem to be the more reasonable one, especially when fortified as it is by the foregoing facts.

Considering, therefore, (1) the condition of the only person claiming the Episcopate who acted in the so-called Consecration ; (2) the extreme irregularity of the act itself, in performing which there was only one Bishop—and he the one just spoken of—present ; (3) the fact that presbyters were associated with him on the avowed ground that they were just as competent to act as a Bishop; (4) that we know not what service was used ; (5) that if the Ordinal were used *in verbis et actibus ipsissimis*, it was still used not only with the secret intention, but with the avowed purpose, of not doing what it intended should be done; (6) that on grounds of reason and of precedent, we were compelled to regard Dr. Cheney as incapable of being elevated to the Episcopate; we were, in a manner, forced to conclude that the act of Consecration, so called, of Dr. Cheney, was *ipso facto*, null and void.

But, further, on the 24th of February, 1876, Dr. Cummins and Dr. Cheney, assisted by one Methodist bishop, one Methodist minister, two Presbyterian ministers, and six members of the so-called "Reformed Episcopal Church," went through some form of consecration, by which they declared that the Rev. W. R. Nicholson, D.D., was elevated to the Episcopate.

The same questions that came up in connection with Dr. Cheney's so-called Consecration arise here. It is enough, however, to say, in addition to what has been already said—(1) that the condition of the so-called Consecrator had been changed—and for the worse—by the fact that on the 24th day of June, 1874, Dr. Cummins had been deposed by the Presiding Bishop, with the consent of a majority of the House of Bishops; (2) that the probabilities of an insufficient service and form are greatly increased by the character and positions of those whose assistance he employed; and (3) that Dr. Nicholson had been canonically deposed several months previous to this, so-called, Consecration. Our conclusion, therefore, as to him, was the same as that to which we had before come in the case of Dr. Cheney.

These two Consecrations, so called, are the only ones at which Dr. Cummins ever officiated; and all later ones, as well as all Ordinations of presbyters and deacons, in what is known as the "Reformed Episcopal Church," depend on them. For the reasons then, above given—without asserting that no other reasons have weighed with individual Bishops—the Bishops in the United States always ordain those who apply to be received from, what is commonly called, the "Cummins Schism," into the Church."

At a meeting of the American Bishops present at the Lambeth Conference, the above statement of the Presiding Bishop was adopted as the statement of the Bishops present, and ordered to be presented to the Conference with the addition of the appended note, on page 360.

A. CLEVELAND COXE,

WM. CROSWELL DOANE,

GEORGE F. SEYMOUR.

Committee on behalf of the American Bishops.

No. XXXVII. (See page 46.)

Sermon preached by the Archbishop of York, in St. Paul's Cathedral, on Saturday, July 28, 1888.

"For the earnest expectation of the creature waiteth for the manifestation of the sons of God."—ROM. viii. 19.

THE Apostle in these grand chapters realises the coming of Christ as a power in the world. Christianity is not, with the Apostle, a saving truth, but a saving power which Christ has brought into the world. In chapter vii. he sees man divided and distracted, with light enough to see the right, but with will too weak to stand firm in it; and then the greatness of the deliverance of the human will from the power of sin through Christ is contrasted with it. "O wretched man that I am! Who shall deliver me from the body of this death? I thank God through Jesus Christ our Lord" (vii. 24, 25). Law and peace have come through Him, and the quickening of the mortal body through the in-dwelling Spirit. Sin is subdued and men are made children of God; and if children then heirs; heirs of God, and joint heirs with Christ (viii. 16, 17). But it is impossible for him not to contrast this ideal of freedom with the continuing sufferings of the present time. The creation is still waiting for a redemption, of which man shall be, in a measure, the instrument. The present suffering may well be borne, through the strength of the hope that is before us. Rising to a sublimer height of diction, the Apostle exclaims that "The earnest expectation of the creature waiteth for the manifestation of the sons of God" (viii. 19).

The Greek word used is a picture in itself. It is the expectation of a man with head erect, looking out afar towards the source from which the succour is to come. It presents to the eye the waiting of all creatures for the manifestation, or further work of the children of God; groaning meanwhile and travailing in pain. We ourselves who have received the Spirit groan with the pain of waiting for the complete redemption in us. "We are saved, indeed, in the way of hope" (viii. 24), for we still wait in patience. Persecution, temptation, the falling away of many, the martyrdom of many, the turning away of the stream of grace from whole districts and churches, leaving a barren wilderness in place of the dews and sweet pastures of the Gospel. For this consummation we pray for the complete fulfilment; but we know not what to pray for as we ought, blindly stretching forwards towards complete redemption.

The Spirit helps our prayers, and "with groanings which cannot be uttered," with yearnings within our souls to which we could give no adequate expression, stretches forth towards the complete revelation, towards complete love, clearer knowledge, deeper peace.

Thus in the time of St. Paul the creation stood in expectation, with head erect, with far-off look, waiting for the dawn of that day which should make her deliverance through Christ complete. St. Paul knew not what would follow, that after eighteen centuries the expectant creation should still so stand, waiting for deliverance. Still the world is full of misery; still it waits for redemption: it is as far off from peace as ever. Strife and struggle, pain and death, are inscribed upon the world's foundation-stones. They are older than the fall of man. Long before man lived to be tempted and to fall, we find their history in the stone-book of creation.

He who subjected the creature (creation) to vanity, to a progress by constant struggle and death towards a higher condition, in which life, and then man and self-consciousness and sin and the great redemption would come to pass, knew His own purpose in so doing. The creation was made subject to vanity, that is, to constant change. But He who so made it knew the issue. He subjected the same in hope. Only in the way of hope can we yet understand the great story of the creation.

St. Paul describes three stages of progress. Until the time of redemption, the whole creation groaned and travailed; and the growth and entombment of animal races, the geologic changes (some gradual, some paroxysmal), the appearance of man, the rise and ruin of Empires, the civilisations that bloomed and died down into desolation were but parts of its torments. There came, secondly, the time in which Paul writes, when the way of holiness and love was opened out, and new strength given to obey God.

And now the Spirit helps the redeemed to pray for the last period, that of complete deliverance; and still they know not fully what to pray for as they ought. And this last stage of waiting has been made bitter by the contamination of the Church itself by vanity; that is, by strife and disunion, and loss of love. Already in St. Paul's time, strife was not unknown. He did not see " Diocletian's fiery sword work busy as the lightning;" nor the Asiatic Churches of the Apocalypse swept away by Mahometan swords; nor the apathy and faithlessness in the Church itself; nor the corruptions of practice which at times have obscured the faith, still held in words and still professed.

We have waited nearly two thousand years, and the language held by those who have lost faith is that they can wait no more; that the power of Christ is no more seen. "When the Hebrews," says one of these writers, "were on their way to the promised land, they perceived that God was with them. God had spoken and had said, 'It lies before you'; and by night a cloud of fire kindled and marched in their van. Now the celestial light is extinct. We are not quite sure that we have God over our heads. We possess no other light but our understanding, and with this glimmering guidance we must direct ourselves through the night. Oh! that we could still be sure that there was a promised land; that others besides us would reach it; that this desert would end in something. This certainty is taken from us; and yet we advance continually, pushed forward by an indefatigable hope."[1]

Beyond doubt, if the power of the Lord is gone, all is gone. He is not a doctrine; but a power. Surrounded by the sick and maimed, He heals them. When He speaks of the Divine Law He does not fear to complete and enlarge it. What is the power which enables men to live no longer to themselves? "The love of Christ constraineth us," replies St. Paul; and the word "constraineth" denotes a real compelling force.

Examine the history of the Church for the first century, from the Day of Pentecost onwards. The records are scanty; but the world vibrated to the tread of that power. Historians hardly mention the name of Christ; but the power is working. If it were indeed true that the power had spent itself; that Christianity, like the moon among planets, were a spent region,—airless, waterless, lifeless,—we should seek perforce another guide. But is it so? Gathered here from all corners of the earth, we ought to be able to find an answer. Has material civilisation supplanted faith? Let brothers answer from America, Australia, and New Zealand. They are colonies of yesterday: their first years were as always a struggle for bread. At first they gave refuge to our criminal class. They did not start with all the apparatus of a traditional religion. Now all are the scene of flourishing churches. A Christian zeal more fruitful, in reference to population, by far than our own, has grown up on the soil. The feeling that civilisation is in itself sufficient for

---

[1] Guyan, "Irreligion de l'Avenir," p. 337.

human progress without religion, finds no countenance from this last chapter of the world's history. The complaint now is not that the voice of religion is not heard; but rather that the voices of jarring creeds are too many. The air is torn with the jangling bells of many churches.

Apply what test you will: the test of numbers; of holy works; of saintly souls; Christian progress is advancing, not receding. Missions have done more in this century than ever before. In a word, that thought which underlies St. Paul's account—namely, that creation stood waiting for its own final redemption, of which man should be the instrument, need not be abandoned now on the ground that man no longer shares the Divine strength.

Is it then true, that the power of man is or ever can be able to work out, by Divine aid, the redemption of creation?

Two lines of conquest over the powers of darkness go on together: the one overcoming physical obstacles, and the other spiritual. The physical progress moves at an increasing rate. It began far back in history; and depends on the mental energies of man. Even the Syrian desert is not mere sand and rock, but consists of excellent soil, desert only by reason of man's neglect. The barren sides of Lebanon have once had beautiful terraces in high cultivation. The terraces remain, but the culture has ceased with man's apathy or relapse towards barbarism. In all civilised countries the soil is useful exactly in the degree in which man's energy defends it from returning to wildness. Modern discoveries have in two ways lengthened life: by preserving health on one side, and by crowding into a given time far more achievement.

We, who could not be heard for 100 feet, can now speak under the ocean 3,000 miles. We can go and return in a single day over distances which to our great grandfathers would require a week; and when we think of what are called the Miracles of Science, we are exhilarated by the conviction that the discoveries of the next decade are likely to be more in number, and more wonderful than those of the last decade, over which we have not yet ceased to be astonished. All these conquests are gifts of God to man, and obtained through man. They are poured out profusely; and at the same time they are educating the race that discovers them into higher skill; and the race which produces more Newtons, and Watts and Nasmyths, more Harveys and Pasteurs, will become the channel of a greater flow of beneficent inventions.

The other road of progress is the spiritual. On that road the pace is slower, the results more unequal, and there are intervals of heartbreaking failure, and retrogression. And yet the gifts of God are great. They cannot be overlooked or denied; and they depend upon the action of man, on the vigour of his faith, on the completeness of his devotion. "How shall they believe in Him of whom they have not heard; and how shall they hear without a preacher." The Most High speaks no more to us in prophetic vision, or by a voice from Heaven. He inspires souls with the power of His spirit; He accumulates, if I may say so, in the vessel of man the Divine electric fire through which spiritual work must be done. There is no other way in the present course of His working. If there are no *men* of faith, neither faith nor the fruits of faith can be upon the earth. When we are twitted with the languid life of the Christian Churches, as compared with the splendid activity and performance of science, the inference is not that there is no longer any guidance, for there is much; but that men who profess to be Christian show a languid and intermittent life, a hypothetical belief, instead of the Apostles' categorical conviction; a perpetual compromise with modern views; an eyesight made false and double by the endeavour to work for double ends. How shall such an engine accomplish a substantial share in the great reform and progress which it is at once the privilege and the duty of the Christian Church to carry on? The spiritual progress has never preserved in past centuries a steady and equal pace. No period of twenty years has ever equalled the grand outpouring of life of the first twenty years after the Resurrection.

No century has been like the first. In the seventh century, churches that had once been faithful, had become deserts, sunless and dewless; fit only, as it seemed, to be visited with the destroying swords of Mohammed. But the law has always been the same. Churches have prospered when peopled by faithful men, they have languished or died when faith has languished and sin has paralysed the will. "The river of grace" never runs dry it is true; but it often changes its course to water new districts, and leaves in its old channel nothing but arid sands. Faith will never be extinct; but it is not tied to any of the places which it enlightens; it leaves behind it a frightful night to those who have despised the day, and it carries its rays to purer eyes.[1]

Let this be the last word which we all carry away from this our conference. Christ is a power; a power of faith and love, which wrought the salvation of the human race. He comes to us and imparts to us His nature; all the stages of his earthly history are repeated in us: the tender infant birth of faith, the growth to perfect manhood, the temptations and the resistance and self-denial, the crucifixion of the old, and the resurrection to the new life, and the affections set thereafter upon things in heaven. If this union is real, if we have done nothing to weaken it, we are like Him; we are of Him; we are one with Him, and His power is with us. There is no other source of strength. And on the other hand, a nature so united

---

[1] Fenelon.

to the Lord cannot be hid, but must be strong and prevail, and a Church where such men are found must needs abound with the fruits of grace. To us, if the Apostle is right, the true progress of the world is committed, and the world is waiting even now for the manifestation of the sons of God. We turn from contemplating with pride the growth of churches, the number of chief pastors added to our counsels, the yearning after closer union one with another, to admit once more the fact that each of us stands with regard to his fellows, quite alone, either gifted with the spirit of Christ, and if so, a storehouse of Divine power for good; or else having a name to live, whilst he has lost hold of the love of Christ, and then nothing can proceed from him, in whom is neither savour, nor will, nor strength.

Now the sins and miseries which yet remain cannot be overcome by mere civilisation. The tools she can use suit not this work; the results she arrives at intensify the evils. Think of a single day in London: how human creatures groan and travail, knowing as yet no redemption by Divine or by any love, from sin and sorrow. The night closes over the day of struggle, but rest comes not with the dark. Men watch round death-beds, and while they sorrow feel that death, at least, is rest. Houseless wanderers are fortunate who can sleep unobserved under a tree; some of them (I know it) have learned to sleep upon their feet, to whom the doorstep is forbidden, who are only allowed such sleep as can consist with "moving on." The servants of pleasure are still astir; the pleasure that is made up of drink and shameless appetite, which must not be called brutal in justice to the brute. Under cover of night, loves that are worse than hatreds work themselves out. Between the loud roar of day and the dull throbbing of night there is a difference, but sin never ceases in this crowd of four millions for whom Jesus did once surely die. Consider, too, the poverty as well as the sin: wealth was never greater; poverty was never more stark and grinding. Westwards there are streets and squares of palaces, charged to the full with every contrivance of luxury, such as no mediæval queen could have dreamed of. Eastward there are dwellings far more numerous, upon which none of those luxurious inventions have lighted. In many of them a few helpless, shivering women try to keep continuous the miserable meals which barely stave off starvation upon the few daily pence which their work is judged to be worth. Our boasted progress has made both the wealth and the poverty. If the progress become more rapid, we do not see why the riches may not grow greater and the poverty more deadly. We compassionate the poor; we are indignant with those who stand next them and do not seem to help; we wax angry with what is called the "sweating system," which, after all, is sometimes an attempt to brigade and organise in workshops a number of helpless creatures whose labour is so little worth that if it were not organised it would earn no wage at all. We have been considering, amongst other topics, the Socialism which is now making itself felt in every country. Socialism is not so much a system or a discovery, as an outcry of hungry despair. Its idea is that nothing can be worse than the present social state, and that any change, even through a universal conflagration of that system, must be an improvement, for what exists is evil beyond conception. Many of its remedies are childish and contradictory. A revival of old experiments that have failed; abolish heirship and succession; organise workshops without the power to dismiss useless workmen, and so on. Mere hunger lies at the root of Socialism.

The terrible element of this question is that our present progress aggravates both extremes; doubling the pile of the rich, and halving the wages of an increasing number of the poor. The quick progress of science does not help it. Against the slower progress of spiritual improvement it is the chief resisting element. You cannot always shut your eyes to this terrible problem of the poor. You may not fear that they will ever destroy society, they are too weak and helpless for that; but still, even the most flaccid conscience must be uneasy. We may sleep in our beds, because starving hands can brandish no weapon and kindle no torch; but still our sleep cannot be so sound if we know that brothers and sisters are starving around us. Who has said, " The murmurs of the poor are just. Why this inequality of conditions? Formed as we all are out of the same dust, there is no way of justifying this except in saying that God has commended the poor to the rich, and has assigned them their maintenance out of their superfluity." It was not a communist. The words are the words of Bossuet.

Now I repeat, that in these two fields, Social progress is well-nigh powerless, and certainly cannot hope to bring out a social system from them which shall be agreeable to the law of love. Competitive trade, brilliant inventions, the hope of profit, have made many rich; but in the nature of the case, the great commercial machine stands sometimes still, and then the capital of the rich remains; but the labour, which is the capital of the poor, lies useless, and they starve. The power of Christ, on the other hand, which has wrought such wonders in the past, ennobling the family life, affirming the equal rights of all redeemed men, building the hospital, freeing the slave, organising the care of the poor, exists still; and if it seems weaker, it is owing to the weaker faith of His followers. Let us more actively affirm the doctrine of love to others; let us apply it to thoughtless marriages; to intemperance; to want of thrift—the chief causes of the helplessness of the people. Let us speak of avarice as our Lord and His Apostles speak of it, as a deadly sin; let us explain the sinfulness of luxury; let us charge wealth with its proper trusts, its Christian claims; let us remind Dives that it is a sin against Christ even to refuse *to think* of Lazarus at the gate; and results as glorious will follow as those which attended the march of the Saviour in earlier times. Are there not facts to prove it? The great increase of expenditure on missions during this century; the splendid examples of individual philanthropy; all these teach us that at this moment we have not reached the summit of human endeavour, but only the first ridge from which we can see, not the downward slope, but alps rising behind alps, which we may not pronounce unattainable until we have tried them. Nor is our power over sin diminished. A hundred years ago, men classed with miracles the conversion of a Magdalen. Now you may call it a miracle still; but it is part of the daily organised work of every complete church, and is blessed with daily success. A century ago the criminal class was looked on as hopeless, and was only dealt with by the severest repression; now the reformatory snatches, in early boyhood, the predestined thief and social pest, and trains them to good, and loads his neck with the beneficent yoke of the moral law, which he will not wish to cast off. We do not discuss it as a possibility; it is part of the Church's constant work. Every Christian man is a storehouse of the power and will of Jesus Christ.

If we have failed to make Christ's purpose known and to manifest His love, we must bear our own sin, and confess it; we must not say that the power of Christ has gone out of the world. It is not the men of high Christian endeavour, who come before us, whining that there is no guidance; it is not the man of prayer, who announces that he has tried to find Christ in prayer, and failed to find Him. No! belief strengthens belief; fresh talents are added where talents are. The complaints that religion is exhausted come from those who have not striven to shape their life according to the truth they knew; weak, perplexed, exhausted, they are ready to become the prey of the first who shall say, "The world is dark and lost; evil has conquered; God we cannot know!" The power of Christ manifested in believers has conquered unbelief, has won over souls, in every age, in every country, against every hinderance. Christianity once consisted of five disciples that followed Christ: it has grown to a countless multitude. The work has been done between these two points by believing men. On the last night of our Lord's ministry all the disciples "forsook Him and fled." That is put before us, not without intention, as the result of His personal teaching, to show that the multitudes, whom no man can number, have been the fruits of Apostles and messengers and believers, in whom the power of Christ was.

Go forth! brethren, beloved, to your glorious work amongst the nations of the earth. You will leave behind you kindly memories for those who have listened to your loving counsels.

Go forth! and tell every believer that the power of Christ is his, if he will use it. We may say nay! We are bound to say "Who is sufficient for these things?" We are not permitted to say that the work against sin and misery can no longer go on, for that is the work of God and Christ, who gives in daily proofs, undeserved that He is working with us still. Go forth! and when social progress makes its claim for great things done, admit the claim; but claim at the same time to be workers in another field of progress, by the spiritual power of Christ. The creation (to recall the apostle's image) stands with head erect in expectation of deliverance from afar; and many a heart will fail before that deliverance come, and many a weak faith will wither; many a sufferer will cry, "How long?" many will ask, "Art thou He that should come?"

With head erect, looking afar towards the growing dawn, we will stand in patient expectation. "Be thou faithful unto death, and I will give thee a crown of life."

No. XXXVIII. (See page 47.)

EPISTOLA CENTUM QUADRAGINTA QUINQUE EPISCOPORUM IN ANGLIA CONGREGATORUM IN PALATIO LAMBETHANO MENSE IULIO ANNO SALUTIS MDCCCLXXXVIII.

Fidelibus in Christo Iesu salutem.

Nos Archiepiscopi, Metropolitani, aliique Episcopi Sanctæ Catholicæ Ecclesiæ, centum quadraginta quinque numero, cum Ecclesia Anglicana pleno iure communicantes, super diœceses proprias iurisdictionem episcopalem exercitantes vel ad episcopalia munia in eis obeunda legitime delegati, a diversis orbis terrarum regionibus congregati in Palatio Lambethano anno Dominicæ Incarnationis MDCCCLXXXVIII, præsidente reverendissimo Præsule Edwardo Divina Providentia Archiepiscopo Cantuariensi totius Angliæ Primate et Metropolitano, in dicti palatii sacello participes facti sacrosanctorum mysteriorum corporis et sanguinis Domini nostri Iesu Christi et orationibus adunati ad Spiritus Sancti directionem impetrandam, de quæstionibus compluribus nobis propositis consilium inivimus, ad salutem populi Dei et ad statum Ecclesiæ per diversas mundi partes diffusæ pertinentibus.

His quæstionibus sedulo et serio deliberandis mensem integrum impendimus, tum publico conventu tum extra conventum quibuscunque res singulæ delegatæ erant. Nunc demum ea quæ de his rebus nobis placuerunt fidelibus in Christo commendamus.

Huic epistolæ duplicem documentorum seriem adiunximus, quarum prima Sententias Conventus sollemnes continet altera delegationum singularum Relationes. Illud autem memoria tenendum eorum solum quæ in priore genere continentur rationem a Conventu nostro esse petendam. Delegationum enim Relationes in tantum Conventus animum exprimere credendæ sunt, quantum in Sententiis vel rursus confirmatæ sint vel ipsis verbis in Sententiis excipiantur. Sed operæ pretium habuimus has Relationes typis exprimere cum locupletem videantur meditationi vestræ materiam suppeditare.*

Imprimis vero quæstionibus moralibus ad vitae regimen utilibus, quæ Conventui propositæ erant, animadverti volumus; et his omnibus præponimus quæ dicenda sunt de officio Ecclesiæ ad temperantiam et castitatem promovendam.

De Temperantia circa potus temulentos.

Multos per annos viri magnanimi, sibi minime parcentes, fortiter connisi sunt ad ebrietatem abolendam, quorum conatus ut multiplici auctu crescant sedulo optamus. Mala enim quæ ex hoc peccato ecclesiæ et genti nostræ oriuntur, vix verbis supra veritatem augeri possunt. Sed moneri vos oportet ne sententiæ falsæ aures præbeatis quæ si latius irrepat bono operi et magno damnum illatura est. Cum enim utilissimam credamus abstinentiam circa potus temulentos quæ absoluta vocetur (*total abstinence*), si pro instrumento ad finem bonum habeatur, eas tamen voces improbare volumus quæ usum vini in se damnant nulla ratione habita eorum quæ vel nobis vel aliis insequantur; et reprehendi a nobis significavimus consuetudinem quorundam, qui, ut fertur, in sacris mysteriis celebrandis alio liquore utuntur; quæ consuetudo ex hac sententia tacite concepta originem duxisse videtur.

[*Sententia* II.—Pronuntiant episcopi in hoc Conventu congregati usum succi ex uvis non fermentati vel alius cuiuscunque liquoris quam veri vini, vel aqua mixti vel meraci, pro elemento calicis in Sacra

---

* In hac interpretatione Sententias illas propriis Epistolæ locis subiunximus, quantum necesse erat ad Epistolam intellegendam, et Relationum tantum quod omitti non poterat.

Communione administrandi, exemplo Domini non esse consentaneum et ab Ecclesiæ Catholicæ consuetudine pervicacius recedere.]

De Castitate Vitæ.

Contra vero his ultimis temporibus vix tandem Christianæ societatis conscientia experrecta est ut gnaviter agendum esse sentiat ad castitatem vitæ vindicandam. Nos ergo hanc occasionem arripere volumus, quæ ex distantibus terrarum regionibus eos congregavit qui Communionis Anglicanæ personam gerunt, ut sacrum bellum adversus hoc peccatum edicamus, quod ante omnia corpus Christi coinquinat et sancti Spiritus templum polluit. Graves et serias voces Relationis in memoriam redigimus; nihil enim nisi communem omnium Christianorum operam huic malo cohibendo sufficere credimus. Provocamus igitur vos ut succurratis disciplinæ sanctæ et severæ; et appellamus omnes, ad quos hæc vox nostra pervenerit, ut coniunctis viribus iudicium hominum de his rebus castigemus, et traditiones ignobiles et corruptas penitus aboleamus, quæ non solum nomen Magistri nostri Christi dedecorent, sed etiam naturam humanam in imagine Dei factam ignominia afficiant.

[*Relatio Delegatorum de hac re omnibus Episcopis ita placuit ut nec addere quidquam nec detrahere voluerint.*]

De Sanctitate Matrimonii.

Huic rei necessario coniuncta est conservatio sanctitatis matrimonii, de qua tota virtus publica pendet. Damnum autem huic sanctitati non minimum illatum est, legibus in quibusdam regionibus latis, per quas pluribus de causis quam antea factum erat divortium conceditur. Præceptum igitur Christi de ea re iterum a nobis asseverandum censuimus, et clericis nostræ Communionis consilia damus quales se præstare debeant adversus eos qui contra legem Domini deliquerint.

[*Sententia* IV.—(A). Cum Domini nostri verba

divortium diserte prohibeant, excepta fornicationis vel adulterii causa, non alia certe de causa, præter exceptam, divortium agnoscere potest ecclesia Christiana, neque quocunque modo ratum facere matrimonium cuiuscunque personæ, contra hanc legem separatæ, persona altera superstite.

(B.) Matrimonio ob fornicationem vel adulterium dissoluto, nequaquam oportet personam nocentem benedictione ecclesiastica in secundas nuptias haberi dignam, superstite persona innocente.

(C.) Cum cognoverimus diversas semper in ecclesia fuisse sententias, matrimonio ob adulterium dissoluto, utrum voluerit Dominus necne a secundis nuptiis personam innocentem prohibere, consilium dat Conventus ne clerici admoneantur ut a sacramentis ceterisque ecclesiæ privilegiis eos arceant, qui civilibus legibus concedentibus ita nuptias inierint.]

De Polygamia.

Sanctitas matrimonii, quale inter Christianos contrahitur fideli coniunctione unius viri cum una femina constat usquedum coniunctio illa morte dissolvatur. Gentium quidem paganarum polygamicas societates inter omnes constat a lege Christi damnari; quæstionibus autem multis et difficilibus dant locum, quæ præterito tempore variis modis solutæ sunt. Nos vero cum ea omnia perspexerimus quæ missionarii ex variis regionibus diversa retulerint, nihil sane de rebus pauxillis statuere voluimus, quas praesidentibus ecclesiarum per loca constitutis decidendas reliquimus, sed præcepta quædam gravioris momenti dedimus, quibus solis credimus missionarios tuto dirigi posse. Imprimis vero nobis curæ fuit ut Christianam matrimonii notionem salvam atque incolumem servaremus, successus illos, qui aliter protinus et cito fierent in evangelio propagando, minimum valere rati si hac notione imminuta vel confusa redimerentur.

[*Sententia* V.—(A.) Conventui placuit ad baptismum non admittendos eos qui in polygamia vivant, sed inter catechumenos habendos, et disciplinæ Christianæ subiciendos donec possint se ad legem Christi conformare.

(B). Conventui visum est polygamorum virorum feminas ad baptismum nonnunquam admitti posse, sed præsidentibus ecclesiæ per loca constitutis iudicium relinquendum esse quo tempore et quibus condicionibus tales baptizari expediat.]

De die Dominica.

Digna Dominicæ observatio, ut diei requietis cultus divini et evangelicæ institutionis, recta via ad Christianæ societatis salutem et incolumitatem confert. Proximis vero temporibus hanc diem minus ac minus diligenter observari animadvertimus, unde sanctitas eius in discrimen veniat. Hoc igitur maxime deprecati, hortamur eos qui otio fruuntur ne commodorum suorum gratia occasiones requietis et cultus divini aliis subtrahant. Dominos et operarum conductores hortamur ut famulis et opificibus iura studiose conservent. Dies enim Dominica pro hæreditate inæstimabili nobis habenda est; qua si quis abutitur metuendo iudicio obnoxius est.

[*Sententia* VII.—(A.) Conventui visum est observantiam religiosam unius diei ex septem, quarto mandato sancitam, lege divina hominibus iniungi.

(B) Usque ab resurrectione Domini primam hebdomadis a Christianis observatam fuisse, ut cultui divino et requieti propriam, et Dominicæ nomine insignitam in sabbati locum paullatim successisse, cum pro festo magno a Christiana ecclesia singulis hebdomadibus celebraretur.

(C). Observantiam Dominicæ, ut diei requietis cultus divini et doctrinæ sacræ, inæstimabili bono fuisse omnibus regionibus Christianis per quas obtinuerit.

(D). Observantiæ huius neglegentiam, in dies crescentem, sanctitatem eius et utilitatem in maximum discrimen adducere.

(E). Maxime deprecandam esse consuetudinem quorundam ordinum hominum, qui divitiis otioque abundent, iam latius se diffundentem, ut Dominica die ad delectationes huius mundi abutantur.

(F). Illud maxime evitandum ne quid ab illa requie deroget, qua in hac die famuli aeque ac magistri, et opifices æque ac operarum conductores, iure frui debent.]

De Socialismo.

His ad mores spectantibus arctissime cohæret quæstio quomodo se gerere debeat Ecclesia Christiana adversus hodiernas de vita publica controversias. Cum enim immodica varietate bona huius mundi distribuantur, cum hic divitiæ ingentes accumulentur, et illic miseranda conspiciatur inopia, necesse est multis et anxiis cogitationibus turbari eum qui mentem Christi induere velit. Nihil igitur consideratione dignius, vel clericis vel laicis, quam quæstiones de Socialismo qui vocatur agitatæ. Meditatio autem de propositis quæ ad æqualitatem tendant circa huius mundi bona, et læta susceptio eorum quæ a quoquam vel bene suscepta vel bene gesta sint, cum excogitatione rationum quibus, sive legum latione, sive societate voluntaria, sive alio modo quocunque pacifice et sine seditione aut iniuria quæstiones istæ ad solutionem perducendæ sint, hæc inter nobilissima studia reputamus quibus viri, qui Christi vestigiis insistere velint, semet ipsos dedere potuerint. Præsto sunt autem in Relatione quæ ad solutionem harum controversiarum conferre videantur.

De Migrantibus.

Unum autem hominum genus præ ceteris Conventus nostri cura et humanitate dignum esse videbatur. Migrantium enim numerus Britannicarum insularum ecclesias ecclesiæ Americanæ et coloniarum nostrarum ecclesiis vivo vinculo alligat. Nihil igitur

Conventus nostri deliberationibus magis erat proprium quam, quid huic tantæ multitudini debeamus reputare qui communem nobiscum sortiti sint fidem. Illud certe, si quid aliud, ecclesiæ est officium, ut profectos ex antiqua patria in novam benevolis oculis per totum iter consequatur, ut cura vigili respiciat, et pericula quæ circa viam et animæ eorum et spiritui insidientur avertat. Sunt vero in Relatione nonnulla quæ credamus ad hanc finem conferre posse.

De certa circa Fidem Doctrina.

Cum igitur de his quæstionibus ita decreverimus ut præceptis Domini et evangelicæ disciplinæ, quatenus aut privatorum hominum mores, aut vitam publicam tangant, primum locum tribuamus, ea iam perscrutemur quæ ecclesiæ partim habeant vel partim possint prospicere ad ea fidei principia tradenda quibus illa morum disciplina fundata sit.

Nobis vero persuasum est hoc opus magna diligentia et emendatione multa indigere. Iuniorum enim institutioni circa religionem multa desunt, præsertim ubi de doctrina Christiana agitur. Quæ incommoda non unum tantum ordinem hominum tangunt, sed et laicos accingere se oportet ut cum clericis huic malo medeantur. Et parentibus quidem hoc opus a Deo mandatum est. Susceptores autem monendi sunt ut officium in parvulos, pro quibus in baptismo responderint, fideliter expleant, et caveant ne indocti maneant vel minus parati ad sigillum Confirmationis accedant. Catechizandi autem usus in propatulo habitus et præparatio eorum sollemnis qui ad Confirmationem instituuntur in maius provehi sine dubio possunt. Simul et cura magis assidua et studio clericorum diligentiore indigent scholæ quæ vocantur dominicales, quam ut multis in locis res nunc se habet. Institutio autem eorum qui in huiusmodi scholis doceant, et alumno-præceptorum (*pupil teachers*) in scholis quæ feruntur elementaribus, opus si quid aliud necessarium parocho et pastori credendum est. Porro oportet pastorem morum præcepta quæ ex Bibliis trahit ita confirmare ut discipulos iterum atque iterum ad sanctiones legis divinæ revocet et ad congrua doctrinæ et disciplinæ exempla quæ in iisdem scripturis reperiuntur. Possunt autem, etiam amplius quam nunc fit, contionantes in ecclesia fidei simul et moribus consulere, et rationi divinorum officiorum lucem afferendo audientes perducere ut intellegant quali inter se vinculo coniungantur cultus Dei et fides et opera—id est quid doceant Liber Precum publicarum, et Catechismus et Symbola.

Non tamen propter iuniores tantum, vel propter eos quos gregibus suis adscriptos habent, clericos oportet certæ et accuratæ fidei doctrinæ studere.

Meditatio certe sacræ Scripturæ exercitationis ingenii Christianis magna pars est, et Biblia ipsa præcipuum omnis doctrinæ circa religionem instrumentum est. Miserum vero dictu, his temporibus, multi ex multis locis quasi signo dato Bibliorum auctoritatem impugnant, neque ut divinæ scientiæ thesaurum accipi sinunt; et per omnes hominum ordines increbrescunt suspiciones, dubitationes, censuræ infestæ et iudicia incredula eorum dogmatum quæ veritate divinitus revelata fundata sunt.

Quandocunque igitur talia originem traxerint ex ignorantia rationis quæ constare debeat inter scientiam rerum naturæ et Revelationem Dei, possunt certe et debent patienter et cum benevolentia tractari. Quod si physicorum sive inventis sive effatis conturbantur mentes hominum, magnopere curandum est ne elementa fidei extinguantur, et regenda magis ingenia quam coercenda ut veritatem perspiciant, talibus inventis leges naturæ in lucem proferri, quibus recte intellectis opus Creatoris magnificum, verbo virtutis Eius sustentatum, amplius et æquius æstimetur.

Periculum vero maius ex hac oppugnatione oritur, sive plane infesta sive mere incredula dicenda sit, utpote difficile nobis sit definire, quatenus doctrina nostra, vel saltem populi de ea iudicium, videatur satis habere rationem earum sententiarum de Sacræ Scripturæ inspiratione et præsertim de Veteris Testamenti dispensatione et disciplina, quæ, quamvis in ecclesia nunquam diserte sancitæ sint, ex longo tamen tempore et multis in locis obtinuerint.

Monendi sunt clerici ut caute et diligenter has controversias tractent, et studiosius hortandi ut ad unum quasi fundamentum doctrinam suam omnem referant, ad Dominum scilicet nostrum Iesum Christum, sacrificium pro peccatis nostris, impietatis nostræ medicinam, vitæ omnis spiritualis fontem, conscientiæ voluntatique nostræ et normam et exemplar omnium virtutum. Ad Ipsum certe et ad opus Ipsius doctrina omnis Veteris Testamenti confluit, ex Ipso Novi Testamenti doctrina omnis derivatur et spiritu et virtute et specie. Ecclesiæ autem est ita operari ut bona ea, quæ ex Incarnatione Verbi Dei fluxerint, ad vitæ usum adhibeat et latius proferat, et doctrina ecclesiæ propagatio est dogmatum quæ super ipsam Incarnationem fundata sint quomodo in Symbolis colliguntur.

De iure mutuo diversarum partium Anglicanæ Communionis.

Ex disceptatione nostra de iure mutuo diœcesium et regionum nostræ Communionis nonnulla saltem prodierunt quæ iudicio vestro commendari volumus. Primum quidem necesse videtur ad regulas a Conventu anni MDCCCLXXVIII. propositas animadvertere, et rursus monere intra Communionis nostræ fines acta cuiusvis ecclesiæ vel Provinciæ, recte et ordine significata, ab aliis ecclesiis et ab his qui in illis conversantur, in honore habenda esse; ne quis sive Episcopus seu clericus in diœcesi iure constituta sine permissione Episcopi qui ibidem sit ministret; ne quis vero Episcopus clericum quemquam ex alia Diœcesi venientem ad sacra ministeria admittat sine litteris commendaticiis idoneis. Harum enim regularum neglegentia gravium interdum scandalorum occasio facta est. Episcopi quidem, quod ad eos attinet, a talibus malis præcavere parati sunt consilium privatim dando simul cum consuetis et formatis litteris; sed et clericos decet cautius versari, cum tales litteras obsignaturi sint; eos quoque, qui his litteris utuntur, cavere oportet ne graventur si accurate quæsitum fuerit qui sint ipsi ut quales. Hae enim quæstiones, quamquam ipsis fortasse supervacaneæ esse videantur, omnino tamen necessariæ sunt ut in hac re saluti ecclesiæ satisfiat.

Cavendum certe maxime est ubi de clericis agitur ad sacra ministeria in coloniis nostris capessenda ordinatis. Enimvero libentissime concedimus eos qui ætatis robur in peregrinos labores impenderint, seu tandem in patria requiescere seu consueta opera novis mutare voluerint, dignos esse quibus consulatur. Sed de hac re generatim decernere impossibile est.

Illa autem quæstio nobis quasi maioris momenti proponebatur utrum Concilium vel Concilia institui possent rerum referendarum gratia, quæ de controversiis consilium darent vel etiam decernerent a præpositis Provinciarum Colonicæ ecclesiæ appellata. Qua de re nobis videtur diutissime et consideratissime deliberandum, ne cito ac temere potestatem constituamus quæ sive pro Concilio habita sive Iudicio publico propior, tum disciplinæ nostræ tum libertati detrimentum allutura sit.

De Christianorum apud nos domestica reconciliatione.

Post anxiam disceptationem satis habuimus articulos aliquos proponere, qui pro fundamento sint a quo progressi, Deo favente, ad domesticam Christianorum reconciliationem propius accedere possimus. Qui articuli, quattuor numero, in Sententiis appositis reperientur.

[*Sententia* XI. Conventui placuit hos articulos, Deo favente, pro fundamento fore a quo progressi ad reconciliationem domesticam propius accedamus:—

(A) Sacras Scripturas veteris novique Testamenti utpote "omnia ad salutem necessaria continentes," cum pro regula veritatis et norma legitima in rebus fidei habendæ sint.

(B) Symbolum Apostolicum quod in baptismate pronuntiatur, et Nicænum quod fidei Christianæ idoneam expositionem continet.

(C) Sacramenta duo a Christo ipso instituta— Baptisma scilicet et cenam Domini—dummodo Christi verba in prima institutione usurpata, et elementa quibus ipse usus est semper usurpentur.

(D) Episcopatum ex antiquis sæculis traditum, ratione quidem administrationis gentium necessitatibus accommodatum et populorum a Deo in ecclesiæ unitatem vocatorum.

Sententia XII. Conventus noster præpositos variis Communionis nostræ regionibus enixe rogat, ut, quantum fieri possit una agentes, notum faciant se paratos esse ad fraterna colloquia (sicuti ab Americana Ecclesia iam propositum fuerit) eos accipere qui aliarum Christianarum societatum in gentibus Anglicizantibus personas gerant consilii capiendi causa, quomodo vel ad reconciliationem integram progredi possimus vel ad talem invicem consuetudinem ex qua temporis progressu arctior quædam unitas nascatur.

Sententia XIII.—Conventus suadet, immo magni momenti esse censet ad reconciliationem confirmandam, ut notitia late diffundatur de doctrinæ normis et de formulis in Ecclesia Anglicana usitatis; suadet etiam ut simili modo divulgetur notitia de formulis doctrinæ cultusque divini et regiminis a ceteris Christianorum societatibus receptis, in quas gentes Anglicizantes divisæ sunt.]

Anglicana autem Communio, ut videtur, societates hominum a se per miseras divisiones separatas hoc animo respicit :—

Parati sumus ad fraterna colloquia omnes recipere qui communionem nobiscum perfectiorem expetant.

Condiciones autem ferimus quibus ex sententia et persuasione nostra talis communio iniri possit. Quamquam enim vehementissime cupimus fratres a nobis aversos complecti, ut voluntas Domini "unus grex unus pastor" ad effectum perducatur, non tamen decet nos infideles esse dispensatores magni depositi nobis commendati. Neque enim circa fidem neque circa disciplinam loco nostro cedere possumus. Concordia autem illa, neque vera fieri possit iudicio nostro neque optanda quæ statione sic relicta fuerit composita.

Libentissime tamen et cum gratiarum actione agnoscimus verum pietatis opus quod a Christianis extra Communionem nostram perficitur. Manifesta enim et in oculis posita est gratia Dei laboribus eorum propter Christi nomen susceptis impertita. Ne quis autem verba nostra aliter accipiat ac dicta sunt. Immo probe compertum habemus quibus vinculis et quam forti persuasione institutis propriis adstricti sint ii qui a nobis dissident. Horum ergo rationem habemus, itidemque institutorum nostrorum et opinionum ab illis rationem haberi volumus. Verum enimvero affirmant testes idonei non in Anglia tantum sed in omnibus Christianismi regionibus desiderium unitatis verum exstare, hominumque corda maius quam antea factum est ad societatem inter Christianos conciliandam commoveri. Hac voluntate penitus se affectum fuisse et in disceptationibus et in sententiis ostendit noster Conventus. Faxit igitur Deus ut super aquas turbulentas discordiarum religiosarum moveatur spiritus amoris.

De Ecclesiis Scandinavicis.

Inter gentes quæ populos Anglicizantes proxime contingunt Scandinavicæ certe numerantur, quæ et in multis diœcesibus nostris frequentia satis magna valent. Non mediocris ergo momenti Conventui nostro fuit qualem se habere deberet Communio Anglicana ergo ecclesias Scandinavicas. Suademus autem in præsens et familiarius versandum et mutuam invicem cognitionem appetendam usque dum, occasione oblata, arctiorem societatem ineamus nulla tamen institutorum nostrorum, quæ necessaria credimus, iactura facta.

[*Sententia* XIV.—Conventui placuit amicitiam inter ecclesias Scandinavicas et Anglicanas sedulo expetendam ; et condiciones, si quæ proponantur, ab ecclesia Suedica, ad mutuam difficultatum explicationem spectantes, libentissime accipiendas, ut si fieri possit, temporis progressu, communio invicem stabiliatur, solido iuris ecclesiastici fundamento confirmata.]

De veteribus Catholicis et aliis.

Neque vero qui nobiscum consociantur caritate et benevolo affectu moveri non possunt erga illos qui in Europa continenti ad Reformationem Ecclesiæ contendunt, præsertim cum difficultatibus maximis impediti eandem plerumque nobiscum rationem secuti sint et Episcopatum quasi institutum Apostolicum obtinuerint. Quamvis enim nondum venisse tempus censeamus ut cum ullis de illorum numero societatem omnibus numeris absolutam ineamus, et cum festinatam quamvis actionem valde deprecemur, quæ antiqua et bene cognita iurisdictionis instituta violaverit, credimus tamen nullo iuris ecclesiastici damno posse nos amicitiæ dextras prætendere, et speramus insuper tempore opportuno fore ut liceat cum nonnullis certe illorum arctiore nosmet societate coniungere.

[*Sententia* XV.—(A). Libentissime agnoscit Conventus quam digne et libere se gesserit Ecclesia Batava veterum Catholicorum, et crebriore fraternæ amicitiæ usu sperandum censet ut multa ex impedimentis, quæ nunc nos ab invicem dirimant, de medio fiant.

(B). Nostrum esse censemus et cum veterum Catholicorum Communione in Germania et cum

"Ecclesia Christiana Catholica" in Helvetia amicitiæ usum augere et promovere, non solum propter studiorum coniunctionem sed etiam ut Deo gratias referamus qui, in magnis difficultatibus et angustiis et temptationibus, roboraverit illos ut pro veritate pati velint; et iura illis pollicemur quæ a Delegatione proposita sunt, eis saltem condicionibus quæ in Relatione significantur.

Relatio autem ista ita se habet:—" Nihil obstare
" nobis videtur quominus et clericos eorum et fideles
" laicos ad sacram Communionem admittamus, eis-
" dem scilicet condicionibus quibus apud nos nostri
" admittantur; agnoscimus simul et benevolentiam
" eorum qua iura spiritualia etiam nostris conces-
" serint.

" Propter varietates autem legum matrimonialium
" infaustas, quas magni momenti æstimamus, definien-
" dum est nobis a sacra Communione prohibendam
" esse quamvis personam, quæ matrimonium contra
" leges et canones Ecclesiæ Anglicanæ contraxerit.
" Contra vero, ius æquum veteribus Catholicis red-
" dentes, neminem nos posse admittere profitemur qui
" apud eos a sacra communione fuerit prohibendus."

(C). Benevolentia nostra digna esse veterum Catholicorum in Austria studium et voluntatem sibi minime parcentium; speramus autem cum res eorum ecclesiastica perfecte fuerit et solide constituta pleniorem cum eis societatem nosmet inituros.

(D). De Reformatoribus autem qui in Italia, Gallia, Hispania et Lusitania, iugum condicionum iniquarum circa communionem ecclesiasticam excutere connitantur, speramus fore ut, cum formulas doctrinæ et disciplinæ salubres assecuti sint et rem suam more Catholico constituerint a nobis liberius agnoscantur.

(E) Nolumus sane intercedere quominus episcopi ecclesiæ Catholicæ, ultima necessitate cogente, in rebus ecclesiasticis peregre se interponant; deprecamur tamen quamvis actionem quæ aut antiqua et bene cognita iurisdictionis instituta aut commoda totius Anglicanæ communionis videatur negligere.]

De Ecclesiis Orientalibus.

Sedulo se velle significavit Conventus ut benevolam consuetudinem, quæ nunc Ecclesias Orientales cum Communione Anglicana coniungat, confirmare et augere possit. Etenim hae Ecclesiæ Christianorum hominum animos per longum tempus sibi conciliaverunt. Multa iam saecula persecutionem passæ in locis multis et tenebrosis evangelicæ lucis vivam flammam servaverunt. Quod si hic et illic lux illa languescere aut hebescere videatur, propter hoc etiam magis nos decet, tempore opportuno utentes, flammam hanc fovere ac conservare. Neque metuendum est ut fraterna officia nostra, benigna voluntate, ut par est, oblata, ab illis digne excipiantur. Agnoscimus autem cum gratiarum actione nulla inter nos et illos exstare impedimenta, qualia nos a Latinorum communione prohibeant, tum propter infallibilitatem ecclesiæ sollemniter confirmatam quasi in persona summi Pontificis inhærentem, tum propter dogma immaculatæ conceptionis Beatæ Virginis Mariæ, et alia dogmata Conciliorum Pontificalium auctoritate Christianis imposita. Romana quidem ecclesia sororem Orientalem inique semper tractavit, quippe quae Episcopos suos antiquis Diœcesibus ingerat, et proselytismum strenue et constanter agat. Merito igitur haec indignatur Ecclesia Orientalis, ut iniuriam passa, cum institutis Catholicis plane contraria sint; nos autem Anglicanos cavere decet ne simili modo peccemus.

Si quis vero inter Orientales lucem clariorem et spiritualis vitæ incrementum desideraverit, potest sane in ecclesia in qua baptizatus fuerit permanendo, lucem circa se aliquo modo diffundere, et civibus suis opem afferre.

Sed cum a proselytismo certe nos abstinere

debeamus, æquum tamen est iura nostra et statum verum ecclesiæ nostræ, per annorum seriem stabilitæ, hominibus illis proponere, qui cum rebus novis præcipue in religione maxime diffidant, historiam tamen Catholicæ antiquitatis magni faciant. Oportet etiam nos institutioni Clericorum in Orientis partibus subvenire, et ubi rerum angustia sit etiam scholis communibus succurrere.

[*Sententia* XVII. Conventus noster consuetudine benevola lætatur qua usi sunt Archiepiscopi Cantuarienses aliique ex Episcopis Anglicanis cum Patriarchis Constantinopoleos aliisque Patriarchis vel Episcopis Orientalibus, et sperare se profitetur fore ut progressu temporis impedimenta quæ pleniorem communionem iam prohibeant, usu familiari crescente, et diffusa luce, e medio tollantur. Fideles autem ad orationes de hac re constanter excitat Conventus, suadet que eis qui Christi leges nobiscum sequuntur ut Reformationi intestinæ ecclesiarum Orientalium consilio et ope subveniant, potius quam singulos hinc et illinc a Communione illarum subtrahant.]

De formulis canonicis apud nos usitatis.

His animadversis formulas doctrinæ et cultus divini canonicas, quæ apud nos receptæ sunt, diligentius a vobis perpendi volumus. Maximi enim momenti est et fidem nostram et mores, cum ecclesiis antiquis tum eis quæ per gentes a missionariis iam formantur et aluntur, tales ostendi ut neque ullis fastidio sint neque libertatem veram impediant, neque plenæ perfectæque Communioni moram afferant.

Declaramus igitur, priorum Conventuum exemplum secuti, nos sub uno Capite divino in unius Catholicæ et Apostolicæ Ecclesiæ Societate coniungi, unamque Fidem firmiter tenere in scripturis sacris revelatam, symbolis definitam, a primitiva ecclesia constanter conservatam et a Conciliis œcumenicis indubitatis affirmatam : agnoscimus autem doctrinæ simul et cultus divini formulas proprias Librum Precum publicarum cum Catechismo, formam Ordinationis, et triginta novem Articulos—hæreditatem quidem præcipuam Ecclesiæ Anglicæ, sed plus minusve ab omnibus nostræ Communionis Ecclesiis receptam.

Formulas autem istas externis Ecclesiis integras et sinceras ostendi volumus. Quippe libertas quodammodo ecclesiis per gentes paganas succrescentibus concedenda est; neque enim æquum foret triginta novem Articulos integros his imponi pro condicione nobiscum communicandi utpote et verbis et forma rerum temporumque indole et colore circa originem primam affectos. Contra autem non possumus illas ut pleno iure nobiscum communicantes et præsertim quoad Ordines sacros agnoscere, nisi prius testimonium satis idoneum dederint se eandem, quoad substantiam eius, doctrinæ formam nobiscum obtinere. Nec difficile esse putandum, nedum impossibile, articulos cum formulis nostris doctrinæ et cultus divini satis concordantes proponere, qui omnibus in ecclesia tali ordinandis imponendi sint.

[*Sententia* XVIII.—Ab Archiepiscopo Cantuariensi expetit Conventus ut consilium cum quibus voluerit capiat, qui deliberent utrum expediat interpretationem Anglicam Symboli Nicæni vel formulæ " Quicunque vult." quovis modo emendare.

Sententia XIX.—De Ecclesiis modo nunc constitutis, præsertim in regionibus nondum Christianis, ita iudicamus. Priusquam recognoscantur ut quæ pleno iure communionis nobiscum frui debeant, et præcipue quæ donum successionis Episcopalis a nobis accipere debeant, oportet eos nobis documentis certis ostendere se, eandem, quoad substantiam eius, doctrinæ formam nobiscum obtinere, et clericos earum articulis, qui cum formularum nostrarum doctrinæ et cultus divini diserte conceptis sententiis concordent, subscribere ; non tamen ex necessitate tales clericos cogendos esse triginta et novem Articulos Religionis integros accipere.]

Hanc epistolam, Fratres, ad finem perducimus humiles et sinceras Deo Omnipotenti gratias agentes, propter magnam Eius erga nos benevolentiam et caritatem. Concessit enim nobis ut hic plures numero quam antea congregemur. Ex omni autem regione orbis terrarum scientiæ simul et experientiæ thesauri in medium collati sunt. Ipsis quoque oculis, plenius quam antea fieri poterat, proposita est magnæ Anglicanæ Communionis et amplitudo et potentia et virtus.

Quantis facultatibus prædita sit, quantis temporum opportunitatibus, quantis commodis fruatur intelleximus. In disceptationibus autem communi concilio habitis unitatem eius veram esse experti sumus, quantumvis partes eius vel statu vel maturitate varient. Ubi enim discordia sententiarum inter nos fuerit, ibi etiam concordia spiritus et propositi unitas; itaque recordationibus quas nobiscum reportamus refecti roboratique et ad maiora incitati ad diœceses nostras alius alia via redibimus.

Sed beneficii a Deo accepti conscientia cum officii debito arcte coniuncta est. Quo magis enim ea commoda sentimus, quibus in communione Anglicana fruimur, eo magis incendimur ut munera nostra exsequamur, quæ non tantum nostrates tangant, vel in evangelio propagando expleantur, sed ad omnes ecclesias Dei pertineant. Quippe singulari loco positi ad singulare opus evocamur. Deum ergo enixe apprecamur ut omnes—clerici pariter ac laici—manifestam Eius voluntatem secum reputent, et quamcumque stationem teneant summis viribus contendant ut propositum Eius in finem debitum perducatur.

His verbis, salutem vobis multam optantes, ea quæ nobis in hoc Conventu placuerunt studio vestro et considerationi tradimus, Deum insuper supplicantes ut Spiritus Sanctus cogitationes vestras gubernet et vosmet ipsos in omnem veritatem dirigat, faciatque ut consilia nostra per operationes vestras ad gloriam Dei vertantur et ad regni Christi incrementum.

Subscripsi in nomine Conventus,

EDWARDUS CANTUARIENSIS.

ΕΠΙΣΤΟΛΗ ΕΚΑΤΟΝ ΤΕΣΣΑΡΑΚΟΝΤΑ ΠΕΝΤΕ ΕΠΙΣΚΟΠΩΝ

ἐν Ἀγγλίᾳ συνηθροισμένων ἐν Παλατίῳ Λαμβηθανῷ μηνὶ Ἰουλίῳ ἔτει ͵αωπη΄ (1888).

Τοῖς πιστοῖς ἐν Χριστῷ Ἰησοῦ χαίρειν ἐν Κυρίῳ.

Ἡμεῖς Ἀρχιεπίσκοποι καὶ Μητροπολῖται καὶ ἄλλοι ἐπίσκοποι τῆς ἁγίας Καθολικῆς Ἐκκλησίας, συγκοινωνοῦντες ὁλοκλήρως τῇ Ἀγγλικανῇ Ἐκκλησίᾳ, ἑκατὸν τεσσαράκοντα πέντε ὄντες τὸν ἀριθμόν, ἅπαντες ἐπισκοπὴν παροικιῶν ἐπιτηδεύοντες ἢ νομίμως ἐπισκοπικὰ τέλη ἐν αὐταῖς ἐπιτετραμμένοι, συνελθόντες ἐκ διαφόρων τῆς οἰκουμένης κλιμάτων ἐν Παλατίῳ Λαμβηθανῷ ἔτει σωτηρίῳ ͵αωπη΄ (1888), προεδρεύοντος τοῦ σεβασμιωτάτου Ἐδονάρδου τῇ θείᾳ προνοίᾳ Ἀρχιεπισκόπου Καντουαρίας, ὅλης Ἀγγλίας πρωτεύοντος, καὶ Μητροπολίτου, μετειληφότες ἐν τῷ ναῷ τοῦ εἰρημένου Παλατίου τῶν ἁγίων μυστηρίων τοῦ σώματος καὶ τοῦ αἵματος τοῦ Κυρίου, καὶ προσευχαῖς ἡνωμένοι ὑπὲρ τῆς τοῦ ἁγίου Πνεύματος χειραγωγίας, ἐξέτασιν πεποιήκαμεν διαφόρων ζητημάτων ἡμῖν προβεβλημένων ἀνηκόντων εἰς τὴν τοῦ Θεοῦ λαοῦ εὐπραγίαν καὶ τὴν τῆς ἐκκλησίας κατάστασιν ἐν διαφόροις τοῦ κόσμου μέρεσιν.

Περὶ τούτων οὖν ἀκριβῶς καὶ σπουδαίως ὅλον μῆνα συμβουλευσάμενοι, κοινῇ τε συνόδῳ καὶ ἰδίᾳ οἷς τὰ πράγματα κατὰ μέρος ἐπετράπη, παρατιθέμεθα τανῦν τοῖς πιστοῖς τὰ περὶ τούτων ἡμῖν δόξαντα.

Ταύτῃ τῇ ἐπιστολῇ δύο εἴδη ὑπομνημάτων προστεθείκαμεν, δηλαδὴ τὰς τοῦ Συμβουλίου διατάξεις καὶ τὰς τῶν Ἐπιτροπῶν ἐκθέσεις.*

Γνωρίζειν δὲ ὑμᾶς θέλομεν ὅτι τὰ πρῶτα μόνον θεωρεῖν χρεὼν ὡς ὑπ' αὐτοῦ τοῦ Συμβουλίου ἀποπεφασμένα. Αἱ γὰρ ἐκθέσεις ἐπὶ τοσοῦτον τὸ τοῦ Συμβουλίου φρόνημα ὑποδεικνύασιν ὅσονπερ ἐν ταῖς διατάξεσιν ἢ κατὰ τὴν διάνοιαν ἢ αὐτοῖς ῥήμασιν ἀνελήφθησαν. Τὰς δὲ ἐκθέσεις ἐκείνας τετυπωμένας ἐκδιδόναι ἄξιον ἡγούμεθα, ὡς τοῖς ἀναγιγνώσκουσιν καρπὸν μελέτης ἱκανὸν παραστήσειν δυναμένας.

Πρῶτον δὴ τὰ ἠθικὰ καὶ πρακτικὰ ἐτάξαμεν περὶ ὧν ἐν τῷ Συμβουλίῳ λόγος ἐγένετο· καὶ πρώτιστα τὰ τῆς Ἐκκλησίας καθήκοντα ὑπὲρ τῆς ἐγκρατείας καὶ τῆς ἁγνείας.

Περὶ τῆς περὶ τὰ μεθυστικὰ ποτὰ ἐγκρατείας.

Εὐγενῶς ἐκ πολλῶν ἐτῶν ἤδη, καὶ ἐν τῇ Ἐκκλησίᾳ καὶ ἐκτὸς, ἠγωνίσαντο ἄνδρες αὐταπαρνητικοὶ ὅπως τὴν περὶ τὰ ποτὰ ἀκρασίαν καταργήσωσιν, τοῖς δὲ ἐπιχειρήμασιν τούτοις ἐπίδοσιν πολλαπλασίαν μετὰ σπουδῆς εὐχόμεθα. Περὶ γὰρ τῶν κακῶν τῶν καὶ τῇ Ἐκκλησίᾳ καὶ τῷ ἡμετέρῳ ἔθνει ἐκ τῆς ἁμαρτίας ταύτης συμβαινόντων ὑπερβολικῶς εἰπεῖν οὐ ῥάδιον· ἀλλὰ ἀναγκαῖον ἡγούμεθα περὶ ψευδοῦς τινος ὑποθέσεως νουθετικώτερον λέγειν ἵνα μὴ τὰ καλῶς εἰργασμένα παρεισδύουσα διαφθείρῃ. Τὴν μὲν γὰρ παντελῆ λεγομένην ἀποχὴν τῶν μεθυστικῶν ποτῶν περὶ πολλοῦ ποιούμεθα ὡς ἐπὶ τέλει ἀγαθῷ ἐπιτηδευομένην· τοὺς δὲ λόγους ἐκείνους ἀποδοκιμάζομεν οἷς ἡ τοῦ οἴνου χρῆσις καθ' αὑτὴν καταγινώσκεται, χωρὶς τῶν ἀπ' αὐτῆς ἢ τοῖς χρωμένοις ἢ καὶ ἑτέροις συμβαινόντων· τὴν δὲ πρᾶξιν τινῶν, ὡς λέγεται, ἐπεμεμψάμεθα ἐκ τῆς ὑποθέσεως ταύτης σιγῇ ὑποκειμένης ὡς φαίνεται

---

* Ἐν ταύτῃ τῇ μεταφράσει τὰς τοῦ Συμβουλίου διατάξεις ὅσον χρέος ἦν τοῖς τῆς ἐπιστολῆς οἰκείοις τόποις παρατεθείκαμεν, τῶν δὲ ἐκθέσεων αὐτὰ τἀναγκαιότατα μόνον δεδώκαμεν πρὸς τὴν κατάληψιν τῶν δεδογμένων.

Greek Version of Encyclical Letter of 1888.

ἐκγινομένην, οἵτινες ἑτέρῳ τινὶ ποτῷ ἐν τοῖς ἁγίοις μυστηρίοις χρῶνται.

[Διάταξις β'. Οἱ ἐν τῷ Συμβουλίῳ συναθροισθέντες ἐπίσκοποι ἀποφαίνομεν τὴν χρῆσιν τοῦ ἐκ βοτρύων ἀζυμώτου χυμοῦ ἢ ἄλλου τινὸς πλὴν οἴνου ἀληθινοῦ κραθέντος ὕδατι ἢ ἀκράτου, ἐν τῇ μεταδόσει τοῦ ποτηρίου ἐν τῇ ἁγίᾳ κοινωνίᾳ, μὴ εἶναι κατὰ τὸ ὑπόδειγμα τοῦ Κυρίου καὶ ἔκκλισιν εἶναι ἰδιογνώμονα τοῦ τῆς καθολικῆς ἐκκλησίας ἔθους.]

Περὶ ἁγνείας.

Περὶ τῆς ἁγνείας μέντοι νῦν δὴ πρῶτον ἄρχεται κινεῖσθαι εἰς τὸ δραστήριον ἡ τοῦ Χριστιανοῦ πλήθους συνείδησις· ἡμεῖς οὖν τῷ καιρῷ τῷδε χρῆσθαι θέλομεν, ἐν ᾧ ἐκ μακροτάτων κλιμάτων πρόβουλοι τῆς Ἀγγλικανῆς κοινωνίας συνηθροίσθησαν, ὅπως κατ' ἐκείνης τῆς ἁμαρτίας ἱερὸν πόλεμον ἀνακηρύσσωμεν, ἢ πρὸ πασῶν τὸ τοῦ Χριστοῦ σῶμα μιαίνει καὶ τὸν ναὸν τοῦ ἁγίου Πνεύματος κοινοῖ. Ἀνακαλούμεθα οὖν τοὺς ἐν τῇ ἐκθέσει λόγους τοὺς ἐμβριθεῖς· οὐδενὸς γὰρ ἄλλου ἢ κοινῆς πάντων Χριστιανῶν ἐνεργείας δεῖ ὅπως τὸ κακὸν τοῦτο παύσωμεν· ἐπικαλούμεθα δὲ ὑμᾶς συμμάχους ἀσκήσεως καθαρᾶς καὶ μεγαλοθύμου· ἐπιμαρτυρόμεθα δὲ ἅπαντας πρὸς οὕστινας ἂν ἡ φωνὴ ἡμῶν ἐφίκηται ἵνα ἡμῖν συναντιλαμβάνωνται πρὸς τὴν τῆς δημοσίας γνώμης κάθαρσιν, καὶ πρὸς τὴν τῶν ἀγεννῶν καὶ σαπρῶν παραδοσέων παντελῆ κατάλυσιν, τῶν μὴ μόνον τὸ ὄνομα τοῦ δεσπότου ἡμῶν Χριστοῦ ἀτιμαζουσῶν, ἀλλὰ καὶ τὴν φύσιν τὴν ἀνθρωπίνην ἐν εἰκόνι Θεοῦ κτισθεῖσαν καταισχυνουσῶν.

[Ἡ ἔκθεσις τῆς Ἐπιτροπῆς πᾶσιν τοῖς Ἐπισκόποις ἤρεσεν, καὶ ὡς πλείστης σπουδῆς ἀξία ἐπῃνέθη.]

Περὶ γάμου ὁσιότητος.

Ἀμέσως δὲ τούτου τοῦ λόγου ἔχεται ἡ τῆς τοῦ γάμου ὁσιότητος διαφύλαξις, ἀφ' ἧς πᾶσα ἡ δημοσία ἀρετὴ ἀπήρτηται. Αὕτη δὲ ζημίαν ἔλαβεν οὐ τὴν τυχοῦσαν ὑπὸ τῶν ἀρτίως ἐν χώραις τισὶν νενομοθετημένων, καθ' ἃ ἡ τοῦ γάμου διάλυσις ἐπὶ πλείοσιν αἰτίαις ἢ τὸ πρότερον συγχωρεῖται. Τὴν οὖν περὶ τούτων Χριστοῦ ἐπιταγὴν πάλιν ἀνακηρύσσειν ἀναγκαῖον ἡμῖν ἡγησάμεθα καὶ τοῖς κληρικοῖς τῆς ἡμετέρας κοινωνίας παραγγελίας τινὰς ὑποθέσθαι ποίους δεῖ παρέχεσθαι ἑαυτοὺς πρὸς τὰς τοῦ Κυριακοῦ κανόνος παραβάσεις.

[Διάταξις δ'. (Α.) Τοῦ Κυρίου ῥητῶς τὴν τοῦ γάμου διάλυσιν κωλύοντος παρεκτὸς λόγου πορνείας ἢ μοιχείας, οὐκ ἐξ ἄλλης αἰτίας χωρὶς τῆς ἐξῃρημένης τὸ διαζύγιον ἀποδέχεσθαι δύναται ἡ Χριστιανὴ ἐκκλησία, ἢ ὁτῳοῦν τρόπῳ τῷ παρὰ τὸν νόμον τοῦτον διαζυγέντι γάμον συναινεῖν, ζῶντος τοῦ ἑτέρου προσώπου.

(Β.) Γάμου διὰ πορνείαν ἢ μοιχείαν διαλυθέντος οὐδαμῶς δεῖ τὸ πρόσωπον τὸ τῆς αἰτίας ἔνοχον εἰς μετάληψιν εὐλογίας ἐκκλησιαστικῆς ἐφ' ἑτέρῳ γάμῳ ἀξιοῦσθαι, ζῶντος τοῦ ἀναιτίου.

(Γ.) Ἐπειδήπερ οἴδαμεν διημφισβητῆσθαι πολλάκις ἐν τῇ ἐκκλησίᾳ, γάμου διὰ μοιχείαν διαλυθέντος, πότερον ἐβούλετο ὁ Κύριος τῷ ἀναιτίῳ προσώπῳ γάμον ἀπαγορεύειν ἢ μή, παραινεῖ τὸ Συμβούλιον τοῖς κληρικοῖς παραγγελίας μὴ διδόναι ὅπως τῶν ἁγίων μυστηρίων καὶ τῶν ἄλλων τῆς ἐκκλησίας προνομίων τοὺς τοιούτους κωλύωσιν, νόμῳ πόλεως γεγαμηκότας.]

Περὶ πολυγαμίας.

Ἡ τοῦ γάμου ὁσιότης ὡς ἐν Χριστιανοῖς νενομισμένου ἐν συζυγίᾳ πιστῇ ἑνὸς ἀνδρὸς πρὸς μίαν γυναῖκα κεῖται, ἕως ἂν τῷ θανάτῳ ἡ συζυγία διαλυθῇ. Αἱ μὲν οὖν τῶν ἐθνικῶν πολυγαμικαὶ συνάφειαι ὁμολογουμένως τῷ νόμῳ Χριστοῦ κατεγνωσμέναι εἰσίν· ἀπορίας δὲ πολλὰς ἔργῳ παριστᾶσιν, ὧν ἐν τῷ πρόσθεν χρόνῳ διάφοροι λύσεις γεγένηνται. Ἡμεῖς μέντοι τὴν πολυγαμίαν σκεψάμενοι πρὸς τὰ ὑπὸ τῶν ἱεραποστόλων ἐκ διαφόρων μερῶν τῆς γῆς ἀπαγγελθέντα, τῶν μὲν μικροτέρων ἀπέχεσθαι ἠξιώσαμεν τοῖς κατὰ τόπους προεστῶσιν τῶν ἐκκλησιῶν ἐπιτρέψαντες, τὰ δὲ καθόλου ὁρίσαντες τοιαῦτα παρηγγείλαμεν οἷς ἀνάγκην εἶναι νομίζομεν ἐπακολουθεῖν τὸν ἱεραπόστολον, τὸν ἀσφαλῶς ἐνεργεῖν βουλόμενον. Πρῶτον δὲ πάντων τούτου ἐφροντίσαμεν τοῦ τὴν Χριστιανικὴν τοῦ γάμου ὑπόληψιν τηρεῖν καὶ διαφυλάττειν, νομίσαντες τὰς παραυτίκα καὶ ἐν τάχει ἐπιτυχίας, αἳ ἴσως ἂν πρὸς τὴν διάδοσιν τοῦ εὐαγγελίου ἐπεγένοντο, ἐν μηδενὶ λόγῳ εἶναι διαφθαρείσης καὶ συγχυθείσης τῆς ὑπολήψεως ταύτης.

[Διάταξις ε΄. (Α.) Τῷ Συμβουλίῳ ἔδοξε τοὺς ἐν πολυγαμίᾳ διαιτωμένους μὴ πρὸς τὸ βάπτισμα παρίεσθαι, ἀλλ' ὡς κατηχουμένους καταλέγεσθαι καὶ τῇ Χριστιανικῇ διδαχῇ ὑποτάσσεσθαι, ἕως ἂν οὕτω καταστῶσιν ὥστε τὸν νόμον Χριστοῦ παραδέχεσθαι.

(Β.) Τῷ Συμβουλίῳ ἔδοξε τὰς τῶν πολυγάμων γυναῖκας ἐνίοτε πρὸς τὸ βάπτισμα παριέναι ἐνδέχεσθαι, τοὺς δὲ κατὰ τόπους προεστῶτας τῆς ἐκκλησίας διαγιγνώσκειν τὰς περιστάσεις ἐν αἷς τὰς τοιαύτας βαπτίζειν ἔξεσται.]

Περὶ τῆς κυριακῆς ἡμέρας.

Ἡ τῆς κυριακῆς παρατήρησις, ὡς ἡμέρας ἀναπαύσεως καὶ θρησκείας καὶ εὐαγγελικῆς διδασκαλίας, τείνει παρευθὺς πρὸς τὴν τῆς Χριστιανικῆς πολιτείας εὐταξίαν. Κατενοήσαμεν δὲ προσφάτως τῆς ἀμελείας προκοπτούσης ἀνειμενέστερον τηρεῖσθαι τὴν ἡμέραν, ὥστε κινδυνεύειν τὴν ἁγιότητα αὐτῆς ἐλαττωθήσεσθαι. Τοῦτο δὲ μάλιστα πάντων ἀπευχόμενοι τοὺς σχολῇ πολλῇ χρωμένους ἐπιμαρτυρόμεθα μὴ διὰ φιλαυτίας ἀναπαύσεως καιροὺς καὶ θρησκείας ἑτέροις ὑφαιρεῖν. Τοὺς δὲ δεσπότας ἐπιμαρτυρόμεθα καὶ τοὺς ἐργοδότας τὰ τῶν ὑπηρετῶν καὶ ἐργατῶν δίκαια φιλοτίμως φυλάττειν. Κληρονομίαν γὰρ ἔχομεν παντιμοτάτην τὴν Κυριακὴν ἡμέραν, ὅστις δὲ ταύτῃ καταχρῆται δεινῆς κρίσεως ὑπεύθυνος γίγνεται.

[Διάταξις ζ́. (Α.) Τῷ Συμβουλίῳ ἔδοξε τὴν θρησκευτικὴν παρατήρησιν μιᾶς ἡμέρας ἐν ταῖς ἑπτά, ἐν τῇ τετάρτῃ ἐντολῇ διαταχθεῖσαν, θεῖον ἔχειν τὸ κῦρος.

(Β.) Ἀπὸ τῆς ἀναστάσεως τοῦ Κυρίου τὴν πρώτην τῆς ἑβδομάδος τετηρῆσθαι Χριστιανοῖς ὡς ἡμέραν θρησκείας καὶ ἀναπαύσεως, καὶ κυριακὴν ἐπονομασθεῖσαν τὴν ἱερὰν τάξιν τοῦ σαββάτου ἤρεμα διαδέξασθαι ὡς μεγάλην ἑορτὴν κατὰ πᾶσαν ἑβδομάδα τῇ Χριστιανῇ ἐκκλησίᾳ.

(Γ.) Τὴν παρατήρησιν τῆς κυριακῆς, ὡς ἡμέρας ἀναπαύσεως καὶ θρησκείας καὶ θείας διδασκαλίας, παντιμότατον ἀγαθὸν γεγονέναι πάσαις Χριστιανικαῖς χώραις ἐν αἷς διεφυλάχθη.

(Δ.) Τὴν καθ᾽ ἡμέραν αὐξανομένην ἀμέλειαν τῆς παρατηρήσεως κινδυνεύειν μέγα τι ὑφαιρήσειν τοῦ ἱεροῦ αὐτῆς καὶ φιλανθρώπου χαρακτῆρος.

(Ε.) Ἀπευκτέον εἶναι τὰ μάλιστα τὴν συνήθειάν τινων τὴν ἐπεκτεινομένην, τῶν εὐπορίᾳ καὶ σχολῇ πολλῇ χρωμένων, τὸ τὴν κυριακὴν εἰς τέρψεις βιωτικὰς μεταστρέφειν.

(Ζ.) Φυλακτέον εἶναι ἵνα μηδὲν ὑφαιρῆται τῆς ἀναπαύσεως ἧς ἐν τῇ ἡμέρᾳ ταύτῃ οὐχ ἧττον οἱ ὑπηρέται ἢ οἱ κύριοι, οὐδ᾽ ἧττον οἱ χειροτέχναι ἢ οἱ ἐργοδόται δίκαιοί εἰσιν ἀπολαύειν.]

Περὶ τοῦ κοινεταιρισμοῦ (Socialism).

Συνῳκείωται δὲ τοῖς πρακτικοῖς ζητήμασι τούτοις ἡ σχέσις τῆς Χριστιανικῆς ἐκκλησίας πρὸς τὰ κοινοπολιτικὰ τὰ καθ᾽ ἡμέραν ἀμφισβητούμενα. Τὸ γὰρ περισσῶς ἄνισον τῆς διαδόσεως τῶν βιωτικῶν χρημάτων, καὶ ἔνθεν μὲν ὁ ἀποθησαυρισμὸς ἄτοπος γεγενημένος, ἔνθεν δὲ ἡ ἀθλιωτάτη πτωχεία—ταῦτα τῷ ἐν ἑαυτῷ τὸ φρόνημα τοῦ Χριστοῦ κατέχοντι φροντίδα πολλὴν καὶ μέριμναν παρέχει. Οὐδὲν ἄρα λόγου ἀξιώτερόν ἐστιν, οὔτε τοῖς κληρικοῖς οὔτε τοῖς λαϊκοῖς, ἢ τὰ περὶ τοῦ λεγομένου κοινεταιρισμοῦ προβεβλημένα. Ἡ δὲ μελέτη τῶν ἐπιχειρημάτων τῶν πρὸς τὸ ἰσόρροπον τεινόντων περὶ τὰ ἐκτὸς ἀγαθά, καὶ ἡ μετὰ χαρᾶς ἀποδοχὴ τῶν καλῶς τισιν ἢ ἐπινοουμένων ἢ πραττομένων, καὶ τὸ βουλεύεσθαι ὅπως εἴτε νομοθεσίᾳ εἴτε ἑταιρείᾳ εἴτε ἄλλῳ τινὶ τρόπῳ εἰρηνικῶς καὶ ἄνευ στάσεως καὶ ἀδικίας αἱ ἀπορίαι αὗται λύσεως τύχωσιν—ταῦτα ἐν τοῖς γενναιοτάτοις ἀριθμοῦμεν οἷς οἱ τοῖς ἴχνεσιν τοῦ Χριστοῦ ἐπακολουθεῖν βουλόμενοι ἑαυτοὺς παραδιδόναι δύνανται. Ἔστιν δὲ ἐν τῇ ἐκθέσει ἃ πρὸς τὴν λύσιν τῶν προβλημάτων τούτων ἂν συμβάλλοι.

Περὶ τῶν μεταναστάντων.

Εἰσὶν δὲ καὶ οἳ ἐξαιρέτως τῆς φροντίδος τοῦ συμβουλίου καὶ συμπαθείας ἐνδικώτατα ἠξιώθησαν. Διὰ γὰρ τῶν μεταναστάντων ἡ τῶν Βρεττανικῶν νήσων ἐκκλησία τῇ τῶν Ὁμοσπόνδων Πολιτειῶν καὶ ταῖς τῶν ἀποικιῶν ἐκκλησίαις κοινωνικῷ συνδέσμῳ δέδεται. Οὐδὲν ἄρα οἰκειότερον τῷ ἡμετέρῳ συλλόγῳ ἢ τὸ ἐπισκέπτεσθαι τί τὸ ὀφειλόμενον τοῖς πολλοῖς τούτοις τοῖς ὁμότιμον ἡμῖν πίστιν κεκτημένοις. Προσήκει δὲ μάλιστα τῇ ἐκκλησίᾳ κατὰ πᾶσαν τὴν πορείαν ἐκ τῆς ἀρχαίας πατρίδος εἰς τὴν νέαν συμπαθέστατα τούτους ἐπισκοπεῖν καὶ μετὰ φροντίδος πολλῆς τηρεῖν, καὶ τοὺς κινδύνους τοὺς περὶ τὴν ὁδὸν καὶ τῇ ψυχῇ καὶ τῷ πνεύματι ἐγκειμένους ἀποτρέπειν. Ἐν δὲ τῇ ἐκθέσει τινὰ ὑποτεθείκαμεν τὰ πρὸς τὸ τέλος τοῦτο ὡς πιστεύομεν συμβαλούμενα.

Περὶ διδασκαλίας καὶ κατηχήσεως.

Διατάξαντες οὖν οὕτως περὶ τούτων, ὥστε ταῖς ἐπιταγαῖς τοῦ Κυρίου καὶ τῇ εὐαγγελικῇ εὐταξίᾳ καὶ κατὰ τὸν βίον καὶ ἐν τῇ πολιτείᾳ τὸν πρῶτον τόπον ἀποδοῦναι, ἐκεῖνα ἤδη ἐπισκεψώμεθα ἃ ταῖς ἐκκλησίαις ἕτοιμα καὶ πρόσκαιρά ἐστιν εἰς τὴν παράδοσιν τῶν ἀρχῶν τῆς πίστεως αἷς πᾶσα ἡ ἠθικὴ διδασκαλία ἐπῳκοδόμηται.

Πεπείσμεθα δὲ ἀνενδοιάστως τὸ ἔργον τοῦτο μελέτης ἀκριβοῦς δεῖσθαι καὶ ἐπιδόσεως μεγάλης. Ἡ γὰρ θρησκευτικὴ προπαιδεία τῶν νεωτέρων ἐντελείας καὶ γνησιότητος πολὺ ἐλλείπει, οὐχ ἥκιστα δὲ περὶ τὴν θείαν διδαχήν. Ἡ δὲ ἔλλειψις αὕτη οὐχ ἑνὶ μόνον γένει ἀνθρώπων πρόσεστιν, ἀλλὰ καὶ τοὺς λαϊκοὺς ἑτοιμάσασθαι δεῖ ὡς συλληψομένους τοῖς κληρικοῖς πρὸς τὴν χρείαν ταύτην. Τοῖς μὲν οὖν γονεῦσιν παρὰ θεοῦ τοῦτο ἐπέσταλται· τοῖς δὲ ἀναδόχοις παραγγέλλειν χρὴ ὅπως τοῖς παιδίοις ἀνθ᾽ ὧν τῷ Χριστῷ συνετάξαντο τὴν πρέπουσαν ἐπιμέλειαν παρέχωσιν, ἵνα μὴ ἀδίδακτοι μένωσιν, ἢ πρὸς τὴν σφραγῖδα τῆς βεβαιώσεως ἀπαράσκευοι χωρῶσιν. Πολλὴν δὲ ἐπίδοσιν ἐπιδέχοιτ᾽ ἂν ἡ φανερῶς γιγνομένη κατήχησις καὶ ἡ ἑτοιμασία τῶν πρὸς τὴν βεβαίωσιν τασσομένων. Ἅμα δὲ καὶ συνεχεστέρας ἐπιστάσεως καὶ σπουδῆς ἐπιμελεστέρας παρὰ τῶν κληρικῶν προσδεῖται τὰ σχολεῖα τὰ κυριακὰ τῆς νῦν πολλαχοῦ εὑρισκομένης. Τῶν δὲ ἐν τοῖς τοιούτοις διδασκόντων καὶ τῶν νεοφυτοδιδασκάλων (pupil-teachers) ἐν τοῖς δημοτικοῖς σχολείοις (elementary schools) τὴν παιδαγωγίαν οὐδὲν ἄλλο ἢ ἔργον ἀπαραίτητον τῷ πρεσβυτέρῳ καὶ ποιμένι νομιστέον· τά τε ἠθικὰ καὶ πρακτικὰ παραγγέλματα τὰ ἐκ τῶν Βιβλίων βεβαιοῦν δεῖ τὸν διδάσκαλον τοὺς μαθητὰς ἀεὶ ἐπανακαλοῦντα ἐπὶ τὰς τοῦ Θεοῦ ἀπειλὰς καὶ τὰ μετ᾽ αὐτῶν διδαχῆς καὶ εὐταξίας οἰκεῖα παραδείγματα ἐν ταῖς αὐταῖς γραφαῖς περιλαμβανόμενα. Ἐνδέχεται δὲ ἔτι πλέον τῆς νῦν μεθόδου τοὺς ἐν τῇ ἐκκλησίᾳ ὁμιλοῦντας τῇ πίστει ὁμοῦ καὶ τῇ τῆς ἀρετῆς πράξει συμβάλλεσθαι, καὶ τοὺς ἐξηγουμένους τὸ τῆς ἁγίας θρησκείας σύστημα καὶ τάξιν προάγειν τοὺς συναγομένους ὅπως μανθάνωσιν ἀκριβῶς οἵαις σχέσεσι πρὸς ἀλλήλας χρῶνται ἡ εὐσέβεια καὶ ἡ πίστις καὶ τὰ ἔργα—τουτέστιν οἷα διδάσκουσιν ἥτε βίβλος τῆς δημοσίας εὐχῆς καὶ ἡ κατήχησις καὶ τὰ σύμβολα.

Οὐ μέντοι διὰ τοὺς νεωτέρους μόνον ἢ καὶ διὰ τοὺς φανερῶς ἐν τοῖς ποιμνίοις αὐτῶν τεταγμένους ἀσφαλοῦς καὶ ἀκριβοῦς διδαχῆς ἐφίεσθαι δεῖ τοὺς κληρικούς.

Ἡ γὰρ τῶν ἱερῶν γραφῶν μελέτη διανοητικῆς γυμνασίας μέρος οὐ σμικρὸν τῷ Χριστιανῷ γέγονεν, τὰ δὲ βιβλία πρῶτον πάντων ὄργανον πᾶσιν τοῖς τὴν εὐσέβειαν ὑφηγουμένοις. Ἀλλ᾽ ἐν τῷ παρόντι, κατὰ δυστυχίαν, πολλοὶ πολλαχόθεν ὡς ἐκ παρατάξεως τοῖς βιβλίοις ἐπιστρατεύουσιν, οὐκ ἐῶντες ἀποδέχεσθαι αὐτὰ ὡς θείας γνώσεως θησαυρόν, ἐπιπολάζουσι δὲ ἐν πάσῃ τάξει τῆς πολιτείας ὑποψίαι πολλαὶ καὶ ἀπορίαι καὶ ἀντιλογίαι καὶ κρίσεις ἀγνώμονες τῶν τῇ ἀποκαλύψει τῆς ἀληθείας ἐποικοδομημένων δογμάτων.

Ὅταν μὲν οὖν τὰ τοιαῦτα ἐξ ἀπειρίας γίγνηται τῆς καθηκούσης σχέσεως τῆς φυσικῆς ἐπιστήμης πρὸς τὴν θείαν ἀποκάλυψιν, ἐνδέχεται δὴ καὶ εἰκός ἐστι μετὰ πάσης εὐγνωμοσύνης κρίνειν καὶ ὑπομονητικῶς ἀνέχεσθαι. Ἐὰν δὲ καὶ ταραχθῶσιν αἱ ψυχαὶ τῶν ἀνθρώπων διὰ τῶν φυσικῶν εὑρημάτων ἢ ἐκ τῶν φυσιολόγων ἀποφάσεως, φροντιστέον ὅπως μὴ τὰ σπέρματα τῆς πίστεως ἀποσβέσομεν, μᾶλλον δὲ τοὺς οὕτως ταραχθέντας ἐπὶ τὸν ἀληθινὸν λόγον προάξομεν, τουτέστιν ἐξ αὐτῶν τῶν εὑρημάτων δεικτέον δηλοῦσθαι νόμους οἵτινες, τοῖς ὀρθῶς κρίνουσιν τὸ ἔργον τοῦ κτίστου καὶ δημιουργοῦ τὸ ἔνδοξον, τῷ ῥήματι τῆς δυνάμεως αὐτοῦ φερόμενον, μετὰ τιμῆς μείζονος διασαφοῦσιν.

Μείζονα δ' ἔχει κίνδυνον ἡ παράταξις αὕτη, εἴτε σκεπτικὴν δεῖ λέγειν εἴτε καὶ ἄντικρυς πολεμίαν, διὰ τὸ χαλεπῶς ἂν διορίσαι ἡμᾶς μέχρι τίνος ἡ διδαχὴ ἡμῶν, ἢ τοὐλάχιστον ἡ περὶ αὐτῆς τοῦ πλήθους ὑπόληψις, φαίνεσθαι δύναται λόγου ἔχουσα ἀρκούντως τῶν περὶ θεοπνευστίας καὶ περὶ τῆς ἐν τῇ παλαιᾷ διαθήκῃ προπαιδευτικῆς οἰκονομίας ἐκ πολλοῦ καὶ πολλαχοῦ ἐπιπολαζουσῶν δοξῶν, εἰ καὶ μηδέποτε ἐν τῇ ἐκκλησίᾳ κυρίως κεκανονισμένων.

Παραινετέον οὖν τοῖς κληρικοῖς ὅπως τὰ ἀμφισβητήματα ταῦτα μετ' εὐλαβείας καὶ φιλοπονίας μεταχειρίζωσιν, καὶ σπουδαιότατα παρακλητέον σύνδεσμον πάσης τῆς διδαχῆς ποιεῖσθαι τὸν Κύριον ἡμῶν Ἰησοῦν Χριστόν, ὡς θυσίαν ὑπὲρ τῶν ἁμαρτιῶν ἡμῶν, καὶ ἰατρὸν τῆς ἁμαρτωλίας, καὶ πηγὴν πάσης τῆς πνευματικῆς ζωῆς, καὶ ἀποκάλυψιν τῇ συνειδήσει τῶν τε ὅρων καὶ τῆς προαιρέσεως πάσης τῆς ἠθικῆς ἀρετῆς. Εἰς αὐτὸν γὰρ καὶ εἰς τὸ ἔργον αὐτοῦ συντείνουσιν τῆς παλαιᾶς διαθήκης αἱ διδαχαὶ πᾶσαι, καὶ ἐξ αὐτοῦ αἱ τῆς καινῆς ῥέουσιν πᾶσαι καὶ πνεύματι καὶ δυνάμει καὶ μορφῇ. Τῆς δὲ ἐκκλησίας τὸ μὲν ἔργον ἐστὶν ἡ προσκομιδὴ τοῖς ἀνθρώποις καὶ ἡ ἐξάπλωσις τῶν χαρισμάτων τῆς ἐνσαρκώσεως τοῦ Λόγου, ἡ δὲ διδαχὴ ἡ ἀνάπτυξις τῶν ἐπ' αὐτῇ τῇ ἐνσαρκώσει θεολογουμένων, ὥσπερ ἐν τοῖς συμβόλοις εὑρίσκεται.

Περὶ τῶν πρὸς ἄλληλα σχέσεων τῶν μερῶν τῆς Ἀγγλικανῆς κοινωνίας.

Ἐν τῇ ζητήσει περὶ τὴν πρὸς ἀλλήλους σχέσιν τῶν παροικιῶν καὶ μερῶν τῆς ἡμετέρας κοινωνίας ἔνια ἐφεύρομεν ἃ καὶ ὑμῖν ὡς ἀξιόλογα παρατιθέμεθα. Ἀναγκαῖον μὲν πρῶτον φαίνεται ἐπὶ τὰς ἀρχὰς τὰς ὑπὸ τοῦ προτέρου Συμβουλίου ἐν ἔτει ͵αωοη' (1878) καταβληθείσας ὑμᾶς παραπέμπειν, καὶ κελεύειν τὰς τῆς ἡμετέρας κοινωνίας ἐκκλησίας καὶ τοὺς ἐν αὐταῖς συναναστρεφομένους τὰς κυρίως δηλωθείσας πράξεις ἢ παροικίας ἄλλης ἢ ἐπαρχίας ἐν τιμῇ ἔχειν· ἐπίσκοπον δὲ μηδένα ἢ κληρικὸν ἐν παροικίᾳ νομίμως κατασταθείσῃ, μὴ ἐπιτρέποντος τοῦ ἐνταῦθα ἐπισκόπου, λειτουργεῖν· ἐπίσκοπον δὲ μηδένα τοὺς ἐξ ἄλλης παροικίας ἐλθόντας κληρικοὺς ἄνευ συστατικῶν ἐπιστολῶν, καὶ τοῦτο ἱκανῶν, εἰς λειτουργίαν δέχεσθαι. Ἡ γὰρ τῶν τοιούτων κανόνων παραμέλησις σκανδάλων χαλεπῶν αἰτία γέγονεν. Οἱ μὲν οὖν ἐπίσκοποι τὰς τοιαύτας βλάβας προφυλάττεσθαι ἕτοιμοί εἰσιν ἰδίᾳ τὴν συμβουλὴν διδόντες ἅμα τῷ εἰωθότι καὶ ὡρισμένῳ συστατικῷ, τοὺς δὲ κληρικοὺς προσήκει εὐλαβείᾳ μείζονι χρῆσθαι τὰς μαρτυρίας ὑποσημαινομένους· τοὺς δὲ τῶν μαρτυριῶν δεομένους τοῦ μὴ λίαν εὐπαθεῖς εἶναι κατέχειν ἑαυτούς, ἐὰν συμβαίνῃ αὐτοῖς περὶ τοῦ τίνες εἰσὶ καὶ ποῖοι τὸ ἦθος ἐξετάζεσθαι· ἡ γὰρ τοιαύτη ἐξέτασις καίπερ περισσὴ εἶναι δοκοῦσα πρὸς ἑαυτοὺς γιγνομένη, ἀναγκαία ἐστὶν ὡς ἐπὶ τὸ πολὺ ὅπως τῆς προσηκούσης ἀσφαλείας τυγχάνωμεν.

Εὐλαβητέον δὲ μάλιστα περὶ τοὺς εἰς τὴν ἐν ταῖς ἀποικίαις λειτουργίαν χειροτονηθέντας. Ἀσμενέστατα μὲν γὰρ συγγιγνώσκομεν τοὺς τὴν τοῦ βίου ἀκμὴν εἰς τὴν ἔξω διακονίαν προθύμως ἐπιδόντας μεγάλης σπουδῆς ἀξίους εἶναι ὁπόταν δέῃ αὐτοὺς προελθόντος τοῦ χρόνου ἀναπαύεσθαι ὡς ἐν τῇ πατρίδι ἢ τὴν οἴκοι ἐργασίαν τῆς ἔξω ἀνταλλάττεσθαι. Καθόλου δὲ περὶ τούτων ὁρίζεσθαι ἀδύνατον.

Ἐκεῖνο δὲ ἡμῖν προτέθειται ὡς μεγίστης σπουδῆς ἄξιον —τὸ εἰ ἐνδέχεται Βουλὴν ἢ Βουλὰς καθιστάναι ἀναφορᾶς ἕνεκα, ὥστε συμβουλεύειν περὶ τῶν ζητημάτων ἃ ἂν τύχῃ προβεβλημένα ὑπὸ τῶν τὰς ἐπαρχίας τῆς ἐν ταῖς ἀποικίαις ἐκκλησίας ἐπιτετραμμένων, ἢ καὶ διαγνῶναι. Περὶ δὲ τούτου ἡμῖν δοκεῖ σκέψεως τε δεῖν πολλῆς καὶ βουλῆς χρονίας, ὥστε μὴ τελευτῶντας ἀναγκάζεσθαι ἀρχὴν καθιστάναι δι' ἧς, εἴτε συμβουλευτικῆς γιγνομένης εἴτε δικαστηρίῳ μᾶλλον ἐοικυίας, ἡ εὐκοσμία ἅμα καὶ ἡ αὐτονομία κινδύνευοι ἂν βλαβήσεσθαι.

Περὶ τῆς παρ' ἡμῖν συνενώσεως τῶν Χριστιανῶν.

Μετὰ φροντίδος καὶ μερίμνης συμβουλευομένοις ἔδοξεν ἡμῖν ἀρκεῖν ὅρους τινὰς προκαταβαλέσθαι ὡς ἀφορμὴν ἀφ' ἧς, Θεοῦ συνεργοῦντος, ἐπὶ τὴν οἴκοι συνένωσιν ἐγγυτέρω ἂν προχωροῖμεν. Οὗτοι δὲ οἱ ὅροι, τέτταρες ὄντες τὸν ἀριθμόν, ἐν ταῖς παρακειμέναις διατάξεσιν εὑρεθήσονται.

[Διάταξις ια'. Τῷ Συμβουλίῳ ἔδοξε τοὺς ὅρους τούσδε ἀναδεῖξαι ὡς ἀφορμὴν τινα παρέχοντας ἀφ' ἧς, Θεοῦ συνεργοῦντος, ἐπὶ τὴν οἴκοι συνένωσιν ἐγγυτέρω ἂν προχωροῖμεν.

(Α.) Τὰς ἁγίας γραφὰς τῆς παλαιᾶς καὶ τῆς καινῆς διαθήκης, τὰ πάντα εἰς σωτηρίαν ἀναγκαῖα κατεχούσας, καὶ κανόνα καὶ κυρίαν στάθμην τῆς πίστεως ὑπάρχουσας.

(Β.) Τὸ σύμβολον τὸ ἀποστολικόν, ἐν βαπτίσματι ἐκφωνούμενον, καὶ τὸ Νικαῖον, ἔκθεσιν τελείαν ὂν τῆς Χριστιανικῆς πίστεως.

(Γ.) Τὰ δύο μυστήρια ὑπ' αὐτοῦ τοῦ Χριστοῦ κεκανονισμένα—τὸ Βάπτισμα καὶ τὸ Κυριακὸν δεῖπνον —μετ' ἀδιαλείπτου χρήσεως τῶν ἐπὶ τῇ πρώτῃ καταστάσει λόγων τοῦ Χριστοῦ καὶ τῶν ὑπ' αὐτοῦ ὡρισμένων στοιχείων διακονούμενα.

(Δ.) Τὴν ἐκ γενεῶν ἀρχαίων παραδεδομένην Ἐπισκοπὴν ἐπιτηδείως οἰκονομουμένην ταῖς ἀεὶ κατὰ τόπους χρείαις γιγνομέναις τῶν ἐθνῶν καὶ τῶν λαῶν τῶν ὑπὸ τοῦ Θεοῦ καλουμένων εἰς τὴν ἑνότητα τῆς ἐκκλησιας.

Διάταξις ιβ'. Τὸ Συμβούλιον μετὰ σπουδῆς παρακαλεῖ τοὺς τὰ μέρη τῆς ἡμετέρας κοινωνίας νομίμως ἐπιτετραμμένους, συνεργοῦντας ἀλλήλοις ὅσον δυνατόν, ἀποφαίνεσθαι ὡς ἕτοιμοι ὑπάρχουσιν συμβουλῆς φιλαδέλφου μετέχειν (οἵανπερ ἤδη ἀπεφήνατο ἡ ἐν ταῖς Ὁμοσπόνδοις Πολιτείαις τῆς Ἀμερικῆς ἐκκλησία) μετὰ τῶν ἐπιτρόπων ἄλλων Χριστιανικῶν κοινωνιῶν τῶν ἐν τοῖς Ἀγγλογλώσσοις ἔθνεσιν, ὅπως λογίζωνται τίνι τρόπῳ ἐνδέχεται προχωρεῖν εἴτ' ἐπὶ ὁλοσχερῆ συνένωσιν, εἴτ' ἐπὶ τοιαύτην τινὰ σχέσιν ἐξ ἧς ἂν ῥᾷον ᾖ εἰς ἑνότητα τελειοτέραν ἐν ὑστέρῳ χρόνῳ προιέναι.

Διάταξις ιγ'. Τὸ Συμβούλιον παραινεῖ ὡς λόγου μάλιστα ἄξιον πρὸς τὴν συνένωσιν, τὸ γνωστοὺς ποιεῖν ἅπασιν τοὺς κανόνας τῆς διδαχῆς καὶ τοὺς τύπους τῆς λειτουργίας τοὺς ἐν τῇ Ἀγγλικανῇ ἐκκλησίᾳ νομιζομένους· ἔτι δὲ καὶ τοὐναντίον τοὺς κανόνας τῆς διδαχῆς καὶ τῆς θρησκείας καὶ τῆς πολιτείας τοὺς ἐν ἄλλαις κοινωνίαις τῶν Χριστιανῶν νομιζομένους, εἰς ἃς τὰ Ἀγγλόγλωσσα ἔθνη κατατέτμηται.]

Δοκεῖ δὲ ἡ τῆς Ἀγγλικανῆς κοινωνίας σχέσις πρὸς τοὺς ἀπ' αὐτῆς διὰ τῶν ἀθλίων σχισμάτων διακεκριμένους τοιάδε τις εἶναι·—

Ἑτοίμους ἡμᾶς αὐτοὺς παρέχομεν πρὸς φιλάδελφον συμβουλὴν μετὰ τῶν συγκοινωνίας τελειοτέρας μεθ' ἡμῶν μέχρι τινὸς γοῦν ὀρεγομένων. Ὅρους δὲ προτίθεμεν ἐφ' οἷς ἐνδέχεται καθ' ἡμᾶς καὶ κατὰ τὴν ἡμετέραν πεποίθησιν τὴν τοιαύτην συγκοινωνίαν γίγνεσθαι. Εἰ γὰρ καὶ τὰ μάλιστα ποθοῦμεν τοὺς ἀφ' ἡμῶν ἠλλοτριωμένους συμπεριλαμβάνειν, ὥστε εἰς ἔργον ἐλθεῖν τὸ τοῦ Κυρίου "μία ποίμνη, εἷς ποιμήν," οὐ μέντοι χρὴ ἡμᾶς οἰκονόμους ἀπίστους γίγνεσθαι τῆς μεγάλης παρακαταθήκης τῆς ἡμῖν παραδεδομένης. Οὔτε γὰρ περὶ τὴν πίστιν οὔτε περὶ τὴν ἐκκλησιαστικὴν πολιτείαν τὴν τάξιν τὴν ἡμετέραν ἀπολείπειν δυνάμεθα. Ἡ δὲ ὁμονοία ἐκείνη ἡ διὰ τοιαύτης λιποταξίας ἐγγιγνομένη οὔτε ἀληθινὴ ἂν εἴη οὔτε ἐπιπόθητος κατὰ τὴν ἡμετέραν γνώμην.

Ἀσμένως μέντοι καὶ μετ' εὐχαριστίας ἀναγνωρίζομεν τὸ ἔργον τῆς εὐσεβείας τὸ ἀληθινὸν τὸ ὑπὸ τῶν Χριστιανῶν τῶν ἔξω τῆς ἡμετέρας κοινωνίας φιλοπονούμενον. Δήλη γάρ ἐστιν καὶ ἐν ὀφθαλμοῖς ἡ χάρις ἡ ταῖς ὑπὲρ τοῦ Χριστοῦ ἐνεργείαις αὐτῶν συγχωρηθεῖσα. Τὸ δὲ περὶ τούτων λεγόμενον οὐ παρανοητέον. Οὐ γὰρ περιορῶμεν οἵοις συνδέσμοις καὶ ὡς σταθερᾷ τῇ πεποιθήσει δεδεμένοι τῶν ἐπιτηδευμάτων τῶν εἰθισμένων ἔχονται. Ταῦτα δὲ ἐν λόγῳ ἔχοντες καὶ τὰς ὑπολήψεις καὶ τὰς γνώμας τὰς ἡμετέρας λόγου τυγχάνειν ἀξιοῦμεν. Μαρτυροῦσιν δὴ ἄνδρες ἀξιόλογοι ὅτι οὐκ ἐν Ἀγγλίᾳ μόνον ἀλλὰ καὶ ἐν πᾶσιν μέρεσιν τῆς Χριστιανότητος πόθος ἀληθινὸς τῆς ἑνότητος εὑρίσκεται, καὶ τὰ σπλάγχνα τῶν ἀνθρώπων μᾶλλον ἢ τὸ πρὶν ὁμιλίας Χριστιανικῆς ὀρέγεται. Τὴν δὲ συμπάθειαν ταύτην καὶ ἐν ταῖς ζητήσεσίν καὶ ἐν ταῖς διατάξεσιν ἐν ἑαυτῷ πληρῶς ὑπάρχουσαν ἐνεδείξατο τὸ Συμβούλιον· εὐχόμεθα δὲ πρὸ πάντων ὅπως τὸ πνεῦμα τῆς ἀγάπης ἐπιφέρηται ἐπάνω τῶν θολερῶν ὑδάτων τῶν θρησκευτικῶν διαλογισμῶν.

Ἡ πρὸς τὴν Σκανδιναυικὴν ἐκκλησίαν σχέσις.

Ἐν τοῖς ἔθνεσιν οἷς ἐπιμίγνυνται μάλιστα οἱ Ἀγγλόγλωσσοι ὑπάρχει δηλονότι τὰ Σκανδιναυικά, καὶ γὰρ ἐν πολλαῖς τῶν ἡμετέρων παροικιῶν τῷ πλήθει ὄχλον ἱκανὸν συντελεῖ. Οὐκ ἀδιάφορον οὖν τῷ Συμβουλίῳ ποία ἂν εἴη ἡ τῆς Ἀγγλικανῆς κοινωνίας σχέσις πρὸς τὰς Σκανδιναυικὰς ἐκκλησίας. Παρηνέσαμεν δὲ ὅπως εἰς ἀκριβεστέραν γνῶσιν ἀλλήλων προέλθωμεν καὶ φιλικώτερον συναναστρεφώμεθα μέχρις ἂν δυνώμεθα, συγχωρούντων τῶν πραγμάτων, συμμαχίαν οἰκειοτέραν ποιήσασθαι, μὴ παραδόντες τὰς ἀρχὰς ἃς ἀναγκαίας ἡγούμεθα.

[Διάταξις ιδ'. Ἔδοξε τῷ συμβουλίῳ σπουδάζειν χρῆναι σχέσεις φιλικωτέρας μεταξὺ τῶν Σκανδιναυικῶν ἐκκλησιῶν καὶ τῆς Ἀγγλικανῆς ἐκκλησίας καταστήσασθαι, τὰς δὲ προκλήσεις τῆς Σουηδικῆς ἐκκλησίας, ἐάν τινες γίγνωνται, πρὸς ἀμοιβαῖον σαφηνισμὸν τῶν διαφορῶν, ἀσμενέστατα δέχεσθαι ἡμᾶς, βουλομένους εἴ ποτ' ἔσται δυνατόν, προελθόντος τοῦ χρόνου, τὴν συγκοινωνίαν ἐπ' ἀρχαῖς βεβαίαις τῆς ἐκκλησιαστικῆς πολιτείας καταστήσασθαι.]

Πρὸς τοὺς ἀρχαίους καθολικοὺς καὶ ἄλλους.

Ἀδύνατον δὲ μὴ συμπάσχειν τὰ μάλιστα τοὺς εἰς τὴν Ἀγγλικανὴν κοινωνίαν συντελοῦντας τοῖς ἐν τῇ ἠπείρῳ τῆς Εὐρώπης εἰς μεταρρύθμισιν τῆς ἐκκλησίας ἀγωνιζομένοις, τοῖς ἐπὶ μεγίσταις δυσκολίαις ὡς ἐπὶ τὸ πολὺ τὴν αὐτὴν μεθ' ἡμῶν τάξιν κατασχοῦσιν καὶ τὴν Ἐπισκοπὴν ὡς ἀποστολικὴν κτίσιν κρατήσασιν. Τοιγαροῦν οὔπω παρεῖναι τὸν καιρὸν ἡγούμενοι ἐν ᾧ συνθήκην πρὸς τούτων τινὰς ἀμέσως γράφειν δυνάμεθα, καὶ ἐξαιφνίδιον πρᾶξιν οἱανδήποτε ἀποποιούμενοι, ἀρχαίους καὶ γνωρίμους κανόνας τῆς ἐκκλησιαστικῆς πολιτείας μέλλουσαν παραβαίνειν, ἡγούμεθα μέντοι δύνασθαι ἡμᾶς τὰ τῆς φιλίας προτείνειν, μὴ παριδόντες τοὺς κανόνας ἐκείνους, καὶ ἐλπίζομεν ἐν καιρῷ καθήκοντι μετά τινων γοῦν τῶν κοινωνιῶν τούτων συνθήκην καὶ συμμαχίαν ποιεῖσθαι.

[Διάταξις ιε'. (Α.) Ἀσμένως κατενόησε τὸ Συμβούλιον τὸ σεμνὸν καὶ αὔταρκες τῆς τάξεως τῆς ὑπὸ τῆς ἀρχαίας καθολικῆς ἐκκλησίας τῆς Ὁλλανδίας διατηρουμένης καὶ πρὸς συχνοτέραν καὶ φιλάδελφον ἐπιμιξίαν ἀποβλέπει ὅπως ἐκποδὼν γίγνηται πολλὰ τῶν ἡμᾶς καὶ αὐτοὺς εἰς τὸ παρὸν διαιρούντων.

(Β.) Καθήκειν ἡμῖν ἡγούμεθα πρός τε τὴν ἀρχαίαν καθολικὴν κοινωνίαν ἐν Γερμανίᾳ καὶ πρὸς τὴν "Χριστιανὴν καθολικὴν ἐκκλησίαν" τῆς Ἑλβετίας φιλόφρονα συναναστροφὴν προτρέψασθαι, οὐ μόνον διὰ συμπάθειαν ἀλλὰ καὶ τῷ Θεῷ εὐχαριστοῦντας τῷ ἐν μεγάλαις ἀπορίαις καὶ δυσκολίαις ἅμα δὲ καὶ πειρασμοῖς πρὸς τὸ πάσχειν ὑπὲρ τῆς ἀληθείας ἐνδυναμώσαντι αὐτούς· καὶ τὰ προνόμια αὐτοῖς παρέχομεν τὰ ὑπὸ τῆς Ἐπιτροπῆς ὑποτεθέντα, ἐπὶ τοῖς ἐν τῇ ἐκθέσει δηλουμένοις.*

(Γ.) Συμπαθείας ἀξία ἐστὶν ἡ τῶν ἀρχαίων καθολικῶν ἐν Αὐστρίᾳ αὐταπαρνητικὴ προθυμία, ἐλπίζομεν δέ, τῆς διοργανώσεως αὐτῶν στερεᾶς ἀρκούντως καὶ τελείας γενομένης, γενικωτέραν κοινωνίαν καθιστάναι δυνήσεσθαι.

(Δ.) Περὶ δὲ τῶν μεταρρυθμιστῶν τῶν ἐν Ἰταλίᾳ καὶ Γαλλίᾳ καὶ Ἱσπανίᾳ καὶ Λουσιτανίᾳ τῶν τοὺς ἀθέσμους ὅρους τῆς κοινωνίας ἀποσειομένων, ἐλπίζομεν αὐτοὺς τύπους οὕτως ὑγιαινούσης διδαχῆς καὶ πολιτείας δέξεσθαι, καὶ διοργάνωσιν οὕτως καθολικὴν παρασκευάσεσθαι, ὥστε δύνασθαι ἡμᾶς ἐντελεστέρῳ τινὶ τρόπῳ ἀποδέχεσθαι αὐτούς.

(Ε.) Μὴ βουλόμενοι ἐμποδίζειν τοὺς τῆς καθολικῆς ἐκκλησίας ἐπισκόπους τοῦ κατὰ τὸ δίκαιον ἐπεμβαίνειν εἰς τὰ πράγματα ἐπειγούσης τῆς ἐσχάτης ἀνάγκης, παραιτούμεθα μέντοι πρᾶξιν ὁποιανδήποτε ἥτις ἂν δοκῇ τοὺς ἀρχαίους καὶ βεβαίους ὅρους τῆς ἐκκλησιαστικῆς πολιτείας καὶ τὰ

---

* Ἔχει δὲ οὕτως ἡ ἔκθεσις·—Οὐδὲν ἡμῖν δοκεῖ κωλύειν μὴ παριέναι τοὺς κληρικοὺς αὐτῶν καὶ τοὺς πιστοὺς εἰς ἁγίαν κοινωνίαν ἐφ' οἷς καὶ οἱ παρ' ἡμῖν παραγίγνονται, ἀναγνωρίζομεν δὲ καὶ τὴν προθυμίαν αὐτῶν τὴν εἰς ἡμᾶς προνόμια πνευματικὰ τοῖς ἡμετέροις παρεχόντων.

Διὰ δὲ τὰς διαφορὰς τὰς λυπηρὰς τῶν γαμικῶν νόμων, ἃς λόγου πολλοῦ ἀξίας ἡγούμεθα, ἀποφαινόμεθα ὅτι ἀδύνατον ἡμῖν παριέναι εἰς τὴν ἁγίαν κοινωνίαν τοὺς γεγαμηκότας παρὰ τοὺς νόμους καὶ κανόνας τῆς Ἀγγλικανῆς ἐκκλησίας· τὸ δὲ ἴσον τοῖς ἀρχαίοις καθολικοῖς ἀπονέμοντες οὐκ ἂν δυναίμεθα παριέναι τοὺς τῆς κοινωνίας παρ' αὐτοῖς ἀπειργομένους.

συμφέροντα πάσης τῆς Ἀγγλικανῆς κοινωνίας μὴ ἐντρέπεσθαι.

Ἡ πρὸς τὰς Ἀνατολικὰς ἐκκλησίας σχέσις.

Πλείστην σπουδὴν ἐδήλωσεν τὸ Συμβούλιον ὅπως τὴν φιλικὴν σχέσιν τὴν ὑπάρχουσαν τῶν ἀνατολικῶν ἐκκλησιῶν πρὸς τὴν Ἀγγλικανὴν κοινωνίαν βεβαιῶμεν καὶ συμπληρῶμεν. Αὗται δ' αἱ ἐκκλησίαι διὰ πολλοῦ χρόνου τῆς συμπαθείας τοῦ χριστιανισμοῦ ἀξίας ἑαυτὰς ἀπέδειξαν, ἀπὸ γενεᾶς γὰρ εἰς γενεὰν ἐν πολλαῖς χώραις δὴ καὶ ἐν σκοτεινοῖς τόποις τὴν τοῦ φωτὸς τοῦ εὐαγγελικοῦ φλόγα ζῶσαν διέσωσαν. Εἰ δὲ καὶ τὸ φῶς τοῦτο ἔνθεν καὶ ἔνθεν ἀσθενὲς εἶναι δοκεῖ καὶ ἀμαυρόν, διὰ τοῦτο μᾶλλον καθήκει ἡμᾶς, τῷ καιρῷ ὡς ἐνδέχεται χρωμένους, ἐπιμελεῖσθαι τούτου καὶ περιθάλπειν· οὐδὲ γάρ ἐστι κίνδυνος μὴ οὐ προσδεκτὰ ᾖ τὰ φιλαδέλφως ὑπουργούμενα, ἀπ' ὀρθῆς γνώμης καὶ ἀγάπης εἰλικρινοῦς παρεχόμενα. Μετὰ δ' εὐχαριστίας κατανοοῦμεν τοιαῦτα ἐμποδίσματα κοινωνίας μὴ εἶναι οἷα πρὸς τοὺς Λατείνους δηλαδὴ ὑπάρχει, διὰ τὸ κυρίως ὁρισθῆναι τὴν ἀπλανησίαν τῆς ἐκκλησίας ἐν αὐτῷ τῷ ὑψίστῳ Ποντίφικι κατοικεῖν, καὶ διὰ τὸ δόγμα τῆς ἀμιάντου συλλήψεως τῆς μακαρίας παρθένου Μαρίας, καὶ ἄλλα δόγματα τὰ ὑπὸ τῶν παπικῶν συνόδων κεκανονισμένα. Ἡ μὲν οὖν Ῥωμαία ἐκκλησία τὴν ἀνατολικήν, ἀδελφὴν οὖσαν, ἀεὶ ἠδίκηκεν. Τοὺς γὰρ ἐπισκόπους εἰς τὰς ἀρχαίας παροικίας εἰσβιάζεται, καὶ τὸν προσηλυτισμὸν ἐνεργῶς καὶ συστηματικῶς ἐπιτηδεύει. Εὐλόγως οὖν ἡ Ἀνατολικὴ ἐκκλησία ἀγανακτεῖ ὡς διὰ τούτων ὑβρισθεῖσα ἐναντίων ὄντων διόλου ταῖς καθολικαῖς ἀρχαῖς· ἡμᾶς δὲ χρὴ τοὺς τῆς Ἀγγλικανῆς κοινωνίας ἡμῖν αὐτοῖς προσέχειν μὴ ὁμοίως πως εἰς αὐτὴν ἁμάρτωμεν.

Εἰ γάρ τις παρὰ τοῖς ἀνατολικοῖς φωτὸς λαμπροτέρου καὶ πνευματικῆς ζωῆς αὐξήσεως ἐπιθυμεῖ, δύναιτ' ἂν οὗτος ἐν τῇ ἐκκλησίᾳ ἐν ᾗ ἐβαπτίσθη ἐπιμένων φωτισμόν τινα τοῖς συμπολίταις διαδιδόναι.

Ἀλλ' ἐν ᾧ τοῦ προσηλυτισμοῦ ὅλως ἀπέχειν δεῖ, εἰκός

ἐστιν ὅμως καὶ δίκαιον τὸ ἀξίωμα τὸ ἀληθινὸν καὶ τὴν τάξιν τῆς ἐκκλησίας ἡμῶν ὡς ἱστορικῆς ὑπαρχούσης ἀποδείκνυσθαι πρὸς τούτους οἵτινες, τοῖς καινοτομουμένοις, μάλιστα περὶ τῆς θρησκείας, σφόδρα ἐναντιούμενοι, τὴν ἱστορίαν μέντοι τῆς καθολικῆς ἀρχαιότητος ἀσμένως ἀσπάζονται. Δεῖ δὲ ὑπουργεῖν ἡμᾶς πρὸς τὴν ἐκπαίδευσιν τῶν κληρικῶν, καὶ δὴ καὶ ὁπότ' ἂν ἔνδεια χρημάτων ᾖ ἔτι τοῖς κοινοῖς σχολείοις ὑπηρετεῖν.

[Διάταξις ιζ. Τὸ Συμβούλιον τοῦτο χαῖρον ἐπὶ τῇ φιλικῇ συναναστροφῇ τῇ γενομένῃ μεταξὺ τῶν ἀρχιεπισκόπων Καντουαρίας ἄλλων τε ἐκ τῶν Ἀγγλικανῶν ἐπισκόπων καὶ τῶν Πατριαρχῶν Κωνσταντινουπόλεως ἄλλων τε ἀνατολικῶν Πατριαρχῶν καὶ ἐπισκόπων, ἀποφαίνεται τὴν ἐλπίδα τοῦ τὰ τῆς ἐντελεστέρας κοινωνίας νῦν ἐμποδίσματα, προελθόντος τοῦ χρόνου, ἐκποδὼν γενήσεσθαι, προκοπτούσης τῆς ἐπιμιξίας καὶ αὐξανομένου τοῦ φωτισμοῦ. Παρακαλεῖ δὲ τὸ Συμβούλιον τοὺς πιστοὺς ἐπὶ προσευχὴν ἐκτενῆ περὶ τούτου, καὶ ὑποτίθεται τοῖς συγχριστιανοῖς ὅτι δεῖ τὰς ἐπινοίας καὶ τὰς ἐνεργείας ἐπὶ τὴν ἐσωτερικὴν μεταρρύθμισιν μᾶλλον τῶν ἀνατολικῶν ἐκκλησιῶν ἀπευθύνειν, ἢ ἐπὶ τὸ ἀφέλκειν ἄλλον καὶ ἄλλον εἰς τὴν ἑαυτῶν κοινωνίαν.]

Περὶ τῶν κανονικῶν σταθμῶν διδαχῆς καὶ θρησκείας.

Τούτων δὲ μνησθέντας δεῖ ὑμᾶς τὰς κανονικὰς στάθμας διδαχῆς καὶ θρησκείας μετὰ πολλῆς φροντίδος σκοπεῖν. Δεῖ γὰρ τὰ μάλιστα καὶ τὴν πίστιν ἡμῶν καὶ τὴν πρᾶξιν τοιαύτας οὔσας δείκνυσθαι καὶ ταῖς ἀρχαίαις ἐκκλησίαις καὶ ταῖς νῦν ἐν τοῖς ἔθνεσιν ὑπὸ τῶν ἱεραποστόλων ἀνατρεφομέναις ἐκκλησίαις, οἷαι μήτε ἂν ἀγανακτήσεως αἰτίαν διδῶσιν, μήτε ἀληθινὴν αὐτονομίαν ἐμποδίζωσιν, μήτε σκάνδαλα παρέχωσιν τοῖς ἐπὶ τὴν ἐντελῆ κοινωνίαν προιέναι βουλομένοις.

Τοῖς δὲ προτέροις Συμβουλίοις ἑπόμενοι ἀποφαινόμεθα ἑνοῦσθαι ἡμᾶς μιᾷ Κεφαλῇ καὶ Θεῷ καὶ Σωτῆρι ἡμῶν ὑποτεταγμένους, ἐν τῇ κοινωνίᾳ τῆς μιᾶς καθολικῆς καὶ ἀποστολικῆς Ἐκκλησίας, κατέχειν τε τὴν μίαν πίστιν τὴν ἐν ταῖς ἁγίαις γραφαῖς ἀποκεκαλυμμένην, ἐν τοῖς Συμβόλοις ὡρισμένην, ὑπὸ τῆς ἀρχῆθεν Ἐκκλησίας κεκρατημένην, καὶ ὑπὸ τῶν ἀναμφισβητήτων οἰκουμενικῶν Συνόδων κεκανονισμένην· δεχόμεθα δὲ ὥσπερ στάθμας διδαχῆς ὁμοῦ καὶ θρησκείας τὴν βίβλον τῆς δημοσίας εὐχῆς μετὰ τοῦ ἐμπεριεχομένου κατηχισμοῦ, τὸν δὲ τύπον τῆς χειροτονίας, καὶ τὰ τριάκοντα ἐννέα ἄρθρα—κληρονομίαν ἐξαίρετον τῆς ἐν Ἀγγλίᾳ ἐκκλησίας, ἃ καὶ πάντα πᾶσαι αἱ τῆς ἡμετέρας κοινωνίας ἐκκλησίαι ἢ παντελῶς ἢ ὡς ἐπὶ τὰ πλεῖστα ὁμολογοῦσιν.

Βουλόμεθα δὲ τὰς στάθμας ταύτας τοῖς ἐξωτερικοῖς ἐκκλησίαις ἀφελῶς καὶ ἁπλῶς ἐνδείκνυσθαι. Ἐλευθερίαν δὲ μέχρι τινὸς ταῖς ἐν τοῖς ἔθνεσιν βλαστανούσαις ἐκκλησίαις συγχωρητέον· οὐ γὰρ εὔλογον ταῖς τοιαύταις τὰ τριάκοντα καὶ ἐννέα ἄρθρα ὅλως ἐπιτάττειν ὡς ὅρους τῆς κοινωνίας, ἐπικεχρωσμένα δὴ καὶ κατὰ τὰ ῥήματα καὶ κατὰ τὴν μόρφωσιν διὰ τῶν περιστάσεων τῶν κατὰ τὸν καιρὸν τῆς συνθέσεως αὐτῶν ἐπιπολαζουσῶν. Ἀδύνατον δ' ἂν εἴη τοὐναντίον ἡμᾶς μετέχειν αὐταῖς τῆς τῶν λειτουργῶν χειροτονίας, ὡς πληρῶς ἡμῖν συγκοινωνούσαις, μήπω ἀποδεδειγμένου τοῦ τὸν αὐτὸν ἡμῖν κατά γε τὴν οὐσίαν τύπον διδαχῆς κρατεῖν. Οὐ μὴν χαλεπὸν ἂν εἴη, ἵνα μὴ ἀδύνατον λέγωμεν, τὸ ἄρθρα συντάττειν, κατὰ τὰς στάθμας τὰς ἡμετέρας τῆς διδαχῆς καὶ τῆς θρησκείας, ἐπιτακτέα ἅπασιν τοῖς ἐν ταῖς ἐκκλησίαις τοιαύταις χειροτονουμένοις.

> [Διάταξις ιη΄. Αἰτεῖ τὸ Συμβούλιον παρὰ τοῦ ἀρχιεπισκόπου τῆς Καντουαρίας, ὅπως μετὰ τοιούτων οὓς ἀξίους ἕξει συμβουλεύσηται εἰ σύμφορον ἔσται τὴν Ἀγγλικὴν ἑρμήνειαν τοῦ Νικαίου συμβόλου καὶ τοῦ "ὅστις βούλεται" (quicunque vult) ἐπανορθοῦν.

> Διάταξις ιθ΄. Περὶ τῶν νεοκτίστων ἐκκλησιῶν, μάλιστα ἐν ταῖς μὴ χριστιαναῖς χώραις, δεῖ ὅρον εἶναι τῆς

ἀναγνωρίσεως αὐτῶν, ὡς πληρῶς ἡμῖν συγκοινωνουσῶν, καὶ μάλιστα τῆς δωρεᾶς παρ' ἡμῶν τῆς ἐπισκοπικῆς διαδοχῆς, τὸ δέξασθαι ἡμᾶς παρ' αὐτῶν τεκμήρια ἱκανὰ τοῦ αὐτὰς τὴν αὐτὴν κατά γε τὴν οὐσίαν διδαχὴν ἡμῖν κρατεῖν, καὶ τοὺς κληρικοὺς αὐτῶν ἄρθρα ὑποσημαίνεσθαι κατὰ τὰ διαρρήδην ἐν ταῖς στάθμαις ἡμῶν ταῖς περὶ διδαχῆς καὶ θρησκείας ἀποπεφασμένα, ἀνάγκην δὲ εἶναι μηδεμίαν δέχεσθαι αὐτὰς ὁλοκλήρως τὰ τριάκοντα καὶ ἐννέα ἄρθρα τῆς θρησκείας.]

Ταύτην, ἀδελφοί, τὴν ἐπιστολὴν εἰς τέλος ἄγομεν εὐχαριστίαν ταπεινὴν καὶ ἐγκάρδιον Θεῷ παντοκράτορι ἀπονέμοντες ὑπὲρ τῆς μεγάλης πρὸς ἡμᾶς χρηστότητος καὶ φιλανθρωπίας. Συνεχώρησεν γὰρ ἡμῖν ὧδε συναθροίζεσθαι πλείοσιν οὖσιν τὸν ἀριθμὸν ἢ τὸ πρίν. Πανταχόθεν δὲ τῆς γῆς γνώσεως ἅμα καὶ ἐμπειρίας θησαυροὶ εἰς τὸ κοινὸν συνηνέχθησαν. Ἐγένετο δὲ ἡμῖν καταλαμβάνειν μᾶλλον ἢ τὸ πρὶν ἐδυνάμεθα τό τε μέγεθος καὶ τὴν δύναμιν καὶ τὴν ἰσχὺν τῆς μεγάλης Ἀγγλικανῆς κοινωνίας.

Εἰς ὅσα ἐπιτηδεία ἐστὶν αὕτη, οἵαις δὲ εὐκαιρίαις καὶ οἵοις προνομίοις χρῆται—ταῦτα ᾐσθόμεθα. Ἐν ταῖς ζητήσεσιν δὴ ταῖς ἐν κοινῇ συνόδῳ γενομέναις τὴν κατ' οὐσίαν ἑνότητα ἐδοκιμάσαμεν τὴν πάσας τὰς διαφορὰς καὶ καταστάσεως καὶ προκοπῆς συνάπτουσαν. Ὅπου γὰρ γνώμης διαφωνία ἐν ἡμῖν ἐγένετο ἐκεῖ καὶ πνεύματος συμφωνία καὶ ἑνότης σκοποῦ· καὶ πρὸς τὰς παροικίας ἄλλος ἄλλοσε ἐπανερχόμεθα ἀναψυχόμενοι ἅμα καὶ ἐνδυναμούμενοι καὶ ἐνθουσιάζοντες ταῖς ἀναμνήσεσιν ἃς μεθ' ἡμῶν κομίζομεν.

Ἡ δὲ τῆς εὐχαριστίας αἴσθησις ἀμέσως τῇ τοῦ καθήκοντος χρείᾳ συνδέδεται. Ἡ γὰρ ἀληθινὴ κατάληψις τῶν προνομίων τῶν ἐν τῇ Ἀγγλικανῇ κοινωνίᾳ ἡμῖν ὑπαρχόντων μείζονα ἡμῖν αἴσθησιν παρέχει τῆς ὀφειλῆς, οὐ τῷ ἡμετέρῳ λαῷ μόνον οὐδὲ τοῖς ἔθνεσιν τοῖς ὑπὸ τῶν ἱεραποστόλων εὐαγγελιζομένοις, ἀλλὰ καὶ πάσαις ταῖς ἐκκλησίαις τοῦ Θεοῦ. Ἐξαίρετος γὰρ ἡμῶν ἡ τάξις καὶ πρὸς ἐξαίρετον ἔργον εὐκαίρως ἡμᾶς ἀνακαλεῖ. Εὐχόμεθα δὲ ἐκτενῶς πάντας—κληρικοὺς ἅμα καὶ λαικοὺς—

τὴν τοῦ Θεοῦ προαίρεσιν τὴν πρόδηλον ἐνθυμεῖσθαι καὶ ἐν οἵᾳ δή ποτε κλήσει γενομένους ἀγωνίζεσθαι ὅπως ἂν τὴν βουλὴν Αὐτοῦ εἰς τέλος κατεργάζωνται.

Τούτοις τοῖς ῥήμασιν ὑμῖν ἀποταξάμενοι τὰ ἐν τῷ Συμβουλίῳ συμπεπερασμένα τῇ μελέτῃ ὑμῶν παραδίδομεν, ἱκετεύοντες ὅπως τὸ ἅγιον Πνεῦμα πάντα τὰ ἐνθυμήματα ὑμῶν κατευθύνῃ καὶ εἰς πᾶσαν τὴν ἀλήθειαν κατάγῃ ὑμᾶς, καὶ ὅπως τὰ βουλεύματα ἡμῶν διὰ τῆς ὑμῶν ἐνεργείας εἰς δόξαν Θεοῦ καὶ προκοπὴν τῆς τοῦ Χριστοῦ βασιλείας συντείνῃ.

Ὑπέγραψα ἐν τῷ ὀνόματι τοῦ Συμβουλίου,

ΕΔΟΤΑΡΔΟΣ Ο ΤΗΣ ΚΑΝΤΟΤΑΡΙΑΣ.

PUBLICATIONS OF THE
Society for Promoting Christian Knowledge.

	s.	d.
BEING OF GOD, Six Addresses on the. By C. J. ELLICOTT, D.D., Bishop of Gloucester and Bristol. Small post 8vo. ....Cloth boards	1	6
BIBLE PLACES; or, THE TOPOGRAPHY OF THE HOLY LAND, By the Rev. CANON TRISTRAM. With Map and numerous Woodcuts. Crown 8vo. ....Cloth boards	4	0
CALLED TO BE SAINTS: The Minor Festivals Devotionally Studied. By CHRISTINA G. ROSSETTI, author of "Seek and Find." Post 8vo. Cloth boards	5	0
CHRISTIANS UNDER THE CRESCENT IN ASIA. By the Rev. E. L. CUTTS, B.A. With numerous Illustrations. Crown 8vo............Cloth boards	5	0
CHURCH HISTORY, SKETCHES OF. From the First Century to the Reformation. By the Rev. J. C. ROBERTSON. With Map. 12mo. ....Cloth boards	2	0
GOSPELS, THE FOUR. Arranged in the Form of an English Harmony, from the Text of the Authorised Version. By the Rev. J. M. FULLER, M.A. With Analytical Table of Contents and Four Maps. Post 8vo. Cloth boards	1	0
HISTORY OF THE ENGLISH CHURCH, In Short Biographical Sketches. By the Rev. JULIUS LLOYD, M.A. Post 8vo. ....……………Cloth boards	1	6
JEWISH NATION, A HISTORY OF THE. From the Earliest Times to the Present Day. By the late E. H. PALMER, M.A. With Map of Palestine and Numerous Illustrations. Crown 8vo. ....Cloth boards	4	0
LAND OF ISRAEL, THE. A Journal of Travel in Palestine, undertaken with special reference to its Physical Character. By the Rev. CANON TRISTRAM. With Two Maps and Numerous Illustrations. Large post 8vo. ....Cloth boards	10	6

PUBLICATIONS OF THE SOCIETY.

	s.	d.
LECTURES ON THE HISTORICAL AND DOGMATICAL POSITION OF THE CHURCH OF ENGLAND. By the Rev. W. BAKER, D.D. Post 8vo. .... *Cloth boards*	1	6
NARRATIVE OF A MODERN PILGRIMAGE THROUGH PALESTINE ON HORSEBACK, AND WITH TENTS. By the Rev. A. C. SMITH, M.A. Numerous Illustrations, and Four Coloured Plates. Crown 8vo. .... *Cloth boards*	5	0
PALEY'S EVIDENCES. A New Edition, with Notes, Appendix, and Preface. By the Rev. E. A. LITTON. Post 8vo. .... *Cloth boards*	4	0
PALEY'S HORÆ PAULINÆ. A New Edition, with Notes, Appendix, and Preface. By the Rev. J. S. HOWSON, D.D. Post 8vo. .... *Cloth boards*	2	0
PLAIN REASONS AGAINST JOINING THE CHURCH OF ROME. By the Rev. R. F. LITTLEDALE, LL.D., &c. Revised and Enlarged Edition. Post 8vo.................................... *Cloth boards*	1	0
SOME CHIEF TRUTHS OF RELIGION. By the Rev. E. L. CUTTS, B.A., Author of "Pastoral Counsels," "St. Cedd's Cross." Crown 8vo. .... *Cloth boards*	2	6
TURNING-POINTS OF ENGLISH CHURCH HISTORY. By the Rev. E. L. CUTTS, B.A., Vicar of Holy Trinity, Haverstock Hill. Crown 8vo. *Cloth boards*	3	6
TURNING-POINTS OF GENERAL CHURCH HISTORY. By the Rev. E. L. CUTTS, B.A., Author of "Pastoral Counsels." Crown 8vo. *Cloth boards*	5	0

London:

NORTHUMBERLAND AVENUE, CHARING CROSS, W.C.;
43, QUEEN VICTORIA STREET, E.C.;
BRIGHTON: 135, NORTH STREET.

www.ingramcontent.com/pod-product-compliance
Lightning Source LLC
Chambersburg PA
CBHW030557300426
44111CB00009B/1014